Indian Chronology To Indian History

By

Prof. Ravi Prakash Arya

Assisted by

Alois Heinrich

Amazon Books, USA

In association with

Indian Foundation for Vedic Science

1051, Sector-1, Rohtak, Haryana, India, Pin-124001

Contact No. 9313033917; 9650183260

Email:vedicscience@rediffmail.com; vedicscience@gmail.com

website : www.vedicscience.net

First Edition

Kali era: 5120 (c. 2019)

Kalpa era : 1,97,29,49,120

Brahma era: 15,55,21,97,29,49,120

ISBN: 9788187710851

Contents

1. Indian Concept of History

Indian tradition views history as a science rather than an art. Our ancestors referred to history as Itihāsa Śāstra. It was considered a science because it explored the creation and origin of the universe, subjects inherently related to scientific inquiry. This is why the Itihāsa and Purāṇas are referred to as the fifth Veda..

इतिहास पुराणं पंचमो वेदः
Itihāsa purāṇam pañcamo vedaḥ.

The Vedas address the science of creation, while the Itihāsa and Purāṇas focus on the history of that creation. Consequently, texts that examine the historical aspects of the science of creation will inherently be scientific in nature. In addition to the creation of the universe, history also explores the origin and expansion of humankind on Earth. As such, history encompasses all aspects of human life, not just the political dimension, as often emphasized in modern historical accounts. Following this understanding, various types of historiography emerged in India, which can be classified into 22 distinct categories..

1. Itihāsa

In ancient India, the study of history was approached from a very different perspective than it is today. The term used by ancient Indians was "Itihāsa," which has evolved into the modern concept of history. Itihāsa refers to a narration, and its etymology—इति ह वै आस (it ha vai āsa)—clearly indicates that it represents a recounting of historical events.

Unlike today, where narration is often associated with storytelling, in ancient times, it held a much more significant purpose. During the Vedic era, there existed a school of interpretation known as the Aitihāsika school, which used figurative narratives to explain and elaborate on the creation and origins of human beings. As Durga explains, Itihāsa is a narrative that primarily traces the origins and causes of important events..

निदानभूतमिति ह वै आसीदिति यत्रोच्यते स इतिहासः पुरावृत्त ख्यापकः समाचारः ।

nidānabhūtaṁ iti ha vai āsiditi yatrocyate sa Itihāsaḥ purāvṛtta khyāpakaḥ samācāraḥ

(*Nir.*2.10; 2.24; 9.23; 10.26, etc.)

Nirukta and Bṛhaddavatā use the terms Itihāsa and Ākhyāna to introduce historical narratives in a figurative manner, correlating them with the scientific facts revealed in Vedic hymns. Yāska, who lived around 2700 BC, employs the term Itihāsa six times in his work Nirukta to refer to figurative legends narrated by Aitihāsikas. Originally, Ākhyāna was a synonym for Itihāsa, but over time, the two terms became distinct. Itihāsa began to encompass a broader range of aspects related to individual lives, while Ākhyāna remained focused solely on the history of the universe's creation.

In ancient times, Itihāsa referred to actual or factual events within the political or social spheres rather than fictional accounts. This evolution in the meaning of Itihāsa later led to confusion when the old dictum was reinterpreted.

इतिहास-पुराणाभ्यां वेदं समुपबृंहयेत् ।

Itihāsa purāṇābhyāṁ vedaṁ samupabṛṁyeta

The purpose of the study of Purāṇas was to explain and clarify the secrets of the Vedas by narrating the figurative legends (Itihāsa). This approach was studied in a new context, as scholars often found themselves confused about the Vedas containing traces of actual political or social events.

The term Itihāsa represented one aspect of this concept, which was further completed by incorporating the Purāṇa alongside Itihāsa. Thus, the combination of Itihāsa and Purāṇa became widely recognized. Now, we will discuss the meanings and scope of the Purāṇa as understood by ancient Indians..

2. Purāṇa

Ancient Indians used the term "Purāṇa," which can be compared to modern-day history or Itihāsa. The purpose of modern history is to chronologically record events in the political, social, and intellectual realms. In contrast, the scope of Purāṇa was much broader. It encompassed five key subjects.

सर्गश्च प्रतिसर्गश्च वंशो मन्वन्तराणि च
वंशानुचरितं चैव पुराण पंचलक्षणम् ॥
sargaśca pratisargaśca vaṁśo manvantarāṇī ca
vaṁśānucaritaṁcaiva purāṇam pañcalakkṣaṇam

1. *Sarga*: To keep track of the creation and evolution of the Universe.

2. *Pratisarga*: To keep track of the decreation or dissolution of the Universe.

3. *Vaṁśa:* This refers to maintaining a record of the descent of heavenly bodies in the universe and other biological species.

4. *Vaṁśānucarita:* This involves keeping track of lineages, pedigrees, or genealogies of heavenly bodies in the universe and other biological species up to the present day.

5. *Manvantara: A measure of the time elapsed since the universe's origin.*

At the origin of humankind, only five primary issues were prevalent and were thus addressed in the Purāṇas. However, as society developed and became more stratified, the concerns of humanity also diversified significantly, leading to an expanded subject matter within the Purāṇas. This increase in topics is noted in various Purāṇas themselves. For example, according to the Śiva Purāṇa (Shri Ram Sharma, Introduction, p. 11), the subject matter of the Purāṇas should encompass the following themes:

सृष्टिश्चापि विसृष्टिचेत् स्थितिस्तेषां च पालनं कर्मणाम्।
वासना वार्ता चमूनां च क्रमेण च वर्णनम्।

प्रलयानां च मोक्षस्य च निरुपणं च उत्कीर्तनम्।
हरेरेव देवानां च पृथक् पृथक् ।
Sṛṣṭiścāpi visṛṣṭiścet sthitisteṣāṁ capālanam karmaṇām
Vāsanā vārtā camunāṁ cakrameṇa cavarṇanaṁ
Pralayānāṁ camokṣasya ca nirupaṇam utkīrtanaṁ
Hare reva devānāṁ ca pṛthak -pṛthak

'The description of creation, decreation, sustenance, caring, action and attachment, an account of dissolution and redemption, and appreciation of Puruṣa and various heavenly bodies are the subjects dealt with in the Purāṇas.'

Vāyu Purāṇa (104.11-17.), on the other hand, gives a more elaborate account of the subject matter of the Purāṇas. It suggests:

पुराणेषु बहवः धर्मास्ते विनिरुपिताः।
रागिणां च विरागाणां यतीनां ब्रह्मचारिणाम् गृहस्थानाम्।
वानप्रस्थानां स्त्रीशूद्राणां विशेषतः॥
ब्राह्मणक्षत्रियविशां ये च संकरजातयः।
गंगाद्या च महानद्या या महानद्यो यज्ञव्रत तपांसि च॥
अनेकविध दानानि यमाश्च नियमैः सह।
योगधर्माबहुविधाः साख्याः भागवतस्तथा॥
भक्तिमार्गा ज्ञानमार्गा वैराग्यनिलनीरजः।
उपासनविधष्चोक्तं कर्म संशुद्धिचेतसाम्॥
ब्राह्मं शैवं वैष्णवं च सौरं शाक्तं तथाऽऽर्हतम्।
षड्दर्शनानि चोक्तानि स्वभावनियतानि च॥
एतदन्तच्च विधिं पुराणेषु निरूपितम्।
अतः परं किमप्यस्ति न वा बोद्धव्यमुत्तमम्॥
purāṇeṣu bahavaḥ dharmāste vinirupitāḥ /
rāgiṇāṁ cha virāgāṇāṁ yatīnāṁ brahmachāriṇām gṛhasthānām /
vānaprasthānāṁ strīśūdrāṇāṁ viśeṣataḥ //

brāhmaṇakṣatriyaviśāṁ ye cha saṁkarajātayaḥ ।
gaṁgādyā cha mahānadyā yā mahānadyo yajñavrata tapāṁsi cha ॥
anekavidha dānāni yamāścha niyamaiḥ saha ।
yogadharmābahuvidhāḥ sākhyāḥ bhāgavatastathā ॥
bhaktimārgā jñānamārgā vairāgyanilanīrajaḥ ।
upāsanavidhaṣchoktaṁ karma saṁśuddhichetasām ॥
brāhmaṁ śaivaṁ vaiṣṇavaṁ cha sauraṁ śāktaṁ tathā rhatam ।
ṣaḍdarśanāni choktāni svabhāvaniyatāni cha ॥
ētadantachcha vidhiṁ purāṇeṣu nirūpitam ।
ataḥ paraṁ kimapyasti na vā boddhavyamuttamam ॥

'Purāṇas are also the records of various ethical codes (dharmas) observed by lovers, recluses, ascetics, brahmacharis (bachelors taking to the study of Vedas and other Śāstras), householders, jungle-dwellers, ladies, and particularly scholars, defence personnel, traders, illiterates, and other mixed professional races. Geographical accounts and accounts of various schools of rituals and religions and various other things concerning individual and society are the main subjects to be dealt with in the Purāṇas.'

It is clear from the discussion above that Itihāsa, in ancient times, not only chronicled important events in chronological order but also traced the origins and causes of significant occurrences, both in nature and society. Itihāsa maintained a connected account of these events in relation to time and space. On the other hand, Purāṇa focused on events that repeat in every new cycle of creation. This is reflected in the phrase associated with Purāṇas: "*purā navaṁ bhavati it Purāṇam*," meaning "whatever repeats is the subject matter of Purāṇa." Therefore, Purāṇa can be viewed as a substitute for modern history. The etymology of Purāṇa is closely related to the saying, "history repeats." In this way, Itihāsa and Purāṇa complemented each other; while Purāṇa recorded events, Itihāsa explored the origins and causes of those recorded events.

3. **Ākhyāna**: was used, as stated above, for the historical account of the creation of the universe.
4. **Upākhyāna**: is a sub narration related to the main narration.
5. **Sarga**: Creation of the universe.
6. **Anvākhyana**: To relate the historical narration narrated by some other person.
7. **Ākhyāyikā**: A historical narration of creation traditionally handed down to posterity.
8. **Purākalpa**: To narrate the events taken place in the previous kalpas.
9. **Purāvṛtta**: To narrate the events taken place in the previous manvantaras.
10. **Aitihya**: A popular event in history.
11. **Itivṛtta**: A brief history.
12. **Parakriyā**: A particular method to narrate the historical works/ deeds done by others.
13. **Parakṛti**: A particular method to reproduce the history recorded by another historian.
14. **Kathā:** The historical narration about the main character
15. **Parikathā:** The historical narration of characters other than the main character.
16. **Gāthā**: There is a difference between gāthā and kathā. Kathā is the historical narration about the main character, but gāthā is a narration told in the context of the main narration.
17. **Charit:** Biography of ideal leaders in society.
18. **Anucharit**: Biography of the posterity of leaders in society.
19. **Vaṁśa**: An account of the descent of species and heavenly bodies.
20. **Vaṁśānucarit:** An account of lineage or line of descent or

pedigrees or genealogies of heavenly bodies or human beings till date.

21. **Gotra-pravarakāra**: An institution of individuals keeping an account of main gotras (descents/effects) and subsequent gotras (descents/effects).

22. **Nārāśaṁsī**: A bibliography of the persons who have made a laudable contribution to society or the nation.

23. **Rājaśāsana**: Records of the Government orders and political history.

24. **Kālavida**: An astronomer keeping the record of the history of time and chronology in history.

From the above-cited types of history, it is clear that history was studied in ancient India as an extensive and exhaustive subject. As such it is our duty to preserve and further the age-old scientific tradition of Itihāsa and Purāṇa of ancient India.

(1) To revive the age-old tradition of Itihāsa, we shall have to trace the origin and causes of events we are dealing with. We are to describe actions in terms of tendencies, motives, causes, and ends behind them.

(2) To revive the tradition of Purāṇas, we shall have to collect, consolidate and compile the data on evolution and dissolution of the universe, lying scattered in the Vedic texts and present the connected account of the same in the more lucid and simple terms or say in modern scientific terms, we shall have to trace the descent of heavenly bodies. We shall have to restructure our calendar as per the calculation done by Vedic Ṛṣis, which is more scientific and begins with the very beginning of our universe. We shall have to trace the connected account of the origin and evolution of speech.

(3) We shall have to preserve the records of Pañjikāras existing at all the famous Tīrtha sthalas of India. Through the records of Pañjikāras, we are still able to know at least 1000 years 1000-year-long history of each and every family and various villages of this country.

(4) We should also take steps to preserve the tradition of Māgadhas and Sūtas who were given the responsibility of teaching and preaching the history of our country. In this very chain, Kathāvācakas, Chāraṇas, Bhāṭas, Mirāsis, Vṛttalekhakas' tradition may not be overlooked, who produced the literature based on real history.

2. Sources of Indian History

When it comes to sources for the history of Ancient India, we are fortunate to have a vast collection of Sanskrit literature. Currently, there are over one crore Sanskrit manuscripts located worldwide. The challenge lies in editing and publishing this extensive body of work and conducting a thorough study of these texts. In his renowned work, 'Satyarth Prakash,' Maharishi Dayanand Sarasvati presents a genealogy of the kings who ruled Indraprastha since the time of the great emperor Yudhiṣṭhira. He derived this list from the fortnightly publications Harischandra Patrikā and Mohan Patrikā, which based their genealogy on a manuscript that is over 300 years old.

Kalhaṇa, in 748 AD, while writing the chronology of the kings of Kaliyuga in his work Rājataraṅgiṇī, highlights that the history of the Kaliyuga kings was fraught with crises. He compiled this work after gathering information from various sources, both fragmentary and complete, that existed before him. Therefore, there is ample source material available to construct an integrated history of ancient India, provided that scholars, institutions, and the Indian government make proper, genuine, and diligent efforts.

Western historians and their followers in India often disregard the most accurate and credible Indian sources. To them, these sources seem like romances and flights of fancy. Consequently, they have neglected to include chapters on figures such as Harischandra, Raghu, Yayāti, Śaryāti, Māndhātā, Pṛthu, Śivi, and many others in the history of ancient India. The periods of the Rāmāyaṇa and Mahābhārata also do not feature in the accounts of ancient Indian history written by foreign scholars and their Indian followers.

Our students are not taught the history of Rāma and Krishna, whose birth dates have been preserved and celebrated within Indian society. Ironically, what should be taught as history is instead categorized as myths, tales, or stories. For many Western scholars, a fact is only considered reliable if it is documented in their own narratives, and their Indian followers seem to accept only what their foreign mentors assert.

If Megasthenes had written a few words about India, the Mauryan Empire would have been included as a chapter in Indian history. The term "Sandrocottus," as he mentioned, is erroneously used as a Greek equivalent for the Indian Chandragupta Maurya. If Fa-Hien had composed something about India, the Gupta period would have become a topic of study in Indian history. Similarly, if Huien-Tsang wrote about India, Harshvardhana would be included in the historical narrative. Accounts from Arabian writers like Alberuni or memoirs from Babur about India are accepted as historical documents. Likewise, if Mortimer Wheeler or John Marshall excavated a mound in Harappa and provided their interpretations, those findings are quickly integrated into the accepted chapters of Indian history.

Despite the fact that the Indus Valley civilization is dated as far back as 2600-1900 BC, the 5,000-year-old period of the Mahābhārata is often dismissed as irrelevant to history. We hesitate to accept what is well-documented by our own sources, viewing Indian scholars and seers as unreliable while considering foreign scholarship as valid. To write an accurate and integrated history of India, we need to disengage from foreign influences. Although foreign or archaeological sources should be regarded as supplementary evidence, they are often seen as essential for formulating our history. If we lack information, we should not assume that it is simply unavailable.

The loss of many Indian sources due to foreign invasions and the fact that many extant sources are neglected in museums and libraries around the world pose significant challenges. It is crucial to explore and utilize this vast repository of data to construct the true and factual history of India. Regarding chronology, Indian writers were proficient in astronomy and included astronomical datelines in both literary sources and epigraphic records. Therefore, there is a need to establish an ancient calendar that allows us to verify the timelines presented in literature and inscriptions, enabling us to create a precise chronology of Indian history.

The present author has made a modest attempt to construct a "9000 Years Calendar of Various Eras," successfully verifying the astronomical datelines cited in epigraphic records, Purāṇas, and other Sanskrit texts to identify the epochs of various historical events and personalities. To comprehend this chronology, scholars and readers are encouraged to consult our "9000 Years Calendar of Various Indian Eras" for cross-referencing. I hope this work will be enlightening for both scholars and general readers alike, offering a clearer understanding of the actual and factual timeline of Indian history..

Notation for historical dating: In this book, the following notation has been used to denote historical dating as described in the Sanskrit literature and Saṁkalpa Pāṭhas.

The extant *Saṁkalpa* tradition reads as under:

अद्य ब्रह्मणोर्द्वितीये परार्द्धे श्वेतवाराहकल्पे सप्तमे वैवस्वतमन्वन्तरे अष्टाविंशतितमे कलियुगे कलिप्रथमचरणे 5119 गताब्दे ।

adya brahmaṇordvitīye parārddhe śvetavārāhakalpe saptame vaivasvatamanvantare aṣṭāviṁśatitamekaliyuge kaliprathamacharaṇe 5119 gatābde ।

The above-cited saṅkalpa tradition calculates the time elapsed since the end of the previous universal creation cycle and the beginning of the current cycle. According to the Saṁkalpa-pāṭha, the first half of Brahmā's life (Parārdha) has already passed, and the first Kalpa (Śveta Vārāha) of the second half (Parārdha) is currently underway. The first half of Brahmā's age is equivalent to 50 Brahmā years, which totals 155,520,000,000,000 years. This period has now concluded, and we are currently in the 51st Brahmā year of the present universal creation cycle.

As of now, 155,521,972,949,120 (approximately 155 trillion) years have elapsed since the start of the current cycle of universal creation. In this cycle, the Svāyaṁbhuva Maṇḍala

(Super-Galactic Center) originated 14,932,949,120 (around 14.9 billion) years ago, while the Parameṣṭhi Maṇḍala (Galaxies) came into existence 10,612,949,120 (about 10.6 billion) years ago. The Sūrya Maṇḍala (the star of our solar system) was formed 6,292,949,120 (approximately 6.2 billion) years ago, and the Earth originated around 4.3 billion years ago. Biological life appeared on Earth roughly 1.9 billion years ago. Human beings emerged on Earth 12,096,000 years after the inception of biological life.

The Saṁkalpa also notes that since the beginning of the Śvetavārāha Kalpa, which is the first day (Kalpa) of Brahmā's second Parārdha, six Manus have elapsed. We are currently in the seventh Manu, Vaivasvata, and 27 Mahāyugas have already passed. The 28th Mahāyuga is in progress, encompassing the Kṛta, Tretā, and Dvāpara Yugas. As for the present Kaliyuga, 5,119 years have passed as of the 13th tithi of Bhādrapada Kṛṣṇa Pakṣa in the year 2019. Thus, the 51st century of the current Kaliyuga has ended, and the 52nd century is currently ongoing.

The time reckoning mentioned above can be represented in the following notation:

Kalpa/Manvantara/Mahayuga/Yuga/Varsha or year/Month/day or Tithi

For example, 21st Dec. 2018 will be written as, 51/7/28 Kali/5119/Margasirsa/S-14

In the above notation

51 denotes 51st Kalpa named Śveta Vārāha Kalpa

7 denotes 7th Manvantara named Vaivasvata Manvantara of Śveta Vārāha Kalpa

28	denotes of 28th Mahāyuga or
28th Kali	denotes Kaliyuga of 28th Mahāyuga
5119	denotes 5119th year of 28th Kaliyuga
S-14	denotes 14th tithi of Śukla Pakṣa
K	will denote Kṛṣṇa Pakṣa

3. Western Scholars and Indian History

Introduction of Sanskrit to the West in the last quarter of 18th century attracted Western scholarship to the study of Indian literature, history, and culture. William Jones (1746-1794) was among those occidental scholars who took the lead in Indic Studies. He founded the Asiatic Society of India in Calcutta in 1786. [1] Two years earlier, he delivered the third annual discourse; [2] in his often-cited "philologer" passage, he noted similarities between Sanskrit, Ancient Greek, and Latin as under:

William Jones (1746-1794)

> The Sanskrit language, whatever be its antiquity, is of a wonderful structure; more perfect than the Greek, more copious than the Latin, and more exquisitely refined than either, yet bearing to both of them a stronger affinity, both in the roots of verbs and the forms of grammar, than could possibly have been produced by accident; so strong indeed, that no philologer could examine them all three, without believing them to have sprung from some common source, which, perhaps, no longer exists; there is a similar reason, though not quite so forcible, for supposing that both the Gothic and

---

[1] T. K. John, *"Research and Studies by Western Missionaries and Scholars in Sanskrit Language and Literature,"* in the St. Thomas Christian Encyclopaedia of India, Vol. III, Ollur [Trichur] 2010 Ed. George Menachery, pp.79 - 83

[2] *A Reader in Nineteenth Century Historical Indo-European Linguistics: The Third Anniversary Discourse, On the Hindus*

> the Celtic, though blended with a very different idiom, had the same origin with the Sanskrit; and the old Persian might be added to the same family.

Friedrich Max Müller (1859) calls this event the beginning of comparative linguistics, Indo-European studies, and Sanskrit philology in the West.

European scholarship, burdened by a superiority complex stemming from its political dominance over the entire world, viewed itself as victors and the rest as victims, masters and slaves. In such a hierarchical relationship, the victor or master always held a position of superiority, while the victim or slave was perpetually inferior. The victor would condescend upon the victim, and the victor or master would expect the victim or slave to conform to their beliefs. If the victim or slave refused, the victor or master would force them to comply.

As new masters, they sought to maintain their supremacy by comprehending the cultures and histories of the colonized people in their own distorted manner. They recognized that political subjugation would not endure indefinitely unless they subjugated the colonized people intellectually and culturally. To achieve this, they aimed to establish their racial, ideological, and historical superiority over the people of this country. To accomplish this goal, they sought to convert the colonized people into their fold.

In the 17th and 18th centuries, European intellectuals deliberately presented a distorted portrayal of Indian history, culture, and literature to create an intellectual crisis in the country. Under the guise of this crisis, they sought to impose their education system upon Indians, stripping them of their cultural richness and past superiority, thereby encouraging them to embrace their faith and pave the way for their permanent settlement and rule.

As part of their plot against Indians, many European scholars pursued Indic Studies with the ulterior motive of Christianizing India.

We come across an astonishing fact that Max Müller who himself was deeply interested in ancient Indian texts, served as a functionary for the colonialists and for Christian evangelists. This fact is verified by one of his letters addressed to the Duke of Orgoil, who was the British secretary of state for India, Müller (Georgina Adelaide Müller, 1902: Chp. XVI, p.358) wrote on 16 December 1868:

Max Müller (1823-1900)

'The ancient religion of India is totally doomed and if the Christianity doesn't step in whose fault will it be.'

In a letter addressed to his wife Georgina Adelaide Müller on December 9, 1867, Prof. Max Mueller wrote (Georgina Adelaide Müller, 1902: Chp. XV, p. 328):

'I still have a great work to do, and I often feel that I might have done a great deal more if I had kept the one object of my life more steadily in view. I sometimes wish you would help me more in doing that, and insist on my working harder at the 'Veda' and nothing else. I hope I shall finish that work and feel convinced that though I shall not live to see it, yet this edition of mine and translation of Vedas will hereafter tell to a great extent on the fate of India and the growth of millions of souls in this country.'

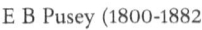

E B Pusey (1800-1882)

At the same place, he further observes:

'It is the root of their religion, and to show them what the root is, I feel sure, is the only way of uprooting all that has sprung from it during the last 3,000 years.

The text of his letter is self-explanatory to the fact that Max Müller pursued Indic studies with an ulterior motive and he was more or less successful in his efforts. His friend Dr. E.B Pusey who was an English churchman and for more than fifty years Regius Professor of Hebrew at Christ Church, Oxford, hurls praises on him for the good job done by him for which he was awarded the position of Sanskrit Chair. He also makes a mention of his support in his elevation to the Chair. He writes on June 2, 1860 (Georgina Adelaide Müller, 1902: Chp. XII, p. 237-38):

'My dear Professor, On the first election to the Sanskrit Chair, you will have heard that we were divided before two great names. Professor Wilson, whose first-rate Sanskrit knowledge was in the mouth of everyone, and Dr. Mill, who, many of us thought, might fulfil the object of the founder better by giving to the Professorship a direct missionary turn. The same thought would naturally recur to us now, and I have kept myself in suspense since our sudden loss of Professor Wilson. **My first impression, however, is my abiding conviction, that we should be best promoting the intentions of the founder by electing yourself, who have already done so much to make us fully acquainted with the religious systems of those whom we wish to win to the Gospel**. It is obvious that without this knowledge a missionary must be continually at fault, ignorant alike of the points of contact of which, after the manner of St. Paul, he may avail himself, or of those which present the chief obstacles to the reception of the Gospel in the minds of those whom he would win. I cannot but think then that your labors on the Vedas-while they attest your wonderful power in mastering this ancient Sanskrit (and of course of the more modern Sanskrit, through which you had access to the older), and while they evince, as **I understand, great philological talent, beyond the knowledge of Sanskrit itself-are the greatest gifts which have been bestowed on those who would win to Christianity the subtle and thoughtful minds of the cultivated Indians**. We owe you very much for the past, and we shall ourselves gain greatly by placing you in a position in which you can give your undivided attention to those labors by which we have already so much profited. You know that I have felt it my duty to confine myself to a different class of languages, those which bear directly upon Hebrew. I have written, therefore, on that upon which I am alone competent to write - not your great knowledge of Sanskrit, of which we have such eminent testimony, but of the great value of that special line of study to which you have devoted yourself. **Your work will form a new era in the efforts for the conversion of India, and Oxford will have reason to be thankful that, by giving you a home, it will have facilitated a work of such primary and lasting importance for the conversion of India, and which, by enabling us to compare that early false religion with the true, illustrates the more than blessedness of what we enjoy.**

Yours very faithfully,

E.B. Pusey

Monier Williams (1819-1899)

The above letter by a Churchman to Müller reveals the hidden agenda of colonialists. By far, this was not the only case. There is another celebrated scholar called Monier Williams he writes (1879: 262):

'Christianity has many more points to their ancient faith than Islam has, and when the walls of the mighty fortress of Brahmanism are encircled, undermined and finally stormed by the soldiers of the cross, the victory of Christianity must be signal and complete.'

H H Wilson (1786-1860)

In his preface to his famous Sanskrit-English Dictionary (1899: p. ix) Monier William, as the Professor of Boden Chair, reveals the objective of founding the Chair for Sanskrit studies by Col. Boden as to convert the natives of India to Christianity. He writes thus:

> In explanation I must draw attention to the fact that I am only the second occupant of the Boden Chair, and that its founder; Col. Boden, stated most explicitly in his will (dated Aug. 15, 1811) that special object of his munificent bequest was to promote the translation of the scriptures into Sanskrit; so as to enable his countrymen to proceed in the conversion of the natives of India to the Christian Religion.

The Book 'Eminent Orientalists: Indian, European and American' (p. 53) informs that Prof. H.H. Wilson, one of the occupants of Boden Chair, delivered two public lectures at Oxford before general audience on 'Religious and Philosophical Systems of the Hindus'. These lectures were written to help candidates for a prize of Pound 200 given by John Muir, a well-known old Haileybury man and great Sanskrit scholar, for the best refutation of the Hindu religious systems. The prize was obtained by one Mr. Mullions.

The above evidence shows that the whole exercise was done by Prof. Wilson for 200 Pounds to encourage students for the refutation of Hindu religion.

However, I must say that whole European community cannot be blamed for their covert designs until and unless some concrete evidence is come across with regard their bias against Indian literature and their objective to evangelize India.

In addition to what has cited above, we must not forget that in the 16th and 17th century, Church was dominating the western intelligentsia. Nobody dared to challenge the ideas subscribed by the Church. We have the example of Galileo Galilei (1564-1642) who had to face the ire of Church when he challenged the egocentrism subscribed by the Church and championed heliocentric. On 3rd October 1992, the Pope Johannes the second said 'sorry' how things were for Galilei. What made the Church very powerful, firstly the Church was making lot of fortune through 'salt trade', secondly the Church was making innocent people to 'confession'. If you confess a sin at church, it will be forgiven. So the Church used to get lot of

Information. Not to mention the mad work of the Malleus maleficarum. One horrible example was the witch burnings. Some tests were used to be done to verify if the woman was a witch or not. They used to open her up and if a particular type of blood comes out, she was considered as innocent. The problem was in this process, usually the participant used to die.

Thus the entire intellectual world of Europe surrendered before the Church We find an echo of this fact in a very popular saying, 'So far as religion is concerned, the sun moves around the earth, but so far as science is concerned, the earth moves around the sun'. Now we may discuss the veracity of the evangelical model of hermeneutics.

Archbishop Usher (1581-1656)

In the 16th century, an Archbishop named Usher (1581-1656) thoughtlessly declared that creation took place on 22 October, 4004 years before the birth of Christ at 9 AM. Thus a lakṣmaṇa rekhā (limit) of chronology was drawn (fixed) and the same was accepted by historians as the borderline in western hermeneutics to fix the chronology of the history of Europe as well as other countries colonized by them. Europeans developed such a framework of their hermeneutics as could not accommodate the concept of history stretching beyond 2000 years before Christ and any chronology beyond 4004 years before Christ was outrightly rejected. So far as sources of the history of Ancient India are concerned, we have a vast Sanskrit literature as source material to accomplish this uphill task. Today we have more than one crore Sanskrit Manuscripts spread over the whole world. The need is to edit and publish such a huge number of books and to undertake an in-depth study of these works.

Kalhaṇa (748 AD) also while writing the chronology of the kings of Kaliyuga in his Rājataraṅgiṇī points out that the history of the Kaliyuga kings was crisis-ridden and he composed this work after collecting the data from many other sources existed prior to him in fragmentary or intact forms. Thus there is no dearth of source material to compile the integrated history of ancient India if proper, genuine and painstaking efforts are made by scholars, institutions and the Indian Govt.

However, under the pressure and impression of Church, an old chronology of Indian history based on astronomy was debunked and new chronology was imposed demoting Indian chronology to match with the chronology of the European history.

When William Jones, who started conducting a fair study of the Indian literature, assigned a higher chronology to Indian history on the basis of the records of the Purāṇas than recommended by Church, he was persistently persuaded by Max Müller to demote the Indian chronology to such an extent as could prove the civilization of west far more ancient than that of India. This scheme of Max Müller of demoting Indian chronology deliberately is exposed by his following request made to William Jones:

"There is but one means through which the History of India can be connected with Greece and its Chronology be reduced to proper limits. Although we look in vain in the literature of the Brahmaṇas or Buddhists for any allusion to Alexander's conquest, and although it is impossible to identify any of the historical events, related by Alexander's companions, with the historical traditions of India, one name has fortunately been preserved by classical writers who describe the events immediately following Alexander's conquest, to form a connecting link between the history of the East and the West. This is the name of Sandracottus or Sandrocyptus, the Sanskrit Chandragupta.

M. Winternitz
(1863-1937)

Max Müller's above-cited insistence forced William Jones to fall in line with him in misapplying the Greek synchronism of

Sandracottus with Chandragupta of Maurya Dynasty instead of the Samudragupt of Gupta Dynasty and thus chronology of Indian history was demoted by 1200 years. Under the same scheme maximum date for the composition of the first book of humanity, the Ṛgveda, was assigned 1500 B.C and million years old astronomical chronology assigned by Indians to the origin of the universe, earth and Vedas were mocked and debunked as farfetched one.

Under the pressure and impression of Church, western models of hermeneutics were developed such a way that the sense of history and chronology in India may be declared as non-existent. To quote a few, *a German Scholar M. Winternitz* (1927: P.30) in his Introduction to his reputed work 'A History of Indian literature' observes as follows:

> 'To them, the facts themselves were more important than their chronological order. They attached no importance at all, especially in the literary matters, to the question of what was earlier or later.'

A A Macdonell (1854-1930)

An Arabian traveller Alberuni (Edward C. Sachau, P.10), who in the year 1030 wrote a book on India remarks:

> 'Unfortunately, the Hindus do not pay much attention to the historical order of things. They are very careless in relating the chronological succession of their kings and when they are pressed for information, they are at loss, not knowing what to say, and invariably take to romancing.'

A.A.Macdonell (1900: P.7) also draws our attention to the same weakness of Indian literature.

> 'History is one weak spot in Indian literature. It is, in fact, non-existent. The total lack of historical sense is so

> characteristics, that the whole course of Sanskrit Literature is darkened by the shadow of this object, suffering as it does from an entire absence of exact chronology'.

According to Max Müller (1859: P. 18)

> 'No wonder that a nation like India cared so little for history?'

While indulging in the Indian history bashing program, these scholars avoided referring to the findings of Jones (1799: chapter on 'The Chronology of the Hindus)' with regard to Indian history. He observes as under:

> 'And for these generations (Brahaddradhas) the Hindus allotted a period of one thousand years. They reckon exactly the same number (1000 years) of years for twenty generations of Jarāsandha, whose son Sahadeva was contemporary to Yudhisthira, and founded a new dynasty in Magadha or Bihar. Then there is a list of twenty Magadha kings from Sahadeva, son of Jarasandha to Satyajit, whose son Puranjaya is killed by his minister Sunga who placed his son Pradyota on the throne. Then the Pradyota dynasty starts in 2100 BC, and then, the Sisunaga Dynasty from 1962 BC followed by Nanda Dynasty from 1602 BC. Then comes the Maurayas from 1502 BC, the Sung dynasty from Pushyamitra 1365 BC, to Kshema Bhumi 1253 BC, then the Kanwa Dynasty from 1253 to 908 BC followed by the Andhra Dynasty from 908 BC, to 452 BC, the last king being Chandrabija".

The above information from William Jones' treatise repudiates westerner's accusations that Indians had no sense of writing history, or chronologically narrating the events. We had clear-cut chronology assigned to each and every event of history. But it was a well-planned attack by the westerners to eradicate India's past. They disapproved of the authenticity of Paurāṇika and other historical records. Had they approved of the authenticity of Paurāṇika and other historical records preserved in Sanskrit literature, they would not have been able to declare the absence of history in India and historical sense of Indians and distort Indian history fact-wise and chronology-wise.

Such western scholars wanted Indians to think of their history in terms of their hermeneutic framework. Whereas, the fact is that in western culture, the concept of chronology evolved 2000 years ago. Since they wanted the supremacy of Church, they accepted the Birth date of Christ as the sheet anchor in the historical chronology of the world. They started teaching in the light of the false Biblical view that Christ was the son of God born first ever on the earth. St. Augustine through Hegel was impressed by Christian fundamentalism and sectarian bias. Karl Jaspers (1963: p.1), the writer of "The origin and goal of history" reveals this fact as:

> 'In the western world, the philosophy of history was founded in the Christian faith. In a grandiose sequence of works ranging from St. Augustine to Hegel, this faith visualised the movement of God through history. God's acts of revelation represent the decisive dividing lines.'

Hegel was proud to say:

> "All history goes toward and comes from Christ. The appearance of the son of God is the axis of world history. Our chronology bears daily witness to this Christian structure of history."

Thus they started calculating the genesis or origin of all events and things after or before the birth of the first son of God, the Christ and vainly claimed themselves as the father of history. Historian philosophers like Jaspers (1963: p. 11) criticizes the idea of history writing based on Christian faith. According to him,

> 'But the Christian faith is the only one faith, not the faith of mankind. This view of universal history, therefore, suffers from the defect that it can only be valid for believing Christians. But even in the west, Christians

have not tied their empirical conceptions of history to their faith. An article of faith is not an article of empirical insight into the real cause of history, as being different in its meaning.'

In fact, our western friends had no idea that the concept of chronology or Kālagaṇanā in India finds its origin with the very origin of the universe. They kept finding in ancient Indian literature the traces of Christian chronological dating type system and so couldn't understand the astronomical dating of the events. Astronomical dating, to them, appeared, as it does, in real sense romances and nothing else. They couldn't make out Kalhaṇa's statement (1.51) of Kauravas and Pāṇḍavas presence in Saptarshi Saṁvat 653 (according to Kashmira School that counts Nakṣatras from Rohiṇi onwards).

शतेषषट्‌सु सार्धकेषु त्र्यधिकेषु च भूतले ।
कलेर्गतेषु वर्षाणामभुवन् कुरुपाण्डवाः ।।
śateṣaṣaṭsu sārdhakeṣu trayadhikeṣu cha bhūtale ।
kalergateṣu varṣāṇāmabhuvan kurupāṇḍavāḥ ।।

[Meaning] When six hundred and fifty-three years of the Saptarṣī Saṁvat in Kaliyuga had passed away, the Kauravas and Pāṇḍavas lived on the earth.

Since Kalhaṇa followed Kashmiri school, so 653 Saptarṣī Saṁvat here means Maghā 53 which corresponds to 3123BC. It will be counted as Maghā 53 (expired) from second Saptarṣī cycle, i.e. 3776 BC-653=3123 BC. Saptarṣī Saṁvat needs correction by ± 18 years to it within one cycle. So, Saptarṣī Saṁvat dates may be corrected upto ± 18. This reference date of Mahābharata war verifes the date line derived by us as 3137 BC. when Pāṇḍavas and Kauravas were present.

To them, Vāyupurāṇa's dating of Nanda's accession in the Saptarshi Saṁvat 1015 (according to Patna school that counts from Revati onwards both in normal and reverse order) i.e. 1641BC and in Saṁ. 610 (according to Kashmiri school) i.e. 1641BC had no meaning. Varāhamihira's unfolding his own time period i.e., 2526 years after the 1st Yudhiṣṭhira Saṁvat, i.e. 3173-2526=647 BC went unnoticed by them.

From the foregoing discussion, it is crystal clear that the westerners came India with the sole mission to plunder the immense wealth of this country. Its richness attracted them so much that they wanted to rule this country so that they would plunder it to the maximum possible limits to enrich themselves. They wanted to propagate their religion so that the people of this ancient most civilisation may also be converted into their fold. To rule a country politically, it is necessary for the ruler to establish his racial, ideological and historical superiority upon the people of ruled country. That is why there was a deliberate attempt on the part of European intelligentsia in the 17th and 18th century to present a distorted picture of history and chronology of India so that an intellectual crisis might be declared in this country. Thus our history was distorted fact-wise and chronology-wise and a confusion was created regarding the historicity of Indian history.

Here I wouldn't like to blame the whole community of the then European scholars until and unless some concrete evidence comes across with regarding their bias against Indian history and literature to evangelise India. This is also well-established fact that the European scholars who were not leading the mission like that of Max Müller were persuaded by the pseudo-evolutionism of Darwin. Since the Vedas were first ever written composition of the world, they were looked upon as the songs of the primitive shepherd or uncultured and savage race of the world. Thus from the aforementioned discussion, it can be maintained that European scholarship was suffering from three serious defects.

Firstly, it was their evil designs.

Secondly, they were not able to come out of the pressure of Church.

The third thing coming to their way was their lack of understanding of the vast and exalted Sanskrit literature and as well as their total unfamiliarity with the tradition and culture of India.

All these three factors led to the distortion of Indian history and chronology as well as Indian culture and civilization at the hands of European scholars knowingly or unknowingly. Hereunder an attempt is being has been made to assign Indian chronology to Indian history based upon information contained in Indian literature, epigraphic records and astronomical data. Indian history begins with the origin of universe.

4. Epochs of Various India Eras

India is credited with the invention of astronomy and mathematics, and the foundations of these sciences were learned by the entire world from Indian scholars. Indian astronomy predates that of the Babylonians, Egyptians, and Hellenistic cultures. John Playfair, a Scottish mathematician who lived from 1748 to 1819 AD, demonstrated that the epoch of the astronomical observations recorded in the tables by Hindu astrologers dates back to 4300 BC. Additionally, the Greek historians Pliny and Arrian, who lived around 95-175 AD, noted that Indians used the Saptarṣi calendar, which began in 6676 BC. This indicates that the use of eras by Indians goes back to ancient times.

To fully grasp Indian history, it's essential to understand the various eras that define it. The chronology of Indian history is complex and involves multiple distinct periods. Below, you will find a brief introduction to each of these eras:

Saptarṣī era: This era was used in Kashmir and the neighboring hilly areas. During the time of Alberuni (1030 AD), it also appeared to be in use in Multan and other parts of the region. This is the only method of time reckoning mentioned in the *Rājataraṅgiṇī*. The era, as previously discussed, is also known as Laukika Saṁvat, Pahari Saṁvat, Śāstra Saṁvat, or Kacchā Saṁvat, and is sometimes referred to as Śakā or Śākā. The Saptarishis, a cluster of seven stars popularly known as the Great Bear, are referenced in several ancient Indian texts that utilize the Saptarishis era for chronological purposes. This system originated from the belief that the Saptarishis move through one Nakṣatra (lunar mansion) in 100 years, corresponding to the twenty-seven constellations from Aśvinī to Revatī. According to the The *Kaliyuga Rājavṛttānta* of the *Bhaviṣya Purāṇa* (Bhāga 3, Chapt. 3):

सप्तविंशति पर्यन्तेकृत्स्ने नक्षत्रमंडले।
सप्तर्षयस्तु तिष्ठन्ति पर्यायेण शत शतम्॥
saptaviṁśati paryantekṛtsne nakṣatramaṁḍale ।

saptarṣayastu tiṣṭhanti paryāyeṇa śata śatam //

[Meaning] The Saptarṣis revolve around the 27 Nakṣatras, spending 100 years in each, taking 2700 years to complete one full revolution.

This cycle of the Saptarṣis, consisting of 2700 human years, when converted to divya years (where 360 human years equal 1 divya year), is equal to 7.5 divya years (*Kaliyuga Rājavṛttānta of Bhaviṣya Purāṇa* (Bhāga 3, Chapt. 3).

सप्तर्षीणां युगं ह्येतद् दिव्यया संख्यया स्मृतम् ।
समा दिव्याः स्मृताः सप्त दिव्याः मासाः षडेव हि ॥
saptarṣīṇāṁ yugaṁ hyetad divyayā saṁkhyayā smṛtam /
samā divyāḥ smṛtāḥ sapta divyāḥ māsāḥ ṣaḍeva hi //

[Meaning] This is said to be the Yuga (cycle) of the Saptarṣis, reckoned by a divine measure (divyā saṅkhyā).

A yuga or cycle of Saptarshis (2700 human years) is equal to 7 divine years (divya samā) and six divine months (divya māsa).

It is important to note that the Saptarṣis do not spend 100 years in each Nakṣatra. Therefore, this era lacks an astronomical basis. Instead, the Saptarṣī Saṁvat was established based on the assumption that the Saptarṣis reside in one Nakṣatra for 100 years, resulting in a cycle of 2,700 years.

ऋक्षादृक्षं शतेनाब्दैर्यान्ति चित्र शिखण्डिनः ।
दिव्यं सप्तर्षिकालोऽयं क्रमादेवं प्रवर्तते ॥
ṛkṣādṛkṣaṁ śatenābdairyānti chitra śikhaṇḍinaḥ /
divyaṁ saptarṣikālo·yaṁ kramādevaṁ pravartate //
(Kaliyuga Rājavṛttānta of Bhaviṣya Purāṇa (Bhāga 3, Chapt. 3).

[Meaning] The brilliantly crested (Citra-śikhaṇḍin, i.e. the Seven Sages / Saptarṣis) move from one constellation (ṛkṣa) to the next in one hundred years.

Thus, this divine cycle of the Saptarṣis proceeds in this order, i.e. it takes full round of 27 constellations in 2700 years.

The names of Nakṣatras are given below:

1. Aśvinī, 2. Bharaṇī, 3. Kṛttikā, 4. Rohiṇī, 5. Mṛgaśirā, 6. Ārdrā, 7. Punarvasu, 8. Puṣya, 9. Āśleṣā, 10. Maghā, 11. Pūrvaphālgunī, 12. Uttaraphālgunī, 13. Hasta, 14. Chitrā, 15. Svāti, 16. Viśākhā, 17. Anurādhā, 18. Jyeṣṭhā, 19. Mūla, 20. Pūrvāṣāḍhā, 21. Uttarāṣāḍhā, 22. Śravṇa, 23. Dhaniṣṭhā, 24. Śatabhiṣak, 25. Pūrvabhādrapada, 26. Uttara Bhādrapada, 27. Revati.

The Saptarṣis era spans 2,700 years, with each of the 27 constellations representing 100 years. In practice, however, the hundreds are often omitted; thus, once the count reaches 100, a new cycle begins at 1. It is understood that the Saptarṣis entered the Maghā Nakṣatra in 3,176 BCE.

We find two types of calculations: the first follows a regular descending order, while the second uses a reverse ascending order, also known as retrograde motion, depending on the starting Nakṣatra, such as Kṛttikā, Aśvinī, Revatī, or Maghā, which serve as the central points for the calculations.

As of 2023, the Saptarṣis are currently in their 100th year in Punarvasu Nakṣatra when calculated in regular order, and in their 100th year in Hasta Nakṣatra when calculated in reverse order. Our 9000 years calendar table presents the positions of the Saptarṣis in both orders.

Also, according to Greek historians Pliny and Arrian (95-175 AD), Indians used the Saptarṣī calendar, which began in 6676 BC. This calendar emphasizes a popular tradition that starts the Saptarṣī era with the Nakṣatra Aśvinī. Specifically, in this tradition, the Saptarṣī Saṁvat started with Aśvinī Nakṣatra, with Bharaṇī as the first Nakṣatra in the regular order and Revati in the retrograde order. Following this system, the first cycle of Saptarṣī Saṁvat began in 6676 BC, the second in 3976 BC, and the third in 1276 BC.

In addition to this, the Patna school counted Nakṣatras from Revatī (expired), starting with Aśvini as the first. The first Saptarṣī cycle of the Patna school began in 6776 BC, the second in 4076 BC, and the third in 1376 BC.

The third school of thought is the Kashmiri School, which considers Kṛttikā as the first Nakṣatra and counts years starting from Kṛttikā (expired), making Rohiṇi the first Nakṣatra in their system. According to this school, the first cycle of the Saptarṣi era began in 6476 BC, the second cycle started in 3776 BC, and the third cycle commenced in 1076 BC. The writings of the Rājataraṁgiṇī and the Skanda Purāṇa represent this school's views.

It is important to note that the datelines mentioned in the Purāṇas may also refer to the Saptarṣi Saṁvat under names such as Kali or Tiṣya Saṁvat. Therefore, scholars must be very careful when deriving dates based on references from the Purāṇas and the Rājataraṁgiṇī. Understanding whether the proposed dateline belongs to the first, second, or third cycle is essential. Suppose the date of a particular event is before 1076 BC, we would need to calculate it based on the second cycle of the Saptarṣi, which starts in 3776 BC. For example, according to Rājataraṁgiṇī (1-51), when 653 years of the laukika Kali (Saptarṣi Saṁvat) had passed, the war between the Kauravas and the Pāṇḍavas took place.

> शतेषु षड्ष (600) सार्धेषु (50) त्र्यधिकेषु (3) च भूतले
> कलेर्गतेषु वर्षाणामभुवन्कुरुपाण्डवाः ॥ 1.51
> *śateṣu ṣaṭsu (600) sārdheṣu (50) trayadhikeṣu (3) cha bhūtale*
> *kalergateṣu varṣāṇāmabhuvankurupāṇḍavāḥ || 1.51*

> [Meaning] When six hundred and fifty-three (653) years of the Saptarṣis had passed on earth, then were born the Kurus and the Pāṇḍavas.

It is important to note that the first year of the second cycle of the Kashmiri Saptarṣi Saṁvat began in 3776 BC. If we subtract 653 years from 3776, we arrive at 3123 BC (3776 - 653 = 3123 BC). The figure 653 represents the 53rd year of the sixth Nakṣatra. According to the Kashmir school, the counting starts from Rohiṇī, which is considered the first Nakṣatra. In the standard sequence, the sixth Nakṣatra is Maghā. Therefore, the number 653 indicates the 53rd year of Maghā (expired). We know that 3124 BC corresponds to the expired Maghā 53. Thus, according to the Rājataringiṇī, the date of the Mahābhārata is established as 3124 BC.

Hereunder we give a table of various cycles of Saptarṣi Saṁvat according to normal order.

Saptarṣi Schools	Kashmir (Kṛttika Ex)	Patna (Revatī Ex)	Popular (Aśvinī Ex)
1st cycle Normal order	6476 BC	6776 BC	6676 BC
2nd cycle Normal Order	3776 BC	4076 BC	3976 BC
3rd cycle Normal Order	1076 BC	1376 BC	1276 BC
4rth cycle Normal order	1624 AD	1324 AD	1424 AD

Sometimes, datelines are also mentioned in some Paurāṇika texts in the retrograde/reverse order of Nakṣatras. Saptarṣis are posited in Maghā Nakṣatra, so Maghā is the counterpoint for all reverse counting.

We also come across such examples where retrograde countings have also been done from Maghā expired (Āśleṣā).

For example, Acharya Abhinava Gupta mentions in his *Bhairava Stava* that he composed this Stava in Saptarṣi Saṁvat 68.

वसुरसे (68) पौषे कृष्णदशम्यामभिनवगुपतःस्तवमिममकरोत्
vasurase (68) pauṣe kṛṣṇadaśamyāmabhinavagupataḥ stavamimamakarot
[Meaning] In the 68th year, on the tenth day of the dark fortnight of the month of Pauṣa, Abhinavagupta composed this hymn (stotra).

The above quote refers to Saptarṣi Saṁvat 4068 or (991 AD) as per the Saptarṣi school of Maghā Nakṣtra (expired) in retrograde motion. Its third cycle starts in 3076 BC. As such time of Abhinava Gupta arrived at 3076 BC-4068=991 AD. Since the month is Pauṣa and tithi is described as Kṛṣṇa daśamī, the probable Gregorian date is 24 Dec. 991.

How to find out the current Saptarṣi Saṁvat?

Acharya Lalla in his 'शिष्यधीवृद्धितन्त्र' gives the method for finding out the current Saptarṣi Saṁvat. According to him,

> चतुर्दशोने तु कलेः समागते शतोद्धृते भानि फलं जगुर्बुधाः ।
> मरीचिपूर्वैमुनिभिर्विरंचिभाद् भवन्ति भुक्तानि नभोविभूषणैः ।।
> *chaturdaśone tu kaleḥ samāgate śatoddhṛte bhāni phalaṁ jagurbudhāḥ* ।
> *marīchipūrvaimunibhirviraṁchibhād bhavanti bhuktāni nabhovibhūṣaṇaiḥ* ।।

> [Meaning] Subtract 14 from expired Kali Saṁvat, divide the remainder by 100, and the quotient will show the number of current Nakṣatra of Saptarṣis' sojourn as per Saptarṣi's Kṛttikā expired school (starting from Bharaṇi) in standard order.

For example, in the year 2023 AD, we find that 5,124 years of Kaliyuga have passed. By subtracting 14 from this number, we get 5,110. When we divide 5,110 by 100, the quotient is 51. Since there are 27 Nakshatras, we deduct 27 from 51, which gives us 24. Punarvasu is the 24th Nakshatra when counted from Bharani in the usual order. It is significant to note that in 2023, the Saptarishis are spending their 100th year in Punarvasu.

Similarly, we can also find out the current Nakṣatra of Saptarṣi's sojourn in retrograde order by counting from Maghā expired (Āśleṣā). Hast Nakshtra is the 23 Nakṣatra if counted from Āśleṣā in retrograde order. We know presently (in 2023), Saptarṣis are spending their 100th year in Hast Nakṣatra as per retrograde order.

Various cycles of Saptarṣi Saṁvat according to the retrograde/reverse order of Nakṣatra is given below:

Saptarṣī Schools	Kashmir (Kṛttika Ex)	Patna (Revatī Ex)	Popular (Aśvinī Ex)	Magha ex. Āśleṣā
1st cycle Reverse order	7976 BC	7676 BC	7776 BC	8476 BC
2nd cycle Reverse Order	5276 BC	4976 BC	5076 BC	5776 BC
3rd cycle Reverse Order	2576 BC	2276 BC	2376 BC	3076 BC
4rth cycle Reverse order	124 AD	424 AD	324 AD	276 BC

Saṁvatsar (Jovian year): The Sun, Moon, and Jupiter will have a conjunction at the same sign every 60 years. Similarly, Saturn and Jupiter will have a conjunction every twenty years, and every 60 years that conjunction will return to the same sign. This is the basic Saṁvatsara cycle where each of the sixty years of Jupiter's cycle receives its name.

To understand the conjunction cycle of Saturn and Jupiter further, you should know that every twenty years (19.859), Saturn and Jupiter will have a conjunction at about 123 degrees apart (approximately ninth sign from the previous sign of conjunction). Every 60 years (59.577), that conjunction will return to the same sign. If a conjunction happened in Aries, in twenty years, the next will happen in Sagittarius, then Leo in twenty more years, and then back to Aries after 60 years from the original Aries conjunction. In this way, the conjunctions will move in lines of the same element, creating a triangle in the zodiac.

The ancient text Sūrya Siddhānta calculates the Jovian year to be about 361.026721 days or about 4.232 days shorter than the Earth-based solar year. This difference requires that about once every 85 or 86 Jovian years, one of the saṁvatsara is dropped as a shadow year, to synchronize the two calendars. This is so in Northern India. In Southern India, the 60-year cycle has become fixed as applicable with the solar year or lunar year only, and its connection with Jupiter years has been lost. Thus, the Jovial Saṁvatsara changes with every Chaitra Śukla Pratipadā in case of the lunisolar calendar and every Meṣa Saṅkrānti in case of a solar calendar. According to Viṣṇudharmottara Purāṇa, the sixty-year Jovial cycle started with the conjunction of the Sun, the Moon, and Jupiter in Dhaniṣṭhā Nakṣatra on Māgha Śukla Pratipada.

> माघशुक्ल समारम्भे चन्द्रार्को वासवर्क्षगौ ।
> जीवयुक्तौ यदा स्यातां षष्ट्यब्दादिस्तदा भवेत् ॥
> *māghaśukla samārambhe chandrārko vāsavarkṣagau I*
> *jīvayuktau yadā syātāṁ ṣaṣṭyabdādistadā bhavet II*
>
> [Meaning] When the conjunction of the Sun, the Moon, and Jupiter took place first time in Dhaniṣṭhā Nakṣatra on Māgha Śukla Pratipada, the sixty-year Jovial cycle started.

If we go by Aśvini Nakṣatra, then the 60-year Jovial cycle starts from the beginning of Kalpa itself, because at the beginning of Kalpa, all the three-Sun-Moon and Jupiter- like other planets and stars were in Aśvini Nakṣatra. But the above-mentioned three planets meet first time in Dhaniṣṭhā nakṣatra after the lapse of 74 crores and 40 lakh (744 Million) years since the beginning of Kalpa. Here it may also be noted that the names of 60 Jovial years are the same in the tradition of Vārāmahira (647 BC) and Bhāskarāchārya, but their order is different. Below are the orders of Jovial years given by Varāhamihira and Bhāskarācharya.

Sr. No.	Varāhamihira	**Bhāsakrāchārya**
1	Vijaya	Prabhava
2	Jaya	Vibhava

3	Manmatha	Śukla
4	Durmukha	Pramoda
5	Hemalambī	Prajāpati
6	Vilambī	Aṅgirā
7	Vikārī	Śrimukha
8	Śārvarī	Bhāva
9	Plava	Yuvā
10	Śubhakṛta	Dhātā
11	Śobhana	Iśvara
12	Krodhī	Bahudhānya
13	Viśvāvasu	Pramāthī
14	Prābhava	Vikrama
15	Plavaṅga	Vṛṣa
16	Kīlaka	Chirabhānu
17	Saumya	Subhānu
18	Sādhāraṇa	Tāraṇa
19	Virodhkṛta	Pārthiva
20	Paridhāvī	Vyaya
21	Pramādī	Sarvajita
22	Ānanda	Sarvadhārī
23	Rākṣasa	Virodhī
24	Anala	Vikṛti
25	Piṅgala	Khara
26	Kālayukta	Nandana
27	Siddhārthī	Vijaya
28	Raudra	Jaya

29	Durmati	Manmatha
30	Dundubhi	Durmukha
31	Rudhirodgārī	Hemalambī
32	Raktākṣa	Vilambī
33	Krodhana	Vikārī
34	Kṣaya	Śārvarī
35	Prabhava	Plava
36	Vibhava	Śubhakṛta
37	Śukla	Śobhana
38	Pramoda	Krodhī
39	Prajāpati	Viśvāvasu
40	Aṅgirā	Prābhava
41	Śrimukha	Plavaṅga
42	Bhāva	Kīlaka
43	Yuvā	Saumya
44	Dhātā	Sādhāraṇa
45	Iśvara	Virodhkṛta
46	Bahudhānya	Paridhāvī
47	Pramdhāvī	Pramādī
48	Vikrama	Ānanda
49	Vṛṣa	Rākṣasa
50	Chirabhānu	Anala
51	Subhānu	Piṅgala
52	Tāraṇa	Kālayukta
53	Pārtiva	Siddhārthī
54	Vyaya	Raudra

55	Sarvajita	Durmati
Sr. No.	**Varāhamihira**	**Bhāsakrāchārya**
56	Sarvadhārī	Dundubhi
57	Virodhī	Rudhirodgārī
58	Vikṛti	Raktākṣa
59	Khara	Krodhana
60	Nandana	Kṣaya

For the sake of calculation, Jovial years are divided into two classes. The Daivī tradition or Northern tradition and Āsurī or Southern tradition have been used in pañchāṅgas and chronology.

As informed above, the duration of Bārhaspatya Saṁvatsara, according to Surya Siddhānta, is 361.026721 days. Thus, Bārhaspatya Saṁvatsara is about 4.232 days shorter than the solar year.

So in each successive solar year, the commencement of a Saṁvatsara will take place in 4.232 days in advance. Thus, every 85 years and 86 years, one Saṁvatsara of 85 X 4232= 359.72 days and 86 X 4.232=363.9 days, respectively, will be in excess. Or say 85 solar years will be equal to 86 Saṁvatsaras, or 86 years will be equal to 87 Saṁvatsaras. As such, one Saṁvatsara needs to be expunged in 85 and 86 solar years alternatively to bring Saṁvatsaras in unison with the solar years. This method is known as the Daivi Method or Northern method.

To find out the Jovial saṁvatsara of Daivī tradition, one has to divide the past Kali era by 85. Add the quotient to the dividend and again divide the sum by 60. The remainder will be the passed Jovial saṁvatsara of Daivī tradition starting from Vijaya Saṁvatsara. By adding one, we can find the current saṁvatsara. According to a tradition represented by Sūryasiddhānta and Varāhamihira, Kaliyuga started from Vijaya Saṁvatsara.

Similarly, finding out the Jovial saṁvatsara of Āsurī tradition is very simple. For this, one has to divide the past Kali era by 60. The remainder will be the expired Jovial saṁvatsara of Āsurī tradition starting from Pramāthi. If we add 1, we get the current saṁvatsara. According to Paitāmaha Siddhānta, Kaliyuga Started from Pramāthi Saṁvatsara.

Below is a table to find out both the Daivī and Āsurī saṁvatsaras based upon calculations cited above.

Sr. No.	**Āsurī Saṁvatsara**	**Daivī Saṁvatsara**
1	Pramāthī	Vijaya
2	Vikrama	Jaya
3	Vṛṣa	Manmatha
4	Chirabhānu	Durmukha
5	Subhānu	Hemalambī
6	Tāraṇa	Vilambī
7	Pārtiva	Vikārī
8	Vyaya	Śārvarī
9	Sarvajita	Plava
10	Sarvadhārī	Śubhakṛta
11	Virodhī	Śobhana
12	Vikṛti	Krodhī
13	Khara	Viśvāvasu
14	Nandana	Prābhava
15	Vijaya	Plavaṅga
16	Jaya	Kīlaka
17	Manmatha	Saumya
18	Durmukha	Sādhāraṇa
19	Hemalambī	Virodhkṛta

20	Vilambī	Paridhāvī
21	Vikārī	Pramādī
22	Śārvarī	Ānanda
23	Plava	Rākṣasa
24	Śubhakṛta	Anala
25	Śobhana	Piṅgala
26	Krodhī	Kālayukta
27	Viśvāvasu	Siddhārthī
28	Prābhava	Raudra
29	Plavaṅga	Durmati
30	Kīlaka	Dundubhi
31	Saumya	Rudhirodgārī
32	Sādhāraṇa	Raktākṣa
33	Virodhkṛta	Krodhana
34	Paridhāvī	Kṣaya
35	Pramādī	Prabhava
36	Ānanda	Vibhava
37	Rākṣasa	Śukla
38	Anala	Pramoda
39	Piṅgala	Prajāpati
40	Kālayukta	Aṅgirā
41	Siddhārthī	Śrimukha
42	Raudra	Bhāva
43	Durmati	Yuvā
44	Dundubhi	Dhātā
45	Rudhirodgārī	Iśvara
46	Raktākṣa	Bahudhānya

47	Krodhana	Pramāthī
48	Kṣaya	Vikrama
49	Prabhava	Vṛṣa
50	Vibhava	Chirabhānu
51	Śukla	Subhānu
52	Pramoda	Tāraṇa
53	Prajāpati	Pārtiva
54	Aṅgirā	Vyaya
55	Śrimukha	Sarvajita
56	Bhāva	Sarvadhārī
57	Yuvā	Virodhī
58	Dhātā	Vikṛti
59	Iśvara	Khara
60	Bahudhānya	Nandana

Our '9000 Years calendar of Various Eras' cites both North and South Indian Jovian year cycles as Daivī and Āsurī traditions. Here it may be noted that if the name of Bārhaspatya Saṁvatsara does not tally with the name mentioned in inscriptions or epigraphical records, then one may try both orders to reach the actual conclusion.

Tiṣya (Tikha) Saṁvatsra: Before the rule of Yudhiṣṭhira, many versions of Saptarṣi Saṁvat were in vogue as cited above. 2nd cycle of Aśvinī centric (popular counting of Nakṣatras) Saptarṣī Saṁvat started in 5076 BC by entering into Bharaṇī Nakṣatra. Tiṣya Saṁvat originated from the 2nd cycle (5076 BC) of Aśvinī Nakṣatra centric Saptarṣī Saṁvat. Tiṣya or Puṣya Nakṣatra is located at the 20th place in retrograde order from Aśvini Nakṣatra. So when the 2nd cycle (5076 BC) of Aśvinī (expired) and Saptarṣī Saṁvat had its 21st year in Bharaṇī Nakṣatra in 5056 BC, after the expiry of 20 years, or say about

1954 years before Kaliyuga, the first Tiṣya or Tikha Saṁvatsara started.

Puṣya or Tiṣya Nakṣatra is considered very auspicious. Goddess Lakṣmī was born in Tiṣya Nakṣatra. So, owing to the auspiciousness of the Tiṣya (Puṣya) constellation, this may have been the reason to carve out a separate Tiṣya Saṁvat from Saptarṣī Saṁvat in ancient times, 1954 years before Kaliyuga in 5056 BC.

2. The second 'Tiṣya Saṁvat' with a corrupt name 'Tikha' started after 1295 years of the main Tiṣya Saṁvat, i.e., in 3762 BC, when Saparṣis were spending their 15th year in Viśākhā Nakṣatra. Viṣṇu's Kacchapa Avatāra (incarnation in Turtle form) took place on Vaiśākha Pūrṇimā. So the 15th year of Saptarṣis is chosen as Vaiśākha Pūrṇimā for the commencement of the second Tiṣya or Tikha Saṁvat. This is also called First Jain Yudhiṣṭhira Saṁvat. Perhaps it was named after some Jain Tirthaṅkara.

3. The Jain tradition of India accepted the commencement of third Tikha Saṁvat 468 years after 3762 BC, i.e. in 3294 BC. This Tikha Saṁvat was also known as 'Second Jain Yudhiṣṭhira Saṁvat'.

After the coronation of Yudhiṣṭhira on the throne of Hastinapur, in addition to various Tiṣya/Tikha Saṁvatsaras, Yudhiṣṭhira Saṁvats also came into being. The Tikha Saṁvat was also quoted by the name of Yudhiṣṭhira Saṁvat in the Jain tradition. Many Sanskrit texts have used this Saṁvatsara. Our table cites Tikha Saṁvatsara corresponding to Kaliyuga, Mahābhārata war, Śaka eras, Vikrama eras, Jovian years and Saptarishi years, so as to make it easy for the readers and researchers to convert the years of a particular era into the corresponding other eras for the past 9000 years.

Yudhiṣṭhira era: There are three Yudhiṣṭhira Saṁvat.

1. The first Yudhiṣṭhira Saṁvat started 36 years before the Mahābhārata war in 3173 BC when Saptarishis were spending their 4th year in Maghā Nakṣatra.

2. The second Yudhiṣṭhira Saṁvat started in 3137 BC when Yudhiṣṭhira ascended the throne after victory in the war.

3. The Third Vijayābhyudaya Yudhisthir Śaka started in 3101 BC with the commencement of Kaliyuga. when he abdicated the throne in favour of Arjuna's son Abhimanyu's son Parikshit, who survived the Mahābharata war. This was named as 'Vijayābhyudaya Saṁvat' because Kaliyuga started with Vijaya named Bārhaspatya Saṁvatsara.

Ancient texts profusely use Yudhiṣṭhira Saṁvats to deal with the chronology of ancient historical events.

Kaliyuga era: As indicated in chapter 14, the present Kaliyuga commenced at midnight ending on the 28th and beginning on the 29th of September in 3101 BC on the 13th of the dark half (Kṛṣṇa) of Bhadrapada month. It may be noted that at the beginning of Kaliyuga Amānta calendar was in use. Thus, the Kaliyuga era began in 3101 BC. Here it may also be informed that its years are both Chaitrādi (lunisolar) and Meṣādi (solar). It is used both in astronomical works and in Pañchāṅgas. In the Pañchāṅgas, sometimes its expired year, the current year is given, and sometimes both. It is also found used in epigraphic records.

Vikrama Era: By the end of the 19th century, this era was in use in Gujrat and over almost the north of India, except perhaps Bengal. The inhabitants of these parts, when migrating to other parts of India, carry the use of the era with them. Vikrama eras are found following three patterns: Kārtikādi (New Year starting from the month of Kārttika), Āṣāḍhādi (New Year starting from the month of Āṣāḍha), and Chaitrādi (New Year starting from the month of Chaitra). Kārtikādi was used in Gujrat. Its months were Amānta. Āṣāḍhādi was used in some parts of Kathiavad of Gujarat. Its months were Amānta. The Chaitrādi Vikrama era was used in northern India. Its months are Pūrṇimānta. According to Prof. F. Kielhorn (Indian Antiquary, vols. 19-20), the Vikrama era was Kārtikādi from the beginning. He thinks that the change in direction of Chaitrādi took place owing to the increasing growth and influence of the

Śaka era. This was not the reason; rather, the truth is that there were three Vikrama eras prevalent at three different times. We can trace two Vikrama eras, the description of which is given below.

It is also well known that the inscriptions dated in the Vikrama era followed two different calendars. One calendar was the Kārttikādi and another was the Chaitrādi (New Year starting from the month of Chaitra). It is evident from the inscriptions that the Kārtikādi calendar is older than the Chaitrādi calendar.

1. Kārtikādi Vikrama Era: Kārtikādi Vikrama era was started by Vikramāditya 1 in 470 years after the death of Mahavira Jain in 1187 BC. So, Kārtikādi Vikrama era dates back to 1187-470= 717-716 BC. He founded it after defeating 96 Śaka kṣatrapas invited by Kālkāchārya to avenge his humiliation from Gardabhilla and having taken initiation into Jainism. Vedaveer Arya's assessment (2015) is correct that this era was also called 'Mālava era' or 'Mālava Gaṇa era'. This era was used in the inscriptions of Chandellas, all Chāhāmanas except Śakaṁbhari Chāhamānas, Gāhaḍawālas, Chaulukyas or Solaṅkis, Chāvaḍas, Parmaras, Pratīhāras, Aulikaras.

According to the Skanda Purāṇa (Maheshwar Khaṇḍa 1, 40.252-253), Vikramāditya I was born in 3020 Saptarṣī Saṁvat.

ततस्त्रिषु सहस्रेषु (3000) विंशत्या (20) चाधिकेषु च।
भविष्यं विक्रमादित्यराज्यं सोऽथ प्रलप्स्यते।

[Meaning] In the future, Vikramāditya will establish his reign in 3000+20=3020 Saptarṣī era.

As we know, Skanda Purāṇa follows the Kashmiri method of counting of Saptarṣī Saṁvat. The year 3020 is higher than the third cycle of Saptarṣī Saṁvat 1076. Accordingly, this number belongs to the second cycle of Saptarṣī Saṁvat of the Kashmiri school, which dates to 3776 BC. If we subtract 3020 from 3776, we reach Saptarṣī era 3776 BC-3020 = 756 BC, or say Punarvasu 21. The above verse of Skanda Purāṇa points to the Vikramaditya I establishing his reign in 756 BC, who started his era in 717 BC.

2. **Chaitrādi Vikrama Era:** The Chaitrādi Vikrama era was started by Vikramaditya II (82 BC-19 AD) in 57 BC by defeating Śakas and declaring his rule in Nepal. He was also called 'Harsha Vikrama. Hereinafter, it will be addressed as Chatrādi Vikrama era. The Ahar inscription is the earliest epigraphic evidence that the Chaitrādi Vikrama era came into use in the beginning of the 3rd century AD. This era is used in the writings of the Śakaṁbhari Chāhamānas.

Śaka Era: This era is extensively used over the whole of India and in most parts of South India, except in Tinnevelly and part of Malabar, it is used exclusively. In other parts, it is used in addition to local eras. Its years are Chaitrādi for luni-solar and Meṣādi for the solar reckoning. Its months are Pūrṇimānta in the North and Amānta in Southern India.

According to Sakanda Purāṇa (Maheśvara Khaṇḍa, 1, 40.254), the Śaka named king will alleviate poverty in the Saptarṣī year 1100. The verse goes like this:

तत शतसहस्रेषु शतेनाप्यधिकेषु च ।
शको नाम भविष्यश्चासौऽतिदारिद्र्यहारकः ।।
tata śatasahasreṣu śatenāpyadhikeṣu cha ।
śako nāma bhaviṣyaśchāsau'tidāridryahārakaḥ ।।

The above given Saptarṣī year 1100 corresponds to the Christian era 1100-1076 BC = 24 AD. This points out to Śālivāhana Śaka who started Śaka era in 78 AD.

Here it may be pointed out that in Indian history we have two Śaka eras. The same view is endorsed by Dr. Vedveer Arya (2015). One Śaka era is known as 'Śaka Nṛpati Rājyabhiṣeka Saṁvatsara', i.e, the epoch commenced at the coronation of a Śaka king. Another Śaka era is known as 'Śaka Nṛpa Kālātīta era', i.e., the era commenced at the death of a Śaka king. Surprisingly, both Śaka eras fall 135 years later than that of the respective Vikrama eras. For example, the Śaka era (583-582 BC) falls 135 years later than the Kārtkādi Vikrama era (717-716 BC), and the Śaka era (78 AD) falls 135 years later than the Chaitrādi Vikrama era (57 BC).

Śaka Era (583-82 BC): As pointed out above in the context of Vikrama era 717 BC that Vikrama defeated 96 Śaka Kṣatrapas in the 470th year of Mahāvira Nirvāṇa kāla (1186-470=) 717- 716 BC and got initiation into Jainism. Gardabhilla was the first ruler who was killed by 96 Śaka Kṣatrapas accompanied by Kālkāchārya. Vikramāditya defeated them in 717-716 BC and started his era. The Gurvāvali says that the dynasty of Vikramāditya ruled for 135 years and 5 months.

The Śaka Kśatraps regrouped themselves and invaded Ujjain again after 135 years and 5 months and re-occupied Ujjain in 583 BC. Śaka Mahākśatrapa Caṣṭana was coronated as the king of Ujjain. He founded the Śaka era in 583 BC, which was referred to as 'Śaka-nṛpa-kāla', 'Śaka-nṛpa-rājyābhiśeka-saṁvatsara', etc.

Chronology of rulers of Ujjain leading to the Kārtikādi Vikrama era (717-716 BC) and Śaka era (583-582 BC) may be constructed as follows:

Sr. No.	Name of the King	Mahavir Nirvāṇa Saṁvat (1186 BC)	Date of Coronation in the Christian Era
1	Gardabhilla (13 years)	453-466	734-721 BC
2	96 Śaka Kśatrapas invited by Kālaka (4 years)	466-470	721-717 BC
3	Vikramāditya 1 (60 years) Founded Kārtikādi Vikrama era (717 BC) after defeating Śaka kṣatrapas and having taken initiation into Jainism	470-530	717-657 BC
4	Dharmaichhu (40 years)	530-570	657-617 BC

5	Gaila Panvisa (25 years)	570-595	617-592 BC
6	Nahade (8 years)	595-603	592-586 BC
7	Ikrami (3 years)	603-606	586-582 BC
8	Śaka king Caṣṭana established his rule and founded his Śaka era (583 BC)	607	583 BC

Jain works like Tiloyapannati of Yativṛṣabha, Harivaṁśa of Jinasena, Dhavala of Āchārya Vīrasena, Trilokasāra of Nemichandra, Mahāviracharitam of Nemichandra and Vichāraśreṇi of Merutuṅga tell us that Mahavira attained nirvāṇa 605 years and 5 months before the Śaka era (583-582 BC) and 470 years before the start of Kārtikādi Vikrama era (717-716BC). We know from Jain sources that Mahāvira attained Nirvāṇa in 1187 BC. As such, the Śaka Nṛpa kāla era commenced in 1187-605 years and 5 months = 583-582 BC. Vedveer (2015) has fixed it as 583 BC on the basis of several epigraphic evidence. To sum up, Śaka Nṛpa Kāla may be fixed between 583-582 BC.

The Chronology of the Western Kśatrapas (583 BC–246 BC)

The Śakas or Scythians belonged to the Valley of the Helmand River in Afghanistan, as the region was called Śakasthāna (Seistān). One branch of the Śakas probably ruled as allies or feudatories, or officials of ancient Indian kings (probably, Yavana kings) of the North-Western region. Gradually, they learnt Sanskrit and adopted Indian traditions, but Indian society viewed them as 'Mlecchas'. The Śakas were possibly appointed as Kśatrapas and Mahākśatrapas during the reign of the Kaniṣka. The names of Mahākśatrapa Kharapallāna and Kśatrapa Vanashpara find mention in some inscriptions found at Sāranāth, which are dated in the third regnal year of Kaniṣka. Taking advantage of the weak Indian political conditions, the Śakas conquered Takṣaśilā & Mathurā in

Northern India and Mālava & Kāthiāwār region in Western India. But Indian society never accepted them as 'Kśatriyas'. Though the Śaka Kśatraps became independent rulers, they were struggling to get social acceptance. It appears that Caṣṭana successfully persuaded some Brāhmaṇas of Ujjain to declare them as Kṣatriyas and ensured that his coronation was carried out according to Indian traditions. Thus, Caṣṭana became the first Śaka king of Ujjain, who was coronated by Brāhmaṇas who declared him as Kṣatriya. They ruled Ujjain for over 337 years. The inscriptions of these rulers are dated from Śaka Nṛpa kāla 6 (577 BC) to Śaka 203(380 BC) and their coins from Śaka 100 (483 BC) to Śaka 337 (246 BC). The Junagarh inscription of Mahākśatrapa Rudradāman I (the grandson of Caṣṭana) is dated in Śaka 72 (511 BC)

स्वामी चष्टनस्य पौत्र....ह पुत्रस्य राज्ञो महाक्षत्रपस्य रुद्रदामनो वर्षे द्वासप्ततितमे (72) मार्गशीर्ष बहुल प्रति

svāmī chaṣṭanasya pautra....ha putrasya rājño mahākṣatrapasya rudradāmano varṣe dvāsaptatitame (72) mārgaśīrṣa bahula prati

[Meaning] In the 72nd year (dvāsaptatitame varṣe), on the Pratipadā (first lunar day) of the dark half (bahula pakṣa) of the month Mārgaśīrṣa, during the reign of King (rājñaḥ) Mahākṣatrapa (mahākṣatrapasya) Rudradāman, grandson (pautraḥ) of Svāmi Caṣṭana and son (putraḥ) of ... [name missing in the text]."

Note: This is an inscriptional record (probably a part of a prasasti or copper-plate grant), dating an event to the 72nd regnal year of Mahākṣatrapa Rudradāman, the grandson of Svāmi Caṣṭana. It specifies the date according to the lunar calendar — Mārgaśīrṣa bahula pratipadā.

Thus chronology of western kṣatrapas (straps) can be constructed in view of Śaka Nṛpa-kāla. Vedveer (2015) has constructed the chronology as follows:

Name of the Ruler	Period of Rule
1. Chaṣṭana, the son of Yaśamotika	583-531 BC

2. Jayadāman, the son of Caṣṭana	
3. Rudradāman I, the son of Jayadāman	531-493 BC
4. Damajadasri I	494-486 BC
5. Jāvadāman	486 BC
6. Rudrasingh I	486-473 BC
7. Iśvaradatta	473-470 BC
8. Rudrasingh I (restored)	470-464 BC
9. Jāvadāman (restored)	464-462 BC
10. Rudrasena I	461-439 BC
11. Saṅghadāman	439-438 BC
12. Damasena	438-429 BC
13. Damajadasri II (ruled along with	
14. Vāradāman and Yaśodāman)	429-422 BC
15. Vāradāman	427-423 BC
16. Yaśodāman	422 BC
17. Vijayasena	422-411 BC
18. Damajadasri III	410-406 BC
19. Rudrasena II	406-384 BC
20. Viśvasingh	384-379 BC
21. Bhartṛdāman	379-366 BC
22. Viśvasena	368-357 BC

Family of Rudrasingh II

23. Rudrasingh II (ruled along with	
24. Yaśodāman II and Rudradāman II)	357-313 BC
25. Yaśodāman II	344-329 BC
26. Rudradāman II	329-313 BC
27. Rudrasena III	313-281 BC

28. Singhasena	281-279 BC
29. Rudrasena IV	279-273 BC
30. Rudrasingh III	273-246 BC

The Śaka era (583-82 BC) was used by western Kṣatrapas, Yadvas, Pallavas, Kadaṁbas, Bāṇas, Gaṅgas, early Rāṣṭrakūṭas, eastern Rāṣṭrakūṭas, etc.

We may give here some examples for the verification of Śaka era (583-82 BC).

The Kolhapur Stone Inscription of Śilāhāra Vijayāditya records Śaka 1065 elapsed (483 AD), Dundubhi saṁvatsara, Full moon day of Māgha month, Monday and a lunar eclipse. as under:

शक-वर्षेषुपञ्च-षष्ट्युत्तर-सहस्र- (1065) प्रमितेष्वतीतेषुप्रवर्त्तमान-दुन्दुभि-संवत्सर-माघ- आसपौर्ण-मास्याम्सोमवारे। सोम-ग्रहणे॥

Śaka-varṣeṣuPañca-ṣaṣṭyuttara-sahasra-pramiteṣvatīteṣuPravarttamāna-Dundubhi-saṁvatsara-māgha-āsapaurṇa-māsyāmsomavāre, soma-grahaṇe.

[Meaning] When five thousand and sixty (pañca-ṣaṣṭi-uttara-sahasra = 1065) years of the Śaka era had elapsed, during the current year named Dundubhi, on the full-moon day (Paurṇimā) of the month of Māgha, on a Monday (Soma-vāra), at the time of a lunar eclipse (Soma-grahaṇa).

The date according to the Śaka era (583-582 BC) corresponds to 10th January 483 AD. We find that a penumbral lunar eclipse occurred on Māgha Pūrṇimā, Monday. The Jovial year on 10th January was Dundubhi, as the same is clear from our '9000 Years Calendar of Various Indian Eras'. From Catra Śukla 1, it changed into Rudhirodgārī.

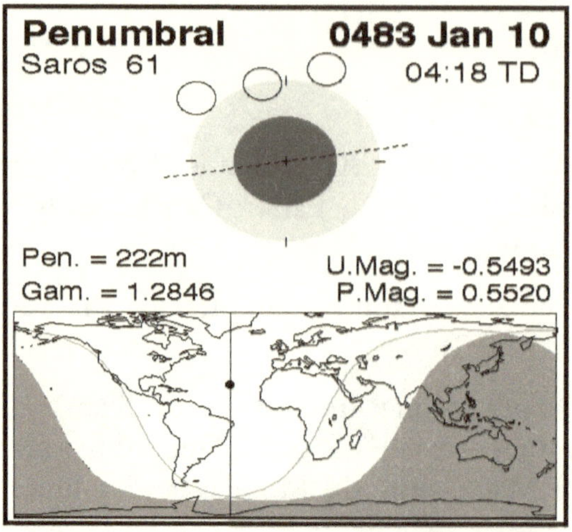

Five Millennium Canon of Lunar Eclipses (Espenak & Meeus)
NASA TP-2009-214172

Kurtaketi Plates (Indian Antiquary, VII, pp. 304-306) record that when 530 Śaka years elapsed, the total solar eclipse occurred at noon hours on the new moon day between Vaiśākha and Jyeṣṭha months, Sunday, in Rohiṇī Nakṣatra and Vṛṣabha Rāśī during noon hours. The plate reads as under:

त्रिंशोत्तर-पञ्च-शतेषु शक-वर्षेस्हु अतीतेषु।
विजय-राज्य संवत्सरे षोडशवर्षेप्रवर्तमाने ॥वैशाख-ज्येष्ठमास-मध्यमामावास्यायाम्भास्करदिनेरोहिण्यर्क्शेमध्याह्नकालेविक्रमादित्यस्य ॥महादेवतयो-रुभयोःवीषभराशौ। तस्मिन् वीषभराशौ सूर्यग्रहणसर्वमासी (सर्वग्रासी) भूते ॥

Trimśottara-pañca-śateṣu Śaka-varṣeshu atīteṣu, vijaya-rājya saṁvatsare ṣoḍaśavarṣepravartamāne....... Vaiśākha-Jyeṣṭhamāsa-madhyamāmāvāsyāyāmbhāskaradineRohiṇyarkśemadhyāhnakāle Vikaramādityasya........Mahādevatayo-rubhayoḥ Vīṣabharāśau, tasmin Vīṣabharāśau SūryagrahaṇaSarvamāsī (Sarvagrāsī) bhūte....

[Meaning] When five hundred and thirty (530) years of the Śaka era had elapsed, in the sixteenth regnal year (ṣoḍaśa-varṣe pravartamāne) of King (rājñaḥ) Vijaya, on the new-moon day (amāvāsyā) falling between the months of Vaiśākha and Jyeṣṭha, on a Sunday (bhāskara-dine), at midday (madhyāhna-kāle), under the constellation Rohiṇī, when both the Sun (Vikrama-

Āditya) and the great deities (Mahādevatayoḥ) were situated in Vṛṣabha-rāśi (the zodiacal sign of Taurus), there occurred a total solar eclipse (sūrya-grahaṇa-sarva-grāsi-bhūta).

Considering the above epoch on the basis of Śaka Nṛpa-kāla (583 BC), this period is 583-530= 53 BC. The coordinates of Badami (Northern Karnataka) are 15°55'N and 75°40'E. We find that close to 53 BC, a total solar eclipse occurred on 7th May 53 BC (9th May 53 BC Julian). Similarly, close to 608 AD, a total solar eclipse occurred on 23rd April, 608 AD (20th April, 608 Julian).

While comparing the data of both eclipses, we find that the eclipse dated 7th May 53 BC, occurred in Northern Karnataka on the new moon day of Vaiśākha month that started at 10:50 AM, and lasted for 3 hours and 6 minutes, or say ended at 1:56 PM. The day was the new moon day of between Vaiśākha and Jyeṣṭha months, and the moon was in Rohiṇī Nakṣatra. The Sun and Moon were also in Vṛṣabha rāśī, i.e., Taurus sign, although the day was Wednesday, while the inscription shows Sunday. if the same date is read in the Gregorian calendar, then it is Sunday. Bārhaspatya Saṁvatsara is also Vijaya (of Bhāskarācharya tradition). Though our table following Varāhāmihira's order mentions Vibhava, but it is according to the tradition of Bhāskarācharya.

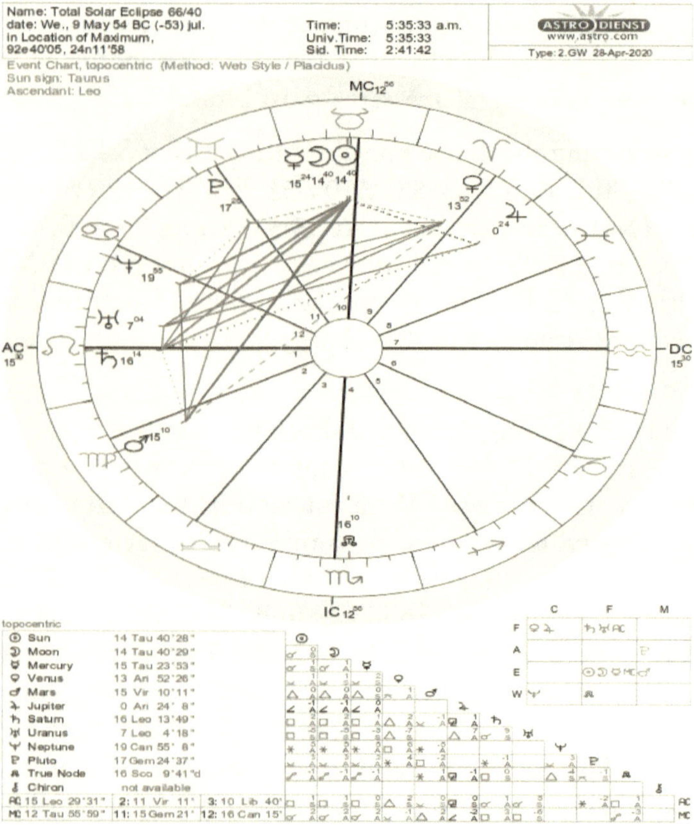

On the other hand, if we go by Śālivāhana Śaka (78 AD), the period is 78+530= 608 AD. The data of eclipse occurred on 23rd April, 608 AD also shows that it occurred on the new moon day between Vaiśākha and Jyeṣṭha months, but it started afternoon hours i.e. 13:51 and lasted for 1 hour and 13 minutes. The Moon was in Vṛṣabha Rāśī but the Sun was also in Vṛṣabha Rāśī. The Moon was in Kṛttikā Nakṣatra and not in Rohiṇi. The day was also Saturday and not Sunday. So, Nakṣatra detail Kurtaketi Plates are not verified by 608 AD eclipse.

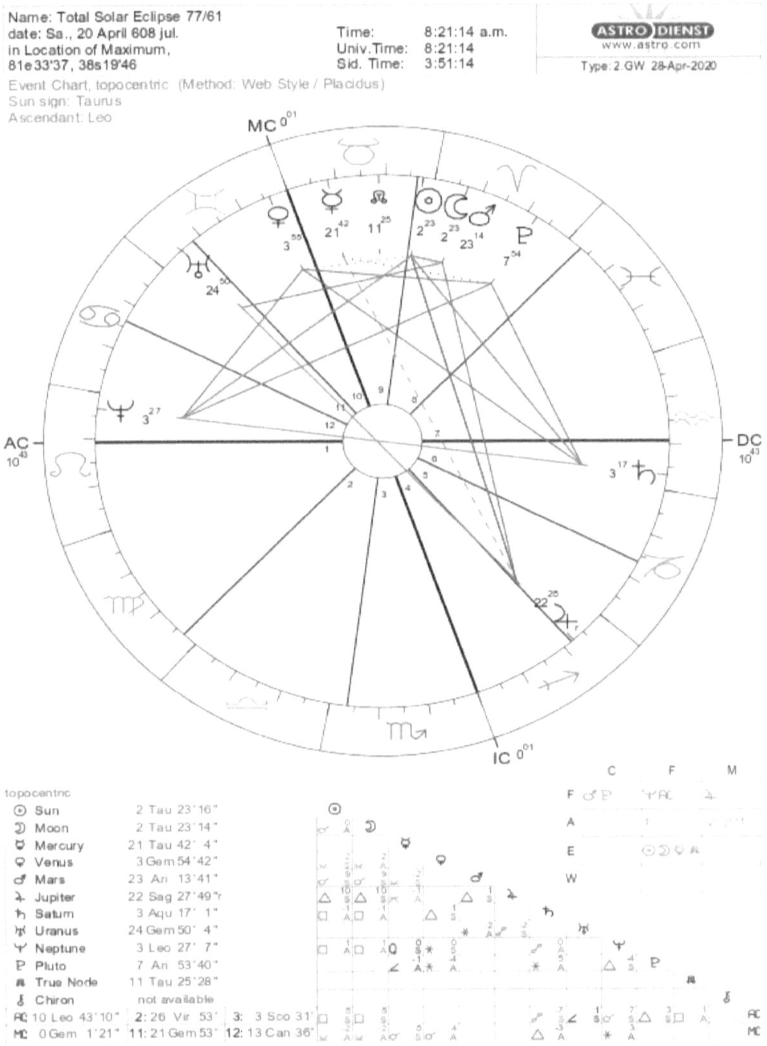

The above- cited analysis clearly shows that Kurtketi plates mention Śaka Nṛpa Kāla (583 BC) instead of Śaka Kālātīta Kāla (78 AD). These examples prove the existence of Śaka Nṛpa era (583 BC).

2. **Śālivahana Śaka era (78 AD):** Another Śaka era is known is 'Śaka Nṛpa Kālātīta era', i.e. the era commenced at the death of a Śaka king. The epoch of 'Śaka Nṛpa Kālātīta' commenced in the year 78 AD when the Śaka rule was permanently ended by Śālivāhana by killing the Śaka king.

Alberuni, a Persian scholar, who visited India between 1017 AD and 1031 AD, wrote:

'The epoch of the era of Śaka falls 135 years later than that of Vikramaditya. The here-mentioned Śaka tyrannized over their country between the river Sindh and the ocean, after he had made Aryāvarta in the midst of this realm his dwelling place. He interdicted the Hindus from considering and representing themselves as anything but Śakas.

.... The Hindus had much to suffer from him, till at last, they received help from the east, when Vikramāditya marched against him, put him to fight and killed him in the region of Karur, between Multan and the castle of Loni. Now this date became famous, as people rejoiced in the news of the death of the tyrant and was used as the epoch of an era, especially by the astronomers. .... Since there is a long interval between the era which is called the era of Vikramāditya and the killing of Śaka; we think that Vikramāditya from whom the era has got its name is not identical with that one who killed Śaka.'

Thus, Alberuni clearly indicated that the death of the Śaka king is the epoch of the Śaka era that commenced in 78 CE he had no information about the era of the coronation of the Śaka king because it was not in vogue at that time. The era that commenced with the killing of the Śaka king was also referred to as 'Śālivāhana Śaka'. Thus, 78 AD is the epoch of 'Śaka Nṛpa Kālātīta' era. It can never be the epoch of 'Śaka Nṛpati Rājyabhiṣeka Saṁvatsara'i.e. the coronation of the Śaka King.

This era will hereinafter be known as Śaka era (78 AD). This era was used by Śakaṁbhari Chāhamānas, later Parmaras, later Rāṣṭrakūṭas, Later Chālukyas of Kalyāṇī, etc.

Harsha Era: There are two Harsha eras.

1. The first one was started by Śri Harsha of Kannauja or Sthanishvara in 457 BC. Alberuni, who came to India around 1017-1031 AD, states that the Śri Harsha era was founded 400 years before the Vikrama era (57 BC):

'The Hindus believe regarding Śri Harsha....... His era is used in Mathura and the country of Kannauja. Between Śri Harsha and Vikramāditya there is an interval of 400 years, as I have been told by some of the inhabitants of that region. However, in the Kashmirian calendar, I have read that Śri Harsha was 664 years later than Vikramāditya. In the face of this discrepancy, I am in perfect uncertainty, which to the present moment has not yet been cleared up by any trustworthy information.'

'Now, the year 400 of Yazdajird, which we have chosen as a gauge, corresponds to the following years of the Indian eras.

1. To the year 1488 of the era of Śri Harsha (1488-1031=457 BC)

2. To the year 1088 of the era of Vikramāditya (1031-1088=57 BC)

It is evident from Alberuni's account that the Śri Harsha era commenced in 457 BC. He also calculated that the year 1031 AD corresponds to the year 1488 in the Śri Harsha era. He simply stated that according to some Kashmirian sources, one Śri Harsha was ruling 664 years after Vikramāditya. Therefore, Alberuni expressed his inability to explain why the people of Mathura and Kannauja believed the existence of the rule of Śri Harsha in 457 BC whereas some Kashmirian sources tell us that Śri Harsha ruled 664 years after Vikramāditya i.e. 606 AD. In fact, Alberuni failed to recognize the second Harsha of 606 AD of Kashmirian sources.

2. Indian tradition doesn't mention any era of 606 AD started by Śri Harsha who ruled 664 years after Vikramāditya, but western historians concocted the myth that Śri Harsha was supposed to have started an era from about 606 AD. Thus, they clubbed Śri Harshavardhan son of Prabhakaravardhan (457 BC) and Śri Harsha son of Rasal (606 AD) into one person and omitted the name of Śri Harshavardhan or Harsha Vikramaditya from Indian history and created a non-existent era of 606 AD.

The Kalachuri-Chedi era (581 BC): Māhiṣmatī (near

Khandwa in Madhya Pradesh) was the capital of the Kalachuri dynasty (Māhiṣmatīm Kalachureḥ kula-rājadhānīm), and Tripuri in Dāhala deśa (near Jabalpur) was the capital of the Chedi dynasty. The Kalachuris and Chedis were the descendants of the ancient Haihaya dynasty. The era used in the inscriptions of the Kalachuris of Māhiṣmatī and the Chedis of Tripuri is referred to as the Kalachuri-Chedi era. This era was also found in the inscriptions of the Mahārājas of Valkhā, the Gurjaras, the Sendrakas, and the early Chalukyas of Gujarat, etc. This era was founded by the kings of the Kalachuri and Chedi dynasties. Based on the study of the solar eclipses and lunar eclipses mentioned in the inscriptions of the Kalachuri-Chedi era, it is easy to conclude that the epoch of the Kalachuri-Chedi era commenced in 551 BC. The Sarkho grant of Ratnadeva II, issued in the Kalachuri year 880 on the occasion of a total lunar eclipse, provides the strongest evidence of the starting point of the Kalachuri-Chedi era.

> तेनाशीत्यधिकाष्ट-वत्सर-शते जाते दिने गृहपते।
>
> कार्त्तिक्यामथ रोहिणीभ-समये रात्रेश्च याम-त्रये॥
>
> श्रिमद्-रत्ननरेश्वरस्य सदसि ज्योतिर्विदामग्रतः।
>
> सर्वग्रासमनुष्णगोः प्रवदता
>
> *Tenāśītyadhikāṣṭa-vatsara-śate jāte dine Gīhpate,*
> *Kārttikyāmatha Rohiṇībha-samaye ratreścha*
> *yāma-traye. Śrimad-Ratnanareśvarasya*
> *sadasi jyotirvidāmagrataḥ, Sarvagrāsamanuṣṇagoḥ pravadatā*
> *tirṇṇa pratijñānadā*

[Meaning] When eight hundred and eighty (880) years had passed, at the end of Thursday, in the month of Kārttika, at the time when the Moon was in the Rohiṇī constellation, during the third watch of the night; in the royal assembly of the illustrious King Ratna-nareśvara, in the presence of eminent astrologers (jyotir-vidām agrataḥ), the occurrence of a total lunar eclipse (sarva-grāsam anuṣṇagoḥ) was declared.

Accordingly, once, in the court of Ratnadeva II and in the presence of other astronomers, Padmanābha predicted that when the day of Gṛhpati or Vāchaspati i.e. Thursday ends in the year 880 and the full Moon occurs in Kṛttikā nakṣatra, a total lunar eclipse will commence during the third quarter of the night i.e. between 0:00 AM to 3:00 AM and the time when moon enters into the asterism Rohiṇī.

The tentative geographical coordinates of Chiñchātalāi (modern Chicholā) are 820 39'E, 220 10'N, as close to the locality of observation. My calculations show that, during the period of 2000 years spanning from 800 BC to 1200 AD, the following total lunar eclipses took place near Kārtika Pūrṇimā, commencing during the third quarter of the night:

4th Dec. 882 BC (12th 883 JC), Tuesday

29th Oct. 629 BC (5th Nov. 630 JC), Monday

21st Dec. 605 BC (28th Dec. 605 JC), Monday

12th Dec. 381 BC, Thursday

24th Nov. 299 AD, Friday

5th Nov. 412 AD, Sunday

8th Nov. 477 AD (7th Nov. 477 JC), Sunday

2nd Jan. 568 AD (31st Dec. 567 JC), Saturday

13th Nov. 672 AD (10th Nov. 672 JC), Wednesday

27th Nov. 820 AD (23rd Nov. 820 JC), Friday

11th Nov. 998 AD (6th Nov. 998 JC), Sunday

4th Jan. 1024 AD (29th Dec. 1023 JC), Sunday

15th Nov. 1128 AD (8th Nov. 1128 JC), Thursday

But none of the above-cited eclipses took place at the end of Thursday on Friday except the eclipses dated 24th Nov. 299 AD. and 8th Nov. 1128 AD. When we judge the eclipses from the point of view of the second parameter of Moon's ingression in Rohiṇi nakṣatra, we find that on 24th Nov. 299 Moon was in Rohiṇī nakṣatra during the eclipse, but we find that on 9th Nov. 1128, during the time of the eclipse, Moon was in Kṛttikā nakṣatra. It shows that the grant was not issued on 8th

November. 1128 AD as held by V. V. Mirashi, rather on 24th Nov. 299 AD. Here I may also quote the view of Vedveer (2015), who held that a grant was issued on 8th Nov. 477 AD. The same is also not maintainable. The two parameters are against his view. First of all, 7th Nov. 477 AD was Sunday and not Thursday, secondly, the eclipse did not take place in the third quarter, ratherit took place in the fourth quarter of night i.e. 3:58 AM. So the dates chosen by V.V. Mirashi and Vedveer don't qualify the verifiable details of the eclipse given in the Sarkho grant. They correspond regularly with the date 24th Nov. 299 AD, when the eclipse, as the inscription remarks, was total with the phases occurring at 0:52, 1:22, 1:53, 3:01 and 4:00.

http://eclipse.gsfc.nasa.gov/eclipse.html

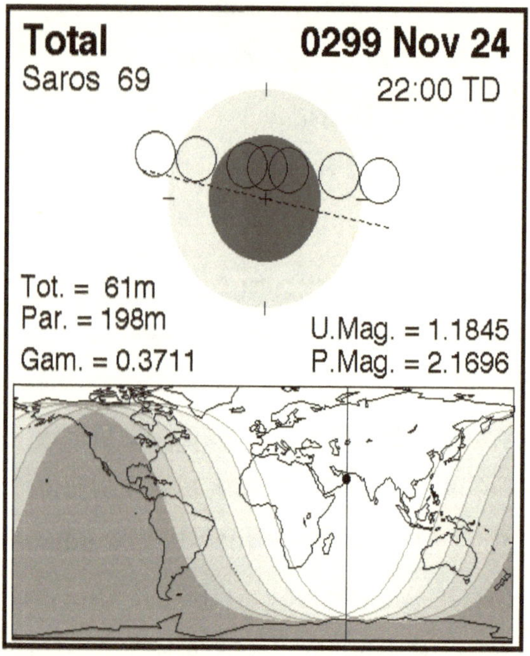

Considering the exact date of the eclipse as 24th Nov. 299 AD, the epoch of the Kalachuri-Chedi era can be derived as 880-299 AD= 581 BC.

The Gāṅgeya era (657-656 BC): Many inscriptions found

in Orissa and Andhra Pradesh are dated in the Gāṅgeya era. Actually, the kings of the Eastern Gaṅga dynasty recorded the regnal year starting from the initial year of the establishment of their dynasty in their inscriptions which has been named as Gāṅgeyaera by modern historians. The Eastern Gaṅgas ruled from the city of Kaliṅga. Kaliṅga deśa is well known from the Mahābhārata era. Khāravela's Mahāmeghavāhana dynasty was reigning in Kaliṅga around the 13th century BC. Seventeen inscriptions of the Māṭharas of Piṣthāpura found till date indicate that the Māṭharas also ruled the Kaliṅga region and the Pitṛbhaktas were their contemporaries. Probably, the Māṭharas and Pitṛbhaktas ruled around the 8th and 7th centuries BC.

It is evident that the eastern Gaṅgas were the successors of the Māṭharas and Pitṛbhaktas.

The Eastern Gaṅgas ruled from 657 BC to 107 BC. They had weakened due to the rise of the Imperial Guptas. They attempted to re-establish themselves along with the Kadaṁbas but the rise of the Chalukyas in the south and the rise of the Maukharis in the north finally ended the rule of the eastern Gaṅgas by 107 BC. The Imperial Guptas were ruling Kaliṅga indirectly through their feudatories and the Gupta era was introduced in Kaliṅga during the reign of Chandragupta II. Gradually, the Gupta era became popular and the Gāṅgeya era was forgotten by the 1stcentury BC.

Gupta era (327 BC): The Gupta era was started by Chandragupta 1 of the Gupta dynasty in 327 BC.

The Valabhi era (319 AD): This era was in use in Kathiawad and the neighbourhood of Gujarat and commenced in 319 AD. Alberuni mentions that the epoch of the Valabhi era falls when 241 years are added to the epoch of the Śaka era (78 CE). 78+241=319 AD.

The Valabhi era is also known as the Gupta Valabhi era. Valabha Guptas are different from Guptas. Alberuni also states that people say that the Valabha Guptas were very powerful people. This date (319 AD) was used as the epoch of the Valabhai Gupta era (Valabhi era) and not the Gupta era. But historians are confusing the Valabhi Gupta era with the Gupta era.

The Lakśmaṇasena Saṁvat (445 AD): Lakśmaṇasena was the most illustrious king of the Sena dynasty of Bengal. The Sena dynasty ruled Bengal and Bihar during the 5th century AD. The Edilpur grant of the time of Ballālasena is dated in the Saṁvat 1136, which may be Kārtikādi Vikrama era. Thus, the epoch of Ballālasena may be fixed around 1136- 717 = 419 AD. Ballālasena was the father of Lakśmaṇasena, and evidently, Lakśmaṇasena must have ascended the throne after 419 AD. The Bisapi grant of Śivasiṁhadevais dated in the year 293 of Lakśmaṇasena era, in the year 1455 (elapsed) of Kārtikādi Vikrama era, and in the year 1321 current of Śakakāla era. This grant was issued in favour of the poet Vidyāpati Śarma on the 7th tithi of the bright fortnight of the Śrāvaṇa month of 737 AD. Thus, the epoch of the Lakśmaṇasena era commenced on in 445 AD, considering 293 years before 737 AD.

The Siṁha Saṁvat (453 AD): The Chaulukya king Jayasiṁha Siddharāja (433-480 AD) founded his era in 453 AD. The Mangrol inscription of the time of the Chaulukya king Kumārapāla is dated on the 13th tithi of the dark fortnight of Āśvina month in 1202 Kārtikādi Vikrama Saṁvat and Siṁha era 32, i.e., 485 AD.

Nepali Era (879 AD): Jayadeva Malla, with the help of Sakhwal, established the Nepal era beginning 879 AD. He ruled over Kāntipurā and Lalitpaṭṭaṇa.

5. The Epoch of the Creation

(51/1/1st Satyayuga)

or

(51st Brāhma year, 1st Svayambhuva Manvantara, 1st Satyayuga)

(1, 972, 949, 121 years ago as of 2019 AD)

As per the Vedic model of creation, creation always leads to decreation and decreation to creation. As soon as a thing is created, it starts depreciating or decreating. So soon as a thing is decreated it tends to creation. The creation and decreation are the eternal cycles. Gitā reflects this phenomenon as:

जातस्य हि ध्रुवो मृत्यु ध्रुवं जन्म मृतस्य च।

jatasya hi dhruvo mṛtu dhruvaṁ janma mṛtasya ca

Everyone who is born will eventually die, and everyone who dies is destined to be reborn..

According to this perspective, the origin of the universe is characterized by its dissolution, and vice versa; dissolution is reflected in its origin. This is why Vedic scientists refer to origin as devolution and dissolution as evolution. One complete cycle of creation and dissolution lasts for 100 Brahma years, which corresponds to 311 trillion years. Out of these 100 Brahma years, half (50 Brahma years) is devoted to dissolution, while the other half is dedicated to creation.

Thus, the first 50 Brahma years—equivalent to 155 trillion years—are defined by the cycle of dissolution, and the subsequent 50 Brahma years will be marked by the cycle of creation. As of 2019 AD, we have completed the dissolution cycle, and we have now entered the creation cycle with the beginning of the 51st Brahma year, known as Śveta Varāha Kalpa, Vaivasvata Manvantara, and the 5120 years of the 28th Kaliyuga. This cycle began approximately 1,972,949,121 years ago.

The Epoch of Conjunction of Planets along with their Apsides and Nodes

51/1/1st Satyayuga

According to the Sūryasiddhānta (1.24), 17,064,000 years after the beginning of the Kalpa, all the planets, along with their apsis (mandoccha) and nodes (śighroccha), aligned at 0 degrees in Āśvinī Nakṣatra for the first time. Previously, these planets would conjoin every 1,080,000 years, but without their apsis and nodes. This period is regarded by the Sūryasiddhānta as the time of the creation of both the animate and inanimate world. In contrast, other Siddhāntas view the Kalpa period solely as the creation era.

ग्रहर्क्ष-देव-दैत्यादि सृजतोऽस्यचराचरम् ।

कृताद्रिवेदाः (474) दिव्याब्दाः शतघ्नाः (ग100) वेधसो गताः ॥ 1.24 ॥

[Meaning] 474 X 100= 47400 divine years (17064000 human years) of Brahmā passed while creating the animate and in animate world of planets, stars and Devas, Dānavas etc.

The reference from the *Sūrya Siddhānta* indicates that biological creation first emerged on Earth 1,955,885,121 years prior to 2019 AD.

The Epoch of Creation of Human Beings on the Earth

51/1/3rd Dvāpara/432000

or 1,960,853,121 years as on 2019 AD

According to the Veda, the earth takes time equal to three Mahayugas for the plants to develop on the surface of the earth. So, naturally, human beings will evolve here in the third yuga.

या ओषधीः पूर्वा जाता देवेभ्यस्त्रियुगं पुरा । ऋ. 10.97.1

yā ōṣadhīḥ pūrvā jātā devebhyastriyugaṁ purā / *RV. 10.97.1*

Human creation on Earth began in the third Mahāyuga, in the 432000th year of the 3rd Dvāpara of the 1st Svāyambhuva Manvantara, approximately 1,960,853,121 years ago as of 2019 AD.

6. Vedic Epoch

51/1/3rd Dvāpara/432000
or 1,960,853,121 years as of 2019 AD

The age of the Vedas is a hotly debated issue. Scholars from time to time have been engaged in determining the antiquity of this oldest literature of the world. In fact, in determining the date of the Vedas, scholars have been led by their various preconceived notions and true or false beliefs. Whereas occidental scholars have their own sets of notions and beliefs, oriental scholars have their own view too. Obsessed with their different types of beliefs and notions the age-old Vedic tradition has totally been ignored or given a goodbye. It was always argued by various scholars at home and abroad that the Vedic traditional belief is clearly very speculative and based on fictitious astronomical calculations. The fact is that none of the viewpoints, occidental or oriental, considered as non-speculative, has any scientific basis; rather, they are also based on speculations more dangerous and misleading than what is called traditional one.

The so-called scientific viewpoint of occidental scholars was based upon their assumption of the origin of the universe and, thereby, the origin of humans on the earth. In the 16th century, an Archbishop named Usher (1581-1656) thoughtlessly declared that creation took place on 22 October, 4004 years before the birth of Christ.

Archbishop Usher

Since clergymen served as the religious teachers and guides for Western scholars, their statements led to speculation about the possible age of the world's oldest literature. When the creation date was established as 4004 years before Christ, it followed that the origin of the first book in the library of the world could not be dated beyond the creation. Based on this timeframe, Western scholars began their efforts to determine the origin of the Vedas.

Most European scholars have long presumed that the earliest Ṛgvedic hymns were composed between 1500 BC and 1000 BC. Macdonell (1854-1930) suggests that the first collection of these hymns, which was later edited around 600 BC to incorporate phonetic changes sanctioned by Classical Sanskrit, originates from a period that can hardly be later than 1000 BC. Max Müller (1823-1900) initially assigned these dates based on his analysis of the linguistic changes in the language of the oldest hymns compared to that of Pāṇini. He believed that multiple linguistic layers existed within Vedic literature, each corresponding to approximately 200 years. By dating Pāṇini to around 300 BC, he proposed that the oldest Ṛgvedic hymns could be traced back to about 1500 BC. Additionally, because some hymns closely correspond with certain gāthās of the Avesta, it is thought that the Iranians and Indians diverged around this time, with most Ṛgvedic hymns being composed thereafter in Punjab. Therefore, according to most Western scholars, the age of the Ṛgveda is estimated to be between 1500 and 1000 BC.

However, modern scientific discoveries have invalidated the earlier assumptions regarding the age of the earth, which had been estimated by Usher at around 4004 BC. Current estimates suggest that the Earth is over 4 billion years old. As a result, the earlier speculations assigning the Vedas a date between 1500 and 1000 BC, based on these outdated views of creation, are now considered entirely unfounded. Given that the fundamental assumptions have been disproven by scientific advancements, there is no basis left to support the prior speculations.

The Second view is held by many Indian scholars, led by Bal Gangadhara Tilak. They assign far different antiquity to the Vedas based upon astronomical events referred to here and there in the Vedic and allied literature. But the main problem with these scholars is that they are very selective while dilating upon the Vedas or ancient Sanskrit literature. They are ready to accept the part statement of the Vedas as suitable to their preconceived notions and projections about the so-called dating of the ancient Sanskrit literature. They are not ready to accept the tradition as a whole. According to these scholars, Rāma's birth during the period when the vernal equinox was taking place in the Punarvasu Nakṣatra is acceptable, but to them, the beginning of the 24th Tretā period mentioned in the same tradition is not acceptable; rather, they venture to call such statements mere suppositions. They don't seem to have the patience to wait and watch further developments in the field of science. They forget that if the mention of the Tretā or the Dvāpara or the Satyayuga is speculative, the mention of the Punarvasu or Aśvini or Kṛttikā may also be speculative. They accept one part as confirmed and another part as fictitious. They are ready to accept the historical events of the Rāmāyaṇa or the Mahābhārata (Mbh.) taking place in this country, but they are reluctant to accept the antiquity of the Mahābhārata Mbh. as handed down to us in a long uninterrupted tradition of 5000 years.

Thus, they are not confident in themselves and pass the buck to other readers and scholars. If they want to accept the part of the tradition, why don't they accept the whole tradition? If something is beyond the ambit of their comprehension, they should make it a point of further research and study, instead of hurriedly concluding and discarding the whole phenomenon as fictitious. Modern research into astronomy and astrophysics has proved the phenomenon of precession to be true, and there is no denying the fact that equinoctial points and solstitial points continue to recede, completing the whole circle in 25920 years.

Under the circumstances when the same phenomenon of equinoctial or solstitial precession repeats itself in 25920 years, there is no problem in accepting the Yuga and the Manvantara theory mentioned in the Vedic and Puranic literature, to ascertain the actual circle of equinoctial or solstitial points.

The third concept is the traditional Indian view, according

to which the Vedas were composed at the time of the creation. Since the Vedas are the knowledge of creation, this knowledge came into existence in the universe at the very moment of its creation. This may be illustrated by an example of a machine. When an engineer makes a machine, the knowledge of machine comes into existence in the cosmos at the very moment of its creation. So, the traditional view maintained that the Vedas are the knowledge of creation and its authorship can be assigned to the creator of God himself in the beginning of creation. The period of creation is calculated to be 197 crores (1.9 billion) years which is handed down to us in the tradition of the Saṁkalpa Pāṭhas. The socio-linguistic survey of Vedic and Puranic literature done by the author of the present lines all but proves the authenticity of the antiquity of the Vedic era handled in the long and uninterrupted tradition of Saṅkalpa Pāṭha.

Some facts on the authenticity of the Vedic Era are rendered hereunder:

Evidence of Antiquity of the Vedic Epoch

The comparative study of the various eras of the world leads one to conclude that it is only the Vedic era which is the longest in the world. All other eras of the world, which are quite latest as compared to the Vedic era are either based on great personalities, dynasties or some important events. In fact, the great seers of India did not consider individuals, dynasties or events important, but according to them a time or Kāla is above all. Everything in this world is encapsulated in time and time is independent of all. So, according to them, personalities or events were to be studied from the point of time and it was not the time that was to be studied from the point of personalities, dynasties or events.

The Vedic era which starts from Kalpa era or Srṣṭi era has the remotest antiquity of 197 crore years. This era has unanimously been accepted in the Vedaṅgas, the Purāṇas and the Manusmṛti, etc. Presently this era has come down to us as Kali era 5120 as on 2019 AD. In fact, only this era was prevalent in India through ages, except a few others which came into vogue after 3000 years of the commencement of present Kaliyuga. These later evolved eras are also based, like most of the others in the world, on some personalities, dynasties or events. Mention may be made of the Kārtikādi Vikramaera (717-716 BC) and Chaitrādi Vikrama era of (57 BC), originally called or the Śaka Nṛpa kāla era 583 BC commencing with coronation of Śaka king Caṣṭana in 583 BC and Śaka kālātīta eracommencing with the termination of Śaka rule in India in 78 AD. Śri Harsha era (457 BC) etc. It seems probable that the Indians got the idea of naming an era after some personality or dynasty or event from the foreigners who came in their contact. Their original era which was safeguarded in the tradition of the Saṁkalpa pāṭhas since 197 crore years till date is based purely on astronomical calculations. It begins with the beginning of the Kalpa and so called the Kalpa era. In fact, this era has been handed down to us with utmost accuracy by a tradition of the Vedic people.

According to some scholars, this era is hypothetical and fictitious based on astronomical calculations of ancient Indian astronomers. Had there been any such era in currency, there would have been chronological data in the Ṛgvedic hymns. But these arguments are baseless. In fact, there were two different but parallel traditions. One was the Vedic and the other was the Paurāṇika tradition. Whereas Vedic tradition preserved the Vedas (knowledge of creation), the Paurāṇika tradition preserved the Kālagaṇanā (the time period of creation), genealogies and the history of creation and decreation.

The Vedas are the books of knowledge and science and so their purpose was not to record the chronology like the present-day books on sciences and technology. Moreover, we come across repeated mention of the Manvantara and the yugas in the Purāṇas and other works, which obviously point out to the various phases of chronology. The Indian era tells about the chronology of millions of years. The number of years is so extensive that it is not feasible to keep the chronological record of all the past events. We had an age-old tradition of the Itihāsa and Purāṇa. The tradition of the Purāṇas is still extant whereas the tradition of the Itihāsa has lost its existence due to some catastrophic reasons or other. No documentary proof of the same is now available for demonstration. The remotest antiquity of the Indian era has always been a moot point among historians and other scholars. It is too lengthy in nature to be accepted by them open-heartedly. In fact, the authenticity of the longest ever era of the world has been fired on one ground or another. This system has also been challenged on the ground that it never got the sanction of people or never been in practice. This is why, while recounting Indian eras, the scholars often start from Vikram era of 57 BC. and fail to touch upon the original and actual system. Keeping in view all the pros and cons of the original Indian era christened as the Vedic era, we would like to observe as under:

(1) So far as its antiquity is concerned, it may appear hypothetical and fictitious to the most of historians and Indologists. On the other hand, geologists, anthropologists, biologists, physicists and other scientists would speak highly of it, since their findings have led them to conclude that the earth originated around 300-400 crore years ago and biological life flourished on it somewhere about 200-300 crore years ago.

Scientists have recently discovered that the existence of ancient microbial life on the red planet or Mars took place around 360 crore years ago. Their studies are based on intensive laboratory work for 10 years with sophisticated lasers and spectrometers on a piece of Martian meteorite weighing 1.9 kg. found in Antarctica in 1984. Whatsoever be the reaction of scholars and scientists regarding this finding, one thing is clear that sign of bacterial life appeared in our neighbourhood or on our planet around 3.5 billion years ago.

Recent research in genetic science has also proved that a Maithunī Sṛṣṭī (sexual production) had evolved on this earth some 200 to 300 crore years ago. If the existence of a Maithunī Sṛṣṭī could occur 200-300 crore years ago, there is a possibility that human life was also certainly in existence on the earth around 196 crore years ago, as suggested by Vedic seers.

Biologists like Lemark (1744-1829), William Smith (1769-1839), and Charles Darwin (1809-1882) etc. also see the origin of biological life on the Earth 100 to 150 crore years ago.

(2) So far as its sanction in the Indian society is concerned, we find the mention of various phases of this era in the Vedic and the Paurāṇika sources. Besides, we have a Saṁkalpa tradition, which is as old as the Vedas themselves. This tradition has kept the year-to-year, month to month, day to day, even Muhurta (period of 48 minutes) to Muhurta record of the time that has elapsed since the inception of this era. The Saṁkalpa Pāṭhas from all over India have been gathered, and on comparative examination, it has been found that there was strict uniformity so far as the reckonings of time are concerned, except those of geographical references, which would have to differ naturally.

So far as the validity of its length is concerned, it may be maintained here that it was not a hypothetical reckoning of time based on backward astronomical calculations. As per the Vedic and the Pauraṇika traditions, humans were present on the earth 196 crore years ago, and the Vedas (knowledge of creation) were imbibed and time reckoning was launched by the seers present then. The following geological, astronomical, biological, and cultural codes of the Vedas stand to authenticate the very antiquity of the Indian era.

1. **Parvata:** This is a well-established fact that the diction and style of a particular language are formed within a particular cultural background marked by the development of various sciences, moral ethos, and philosophy under various circumstances, and as taken from various angles, a particular word may have various meanings. For instance, the term 'fire' in the sense of shooting came in vogue when the bombs were thrown at the enemy through canons by giving fire to the explosive material stored in its barrel. Now the use of this term has no longer remained relevant since we don't give fire for shooting bombs or bullets. But the same word is still in currency though the circumstances have changed and it is taken from a different angle. Similarly, under the circumstances

created by modern science, some new usages are in currency, e.g. 'He went there by air or by the sea.' The above-given usages 'by air' or 'by sea' obviously implies the 'aeroplane' or 'ship'. Suppose the modern science and its technology face extinction due to some catastrophic reasons, and the above phrases are handed down to the future generations after 100 or 1000 years without the actual scientific background behind them. These phrases would naturally appear to the then future generations mere nonsense and nothing else. They would simply laugh at the currency of such foolish usages. Similar is the case with a number of Vedic usages, which have been handed down to us in their literal sense without any proper scientific or cultural background behind their evolution. Take for example the term 'parvata'. The very term 'parvata' stands for mountains in the classical Sanskrit, but the same meaning doesn't hold good so far as the Vedas are concerned. In the Vedas, 'parvata' and all of its synonyms like 'adri' and 'giri''grāvā' etc. refer to the clouds and boundary of the universe instead of earthly mountains. The ancient Vedic scholar Yāska (Kali era 400 or c 2700 BC) has revealed this fact in his celebrated lexicon called the Nighaṇṭu (1.10). Several modern occidentals, as well as oriental scholars, wonder why Yāska has identified 'parvata' with the cloud. They, howev¬er, forget that it was not Yāṣka's personal view, but it was a long tradition handed down to Yāska that preserved the original geographical background within which the term 'parvata' evolved. In fact, this great culture is not 3, 4 or 10 thousand years old but the chronology preserved by this culture since the time of its inception shows that it dates as early as 196 crores (1.9 billion) years ago. The researches into geology have proved that there was the time when there were no mountains on the earth. The use of the term 'parvata' in the sense of cloud in the Vedas clearly points out to the geographical scenario which prevailed during the time of their composition. This earth which is presently covered with mountain ranges was obviously devoid of any sort of mountain around 197 crore years ago. As per theories of orogeny, mountains appeared 60 crore years ago. Under the circumstances, it can unhesitatingly be inferred that the Vedic culture belonged to the period when the orogenic process had not started. This fact indirectly testifies to the authenticity and validity of the Indian era too. Since there were no mountains on the earth, in the beginning, the term 'parvata' or its synonyms like 'adri', 'grāvā', 'giri', etc. had nothing to do with mountains and so rather used sparingly to signify clouds.

Yāska (*Nir.* 1.20.) observed in this connection as follows:

गिरिष्ठाः गिरिस्थायी गिरः पर्वतः।समुद्गीर्णो भवति पर्ववान् पर्वतः पर्व पुनः पृणाते पृणन्ति तत् प्रकृतीतरत सन्धि सामान्यात् मेघस्थायी मेघोऽपि गिरिरेतस्मादेव।

giriṣṭhā girishāyī giriḥ parvataḥ samudgīrṇo bhavati parvavān parvataḥ parva punaḥ pṛṇāteḥ prīṇantiti tat prakrtītarat sandhi sāmānyāt meghasthāyī megho'pi giriretasmādeva.

> 'Giri' is known as 'parvata', since it is the vomited vapour of the earth. It is so-called as it is constituted of fragments. It is called so as it brings up the living beings on the earth with water, etc. These qualities are discernible in clouds. Hence, clouds are called 'giri'.

Later on, these qualities were also found associated with the mountain ranges that emerged on the earth, and so the term 'parvata' and its synonyms were also began to be applied to the mountains, and de Grado en grade this term got conventionalized for mountains only. This is why Lord Macaulay (1800-1859) laughs at the mention of 'parvata' flying in the sky. Had he been well conversed with Vedic dicta, he wouldn't have laughed; rather would have enjoyed the Vedic wisdom.

2. **Nadī, Sindhu, Samudra**: In the Vedas, we have references of 'nadi' and 'sindhu' being used for rainy waters and water flowing on the earth, respectively.

Thus, applications of the terms 'nadī' and 'sindhu' respectively in the sense of rainy waters and rivers show that Vedic culture flourished by the period when oceans were not formed on the earth and the rivers were in the process of formation. Due to the non-formation of oceanic waters by the time of evolution of this culture, the terms 'samudra' and 'arṇava' were also used to denote mid-sphere rather than terrestrial oceans. As per research in Geology, the ancient mountains and the oceans were formed on the earth in the Precambrian or Algonican era, i.e., between 250 to 60 crores of years ago. The Vedic culture, which has recorded its history since 196 crore years ago, clearly reveals that the oceans and mountains were formed on this earth within the range of 196 crore years. The Vedic litanies were composed when there were no mountains and the ocean visibly appeared on the earth, and the rivers were in the process of formation.

3. **Sarasvatī**: Sarasvatī was the name of the first river system that originated on the earth. The very first appearance of this river system on the earth owes to the clouds. The most celebrated Ṛgvedic seer Vasiṣṭha had clearly observed its origin from the celestial parvatasi, i.e. clouds. According to him:

आनोदिवो बृहतः पर्वतादा सरस्वती यजता गन्तु
हवंदेवीजुजुषाणा घृताची शग्मो नोवाचमुशती श्रृणोतु।

ā no divo bṛhataḥ parvatādā sarasvatī yajatā gantu Yajñam
havaṁ devī jujuṣāṇā ghṛtācī śagmo no vācamuśatī śṛṇotu

'From the great celestial parvatas (clouds) Sarasvatī flows towards the site of Yajña. It hears the voice of a person who offers the oblation of ghṛta with the desire of receiving it.'

Parvata here clearly refers to a cloud and not to a mountain as it is conventionally held. The attributive '*divaḥ*' (celestial) bears out the hypothesis that 'parvata' was only intended for clouds and not for mountains, as there can be no mountain in the sky except clouds.

Not only Vasiṣṭha, but another seer had it the same way. According to him, the Sarasvatī is the only flow of waters on earth that issues from the giris (clouds).

ऐका चेतत् सरस्वती नदीनाम् शुचिर्यति गिरिभ्यः समुद्रात्।
ekā cetat sarasvatī nadinām śuciryatī giribhyaḥ ā samudrāt
(RV. 7.95.2).

The concept of the first origin of the Sarasvatī from clouds also shows that the Vedas were composed at the time when there was no mountain, no glacier on the earth. It marks the period before the origin of glaciers on this part of the earth. Geologists have traced the appearance of the glaciation on this part of the Globe in Triassic period i.e. around 22 crore years ago. So there is nothing wrong if we infer that the Vedic hymns containing the description of the origin of rivers from clouds were composed before glaciation.

This fact also bears the testimony to the authenticity of the Indian era.

4. **Brahmaputra**: The Vedas don't have any mention of the Brahmaputra. In fact, the Brahmaputra is the creation of Himalayan mountains. When there were no Himalayan ranges, there was no Brahmaputra. The Pauraṇika (*Vāyu and Matsya*) traditions describe the origin of the Brahmaputra from the lake of Hemasṛṅga. Similarly, the Sarasvatī and Jyotiṣmatī have also been described to have their origins from the lakes of Hemasṛṅga. Hemasṛṅga reminds us of the glaciation around Mānasa-sara. It was the upliftment of the Himalayan ranges that caused the Brahmaputra severed from that of Sarasvatī. The records of the Vāyu and the Matsya Purāṇas belonging to the period of origin of the Himalayan ranges of mountains containing the description of Lohita river or the Brahmaputra rising from the lohita lake situated at the foot of Lohita Hemsṛṅga (Vāyu Purāṇa) and Sarvoṣadha (Matsya Purāṇa). The absence of the Brahmaputra in the Vedas also proves the Vedas older than the Himalayas and so the antiquity of Indian era.

5. **Himvat**: A few references in the Vedas (*RV.* 10.121.4) of Himvat shows the presence of glaciated regions in the Vedic period. The word Himalaya today is taken to mean the Himalayan ranges of mountains. But the main thing to note is that Himalaya is a term of quite a later period. In its earlier references ranging from the Vedas to the Epics and the Puraṇas, the term used was 'Himvat', which literally means 'a place of snow' or 'glaciated region'. Moreover, the later evolved term Himalaya also doesn't indicate any sort of hill or mountain;

rather it also, in its literal sense, points to the glaciated region or the home of snow. In fact, the term 'hima' never denoted hilly terrain, but rather it denoted glaciers. Since the latter originated mountains also became the abode of the glaciers, they came to be called the Himalaya mountains, which literally means abode of glaciers. The Purāṇic tradition narrates the origin of the rivers of North India like Ganga, Sarasvatī, Gaṇḍaka, Yamuna, Sindhu, Sutlej, Chenab, Devikā, Kuhu, Gomatī, etc., from the foot of glaciers.

हिम्वत्पादनिस्सृता (ब्रह्म पुराण २ ॥१६ ॥२७)

himvatpādanissṛtā (Brahma Purāṇa 2.16.27)

Such references are clear-cut records of the geological scenario of glaciation in the Triassic period, i.e., 22 crores of years ago.

6. **Four Seas:** Some of the Vedic ṛcās seem to be composed after the formation of seas or oceans took place. Such ṛcās shed ample good light in the presence of seas on the earth. In the chain of such ,cas, we meet with some as describing the presence of four seas, one each in four directions of the Indian subcontinent, e.g.

रायः समुद्रांश्चतुरोऽस्मभ्यंसोमविश्वतः ।
rāyaḥ samudrāṁścaturo'smabhyaṁ soma viśvataḥ.
(*RV.* 9.33.6.)

See also:

स्वायुधं स्ववसं सुनीथं चतुःसमुद्रं धरूणं रयीणाम् ।
svāyudhaṁ svavasaṁ sunīthaṁ chatuḥsamudraṁ dharūṇaṁ rayīṇām / (RV. 10.47.2.)

The period when this country was bounded by four seas, goes back to 10 crore years ago.

The paleomagnetism of oceanic rocks indicates that the continents started separating during the last 10 crore years. Near the end of the Carboniferous and the beginning of the Permian (i.e., 30 crore years ago), the land masses were assembled into two supercontinents, Gondwana in the south and Laurasia in the north (Enayat Ahmed, 1993:80).

This assemblage of two supercontinents persisted till about 15 crore years ago, but the continents were discernible from their outlines. About 10 crore years ago, the expansion of Indian Ocean by further separation of Antarctica from South Africa and South America and the drifting of India and Australia became more prominent than the Atlantic, which still remained as a relatively narrow ocean, particularly in the north. The picture given below displays the portion of the Indian sub-continent and the seas surrounding it in the four directions

Map of the Eocene Period

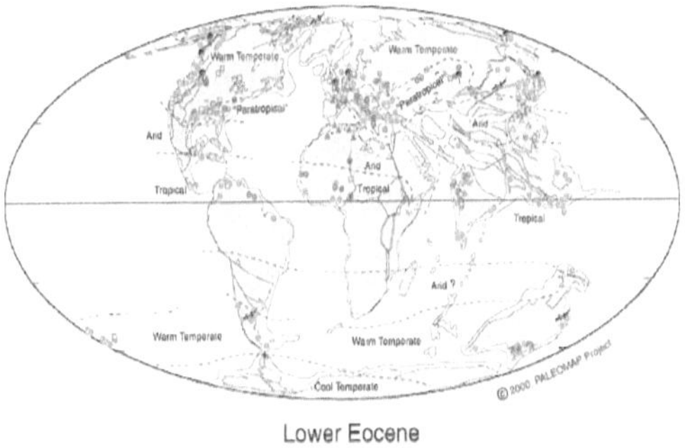

Lower Eocene

Thus, from the above geological description, it is crystal clear that India was surrounded by four seas mentioned in the ṛcas of the Ṛgveda composed around 10 crore years ago. This marks evidently the pre-Himalayan period.

7. **Triviṣṭapa**: According to the Paurāṇika tradition, Humans originated first in the area of Triviṣṭapa (Tibet).

त्रिविष्टपे जाता सृष्टिः ।
triviṣṭape jātā sṛṣṭiḥ.

In the Paurāṇic and Epic traditions Triviṣṭapa has been remembered as a place where from devas descended first. It is often known as svarloka being the highest plateau on the earth. Triviṣṭapa being Tibet in its corrupt form. According to Geologists, Tibet formed as an offshore region of the Gondwana land during the Palaeozoic era. (Enayat Ahmed, 1993: 94)

Palaeozoic era makes its beginning as early as 60 crore years ago and ends as late as 27 crore years ago. So Triviṣṭap's mention as a cradle of deva sṛṣṭi in the beginning of the creation of human beings forces one to accept the great culture as old as the formation of Tibet itself.

8. **Vaḍvāgni:** As per modern geological researches, the Himalayan ranges of mountains started to form in the Eocene period, i.e. around 7 crore years ago. It is also a proved fact that the Himalayan ranges of the mountains formed from volcanoes. Here it may be pointed out that age-old Paurāṇika traditions have reported the submarine volcanic activities in the name of the Vaḍvāgni. The Vḍvāgni which literally means'submarine fire' is nothing else, but the submarine volcanic activities that began to take place around 7 crore years ago, if geology provides the correct information. The tradition of the Skand Purāṇa (7.33.40-41) holds that the Sarasvatī drained the Vaḍvāgni to western sea at Prabhāsa Pāṭan. This traditional record of the Skanda Purāṇa obviously points out to 7 crore-year-old submarine volcanic activities that gave rise to the Himalayan mountains. Due to volcanic activities at the submarine level of Manas sara, the submarine surface of Manas sara or Tethys'sea as it is called today, began to uplift and the outflow of water due to the uplifted submarine surface of Manas sara began to be drained by a river channel called Sarasvatī towards western sea at Prabhāsa Pāṭan in the modern Gujarat state. The drainage of submarine volcanic eruptions by Sarasvatī has also been attested in the tradition of several other Purāṇas. Special mention in this connection may be made of the Padma Purāṇa (5.18.154-160).

The record of volcanic activities at the submarine surface level of Tethys' sea proves Vedic culture older than the Himalayas.

9. **Saṅkalpa Pāṭha:** The Saxkalpa tradition that has been handed down to us reads a phrase as under:

मेरोर्दक्षिणभागे जम्बुद्वीपे भारतवर्षे भरतखण्डे
merordakṣiṇa bhāge jambudvīpe bhāratavarṣe, bharatakhaṇḍe

The Saṅkalpā Pāṭha indicates that Jambudvīpa, Bhāratavarṣa, and Bharatakhaṇḍa are located in the southern hemisphere of the Meru. Before discussing the above statement, it is necessary to know about Meru and its southern point. Meru was the name of the lithosphere with two polar caps. This fact has been corroborated by the Yogavāsiṣṭha. Accordingly, Meru is the name of the surface of the earth.

मेरु भूपृष्ठः

meru bhūpṛṣṭhaḥ (Yogavāsiṣṭha, 59.27)

The word 'Maru' is the actual representative of the Meru. 'Maru' is also indicative of a sandy desert devoid of water. This meru had two polar caps and so divided into two halves. The upper half, the northern hemisphere, is known as sumeru, and the lower half, the southern hemisphere, is known as kumeru. Now, one will be able to comprehend the Saṅkalpa pāṭha. Accordingly, Jaṁbudvīpa, which includes Bhāratavarṣa and Bharatakhaṇḍa, was situated in the southern hemisphere of the Meru.

Here it can easily be inferred that when the extant Saṅkalpa pāṭha was introduced, the Indian subcontinent was towards the south pole. In the present circumstances, when we have drifted towards 70 north, it is very difficult to make out the actual significance of the extant Saṅkalpa pāṭha. Its actual intent can only be understood when one looks back the geographical conditions, as gathered from the theories of drifters like Wegener, etc., that Indian subcontinent was the part of southern hemisphere around 35 crore years ago or in the end of the Carboniferous period of the Palaeozoic era.

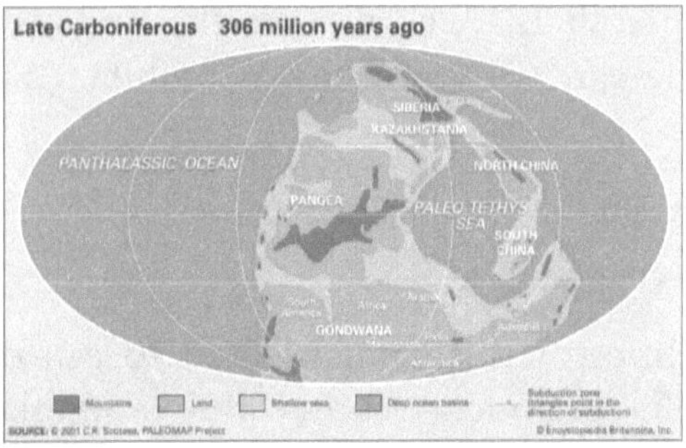

The researches in geology have shown alarming results regarding the drift in the location of different regions of the globe. Accordingly, Indian subcontinent continued to be the part of southern hemisphere until the early Pleistocene period of a Neozoic era or Quaternary era, i.e. till 10 lakh years ago when this continent drifted right on the equatorial point.

10. **Location of the Kailāśa**: The drift in the geographical location of the Indian subcontinent has also been suggested by the Paurāṇika records of the Perennial era. Accordingly, the location of the Kailaśa mountain was earlier in the south, but it was shaken by the kick of Śiva during his Tāṇḍava Nṛtya and transferred towards the north. (Dr. Padmachandra Kashyapa, Bhārata Darśana Mālā, 6)

Here Tāṇḍava Nṛtya of Śiva signifies the forces of drift or plate-tectonic activities that changed the position of the Kailāśa mountain from south to north. One may remember well that the Himalayan ranges of mountains began to form as early as 7 crore years ago, as per modern estimates and 12 crore years ago as per ancient Indian view, and the Śivālaka ranges of mountains were formed as the result of the last stages of the upliftment of the Himalayan ranges ranging from 1 crore year ago to 20 lakh years ago. We are very much aware of the fact that 20 lakh years ago, i.e. by the period of completion of the Himalayan ranges and the Śivālaka ranges we were very much around 70 south of the equator. Presently we have drifted towards 70 north of the equator.

The concept of drifting continents or plate tectonics of the earth has also been suggested in the methods of the construction of Vedic fire altars. According to the Brāhmaṇas, fire-altar represented the earth. The Taittirīya Saṁhitā. (2.6.4) has clarified this fact as:

ऐतावती वै पृथिवी यावती वेदी।
aitāvatī vai pṛthivī yāvatī vedī ।

As the cultural tradition had it, Indians used to call their nation or geographically bounded country the motherland, e.g., we call our country Bhārata as Bhārata mātā. The concept of motherhood is associated with the country because the concept of birth is associated with the country as closely as it is with the mother. Just as a mother is the birth giver, similarly country is also a birthplace. Hence, it is always attributed to the mother and the country of birth. The study of the Vedas tells us that no country or geographical area in the original hymns of the Vedas has been mentioned as mother, rather, earth itself has been found endowed with such attributes as mother–

भूमिमाता पुत्रोऽहम पृथिव्याः ।
bhūmī mātā putro'ham pṛthivyāḥ (AV. Bhumi Sūkta)

'Earth is my mother and I am the child of earth.'

The association of motherhood with the earth simply reveals the fact that this culture is fairly old and belongs to the period when the earth was practically one super-continent and had not fractured into various continents. This geological situation persisted till the period of palaeozoic era or 60 crore years. In fact, the origin of the Indian subcontinent as a separate landmass took place by the end of a Carboniferous era or 35 crore years ago when it was situated between 30^0 south of the equator. See the map of the end of the Carboniferous era as given above.

So this cultural code also supports the author's hypothesis that Vedic culture and the Vedic era was undoubtedly 196 crores (1.9 billion) years old.

14. **Astronomical evidence**: Above-cited geological code of the Vedas and Indian chronology of 196 crore years is also supported by astronomical evidence of two kinds.

1. Firstly we find the important role of the Aśvinīkumaras (The two bright stars Alpha and Beta Aries) in the *RV.* They have been praised in 53 hymns.

To sum up, it can be inferred from the above evidence that the composition of the Ṛgvedic verses took place during the period of the Aśvinī calendar or during the period when the year started with the sun in the Aśvinī Nakṣatra (or Alpha and Beta Arietis).

In the *VS.* (31.22) also, it is clearly stated that Aśvinī was the mouth of the present creation (aśvinau vyāttam). All this points out that in the beginning of present Kalpa 1, 972, 949, 121 years ago the sun was in the Aśvinī Nakṣatra. Keeping in view of this historical fact, Indian Scholars made the Aśvinī Nakṣatra as the basis of their chronology. Aśvinī calendar of the Ṛgvedic period also proves the fact that the Vedas were visualised 1.9 billion years ago by the high-spirited seers present at that period.

2. Apart from the above evidence, the second evidence is quite revealing. Accordingly, the year in the Ṛgvedic period contained 360 days or 720 pairs of Ahas (days) and Rātris (nights). This fact has clearly been recorded in the verses of the *RV.* as under:

द्वादशारं न हि तज्जराय वर्वर्ति चक्रं परि द्यामृतस्य।
आ पुत्राग्ने मिथुनासो अत्र सप्त शतानिविंशतिश्च तस्थुः ॥ RV.1.164.2

dvādaśāraṁ na hi tajjarāya varvarti cakraṁ pari dyāmṛtasya.
ā putrā agne mithunāso atrasapta śatānivimśatiśca tasthuḥ.

'The wheel (of time), having twelve spokes (months) revolves around the heavens, but it doesn't wear out. O Agni! 720 pairs of sons (ahorātras) ride this wheel.'

द्वादशप्रधयश्चक्रमेकं त्रिणि नाभ्यानि क उताच्चिकेत
तस्मिन्तशाकं त्रिशता न शंकवोऽर्पिताः षष्टिर्न चलाचलासः ॥
dvādaśa pradhayaścakramekaṁ triṇi nābhyāni ka utacciketa
tasmintsākaṁ triśatā na śaṅkavo'rpitāḥ ṣaṣṭirna calācalāsaḥ.

'Twelve spokes (months), one wheel (year), three navels (seasons): who understand these? In these, there are installed 360 śaṅkus (rods, i.e. days) like pegs which do not loosen.'

The tradition of the *Tait. Br.* (7.17) also remembers the relic of this ancient most historical fact of astronomy as follows:

त्रीणि च वै शतानि षष्टिश्च संवत्सरस्याहनिसप्त च
वै शतानिविंशतिश्च संवत्सरस्याहोरात्रयः।
trīṇi ca vai śatāni ṣaṣṭiśca saṁvatsarasyāhāni sapta ca vai śatāni viṁśatiśca saṁvatsarasyāhorātrayaḥ.

'A year has 360 days, and 720 days and nights together.'

Thus, a year of 360 days consisting of 12 months of 30 days each formed the earliest astronomical phenomenon and thereby the earliest Vedic calendar, as is evident from the above-cited references. It may here be informed that the month was also further divided into five *ṣaḍahas* of 6 days each.

The year of 360 days was not an approximation or presented a vague idea of the measurement of days in a year. It was rather a real measurement of the days of a year. In fact, the above-cited concept may be understood in light of the theories of expanding the universe. The Vedic seers have already expounded this theory. According to them the origin of space or antarikṣa is the result of the separation of planets from stars. Earlier they were together, and so there was no space between them. With the passage of time due to sliding apart of planets and stars, space between them became visible. Since the space between them became visible, it was known as antarikṣa. For instance, the Ś.Br. (Author, 1995:16) had it as:

> 'In the beginning star and planets were together. In the process of evolution, both began to recede and the space between them became visible. Because space became visible, it was called antarikṣa'

Modern astrophysicists have also come to none the less similar conclusions. According to them, crores of years ago nebulas were close to each other. Even the moon is also going away from the earth, day by day and year by year. It has been calculated that the distance between the moon and the earth is increasing by 13 cms. per year. Similarly, the distance between the earth and the sun is also increasing. Now the earth is 149597870.6 crore Kms. away from the sun. It is revolving around the sun on its ecliptic path of 149597870.6x2x22/7 = 940329472.34 crore Kms. @ 107270 kms. per hour. Imagine the time when the earth was closer to the sun. Its distance being short, the ecliptic path was also short. Under the circumstances, the earth was capable of revolving around the Sun in a shorter period than what it is now. In fact, 197 crore years ago the earth revolved around the sun in 360 days only, so the year was also described as consisting of 360 days. This shows that the ecliptic path of the earth was 107270x8640 (360 days) hrs= 926812800 kms long in 1970000000 years ago if the period of the rate of revolution of the earth remains unchanged. This will make the distance of the earth from the sun 926812800x7/2/22= 147447490 kms before 197 crore years ago. So there is a total increase of distance of the earth from sun 149597870 kms (present) - 147447490 (1970000000 years ago) = 2150379 kms. This makes an average increase in the distance between the earth and sun 215037900000/1970000000=109 cms per year in 1970000000 years. Presently this increase is being calculated @ 15 cms per year. It shows that in the beginning, the rate of increase in distance was much higher than the present one.

Keeping in view of the importance of 360, the Indian astronomers fixed 360 days for the calendric year. Later on, to record any sort of increase in the revolution period due to increase in the distance between the earth and the sun, the provision of the intercalary period was made to be added to the actual period of 360 days. Thus the beginning of the year in the Aśvinī constellations and number of 360 days in a year in the Ṛgvedic period support the above hypothesis.

All the above-cited evidence indicates the presence of humans on the earth crores of years ago, thereby leading one to infer that Vedic era was launched by the seers present 196 crore years ago and was recollected safely and carefully by a long uninterrupted tradition of Saṁkalpa Pāṭhas.

Following the lines of arguments cited above, it can further be observed that the Vedas were visualised somewhere near the inception of the present Kalpa. The internal evidence of the Vedas based on linguistic analysis undoubtedly prove this fact. Though for the time being scholars may have their reservations on this contentious issue, since they may raise questions as to how memory of such a long period was retained in the Vedic and the Paurāṇika tradition. It may not seem feasible, but it may also not be impossible. The manner in which the long uninterrupted tradition has been safeguarded is unparalleled in the history of humankind. Further investigations in various fields of science will be able to shed ample good light on the authenticity of Indian traditional viewpoint.

Let me conclude that only the traditional viewpoint is acceptable and any inference drawn on the basis of some fragmentary references of traditional view would only be misleading and dangerous.

7. The Epoch of Brāhmaṇas

51/6/47

(47th Mahāyuga of 6th Chākṣuṣa Manvantara)

or

22 crore years ago

As has already been pointed out by the present author in his work 'New Discoveries About Vedic Sarasvatī', Vedic tradition finds its origin with the origin of human life or, say, the presence of humans on this globe some 196 crore years ago, and the Brahmanic tradition appears to have started in this country some 22 crore years ago at the time of the first glaciation on this Earth. The second origin of Sarasvatī, as classified by the present author, flowing from Plakṣa to Vinaśana, also took place in the Brahmanic period. This fact has also been corroborated by several Puranic traditions. Plakṣa Prasravaṇa of the Brahmanic period is the pointer to the oozing or thawing out of Sarasvatī from the Himalayas as a glaciated region. There are clear-cut indications in the tradition of Skand Purāṇa (7.30.41) that Sarasvatī, having approached the glaciers, flowed on the Earth through Plakṣa. The approach of Sarasvatī to glaciers was its precipitation in the form of snowflakes from clouds, and its flow in the form of waters on the Earth has been assigned to the place called Plakṣa. In fact, Plakṣa may be recalled as the place of origin of Sarasvatī during the period when the present-day Himalayan region, before its emergence into a mountainous region, witnessed the first-ever glaciation since the origin of the Earth.

Sarasvatī's origin from Plakṣa has also been recorded in the memories of other Purāṇas, such as the VāmanaPurāṇa (3-4), which states that perennial Sarasvatī emerged from the Plakṣa tree.

प्लक्ष वृक्षात् समुद्भूता सरिच्छ्रेष्ठा सनातनी

Plakṣa vṛkṣāt samudbhūtā Saricchreṣṭhā sanātanī

In the Bṛhannāradīya Purāṇa (64-17), Sarasvatī is also

described as Plakṣa Jātā, which means "originated from Plakṣa.

Mārkaṇḍeyena muninā saṁtaptaṁ paramaṁ tapaḥ

तत्र- तत्र समायाता प्लक्षजाता सरस्वती

tatra- tatra samāyātā Plakṣajātā Sarasvatī

In the Tāṇḍya Brāhmaṇa (25-10-16), the distance between the place where Sarasvatī dries up (Vinaśana) and the point of its rising is measured as 44 Āśvins. Additionally, the distance between Plakṣa and Vinaśana is also as long as 44 Āśvins.

चतुश्चत्वारिंशदाश्विनानि सरस्वत्या विनशनात् प्लक्षः प्रास्रवणः

catuścatvāriṁśadāśvināni sarasvatyā vinaśanāt Plakṣaḥ Prāsravaṇaḥ

Now, the primary question arises: was Plakṣa a name for a place or a tree, as it has been recalled in various books? If it was a place name, the challenge is to determine its location and how to find it.

Plakṣa, in fact, was the name of a place, perhaps known for its presence of Plakṣa trees. That's why it was called Plakṣa. So, it's important to distinguish between Plakṣa as a tree and Plakṣa as a place. Plakṣa as a tree is commonly referred to in vernaculars as Pilakhua or a fig tree. Botanically, it is known as ficus religiosa.

The rising of Sarasvatī from a place of Plakṣa trees gave Plakṣa a religious significance, and the tree is revered as holy. Such a place, characterized by Plakṣa trees, is Pilakhua in western Uttar Pradesh. Pilakhua is situated near Hapur and Garhgaṅgā. The name Pilakhua is derived from Pilakhana, a corrupt form of Plakṣa.

The challenge now lies in determining the exact location of Plakṣa as modern Pilakhua based on literary records from the Vedas, Purāṇas, or Epics.

(1). In this context, a reference to the Vāmana Purāṇa (3-4) can be made. According to the text, Sarasvatī, after traversing thousands of stones, entered the Dvaitavana.

सैषा शैलसहस्राणी विदार्य च महा नदी

प्रविष्टा पुण्यतोयैषा वनं दैवतमिति श्रुतम्

saiṣā śailasahasrāṇī vidārya ca mahā nadī

Praviṣṭā puṇyatoyaiṣā vanaṁ daivatamiti śrutam

N.L. Day has identified the location of Dvaitavana, situated approximately 50 miles north of Meerut, in modern Uttar Pradesh. This ancient city was once known as Marudhanvan[3].

(2). King Yudhiṣṭhira started from Kurujāṅgala towards the north on the bank of river Sarasvatī in search of some thick forest full of roots and fruits after sometime he entered Dvaitavana.

There is also a reference of Pāṇḍvas proceeding towards Sarasvatī to the north of Marudhanvan (Modern Meerut). Thus it is clear from the above-cited references that route of Sarasvatī was once via or close to the area of Deoband located to the north of Marudhanvan (Meerut)

(3). Next, let's discuss the location of Kāmyaka vana. According to chapter 244 of the Āryaṇyaka parva, Kāmyaka vana was situated almost in Marudeśa. It's important to note that Marudeśa, or Marusthal, was not a distant land but rather a region close to Hastinapur. From the northern edge of Kāmyakavana, the majestic Himalayan forests began. This information, coupled with the fact that Dvaitavana was located on the banks of Sarasvatī and was situated near the Himalayan hills and forests, respectively, suggests that Sarasvatī, in the Brahmanic period, flowed through Uttar Pradesh. Furthermore, as mentioned in the Geography of Mahābhārata (P.213), from Plakṣa Prasravaṇa, Iśānudhyāsī Tīrtha was approximately half a mile away. The name of this Tīrtha implies a place of worship dedicated to Śiva, and it could also be found within or around Pilakhua.

(4). Mahābhārata (Vanaparva: 8.3-84) mentions Plakṣa among the 113 Tīrthas situated in the Kuru region. The Kuru

---

3 Āraṇyaka Parva 243.21:295.8:296.40 BORI, Poona

region is now identified with the modern regions of Thaneshwar, Delhi, Meerut, and Bijnor, located between the Sarasvatī and Gaṅgā rivers. Its capital was Hastinapur (which is now near modern Bijnor). For further reference, see also Geographical Horizon of Mahābhārata, P.137. Jain Ādi Purāṇa also places Kurujāṅgala between the Sarasvatī and Gaṅgā rivers (16.193).

The most striking feature of the Tīrthas mentioned in the Vanaparva of Mahābhārata is that Gaṅgā-Sarasvatī Saṅgam (84.38) has also been included as one of the Tīrthas of the Kuru region. This explicitly suggests that the Gaṅgā and Sarasvatī must meet in the Kuru region, which can only be the area around Garhgaṅgā and Pilakhua in western Uttar Pradesh.

(5). While recounting Plakṣa as the tīrtha of Kurukshetra, it is mentioned that Sarasvatī originated from a Bamboo near Saugandhika vana, which has also been identified near the Mandākinī river in the Garhwal hills of Uttar Pradesh. This location may not be surprising when considering a folk tale from the Bhutias of Mana village in the Garhwal region of UP. The villagers recount the origin of Sarasvatī in the Mana pass, located at an altitude of 18,400 feet above sea level. This pass is surrounded by majestic peaks covered in a vast expanse of snow and ice and lies on the ancient trade route along the Indo-Tibetan border to the Garhwal region of UP. From Mana Pass to Mana village, Sarasvatī traverses a distance of 45 kilometers. In the high-altitude regions of the Himalayas, the altitude varies from 11,000 feet at Keshava Prayāg (the convergence of Sarasvatī and Alaknandā) to over 18,000 feet at its source.

According to the folk tale, the river descends into Pātāla loka from Bhima Bridge, forming a small stream that eventually meets Alaknandā. The rest of the river reappears at Prayāg rāj to form the Triveṇī. However, before its union with Alaknandā at Keshav Prayāga, Sarasvatī plunges into a deep and narrow gorge below Bhima Bridge. This natural rock bridge is believed to have been constructed by one of the five renowned Pāṇḍva brothers, Bhima, during their 12-year wandering period. The gorge reaches a depth of 150 to 200 feet. After its tumultuous journey through the gorge, the river emerges, its waters cascading with white caps, and merges with Alaknandā to form Keshav Prayāga.

Thus, from the local tradition of folk tales, it is evident that Plakṣa was a region below the glaciated area. During the Brahmanic period, it is most likely that Plakṣa was Pilakhua, which was situated along the route of the Gāṅgā river.

6). As mentioned above, according to the Tāṇḍya Brāhmaṇa (25.10.1-23), the distance between Vinaśana and Plakṣa Prasravaṇa is 44 Āśvins. At the same distance from Plakṣa lies Svarga loka. Therefore, individuals seeking to reach Svarga loka embark on a journey along with the stream of Sarasvatī.

चतुश्चत्वांशदाश्विनानि सरस्वत्या विनशनात् प्लकः प्रास्रवणः तावदितः सवर्गो लोकः सरस्वती सम्मितेन अध्वना सवर्गं लोकं यन्ति

catuścatvāṁśadāśvināni sarasvatyā vinaśanāt Plakaḥ prāsravaṇaḥ tāvaditaḥ savargo lokaḥ sarasvatī sammitena adhvanā savargaṁ lokaṁ yanti

Scholars and others must know that Svarga loka in Sanskrit refers to the northern region of Garhwal, in the upper Himalayan region, along the Mandākinī river. As mentioned in the Tāṇḍya Brāhmaṇa cited above, Plakṣa was situated at an equal distance from Vinaśana and the Garhwal Himalayan region. The performers of yajña used to travel to Svarga loka along with the Sarasvatī stream. It's important to note that Plakṣa was not located on the hilly terrain, but rather in the plains. Sarasvatī's path from the Garhwal region to Plakṣa clearly indicates that Pilakhua is the exact location.

In the Brahmanic period, Sarasvatī didn't reach the western sea; instead, it ended at Vinaśana, approximately 44 Āśvins from Plakṣa. This suggests that Sarasvatī wasn't a significant river during that time, unlike later periods. The Brahmanic period can be considered a glaciated era. According to modern geologists, during the Triassic period, around 22 crore years ago, the northern hemisphere, including present-day Europe, was a desert, while the southern hemisphere, encompassing the

Indian continent, was covered in snow. These memories of glaciation are still preserved in the Purāṇas. During this Brahmanic phase, only Sarasvatī had a narrow course to flow.

Thus, it has been established that the Brāhmaṇic tradition originated in this country during the first glaciation period, approximately 22 crore years ago. While modern research in archaeology, anthropology, and physiology has provided evidence of human existence on Earth before the lakhs of years ago, modern science has yet to conclusively determine the antiquity of human existence. New findings emerge daily, but it is not our obligation to align our perspective with modern scientific findings. We are also not limited by the evidence suggested by modern research. The Vedas have a longstanding tradition of scientific inquiry. The author presents the findings of the Vedic seers and wholeheartedly endorses them. If modern science has yet to reach a definitive conclusion, it can rely on the Vedic findings regardless of geographical or racial biases. However, I must urge my counterparts in India and the West to refrain from hasty criticism of traditional Vedic perspectives under the pressure of incomplete modern scientific findings. The authenticity of the Vedic view regarding the age of the Vedas was established in the previous chapter. Additionally, caution should be exercised when dating Vedic literature based on astronomical observations recorded in the texts. Scholars should not draw conclusions solely on the basis of these observations until they can precisely calculate the cycles of the Yugas, including Mahāyugas, Manvantaras, and Kalpas, which are equally scientific as the astronomical observations.

Epoch of the Śatapatha Brāhmaṇa

In the context of the *Śatapatha Brāhmaṇa*, astronomical references like "Kṛttikās are not swerving from the east" (कृत्तिका प्राच्यै दिशो न च्यवन्ते) indicate that the vernal equinox occurred in the Kṛttikā nakṣatra during that period. According to Raman ayanāñśa, the vernal equinox in Kṛttikā nakṣatra occurred in

1476 BC. However, this doesn't necessarily mean that the Śatapatha Brāhmaṇa era began in 1476 BC. The precession cycle suggests that astronomical phenomena like equinoxes and solstices repeat every 25,920 years before or after a specific year. Therefore, the vernal equinox in Kṛttikā nakṣatra would have occurred in 27,396 BC, i.e., 25,920 years earlier.

Another mention in the *Śatapatha Brāhmaṇa* pertains to the marriage between the Saptarṣis and Kṛttikā (Kak 2022: p. 55). This suggests that the Saptarṣis samvat began in Kṛttikā nakṣatra during the *Śatapatha Brāhmaṇa* period. In 3876 BC, which is 2400 years before the vernal equinox in Kṛttikā nakṣatra (1476 BC), the Saptarṣis samvat also commenced with Kṛttikā nakṣatra. This pattern repeats every 2700 or 27000 years before or after. Therefore, there is a difference of 2400 years or its multiples between the Saptarṣis' sojourn in Kṛttikā and the vernal equinox in Kṛttikā nakṣatra. This also indicates that the Saptarṣis Calendar was in use in this country for a long period.

While Greek historians like Pliny and Arrian suggest that the Saptarṣis Calendar began in 6676 BC, it actually originated from the Dvāpara yuga itself. As such, if we can determine a period in the past when the Vernal equinox and the Saptarṣis's sojourn in Kṛttikā Nakṣatra coincided, we can determine the epoch of the Śatapatha Brāhmaṇa. Calculating 20 cycles of precession (25920 years) and the Saptarṣis (27000 years) backward, we find that the Vernal equinox occurred in Kṛttikā in 519876 BC, and the Saptarṣis began their sojourn in Revatī in 541476 BC. The difference between these two periods is 541476-519876=21600 years. 21600 is a multiple of 9 times 2400 (the difference between the Saptarṣis's sojourn in Kṛttikā and the Vernal equinox in Kṛttikā). Therefore, we can conclude that 519876 BC is the epoch when the Vernal equinox and the Saptarṣis's sojourn in Kṛttikā coincided. Based on this mathematical analysis, the latest epoch of the *Śatapatha Brāhmaṇa* may be fixed as 519,876 BC. It's worth noting that this period can be extended back every 518,400 years, as after or before every 518,400 years, the Vernal equinox and the Saptarṣis's sojourn in Kṛttikā will coincide.

8. The Epoch of Himalayas

51/6/71st Satyayuga - 51/7/23rd Kaliyuga

Last phase of 6th Chākṣuṣa Manvantara to 23rd Kaliyuga of Present Vaivasvata Manvantara

or

12 crore years ago to 2 crore years ago

There are numerous clues in the Purāṇas regarding the origin of the Himalayan mountain ranges. Before the formation of the Himalayas, Sarasvatī used to emerge from the glaciated region of Tethys' sea, known as Plakṣa or present-day Pilakhua. This fact has already been established by the present author. The Skanda Purāṇa (Prabhāsa khaṇḍa 33.89) narrates a significant geological event. While emerging from Plakṣa in the glaciated region (Himvat), Sarasvatī flowed westward but was obstructed by a mountain that attempted to forcibly marry her. This account provides valuable insights into Sarasvatī's flow during the glacial period preceding the Himalayas' formation. It also symbolically suggests that as the upper Himalayas began to rise, they obstructed Sarasvatī's path, as if attempting to forcibly marry her. The Puranic records further reveal that Sarasvatī feigned taking a bath before the matrimonial ceremony and entrusted fire to the mountain, which was promptly extinguished. This suggests volcanic upheaval occurred at that time. This event is believed to have transpired during the Cākṣusa Manvantara (Skanda Purāṇa, Prabhāsa khaṇḍa 35.34). Therefore, we can assign this occurrence to the end of the Cākṣusa Manvantara. Interestingly, in the Vaivasvata Manvantra, the same fire is described as Aurvānala. This time, the fire was exceptionally destructive, consuming the earth immediately upon its emergence (Skanda Purāṇa 35.6). However, Sarasvatī is said to have confined the fire to the ocean, specifically the Tethys Sea. She is also believed to have carried the Aurvānala in a golden pitcher. As the Aurvānala rose at Pippalādāśram in the Himalayas, it flowed westward, reaching Kedāra where it pierced the earth's crust, going underground with burning fire in her hands (Skanda Purāṇa 33.21-26). It then broke forth again at Bhuteshwar after passing through Sri kaṇṭha deśa, Kuruksetra, Viraṭanagara, Gopāyangiri, Kharjuribana, Mārkaṇḍeyāśram, and Arbudāraṇya (Skanda Purāṇa 35. 30-41). The Purāṇa also suggests a gradual process of Himalayan formation through volcanoes at the end of the Cākṣuṣa Manvantara. However, this process gained momentum with the beginning of the Vaivasvata Manvantara. At the end of the Cākṣuṣa Manvantara, the volcanic lava was considered Vaḍvānala, but at the beginning of the Vaivasvata Manvantara, it was treated as Aurvānala.

Firstly, the Puranic record indicates that the formation of the initial phase of the Himalayan ranges commenced approximately 12 crores years ago at the end of the Cākṣuṣa Manvantara. In contrast, modern scientists believe the origin of the Himalayas occurred around 7 crores years ago. The modern perspective is based on estimates, while the ancient view is grounded on actual observations and records made by the then Ṛṣis. The above records suggest that during the process of carrying Vaḍvānala, which erupted due to the formation of the Himalayas, Sarasvatī vanished underground.

The Skanda Purāṇa (35.14) also foretells the birth of another Vaḍvānala at the culmination of the current Manvantara, suggesting a connection between the volcanic eruption at the submarine level and the traditional deluge associated with the end of the Manvantara cycle.

Thus, even considering modern geological research, the Himalayan mountain ranges began forming approximately 7 crore years ago during the Eocene period. It is widely accepted that these mountains were formed through volcanic activity. Ancient Puranic traditions, particularly the Skanda Purāṇa (7.33.40-41), mention Vaḍvāgni, which is believed to be a synonym for submarine volcanic activity. These traditions suggest that Sarasvatī, the river of life, drained Vaḍvāgni into the western sea at Prabhās Pāṭan. This event aligns with a geological occurrence that occurred approximately 12 crore years ago due to volcanic activity at the submarine level of

Mānasa-sara or Tethys sea. The continuous deposition of volcanic lava led to the upliftment of the ocean floor, causing the dewatering of Mānas-sara. Subsequently, Sarasvatī discharged the uplifted water into the western sea at Prabhās Pāṭan. During the early Himalayan phase, approximately 12 crore years ago, when the Himalayan ranges were still in the process of formation, Sarasvatī flowed towards the western sea or reached its terminus there. Therefore, it can be inferred that from the onset of the glacial period, around 22 crore years ago, until the formation of the initial Himalayan ranges, approximately 12 crore years ago, Sarasvatī traversed the region from Plakṣa to Vinaśana. However, with the rise of the Himalayan ranges, Sarasvatī's course extended to the western sea. This extended route remained operational until the final phase of the Himalayan ranges emerged, approximately 2 crore years ago. This period coincides with the reign of Lord Rama, according to Indian chronology. Rama's birth is recorded in the beginning of the 24th Tretā, which translates to around 1.8 crore years.

Here, it may be convenient for readers to summarize that during the Saṁhitā period, which the present author estimates lasted from 196 crores of years to the glacial period, approximately 22 crore years ago, Sarasvatī is described as originating from clouds to form water reserves on the Earth. In the post-Saṁhitā or Brāhmaṇa period, which the present author refers to as the period of the first glaciers in this region, Sarasvatī originated from Plakṣa and flowed until Vinśana, or the area near modern Bisan in Rohtak District, Haryana. This tradition, dating back to the origin of the Himalayas, recounts that Sarasvatī drained the Vaḍvānala of the Tethys sea into the western sea. Therefore, during the early Himalayan phase, Sarasvatī emerged as overflowing waters from the Tethys sea.

Middle Himalayan phase

The Middle Himalayan phase, dating back 6 crore years, marks the period preceding the origin of the Siwalik ranges. References to this phase can be found in the Purāṇas, particularly in the Matsya Purāṇa (121.64-65), which narrates the origin of the Sarasvatī and Jyotiṣmatī rivers. According to this tradition, these rivers emerged from the Sarpa or Nāga lake, situated at the back of Hemakūṭa, flowing towards the western and eastern seas, respectively.

परस्परेण द्विगुणा धर्मतः कामतोऽर्थतः हेमकुटस्य पृष्ठे तु सर्पाणाम् तत्सरः स्मृतः सरस्वती प्रभवति तस्मात्ज्योतिष्मती तु या अवगाढे ह्युभयतः समुद्रौपुर्वपश्चिमौ (१२१ ॥६५)

parasaparena dviguṇā dharmataḥ kāmato'rthataḥ
hemakuṭasya pṛṣṭhe tu sarpāṇām tatsaraḥ smṛtaḥ
sarasvatī prabhavati tasmātjjyotiṣmatī tu yā
avagāḍhe hyubhayataḥ samudraupurvapaścimau (121.65)

The Vāyu Purāṇa presents a similar account, albeit with minor variations. For instance, the Sarpa or Nāga lake is referred to as Śayanā lake, and Sarasvatī is called Manasvinī. In the referenced text, Hemakūṭa, the modern Kailash range (Ali, 1973: Chapter 4), and the Sarpa lake or Śyanā lake located behind Kailāśa are identified as the lake Nak Tso. This lake forms an extensive water sheet that merges with the Pangong Tso at its southeastern bend. Subsequently, the combined waters flow towards the western sea. (Ali: 71)

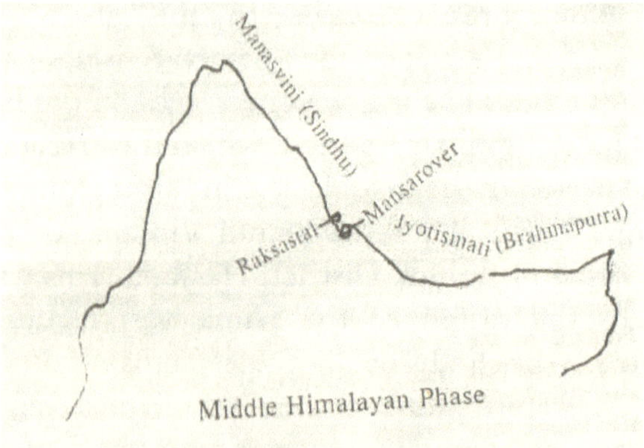

Vedic Sarasvatī, divided into two streams, Sindhu and Brahmaputra, ultimately led to its demise.

Ali (1973) appears to be correct in his conclusions. The word Hemkūṭa refers to Kailāśa. In fact, Sarpa lake, Nāga lake, or Nak Tso is known in the Vāmana Purāṇa as Brahma Sarovar as well. Brahma-sara signifies Mānas-sara. Perhaps, in more ancient times, Nak Tso extended up to the modern Manasarovar lakes (Mānasarovar and Rākṣastāla). Today, we find two river systems, Sindhu and Brahmaputra, originating from the Manasarovar lakes. Sindhu enters the western sea, while Brahmaputra enters the eastern sea. The Matsya Purāṇa names Sindhu as Manasvinī due to its origin from Mānasrovara, while the Vāyu Purāṇa names it as Sarasvatī only. On the other hand, Brahmaputra has been named as Jyotiṣmatī by both, since it flows towards the east, or the direction of Prāga jyotiṣpur (Assam). Jyotiṣmatī is the name of the eastern direction because the Sun rises first in the east. This is why Assam was called Prāga jyotiṣpur. Therefore, Sarasvatī in the middle Himalayan phase is Sindhu. In fact, both the rivers Sindhu and Brahmaputra originate from the two parts of the same lake. Perhaps, this is why the tradition of the Padma Purāṇa (5.18;117-28; 123) and the Skanda Purāṇa (7.35.26) recalls Sarasvatī as both Prācī or eastward flowing and Paścimābhimukhi, or westward flowing. According to the tradition of the Padma Purāṇa (ibidem) and the Skanda Purāṇa (7.35.26), Prācī Sarasvatī is Brahmaputra, and Paścimī Sarasvatī is Sindhu. Trikāṇḍaśeṣa also calls Sarasvatī as Jyotiṣmatī. In fact, Sarasvatī's origin is attributed to the middle Himalayan phase, when it emerged from Sarpa or Nāga lake. This tradition is found in the Vāmana Purāṇa (13.120), where it is referred to as Nāgodbheda. The Purāṇas also mention that Sarasvatī originated from Manas, Brahma, or Nak lake, all of which are associated with Nāgodbheda, which literally means "origin from Nak lake." Interestingly, Nāk also signifies heaven, and the upper Himalayan region was renowned as heaven or Svarga loka.

Last Himalayan Phase

In the last Himalayan phase, we discover the origin of the Siwalik hills. During the earliest glacial period, the entire Himalayan region was renowned as Himvat. Once the Himalayan ranges of mountains began to emerge, the region came to be known as Kailash region, or the abode of Śiva.

Later, the hilly terrain that developed in the lower region of Kailāśa came to be known as the flocks of Śiva, Śivālaka, or Śiwalik in the present sense. With the origin of the Siwalik ranges, the origin of various rivers also shifted from the Upper Himalayan region (Svarga loka or Nāgaloka). The Siwalik ranges were also called Himvatpāda, marking the final phase of the Himalayan mountains' origin. For instance, the origin of the Gāṅgā is described in the Purāṇas as originating from Svarga loka. Svarga loka encompasses both the mid-sphere (atmosphere) where clouds form and precipitate into rain or the highest altitudes on Earth, including the Upper Himalayan region and the two polar regions (Merus), the North and South poles. Regarding the origin of the Gāṅgā, it is stated that it descended from Svarga onto the flocks of the Śiva. As mentioned earlier, these flocks of the Śiva are synonymous with the Siwalik ranges of mountains. From these flocks, the Gāṅgā is said to have descended onto the Earth in various streams. Similarly, during the Siwalik phase, the origin of the Sarasvatī is also narrated as Śivodbheda, meaning the origin of Sarasvatī from the Siwalik ranges of mountains. The Siwalik ranges were also known as Himavatpāda, signifying the final phase of the Himalayas' origin. The Brahma Purāṇa (2.16.24-27) provides a list of rivers that originated during the Himavatpāda or Siwalik phase. The list includes names such as Yamunā, Saryu, Rāvī, Vyāsa, Jhelam, Devikā, Kuhu, Gomati, Dṛṣadvatī, Kauśikī, Tridiva, Niṣṭhivī, Gaṇḍakī, Cakṣu, and lohita:

तैर्विमिश्रा जनपदा आर्या म्लेच्छाश्च भागसः पीयन्ते यैरिमा नद्यो गङ्गा सिन्धुः सरस्वती -२४

शतद्रुश्चन्द्रभागा च यमुना सर्युस्तथा इरावती वितस्ता च विपाश देविका कुहू - २५

गोमती धूतपापा च बुद्बुदा च दृष्द्वती कौशिकी त्रिदिवा चैव निष्ठिवी गण्डकी तथा -२६

चक्षुर्लोहिता इत्येता हिंवत्पादनिस्सृताः -२७

tairvimiśrā janapadā āryā mlecchāśca bhāgasaḥ
pīyante yairimā nadyo Gaṅgā sindhuḥ sarasvatī -24
śatadruścandrabhāgā ca yamunā saryustathā

irāvatī vitastā ca vipāśa devikā kuhū – 25
gomatī dhūtapāpā ca budbudā ca dṛṣdvatī
kauśikī tridivā caiva niṣṭhivī gaṇḍakī tathā -26
cakṣurlohitā ityetā hiṁvatpādanissṛtāḥ -27

The Brahma Purāṇa, as mentioned earlier, clearly illustrates that during the final phase of the Himalayas' origin, Saryū, Devikā, Kuhu, Gomatī, Dṛṣadvatī, Kauśikī, Tridivā, Niṣṭhivī, Gaṇḍakī, Cakṣu, and Lohita either appeared as new rivers or existing rivers with new names. In the context of existing rivers with new names, Lohita, or the present-day Brahmaputra, is a notable example. It didn't acquire its name as Lohita during the earliest phase of the Himalayas' origin. In fact, it was initially named Jyotiṣmatī, as mentioned earlier. During the Inpre Himalayan period, Sindhu and Lohita were not distinct entities; instead, they were combined as Sarasvatī. It was only during the Himalayan period that both river systems emerged by dividing Sarasvatī into two opposing streams. This was the final phase of the Himalayas' origin when they developed their separate identities from Sarasvatī. Notably, during this phase, there was a shift in the connection of Sarasvatī from Sindhu or Jyotiṣmatī to the Gaṅgā. The origin of Sarasvatī was also recounted as Śivodbheda, similar to the origin of the Gaṅgā's Śivālak. The Brahma Purāṇa, which delves into the information about the Siwalik phase, also narrates a story that sheds light on a geological fact: Sarasvatī submerged itself into the basin of the

Gaṅgā due to Brahma's growing affection for her. The Brahmavaivarta Purāṇa also provides a similar account of the origin of Sarasvatī and the Gaṅgā. In fact, after the completion of the last phase of the Himalayan ranges, the entire Himalayan region gained fame as the region of Śiva. The eastern region also came to be known as the region of Brahmā or Brahmarṣideśa, which is now represented by modern Burma. Sarasvatī's fear of developing love for Brahmā clearly indicates the discharge of the maximum waters of Sarasvatī towards the east through its eastern stream, which is the Brahmaputra. To preserve its identity as a westward-flowing river, there was no other option but to accept the myth that Sarasvatī submerged itself into the basin of Gaṅgā. This myth persisted, and as mentioned in the tradition of the Brahmavaivarta Purāṇa, it was asserted that Sarasvatī and Gaṅgā had the same origins.

The oneness of Gaṅgā and Sarasvatī is also supported by a tradition in the Vāmana Purāṇa (Chapter 42), which states that taking a dip in the eastern flow of Sarasvatī provides the same benefits as taking a dip in Gaṅgā.

यः स्नाति गङ्गा स्नानफलं लभेत पूर्वप्रवाहे
yaḥ snāti gaṅgā snānaphalaṁ labheta pūrvapravāhe

In fact, the reference to the eastern flow in connection with Sarasvatī is a pointer to the Ganges alone and not to any other river.

The connection between Sarasvatī and Gaṅgā can also be traced back to the Vedic period. During that time, the origin of Sarasvatī was described as originating from Plakṣa. Ancient Plakṣa, or Pilakhua in modern times, was situated near the basin of Gaṅgā. Close to this location is a place called Garhgaṅgā, which is believed to be the home of Gaṅgā. This proximity between the original source of Vedic Sarasvatī (Plakṣa) and Modern Gaṅgā (Garhgaṅgā) led to the recognition that the origin of Siwalik Sarasvatī (the lost Sarasvatī) and Gaṅgā was the same.

The origin of the last phase of the Himalayan ranges, or Siwalik ranges, is believed to have started approximately

2,00,00,000 years ago, during the Tretā yuga of the 24th Mahāyuga of Vaivasvata Manvantara. This period coincides with the time of Rāma, as mentioned earlier, and is also described in Purāṇas as the 24th Tretā. During Rāma's period, the Sarayū river was mentioned, and it is also included in the list of rivers considered to have belonged to the Siwalik phase by the present author.

The mention of Sarayū during Rāma's period further supports the authenticity of the discussion. It is evident that several new rivers emerged from the mountain ranges during the last phase of the Himalayas' origin. Their names include Saryū, Devikā, Kuhu, Gomatī, Dṛṣadvatī, Kauśikī, Tridivā, Niṣṭhivī, Gaṇḍakī, Cakṣu, and Lohita, among others. All of these rivers undoubtedly originated approximately 2,00,00,000 years ago, as evidenced by the mention of Saryū during Rāma's period, which is unequivocally associated with this timeframe.

9. Epochs of Eminent Personalities of the Present Manvantara

According to the Indian philosophical tradition, the Urdhvaretasa Ṛṣis (High-spirited Yogis who have mastered their senses and attained the revelation of God's creation) after attaining mokṣa, come back to the earth upon the culmination of the Mahāyuga cycle (i.e. in the next creation).

ये श्रुयन्ते दिवं प्राप्ताः ऋषयो ह्यूर्ध्वरेतसः ।
मंत्र ब्राह्मण कर्तारः जायन्ते च युगक्षयात् ॥
ye śruyante divaṁ prāptāḥ ṛṣayo hyūrdhvaretasaḥ ।
maṁtra brāhmaṇa kartāraḥ jāyante cha yugakṣayāt ॥

Ādi Śaṅkara, in his commentary on Vedanta Darśana, also supports this notion, asserting that at the culmination of a Mahāyuga cycle (end of creation), the Maharṣis regain the knowledge in the next creation cycle attained by them in the previous creation cycle.

युगान्तेतर्हितान् वेदान् सेतिहासान् महर्षयः ।
लेभिरे तपसा पूर्वम् अनुज्ञाता स्वयंभुवा ॥
yugāntetarhitān vedān setihāsān maharṣayaḥ ।
lebhire tapasā pūrvam anujñātā svayaṁbhuvā ॥

One such tradition of great scholars, known as the 'Vyāsa tradition,' began in this country during each Dvāpara Yuga of the present Manvantara (Vaivasvata Manvantara). Consequently, the some Vyāsa would be reborn in the Dvāpara yuga of each subsequent Mahāyuga. The Brahmāṇḍa Purāṇa provides a detailed account of this tradition, spanning from the beginning of the Vaivasvata Manvantara until the end of the 28th Dvapara. Their epochs are listed below:

एवमावर्तमानस्ते द्वापरेषु पुनः पुनः ।
कल्पानामार्षविद्यानां नाना शास्त्रकृतश्च ये ॥

वैवस्वतेऽन्तरे तस्मिन् द्वापरेषु पुनः पुनः ।
अष्टाविंशतिकृत्वा वै वेदा व्यस्ता महर्षिभिः ॥
evamāvartamānaste dvāpareṣu punaḥ punaḥ ।
kalpānāmārṣavidyānāṁ nānā śāstrakṛtaścha ye ॥
vaivasvate·ntare tasmin dvāpareṣu punaḥ punaḥ ।
aṣṭāviṁśatikṛtvā vai vedā vyastā maharṣibhiḥ ॥

The name of the first Vedavyāsa of the first Dvāpara yuga was Svayambhūva Vedavyāsa. As such his epoch can be fixed 51/7/1st Dvāpara or 116,645,120 years ago.

द्वापरे प्रथमे व्यस्ता स्वयं वेदाः स्वयम्भुवा ।
dvāpare prathame vyastā svayaṁ vedāḥ svayambhuvā ।

The second Vedavyāsa in the chain was born in the second Dvāpara yuga. His name was Prajāpati. His epoch can be fixed 51/7/2nd Dvāpara or 112,325,120 years ago.

द्वितीये द्वापरे चैव वेदव्यासः प्रजापति ॥
dvitīye dvāpare chaiva vedavyāsaḥ prajāpati ॥

The third Vedavyāsa in the chain was born in the third Dvāpara yuga. His name was Uśanā. His epoch can be fixed 51/7/3rd Dvāpara or 108,005,120 years ago. The fourth was known as Bṛhaspati. He was born in fourth Dvāpara yuga, His epoch can be fixed 51/7/4th Dvāpara or 103,685,120 years ago.

तृतीये चोशना व्यासः चतुर्थे च बृहस्पतिः ।
tṛtīye chośanā vyāsaḥ chaturthe cha bṛhaspatiḥ ।

The fifth Vedavyāsa in the chain was born in the fifth Dvāpara yuga. His name was Savitā. His epoch can be fixed 51/7/5th Dvāpara or 96,364,120 years ago. The sixth was known as Mṛtyu. He was born in sixth Dvāpara yuga, His epoch can be fixed 51/7/6th Dvāpara or 95,045,120 years ago.

सविता पंचमो व्यासः मृत्युः षष्ठे स्मृतः प्रभुः ॥
savitā paṁchamo vyāsaḥ mṛtyuḥ ṣaṣṭhe smṛtaḥ prabhuḥ ॥

The seventh Vedavyāsa in the chain was born in the seventh Dvāpara yuga. His name was Indra. His epoch can be fixed

51/7/7th Dvāpara or 90,735,120 years ago. The eighth was known as Vasiṣṭha. He was born in eighth Dvāpara yuga, His epoch can be fixed 51/7/8th Dvāpara or 86,405,120 years ago.

सप्तमे च तथैवेन्द्रः वसिष्ठश्चाष्टमे स्मृतः ।
saptame cha tathaivendraḥ vasiṣṭhaśchāṣṭame smṛtaḥ ।

The ninth Vedavyāsa in the chain was born in the ninth Dvāpara yuga. His name was Sārasvata Vedavyāsa. He was the son of Sarasvati. His epoch can be fixed 51/7/9th Dvāpara or 82,085,120 years ago. The tenth was known as Tridhāmā. He was born in tenth Dvāpara yuga, His epoch can be fixed 51/7/10th Dvāpara or 77,765,120 years ago. The 11th was Trivṛṣā born in 51/7/11th Dvāpara, 73,445,120 years ago. 12thwas known as Sanadvāja. He was born in 51/7/12th Dvāpara yuga or 69,115,120 years ago.

सारस्वतस्तु नवमे त्रिधामा दशमे स्मृतः ।
ऐकादशे तु त्रिवृषः सनद्वाजः ततः परम ॥
sārasvatastu navame tridhāmā daśame smṛtaḥ ।
aikādaśe tu trivṛṣaḥ sanadvājaḥ tataḥ parama ॥

The 13th Vedavyāsa in the chain was born in the 13th Dvāpara yuga. His name was Antarikṣa. His epoch can be fixed 51/7/13th Dvāpara or 64,805,120 years ago. The 14th was known as Dharma. He was born in 51/7/14th Dvāparaor 60,584,120 years ago. The 15th was Tryayārūṇi. He was born in 51/7/15th Dvāpara or 56,165,120 years ago. 16thwas known as Dhanañjaya. He was born in 51/7/16th Dvāpara yuga or 51,845,120 years ago.

त्रयोदशे चान्तरिक्षो धर्मश्चापि चतुर्दशे ।
त्र्ययारूणि पंचदशे षोडशे तु धनंजयः ॥
trayodaśe chāntarikṣo dharmaśchāpi chaturdaśe ।
trayayārūṇi paṁchadaśe ṣoḍaśe tu dhanaṁjayaḥ ॥

The 17th Vedavyāsa in the chain was born in 51/7/17th Dvāpara yuga or 47,515,120 years ago. His name was Kṛtañjaya. The 18th was known as Ṛṣīja. He was born in 51/7/18th Dvāpara yuga, 43,205,120 years ago. The 19th was Bhardvāja. He was born in 51/7/19th Dvāpara, 38,885,120 years ago. 20th was Gautama son of Gotama. He was born in 51/7/20th Dvāpara yuga, 34,565,120 years ago.

कृतंजयः सप्तदशे ऋषीजोष्टादशे स्मृतः ।
ऋषीजातु भरद्वाजः भरद्वाजात्तु गौतमः ॥
kṛtaṁjayaḥ saptadaśe ṛṣījoṣṭādaśe smṛtaḥ /
ṛṣījātu bharadvājaḥ bharadvājāttu gautamaḥ //

The 21stVedavyāsa born in the 51/7/21st Dvāpara yuga, 30,245,120 years ago. His name was Uttama. The 22nd was known as Haryavana. He was born in 51/7/22nd Dvāpara yuga, 25,925,120 years ago. The 23rd was Vena. He was born in 51/7/23rd Dvāpara, 21,605,120 years ago. 24th was Vajaśrava Somamukhyāyana. He was born in 51/7/24th Dvāpara yuga, 17,285,120 years ago.

गौतमादुत्तमश्चैव ततो हर्यवनः स्मृतः ।
हर्यवनात् परो वेनः स्मृतो वाजश्रवस्ततः ॥
gautamāduttamaśchaiva tato haryavanaḥ smṛtaḥ /
haryavanāt paro venaḥ smṛto vājaśravastataḥ //

The 25th Vedavyāsa in the chain was born in 51/7/25th Dvāpara yuga, 12,965,120 years ago. His name was Tṛṇabindu Tataja. The 26th was known as Śakti. He was born in 51/7/26th Dvāpara yuga, 8,645,120 years ago. The 27th was Parāśara Jātukarṇa. He was born in 51/7/27th Dvāpara, 4,325,120 years ago. Finally, in the 51/7/28th Dvāpara yuga was born Kṛṣṇa Dvaipāyana Vedavyāsa, 5,120 years ago.

अर्वाक् च वाचश्रवसः सोममुख्यायनस्ततः ।

तृणविन्दुस्ततजः तस्मात् तृणबिन्दुतः ।

ततजाच्च स्मृतः शक्तिः शक्तेश्चापि पराशरः ।

जातूकर्णोऽभवत्तस्मात् द्वैपायनः स्मृतः ॥

अष्टाविंशतिरित्येते वेदव्यासाः पुरातनाः ।

The tradition of the *Brahmaṇḍa Purāṇa* not only mentions the history of 28 Vyāsas, but also forecasts the birth of 29th Vedavyāsa as Droṇī in 51/7/29th Dvāpara.

भविष्ये द्वापरे चैव द्रोणि द्वैपायनोपि च ॥
bhaviṣye dvāpare chaiva droṇi dvaipāyanopi cha //

In addition to the above history of 28 Vedavyāsas, the tradition of various Purāṇas mentions the history of some other prominent personalities in the Vaivasvata Manvantara. For example, the *Vāyu Purāṇa* (92.10) says that in 51/7/2nd Dvāpara yuga, i.e. 119,654,000 years ago, there was born Śaunahotra, an effulgent emperor who engaged in high penances desiring a son.

द्वितीये द्वापरे प्राप्ते शौनहोत्रो प्रकाशिराट् ।
पुत्रकामः तपस्तेपे नृपो दीर्घतपस्तथाः ॥ वायु. 92.10
dvitīye dvāpare prāpte śaunahotro prakāśirāṭ I
putrakāmaḥ tapastepe nṛpo dīrghatapastathāḥ II

Vāyu. 92.10

Similarly, from the tradition of *Brahmaṇḍa Purāṇa,* we are given to understand that in 51/7/7th Tretāyuga, i.e. 91,975,120 years ago the whole universe was ruled by Bali. During his reign, Viṣnu assumed the form of a dwarf.

बलिसंस्थेषु त्रेतायांसप्तमे युगे ।
देत्यैस्त्रैलोक्यमापन्ने तृतीये वामनोऽभवत् ॥
balisaṁstheṣu tretāyāṁsaptame yuge I
detyaistrailokyamāpanne tṛtīye vāmano'bhavat II

The *Matsya Purāṇa* (3.47.223) informs us that in the 51/7/19th Tretā yuga, Paraśurāma son of Jamadagni who exterminated all the Kṣatriyas from the earth was born 79,488,120 years ago. He is considered the 6th incarnation of Viṣṇu and 4th one among the incarnations of Vaivaisvata Manvantara. He was preceded by famous Viśvāmitra.

एकोनविंश्यां त्रेतायां सर्वक्षत्रान्तको विभुः ।
जामदग्न्यस्तथा षष्ठो विश्वामित्र पुरस्सरः ॥ मत्स्य पु. 3.47.223
ēkonaviṁśyāṁ tretāyāṁ sarvakṣatrāntako vibhuḥ I
jāmadagnyastathā ṣaṣṭho viśvāmitra purassaraḥ II

Matsya Purāṇa. 3.47.223

10. The Epoch of Rāmāyaṇa

51/7/24th Tretā

or 18,209,120 years ago as on 2019 AD

The Yogavāsiṣṭha provides information about the time period of Rāma. In this context, the following verse can be referred to:

अद्य राम कृते क्षीणे त्रेता सम्प्रति वर्तते - 6/1.27.18
adya rāma kṛte kṣīṇe tretā samprati vartate.

[Meaning] Now, O Rāma, the Satyayuga has passed, and we are currently in the Treta Yuga when you are born to vanquish your enemies.

From the provided statement, it is evident that during the time of Rāma, the Satyayuga had already passed, and the Tretāyuga had commenced. As mentioned in the Mahābhārata, Rāma was born during the sandhi period of Dvāpara and Tretāyuga. Currently, we are in the 28th Kaliyuga, which means that the 28th Tretāyuga has also passed.

However Puranic sources give more specific information. Accordingly, Rāma was born in the 24th Tretāyuga[4]. This period

---

4 त्रेतायुगे चतुर्विंशे रावणः तपसः क्षयात् ।
रामं दाशरथिं प्राप्त सगणः क्षयमीयीवान् ॥ Vāyu Purāṇa, 70-88
tretāyuge caturviṁśe rāvaṇaḥ tapasaḥ kṣayāt
rāmaṁ dāśarathiṁ prāpta sagaṇaḥ kṣayamīyīvān.
[Meaning] In the 24th Tretāyuga Rāvaṇa along with his family members will invite his destruction at the hands of Rāma, due to the reduction of the fruits of his penances.
चतुर्विंशे युगे वत्स त्रेतायां रघुवंशजः ।
रामो नाम भविष्यामि चतुर्व्यूहः सनातनः ॥ *Brahmāṇḍa Purāṇa, 22.36.3*
chaturviṁśe yuge vatsa tretāyāṁ raghuvaṁśajaḥ
rāmo nāma bhaviṣyāmi chaturvyūha sanātanaḥ.
[Meaning] In the 24th Tretāyuga, Rāma will be born in the lineage of Raghus. He will lead the four fold army.
चतुर्विंशे युगे चापि विश्वामित्रपुरःसरः ।

works out, given astronomicalcalculations, to be around 18 Million years. The calculations are as under:

Years of 28th Kaliyuga elapsed	=5120
Years of 28th Dvāpara elapsed	=864,000
Years of 28th Tretā elapsed	=1,296,000
Years of 28th Satyayuga elapsed	=1,728,000
Years of 27th Mahāyuga elapsed	=4,320,000
Years of 26th Mahāyuga elapsed	=4,320,000
Years of 25th Mahāyuga elapsed	=4,320,000
Years of 24th Kaliyuga elapsed	=432,000
Years of 24th Dvāpara elapsed	=864,000

Total years at the end of Tretā	= 18149120
Years of 24th Tretā	= 129600
Total years at the beginning of Tretā	= 17072661

Accordingly, the birth of Rāma took place from 17.072,661 (1.7 million) years to 18,149,120 (1.8 million) years ago from 2019 AD (Kali 5120).

We have some more specific astronomical information about the birth of Rāma from Rāmāyaṇa (1.18.8-9) which is rendered below:

ततो यज्ञे समाप्ते तु ऋतूनां षट् समत्ययुः ।
ततश्च द्वादशे मासे चैत्रे नावमिके तिथौ ॥ 8 ॥
नक्षत्रे अदितिदैवत्ये स्वोच्चसंस्थेषु पंचसु ।
ग्रहेषु कर्कटे लग्ने वाक्पताविन्दुना सह ॥ 9 ॥

लोके राम इति ख्यातः तेजसा भास्करोपमः । Harivaṁśa Purāṇa, 22.104
chaturviṁśe yuge cāpi viśvāmitrapuraḥsaraḥ
loke rāma iti khyātaḥ tejasā bhāskaropamaḥ.
[Meaning] In the 24th Tretāyuga, Rāma led by Viśvāmitra will become famous due to his effulgence like sun.

प्रोद्यमाने जगन्नाथं सर्वलोकनमस्कृतम् ।
कौसल्याजनयद् रामं दिव्यलक्षणयुतम् ॥ 10 ॥
tato yajñe samāpte tu ṛtūnāṁ ṣaṭ samatyayuḥ /
tataścha dvādaśe māse chaitre nāvamike tithau // 8 //
nakṣatre aditidaivatye svochchasaṁstheṣu paṁchasu /
graheṣu karkaṭe lagne vākpatāvinduṇā saha // 9 //
prodyamāne jagannāthaṁ sarvalokanamaskṛtam /
kausalyājanayad rāmaṁ divyalakṣaṇayutam // 10 //

When the six seasons had passed after the completion of Yajña, in the twelfth month of Chaitra, on the ninth day of the lunation, in the 'Punarvasu' constellation, presided over by the Aditi devatā, when the five planets were in their uccha (mandoccha), meaning the Sun, Jupiter, Saturn, Mars, and Venus were in their Mandoccha (Apsis), the Mandoccha of Bṛhaspati had risen with the Moon in the Karka (Cancer) ascendant (Lagna). Kausalya gave birth to Rāma.

This information has perplexed some scholars. It's worth noting that Mrs. Saroj Bala, a retired IRS officer, has been spreading confusion regarding the date of birth of Śri Rāma for several years. In her book, "Dating the Era of Lord Ram" (Rupa & co. Delhi, 2005), she claims that Śri Rāma was born on January 10, 5114 BC. She asserts that she obtained these results using Planetarium Gold software and provides a sky view of planetary positions calculated by the software. However, Planetarium and other software are unable to predict the mandoccha (apsis) of planets or accurately determine the Indian lunar months that existed during that period.

It's important to clarify that the planetary positions suggested by the author based on an apparent misunderstanding of the śloka of Rāmāyaṇa are not accurate. Even a layperson knows that the Sun never enters the Aries sign in January. In 5114 BC, the Sun entered the Makara sign on January 27th, so on January 10th, 5114 BC, it was in the Dhanū sign. When the Sun is in Makara or Dhanu, there can be either the Pausha or Māgha months. Therefore, there's no basis for claiming that the Chaitra month began in January.

A careful examination of the horoscope for 5114 BC, prepared using Astrodienst, reveals that the positions of various stars according to tropical (Horoscope 1) and sidereal (Horoscope 2) calculations are as follows:

Name of Star	Position (Tropical)	Position (Sidereal)
Sun	Sagittarius	Aquraius
Jupiter	Gemini	Leo
Mars	Aquarius	Aries
Venus	Sagitarus	Pisces
Saturn	Leo	Scorpio

Horoscope 1

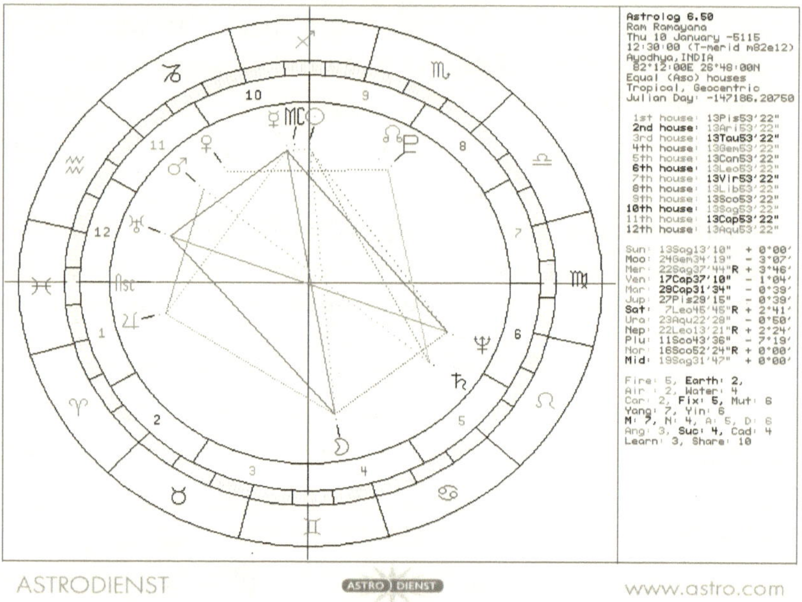

Horoscope 2

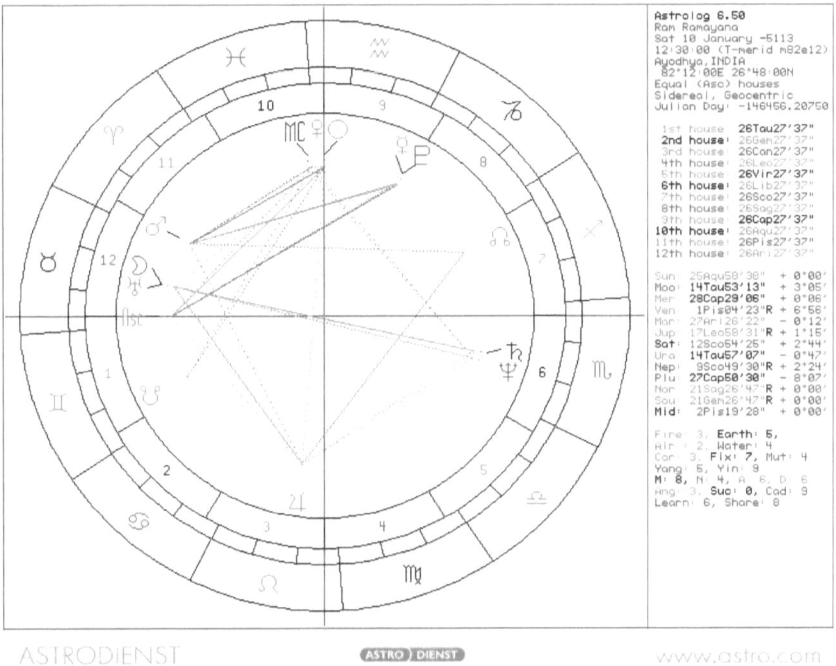

So, none of the planetary positions as erroneously interpreted from the Rāmāyaṇa's śloka actually align with Saroj Bala's claims. Furthermore, as mentioned earlier, her translation of the śloka is also based on a misunderstanding of its meaning. In the śloka, the word 'uccha' in connection with grahas has been incorrectly translated as the 'uccha' position of grahas, as is commonly understood in astrology. However, the author of the Rāmāyaṇa is not referring to astrology but rather astronomy to determine the dateline of Rāma. Therefore, 'uccha' here denotes the mandoccha (highest slow speed) of the grahas. The author provides two clues: 1. By the time of Rāma's birth, the lagna (ascendent) Karka (Cancer) was rising, and 2. The Moon and mandoccha of Bṛhaspati were also rising in the Karka sign, which was also the ascendent during that period. Additionally, the Moon was in conjunction with the Punarvasu Nakṣatra of the Karka sign. It's important to note that the fourth quarter of the Punarvasu Nakṣatra spends time in the Karka sign. The longitude of the Karka sign ranges from 90^{0} to 120^{0}, while the longitudes of the Punarvasu Nakṣatra range from 80^{0} to 93.2^{0}. Therefore, the fourth quarter of the Punarvasu Nakṣatra's time in the Karka sign falls within the longitude range of 90^{0} to 93.2^{0}. Based on this information, the mandoccha of Bṛhaspati must be between 90^{0} and 93.2^{0}. It's also worth mentioning that when a planet or graha is at its mandoccha (apsis) at 0^{0} or 360^{0} and 180^{0}, the difference between its true and mean position is zero. According to Bhāskarāchārya, the mandoccha of Bṛhaspati completes 855 revolutions in a Kalpa (4,320,000,000 years). In contrast, the present Sūrya Siddhanta states that the mandoccha of Bṛhaspati completes 900 revolutions in a Kalpa year (4,320,000,000 years minus 17,064,000 years of creation). However, Bhāskarāchārya or Brāhma Siddhānta does not consider any period spent during creation, unlike the present Sūrya Siddhānta. Therefore, we will perform calculations based on both Siddhāntas.

According to Bhāskarācharya, one revolution of Bṛhaspati's mandoccha will occur in 4,320,000,000/855= 5052631.5789473 years. As mentioned earlier, Paurāṇika sources, quoted above, indicate that Rāma's birth took place during the 24th Tretāyuga. We know that until the beginning of the 24th Tretāyuga, 1,936,440,000 years had elapsed since the commencement of the Kalpa. Therefore, dividing 1,936,440,000 years by 5052631.5789473 years yields the position of Bṛhaspati's mandoccha at the beginning of the 24th Tretāyuga as (1,936,440,000 / 5052631.5789473=) 383.25375. This calculation implies that Bṛhaspati's mandoccha has completed 383 revolutions by the beginning of the 24th Tretāyuga and has moved 0.25375X360=91.35 degrees, which corresponds to the position of Punarvasu Nakṣatra in the Karka Sign. This serves as a solid proof of the precise dateline of Śri Rāma as per the Yogavasiṣṭha, which states that Śri Rāma was born at the beginning of the 24th Tretayuga, approximately 17.072,661 (1.7 million) years ago from 2019 AD. It appears that Yogavāsiṣṭha's calculation aligns with the Brāhma Siddhānta adopted by Bhāskarāchārya. However, if we perform the calculation using the present Sūryasiddhānta, the time of Rāma's birth is determined to occur at the end of the 24th Tretāyuga. The calculations are as follows:

According to the Sūrya Siddhānta, as quoted above, one revolution of Bṛhaspati's mandoccha will occur in 4,302,936,000 divided by 900, which equals 4781040 years. We know that 1,936,440,000 years had passed until the beginning of the 24th Tretāyuga. Therefore, dividing 1,936,440,000 by 4781040 yields the position of Bṛhaspati's mandoccha in the 24th Tretāyuga as (1,936,440,000 / 4781040=) 405.0248481502. This means that Bṛhaspati's mandoccha has completed 405 revolutions by the beginning of the 24th Tretāyuga and has moved 0.0248481502 times 360 degrees, which corresponds to the position of Aśvini Nakṣatra in the Meṣa Sign. Punarvasu Nakṣatra is located in the Karka sign at 900 degrees. The difference between these two positions is 90 degrees minus 8.94 degrees, which equals 81.054665928 degrees. Bṛhaspati's mandoccha takes 4781040 divided by 360, which equals 13280.9999677 years, to travel one degree. Consequently, Bṛhaspati's mandoccha will take 81.054665928 times 13280.9999677 years, which equals 1,076,459 years, to reach the fourth pāda of Punarvasu Nakṣatra in the Karka sign. Calculations based on the current Sūryasiddhānta indicate that Rāma was born at the end of the Tretā yuga, which is 17.072,661 years ago, plus 1,076,459 years, resulting in a total of 18,149,120 (1.8 million) years ago from 2019 AD. It is worth noting that the above date of the Rāmāyaṇa was already known to the people of India during the time of Alberuni, who visited India in 1031 AD. Alberuni calculated the date of Rāma as 18,148,132 years before the gauge-year (1031 AD).

In addition to the astronomical evidence, we also have some other literary and archaeological evidence that supports this view. It is also mentioned in the Purāṇas that by the time of Rāma, the final phase of the Himalayan upliftment had come to an end. This fact is corroborated by the internal evidence of the Rāmāyaṇa and archaeological findings. In the Vālmīki Ramāyaṇa (Dr. Ravi Prakash Arya, 1998), specifically in the Sundara Kāṇḍa (4.28), it is mentioned that when Hanumāna first arrived at Rāvana's palace, he was greeted by decked gateways surrounded by four-tusked elephants that resembled the masses of white clouds and wild beasts and birds. The verse goes as follows:

> वारणैश्च चतुर्दन्तैः श्वेताभ्रनिचयोपमैः ।
> भूषितैः रुचिरद्वारं मत्तैश्च मृगपक्षिभिः ॥
> *vāraṇaiśca chaturdantaiḥ śvetābhranicayopamaiḥ*
> *bhūṣitaiḥ ruciradvāraṁ mattaiśca mṛgapakṣibhiḥ.*

> [Meaning] The inner apartments of Rāvaṇa were adorned with four-tusked elephants resembling masses of white clouds; and possessing graceful gateways attended by deer and chirping birds.

At another place (Rāmāyaṇa, Sundara kāṇḍa, 27.12), Trijaṭā, a Rākṣasī, sees in her dream illustrious Rāma and Lakṣamaṇa mounted on a huge elephant with four tusks resembling a hill. The original verse reads as under:

> राघवश्च पुनर्दृष्टश्चतुर्दन्त महागजम् ।
> आरूढः शैलसंकाशं चकास सहलक्ष्मणः ॥
> *rāghavaśca punardṛṣṭaśchaturdanta mahāgajam*
> *ārūḍhaśailasaṅkāśaṁ chakāsa sahalakṣamaṇaḥ*

> [Meaning] I saw again Lakṣamaṇa appear in effulgence, seated on a huge elephant, having four tusks and resembling a hill.

Vālmīki's mention of four-tusked elephants in the Rāmāyaṇa provides compelling evidence of their existence during the era of the epic. The Encarta Encyclopedia further corroborates this by stating that four-tusked elephants roamed the Earth between 38 million and 15 million years ago, belonging to the Mastodontoidea group. Mastodontoidea is believed to have evolved around 38 million years ago and went extinct approximately 15 million years ago, coinciding with the rise of the shaggy and two-tusked Mastodons.

The provided proof strongly supports the authenticity of the Purānas tradition. It becomes evident that the astronomical time calculation system employed by Vedic seers holds the key to unlocking the true chronology of Indian history. In contrast, modern historians' calculations are highly misleading and serve as evidence of their misinterpretation of the Indian knowledge system.

Four tusked elephants of Rāmāyaṇa

The paradox with such historians is that they lack sufficient knowledge of astronomy or Kālagaṇanā. In fact, a comprehensive understanding of ancient Indian history requires a solid grasp of astronomy and Sanskrit. Even in today's era, it would be highly beneficial for students of ancient history to pursue additional qualifications in astronomy, Kālagaṇanā, or Sanskrit. Historians lacking knowledge in these fields would be unable to accurately portray ancient Indian history, and their attempts would be nothing short of a mockery.

Non-existent of history is not the weakness of Indian literature, but the actual weakness of the reviewers. There is a dictum in Sanskrit

नैष स्थाणोरपराधो यदेनमन्धो न पश्यति
naiṣa sthaṇoraparādho yadainam andho na paśyati.

It's not the pillar's weakness if a blind person can't see it. The real weakness lies within the blind person.'

The Indian concept of history was far more scientific than it is today. Indians not only recorded the births, deaths, and posterity of kings, but they also made provisions to register the birth, death, and posterity of even ordinary citizens. This tradition continues to this day, centered around the renowned Tīrtha sthalas of the country. If you visit Hardwar, Allahabad, Srinagar, and other holy places, you'll find their Pāṇḍas, Pāñjikāras, or Registrars diligently maintaining the history of ordinary people by recording their births, deaths, and posterity at their own level, without any government assistance. It's astonishing to learn that Maithala Brāhmaṇas in Bihar have a tradition of verifying the records of seven generations by the institution of Pāñjikārās before the betrothal ceremony. These practices collectively demonstrate the deep sense of history that permeates Indian society.

11. The Epoch of Sūryasiddhānta

51/7/28th Satyayuga/1728000

In the Sūryasiddhānta, only the Vedic astronomical era is mentioned. The text states that the Sūryasiddhanta was revealed to Maya, a renowned Western scholar, at the end of the Satyayuga of the present 28th Mahāyuga.

This period, when astronomical calculations are considered, is estimated to have occurred approximately 214,112,000 years ago. The calculations are as follows:

Years of 28th Kaliyuga elapsed	=5120
Years of 28th Dvāpara elapsed	=8,40,000
Years of 28th Tretā elapsed	= 1296000
Total years elapsed	= 2141120

The text of the Sūryasiddhānta can be cited below:

अल्पावशिष्टे तु कृते मयनामा महासुरः ।
रहस्यं परमं पुण्यं जिज्ञासुर्ज्ञानमुत्तमम् ॥ 1.2

alpāvaśiṣṭe tu kṛte mayanāmā mahāsuraḥ /
rahasyaṁ paramaṁ puṇyaṁ jijñāsurjñānamuttamam //

When the little Satyayuga was left (approximately 2141120 years ago), a renowned Western scholar named Maya, driven by an insatiable curiosity about the enigmatic science of Astronomy, dedicated a significant portion of time to studying the Sun.

वेदांगमग्र्यमखिलं ज्योतिषां गतिकारणम् ।
आराधयन् विवस्वन्तं तपस्तेपे सुदुश्चरम् ॥

vedāṁgamagryamakhilaṁ jyotiṣāṁ gatikāraṇam /
ārādhayan vivasvantaṁ tapastepe suduścharam //

It unveils the secrets of Astronomy, the primary aid to the Vedas (the science of creation), and the explanation of the movements of celestial bodies. By concentrating his Dhāraṇā, Dhyāna, and Samādhi on the Sun, he achieved this.

तोषितस्तपसा तेन प्रीतस्तस्मै वरार्थिने ।
ग्रहाणां चरितुं प्रदान्मयाय सविता स्वयम् ॥

toṣitastapasā tena prītastasmai varārthine I
grahāṇāṁ charituṁ pradānmayāya savitā svayam II

Consequently, he was revealed to the mysteries of planetary science related to the solar system.

12. The Epoch of Śri Krishna

51/7/28th Dvāpara/863875/Bhādrapada/K-8
or
24 Sept. 3225 BCE (Julian Calendar)

In the Bhāgavatam (11.6.25), Brahmā informs that Krishna remained on the earth for 125 years.

यदुवंशेऽवतीर्णस्य भवतः पुरुषोत्तमः ।
शरच्छतं व्यतीयाय पंचविंशाधिकं प्रभो ॥

yaduvaṁśe'vatīrṇasya bhavataḥ puruṣottamaḥ /
śarachchhataṁ vyatīyāya paṁchaviṁśādhikaṁ prabho //

Puruṣottama Krishna born in Yadu Dynasty lived for 125 years. We are well aware that Śri Krishna passed away at the end of the Dvāpara yuga or the beginning of Kaliyuga. If we add 125 years to the date of the commencement of Kaliyuga, which is 3101 BCE, we can calculate Śri Krishna's birthdate. Adding 125 years to 3101 BCE gives us September 24, 3225 BCE, a Friday or 51/7/28th Dvāpara/ 863875/ Bhādrapada/ K-8.

The calculations are as under:

3rd Sept. 3225 BCE, Thursday Śrāvaṇa Amāvasyā

18th Sept. 3225 BCE, Friday Sun ingresses in Kanyāsign

17th Sept. 3225 BCE, Thursday Bhādrapada Pūrṇimā

24th Sept. 3225 BCE, Friday Bhādrapada K-8

2nd Oct. 3225 BCE, Friday Bhādrapada Amāvasyā

On 24th September 3225 BCE, at the time of Krishna's Birth, at 12 O'clock midnight, the Moon was posited 23° 14' in Vṛṣabha Rāśī, which means that the Moon was in the 4th Pāda of Rohini Nakshtra, as the 4th pāda of Rohiṇī Nakṣatra is located from 20°-23°.20'in Vṛṣabha Rāśī.

13. The Epoch of Yudhiṣṭhira's Coronation

51/7/28th Dvāpara/863928 or 3173 BC

The Kaliyuga serves as a pivotal marker in determining the chronology of Indian history both preceding and following the Mahābhārata war. Once the commencement date of Kaliyuga is established, it becomes straightforward to determine the dates of numerous other historical events. Numerous astronomical and literary sources provide valuable evidence to support this determination. The 14th verse of the Kaliyuga Rāja Vṛttānta explicitly states this:

> पंचसप्ततिवर्षाणि प्राक्कलेः सप्त ते द्विजाः ।
> मघास्वासन् महाराजे शासत्युर्वीं युधिष्ठिरे ॥
> *paṁchasaptativarṣāṇi prākkaleḥ sapta te dvijāḥ* /
> *maghāsvāsan mahārāje śāsatyurvīṁ yudhiṣṭhire* //

> The Sapta Rishis, the Great Bear, entered the constellation of Maghā approximately 75 years prior to the commencement of Kaliyuga, which occurred in 3176 BC. During this period, the renowned king Yudhiṣṭhira reigned over the earth (in 3173 BC).

The Bṛhat Saṁhitā (13.3), as quoted by Kalhaṇa (747-748 AD) in his work titled 'Rājataraṅginī' (1.56), states that Yudhiṣṭhira reigned over the country during the time when the Saptarṣis were positioned in the Maghā Nakṣatra. The verse is as follows:

> आसन् मघासु मुनयः शासति पृथिवीं युधिष्ठिरे नृपतौ ।
> षड्विक्पंचद्वियुतः शककालस्य राज्यस्य ॥
> *āsan maghāsu munayaḥ śāsati pṛthivīṁ yudhiṣṭhire nṛpatau* /
> *ṣaḍdvikpaṁchadviyutaḥ śakakālasya rājyasya* //

> When King Yudhiṣṭhira ruled the earth, the Great Bear, Munis, was visible in the Maghā constellation. By the time of Varāhamihira, 2526 years had passed since the

beginning of the Yudhiṣṭhira Śaka (regnal period) (3173 BC). This calculation gives us the time period of Varāhamihira as 3173-2526= 647 BC.

Note: Śaka kāla of a king is the regnal period. It is not Śaka saṁvat 78 AD as is often called by ignorant historians.

The Kaliyuga Rāja Vṛttānta (Bhaviṣya Purāṇa, Chapter 3), states that after 25 years in the Kaliyuga (3101 BCE), the Saptarṣī will retrograde into the Āśleṣā star and remain there for a century.

पंचविंशतिवर्षेषु गतेष्वथ कलौ युगे ।
समाश्रयिष्यन्त्याश्लेषां मुनयस्ते शतं समाः ॥
paṁchaviṁśativarṣeṣu gateṣvatha kalau yuge ।
samāśrayiṣyantyāśleṣāṁ munayaste śataṁ samāḥ ॥

Our 9000 years calendar also confirms this fact.

King Yudhiṣṭhira's coronation occurred 36 years prior to the Mahābhārata war in 3173 BC, coinciding with the completion of three years in Maghā Nakṣatra by the Saptarishis. The Saptarishis entered Maghā Nakṣatra 75 years before the Kaliyuga, on the first lunation of the bright half of the Chaitra month in 3176 BC. This assertion can be substantiated by the following evidence.

Saptarishis entered Maghā nakṣatra on Chaitra S-1. Calculations prove that this happened on 27th March, 3176BC Saturday. Calculations are as under:

26th March 3176 BC, Friday	Phālguna Amāvasyā
27th March 3176 BC, Saturday	Chaitra S-1
16th April 3176 BC, Friday	Sun ingresses in Meṣa sign
9th April 3176 BC, Tuesday	Chaitra Pūrṇimā
25th April 3176 BC, Sunday	Chaitra Amāvasyā

One of the leading Indologists, Prof. Weber, based on the tradition of Kashmiri Pandits and other evidence, concluded that Laukika Saṁvat came into vogue on the first lunation of the bright half of the Chaitra month when 25 years of Kaliyuga had elapsed. In 3076 BC, Kaliyuga completed 25 years, and

Saptarṣis entered P. Phalguni Nakṣatra. According to this calculation, Saptarṣis spent 75 years in Maghā Nakṣatra during the Dvāpara yuga and 25 years in Kaliyuga. Babu Shyam Sunder Das writes in 'Prāchina Lekhāvali' that Śāstra Saṁvat commenced in 824 AD. In this context, Śāstra Saṁvat refers to the Saptarṣi Saṁvat. Our '9000 Years Calendar of Various Indian Eras' clearly demonstrates that in 824 AD, a new Saptarṣi Saṁvat commenced with the entry of Saptarṣis into Dhaniṣṭhā Nakṣatra.

1. In his Rājataraṅgiṇī (1.52), Kalhaṇa (747-748 AD) notes during his period in the 24th Laukika Saṁvat, 1070 years of the Śaka kāla (Vikramaditya of Gupta Saṁvat 322 BC) has passed. Upon examining our table, we discover that the Saptarṣis were positioned in Sravaṇa 24. The original verse is as follows:

लौकिकेऽब्दे चतुर्विंशे शककालस्य साम्प्रतम्।
सप्तत्यभ्यधिकं यातं सहस्रं परिवत्सराः ॥
laukike'bde chaturviṁśe śakakālasya sāmpratam |
saptatyabhyadhikaṁ yātaṁ sahasraṁ parivatsarāḥ ||

At present in the 24th Laukika Era, 1070 years of Śaka kāla (Gupta Saṁvat 322 BC) have elapsed.

This gives Kalhaṇa's epoch to be 747-748AD.

2. In 1486 Vikrama Saṁvat, during the reign of Raja Sansāra Chand, son of Karma Chand and grandson of Raja Prem Chand of Trigarta Kangra, Raghava Chaitanya inscribed a stotra of Bhavani Jwalamukhi on a stone. This stone commemorates the fifth year of Laukika Saṁvat. Upon examination of our table, we observe that in 1486, Chaitrādi Vikrama Saṁvat, the Saptarṣis were residing in Bharaṇī asterism for their fifth year.

3. Two inscriptions have been unearthed in Baijanath, dating back to the Chaitrādi Vikrama era of 861. The inscriptions were inscribed by Rāma, the son of Bharnatraka, during the reigns of Raja Jaichand and Raja Lakṣmaṇachand of Kangra, located in Himachal Pradesh. One of the inscriptions specifically mentions the 80th year of Laukika Saṁvat, while the other mentions the Śaka Saṁvat of 726. The authenticity of

these dates can be easily verified from the 9000 years calendar, which reveals that the Chaitrādi Vikrama era of 861 corresponds to the Śaka (Śalivāhana) Saṁvat of 726. Consequently, at that time, the Saptarṣis were residing in the Śravaṇa Nakṣatra for an 80th year.

4. Babu Shyam Sunder Das mentions in 'Prāchina Lekhāwali' that the Laukika Saṁvat began after the completion of the 1681 Chaitrādi Vikrama era. Our 9000 Years Calendar provides evidence to support this, as it states that after the completion of the 1681 Chaitrādi Vikrama era, the Saptarṣis completed their journey in the Kṛttikas and entered the Rohiṇi Nakṣatra. This indicates that a new Laukika Saṁvat commenced after the 1681 Chaitrādi Vikrama era.

5. The Raja Abhaya Chand and a few other Rajputs installed a Jain Murti in the marketplace of Kangra, Himachal Pradesh, during the Chaitrādi Vikrama era in 1811. A rock inscription was also placed there, mentioning laukika Saṁvat 30. Our table provides insight into the fact that in the Chaitrādi Vikrama era of 1811, the Saptarṣis were enjoying their 30th year of sojourn in Mṛgaśirā Nakṣatra.

6. Raja Śri Singh Deva of Chamba had a copper plate inscribed with the date Laukika Saṁvat 34. We can confirm this from our table that in the Chaitrādi Vikrama era of 1915, the Saptarṣis were spending their 34th year in the Ārdrā Nakṣatra..

7. One more inscription of the same king is available, dated Chaitrādi Vikrama era 1916, which records Śāstra Saṁvat 35, which corresponds to Ārdrā 35..

The fragmentary evidence presented here is sufficient to demonstrate that the Saptarṣis arrived in Maghā Nakṣatra 75 years prior to the onset of Kaliyuga, which occurred in 3176 BC.

Here it may be noted that Saptarishi Saṁvat, though not astronomically significant, held chronological importance. Varahamihira mentioned its 100-year cycle for each nakṣatra, referring to chronology. Known as 'Śāstra Saṁvat,' it focused on the chronology of Śāstras and ancient Indian history. 'Laukika Saṁvat' was chosen because it was easy for the common person to record and restart counting after completing 100 years.

14. The Epoch of Mahābhārata War

51/7/28th Dvāpara/863963/Kārtika Pūrṇimā
or
20th Nov. 3137 BC

The Aihole inscription of Meguti Temple records the dates of the Mahābhārata war (3137 BC) and an era of Śaka kings (561 BCE), which was prevalent during that time in India. We find numerous Śaka eras in India, including the Śaka Nṛpati kāla (583 BC), which began when the Śakas started ruling India, and the Śakānta era (78 AD), which commemorated the end of Śaka rule in India. The Śaka kāla mentioned in the Aihole inscription bears a resemblance to another Śaka era. It (561 BC) might possibly be associated with Cyrus II of Persia or an independent samvat. It's important to note that the term "Śaka" in Sanskrit refers to a samvat, not necessarily to the Śaka kings. Not all Śaka periods belong to the Śaka kings.

त्रिंशत्सु (30) त्रिसहस्रेषु (3000) भारताद् आह्वादितः ।
सप्ताब्दशतयुक्तेषु (107) गतेष्वब्देषु पंचसु (5) ॥

पंचाशत्सु (50) कलौ काले षट्सु (6) पंचशतासु (500) च ।
समासु समतीतासु शकानाम् भूभुजाम् ॥
triṁśatsu (30) trisahasreṣu (3000) bhāratād āhvāditaḥ । saptābdaśatayukteṣu (107) gateṣvabdeṣu paṁchasu (5) ॥ paṁchāśatsu (50) kalau kāle ṣaṭsu (6) paṁchaśatāsu (500) cha । samāsu samatītāsu śakānām bhūbhujām ॥

[Meaning] When 30 + 3000 + 107+5= 3142 years have passed since the time of Bhārat war (3137 BC) and 50+6+500=556 years of Śaka kings (561) BC) in Kaliyuga, Ravikīrti constructed the temple (in 5 AD expired).

The year 3137 BC aligns with the era mentioned in the Mahābhārata. Here's a brief overview of the Mahābhārata's history:

After his coronation at Indraprastha, Yudhiṣṭhira embarked on a grand journey to perform the Rājasuya Yajña. Accompanying him were his brothers Arjuna, Bhīma, Nakula, and Sahadeva, who led armies across the globe to subdue various kings and collect tributes for the emperor. Notably, the cunning Magadha king, Jarāsandha, fell victim to Bhima and Krishna's might. During Yudhiṣṭhira's sacred ceremony, he honored Krishna as his esteemed guest, marking the completion of 23 years of his reign, which extended until 3150 BC.

However, Yudhiṣṭhira's reign took a tragic turn when he fell victim to Shakuni's treacherous tactics and became ensnared in a game of dice. This fateful game resulted in the loss of his kingdom, his brothers, and his beloved wife. During the second game, Yudhiṣṭhira's fate sealed as he squandered his entire kingdom, leading to a 13-year exile, including a year of anonymity until 3137 BC.

Upon the completion of his exile, Duryodhana, refused to restore his kingdom. Despite numerous diplomatic efforts aimed at resolving the conflict peacefully, Yudhiṣṭhira's pleas fell flat on deaf ears. Ultimately, he was compelled to resort to war against the tyrannical Duryodhana.

We are informed from the Mahābhārata that Krishna witnessed the signs of the destruction of the Yadavas. Gāndhārī, consumed by grief over the loss of her sons and bereft of all her kin, cursed him. She foretold that after 36 years, his own kinsmen, the Yadavas, would perish in a self-destructive war. The verses conveying this prophecy goes as follows:

एवं पश्यन्हृषीकेशः संप्राप्तं कालपर्ययम्।
त्र्योदश्याममावास्यां तान्दृष्ट्वा प्राब्रवीदिदम्॥
चतुर्दर्शी पंचदशी कृतेयं राहुणा पुनः।
तदा च भारते युद्धे प्राप्ता चाद्या क्षयाय नः॥
विमृशन्नेव कालं तं परिचिन्त्य जनार्दनः।
मेने प्राप्तं स षट्त्रिंशं वर्षं वै केशिसूदनः

पुत्रशोकाभिसंतप्ता गान्धारी हतबान्धवा ।
यदनुव्याजहारार्ता तदिदं समुपागतम् ॥ महाभारत, 16.3.16-19
evaṁ paśyanhṛṣīkeśaḥ saṁprāptaṁ kālaparyayam |
trarayodaśyāmamāvāsyāṁ tāndṛṣṭvā prābravīdidam ||
chatudarśī paṁchadaśī kṛteyaṁ rāhuṇā punaḥ |
tadā cha bhārate yuddhe prāptā chādyā kṣayāya naḥ ||
vimṛśanneva kālaṁ taṁ parichintya janārdanaḥ |
mene prāptaṁ sa ṣaṭtriṁśaṁ varṣaṁ vai keśisūdanaḥ
putraśokābhisaṁtaptā gāndhārī hatabānghavā |
yadanuvyājahārārtā tadidaṁ samupāgatam ||
Mahābhārata, 16.3.16-19

Behold these signs that foretold an inauspicious course of time. Since the day of the new moon coincided with the thirteenth lunation, Hṛṣikeśa, summoning the Yadvas, addressed them with these words: "The fourteenth lunation has been made the thirteenth once more by Rāhū. Such a day has appeared at the time of the great battle of the Bharatas. It has once again appeared, it seems, for our destruction. The slayer of Keśī, contemplating the omens that time showed, realized that the thirty-sixth year had arrived and that what Gāndhārī, consumed by grief over the loss of her sons and bereft of all her kin, had foretold was about to come to pass.

Similarly, in another part of the Mahābhārata, the renowned king Yudhiṣṭhira is portrayed as considering the unfavorable omens that occurred after the lapse of 36 years of Mahābhārata war. The description provided is as follows:

षट्त्रिंशे त्वथ संप्राप्ते वर्षे कौरवनन्दनः ।
ददर्शविपरितानि निमित्तानि युधिष्ठिरः ॥
आदित्यो रजसा राजन् समवच्छन्नमण्डलः ।
विरश्मिरुदये नित्यं कबन्धैः समदृश्यत ॥ महाभारत, 16.1.1; 4
ṣaṭtriṁśe tvatha saṁprāpte varṣe kauravanandanaḥ |
dadarśaviparitāni nimittāni yudhiṣṭhiraḥ ||
ādityo rajasā rājan samavachchhannamaṇḍalaḥ |
viraśmirudaye nityaṁ kabandhaiḥ samadṛśyata ||

Mahābhārata, 16.1.1; 4

When the 36th year commenced, the renowned Kuru king, Yudhiṣṭhira, observed ominous signs. The sun's disk appeared covered in dust, devoid of its usual splendor.

There's also a reference in the Mausala Parva of the Mahābhārata (2.19-20) that a solar eclipse occurred 36 years after the Mahābhārata war. Following this eclipse, Dwarka submerged beneath the sea. Interestingly, a partial solar eclipse occurred on August 31, 3101 BCE, which precisely coincides with the 36th year of the Mahābhārata war. This eclipse could also be associated with Dwarka's submergence.

The references cited above from the Mahābhārata provide compelling evidence suggesting that the great war of Bharat took place approximately 36 years before the commencement of Kaliyuga (September 28, 3101 BCE). Following the conclusion of the great war of Bharat, which occurred near the end of Dvāpara or the beginning of Kaliyuga, Yudhiṣṭhira relinquished the throne of Hastinapur to Parikṣita for rule. Additionally, the Yadvas, along with Śri Krishna, met their end due to family or dynastic conflicts. Considering these facts and additional references from the Mahābhārata, it is worthwhile to quote them.

1. There's a reference in the Mahābhārata (Bhiṣma Parva, 3.29) that mentions a lunar eclipse followed by a solar eclipse in the same month, before the actual war. It's worth noting that this astronomical event occurred in July 3137 BCE. Specifically, on the Āṣāḍha Pūrṇimā, which fell on July 25th, 3137 BCE, a total lunar eclipse was followed by a partial solar eclipse on the 9th of August, 3137 BCE, which coincided with the Āṣāḍha Amāvasyā.

2. Śri Krishna proceeded to Hastinapur on a peace mission to avoid war on Kārtika Śukla Pratipadā.

ततो व्यपेते तमसि सूर्ये विमल उद्गते ।
मैत्रे मुहूर्ते संप्राप्ते मृद्वर्चिषि दिवाकरे ॥

कौमुदे मासि रेवत्यां शरदन्ते हिमागमे ।
स्फीतसस्यसुखे काले कल्पः सत्त्वतां वरः ॥ महाभारत, 5.81.6-7

tato vyapete tamasi sūrye vimala udgate |
maitre muhūrte samprāpte mṛdvarchiṣi divākare ||
kaumude māsi revatyāṁ śaradante himāgame |
sphītasasyasukhe kāle kalpaḥ sattvatāṁ varaḥ ||

Mahābhārata, 5.81.6-7

Then, when the Śarada season concluded and the Hemanta season commenced (October 23, 3137 BCE), during the month of Kumuda (Kārtika) in the constellation of Revati, as the night's darkness receded and the radiant sun emerged, on the auspicious Maitra Muhurta, the well-disposed (or ever-ready hero of the heroes embarked on a journey in the gentle rays of the sun towards Hastinapur..

The time described above is the month of Kārtika when the darkness of the night was over. It means that the time was Kārtika S-1 (26 August 3137, Tuesday). As per our calculations the positions of Amāvasyā, Pūrṇimā and the sun's ingress were as under:

6th Nov. 3137 BCE, Sunday	Āśvina Amāvasyā
7th Nov. 3137 BCE, Monday	Kārtika S-1
15th Nov. 3137 BCE, Monday	The sun ingressed into Vṛśchika sign
20th Nov. 3137 BCE, Saturday	Kārtika Pūṛṇimā
6th Dec.3137 BCE, Monday	Kārtika Amāvasyā

Thus, Kārtika S-1 occurred on November 7, 3137 BCE, a Monday. However, when the peace mission failed due to Duryodhana's unwavering resistance, the war was declared on Kārtika Purṇimā, which fell on November 20, 3137 BCE, a Saturday. This was 13 days after the peace mission. I provide the exact reference from Mahābhārata (6.2.23-24) for your reference. The reading is as follows:

अलक्ष्यः प्रभया हीनः पौर्णमासीं च कार्त्तिकीम्।
चन्द्रोऽभूदग्निवर्णश्च समवर्णे नभस्तले॥
स्वप्स्यन्ति निहता वीरा भूमिमावृत्य पर्थिवाः॥

alakṣayaḥ prabhayā hīnaḥ paurṇamāsīṁ cha kārttikīm ।
chandro'bhūdagnivarṇaścha samavarṇe nabhastale ॥
svapsyanti nihatā vīrā bhūmimāvṛtya parthivāḥ ॥

Vyāsa describes the ill omens. O! Dhṛtarāṣṭra! on the full moon of the night of Kārtika, the moon was barely visible, devoid of its usual glory, with a faint greenish tint. Both horizons were of the same color. The ground was completely covered with the bodies of the kings who had been killed in the war, lying there lifeless.

Here it may be informed that the war took place in two phases. The sequence is as under:

Kārtika Pūrṇimā or 20th Nov. 3137 BCE, Saturday: The first phase of the war started on 20th Nov. 3137 BCE. It lasted for 10 days, i.e. till Kārtika K-9 or 29th Nov. 3137BC. Monday.

Kārtika K-9, or 29thNov. 3137 BCE–Mārgaśīrṣa S-6 or 10th Dec.3137 BCE Friday: There was a cease-fire for 12 days.

Mārgaśīrṣa S-6, or 10th Dec. 3137 BCE Mārgaśīrṣa S-14 or 19th Dec. 3137 BCE Sunday: The second phase started on 10th Dec.and ended after 8 days on Mārgaśīrṣa S-14 or 19th Dec. 3137 BCE., Sunday. We have a complete sequence of other events in Mahābhārata. Some of the important events are cited below:

Māgha S-8, or 9 Feb, 3136 BCE, Wednesday: Bhiṣma Pitāmaha died after 56 days battling on Śara Śayyā.

Hereunder, we provide a proof from the *Mahābhārata* demonstrating that Bhiṣma left for heavenly abode on the 56th day after his fall in the battlefield on 8th day of bright half of Māgha month.

पंचाशतं षट् च कुरुप्रवीर शेषं दिनानां तव जीवितस्य।
ततः कर्मफलोदयैस्त्वं समेष्यसे भीष्म विमुच्य देहम्॥ महा. 12.51.14

paṁchāśataṁ ṣaṭ cha kurupravīra śeṣaṁ dinānāṁ tava jīvitasya ।
tataḥ karmaphalodayaistvaṁ sameṣyase bhīṣma vimuchya deham ॥ Mahā. 12.51.14

Oh, the best warriors of Kuru, you have a lease of 56 days. After that, you will leave your body and gain access to the rewards of your virtuous deeds.

शुक्लपक्षस्य चाष्टम्यां माघमासस्य पार्थिव ।
प्राजापत्ये च नक्षत्रे मध्यं प्राप्ते दिवाकरे ॥ महाभारत, 12.47.64
śuklapakṣasya chāṣṭamyāṁ māghamāsasya pārthiva ।
prājāpatye cha nakṣatre madhyaṁ prāpte divākare ॥
Mahābhārata, 12.47.64

Bhiṣma left his body on the 8th day in the bright half of the month of Māgha, when the sun had entered the middle of the bright half, under the Moon's constellation Rohini ruled by Prajāpati.

The above verse states that Bhiṣma departed from his physical form on the eighth day of the bright half of the Māgha month, when the sun had reached the middle of that half. Some scholars interpret the phrase 'मध्यं प्राप्ते दिवाकरे' as the sun having reached its zenith, indicating that it had completed its Dakṣiṇāyana course and commenced its Uttarāyaṇa course. Here it may be noted that as per dereal calendar, the sun commenced its Uttarāyaṇa course on November 28, 3137 BCE, whereas Uttarāyaṇa started on 14th Jan. 3136 BCE as per tropical calendar. However, the Uttarāyaṇa is not mentioned in the above verse.

15. The Epoch of Kaliyuga

51/7/28th Kaliyuga/1/Bhādrapada / K-13
or
28th Sept. 3101 BCE, Friday

The Saṁkalpa Pāṭhas, prevalent across India, provide detailed descriptions of the time period and location of specific events. The collection of Saṁkalpa Pāṭhas from various regions demonstrates uniformity in their chronology. Consequently, 2019 AD corresponds to the 5120th year of Kaliyuga, indicating that Kaliyuga commenced 5119 years prior in 3101 BCE.

French mathematicians and astronomers, such as J. Sylvain Bailly (1736-1793) and Mr. Le Verrier (1811-1877), the discoverer of the planet Neptune, concluded that the present Kaliyuga began at midnight of ending 17th and beginning of 18th Feb. in 3102. However, the Indian astronomical tradition asserts that the current Kaliyuga commenced at midnight on Friday, the dark half of 13th of Bhādrapada, during the period of the Āśleṣā constellation.

Here are the astronomical calculations: (Note: The provided dates are based on the Julian Calendar)

31st August 3101 BCE, Friday	Śrāvaṇa Amāvasyā
17th Sept. 3101 BCE, Monday	Sun ingressed in Kanyā sign
14th Sept 3101 BCE, Friday	Bhādrapada Pūrṇamāsī
30th Sept. 3101 BCE, Sunday	Bhādrapada Amāvasyā
28th Sept. 3101 BCE, Friday	Bhādrapada K-13

Thus, we can confidently say that Kaliyuga commenced at midnight on September 29, 3101 BCE, a Friday. As per Āryabhaṭa (Āryabhaṭiyam, 1.5), the Dvāpara Yuga concluded on a Thursday, and the Kaliyuga commenced on a Friday..

काहो मनवो ढमनुयुग श्ख गतास्ते च मनुयुगछ्ना च।

कल्पादेर्युगपादा ग च गुरुदिवसाच्च भारतात्पूर्वम्।

kāho manavo ḍhamanuyuga śkha gatāste cha manuyugachhanā cha ।

kalpāderyugapādā ga cha gurudivasāchcha bhāratātpūrvam ।

There are 14 (ढ) Manus in a day of Brahman called a Kalpa, and 72 (श्ख) yugas constitute the period of a Manu. Since Thursday, the beginning of this Kalpa by the end of Dvāpara yuga in which Mahābhārata war took place, 6 Manvantaras have elapsed, and of the current 7th Manvantara, 27 (छ्ना) Yugas (Mahāyugas) have passed and of the current 28th Mahāyuga three (ग) yugapāda (Satya, Tretā and Dvāpara) have also passed before the beginning of the current Kaliyuga. The end of the Dvāpara yuga took place on 27th September [Bhādrapada Kṛṣṇa 12], 3101 BCE Thursday.

According to the original Sūryasiddhānat of Pañchsiddhāntikā, Kaliyuga commenced at midnight on Thursay, and Aryabhaṭa has assumed to begin it at sunrise on Friday, that is 15 ghaṭis later.

16. Epochs of Some Prominent Personalities of Indian History in Kaliyuga

Epoch of Pāṇini

51/7/28th Kali/ 200 or 2900 BC

During the period of Sukrita (2941 BC-2883 BC), the ruler of Magadha, famous grammarian Pāṇini, the author of Aṣṭādhyāyi was born in Gāndhāra (Now Afganistan) in 2900 BC. Pāṇini's Aṣṭādhyāyī is called one of the marvels of the human mind. The acquaintance of Europeans scholars with Pāṇini's Aṣṭādhyāyī led to the origin of a new science of comparative philology.

The Epoch of other Scholars

Similarly, taking Pāṇini's epoch as mile stone, and considering the Yudhiṣṭhira Mimānsaka's view[5], epochs of some other prominent scholars may also be fixed as under:

Śiva Maheśvara	51/7/28th	Dvāpara /855600 or 11500 BC
Bṛhaspati	51/7/28th	Dvāpara/855100 or 10000 BC
Indra	51/7/28th	Dvāpara/855600 or 9500 BC
Bharadvāja	51/7/28th	Dvāpara/855800 or 9300 BC
Vāyu	51/7/28th	Dvāpara/856600 or 8500 BC
Bhāṅguri	51/7/28th	Dvāpara/861100 or 4000 BC
Gālava	51/7/28th	Kali/2 or 3100 BC
Vaiyāghrapada	51/7/28th	Kali/2 or 3100 BC

[5] *Sanskrit Vyākaraṇa kā itihāsa*, Ramlall Kapoor Trust, Bahalgarh, Sonepat.

Śantanu 51/7/28th Kali/2 or 3100 BC

Śāklya 51/7/28th Kali/2 or 3100 BC

Chārāyaṇa 51/7/28th Kali/2 or 3100 BC

Pauṣkara Sādi 51/7/28th Kali/2 or 3100 BC

Gārgya 51/7/28th Kali/2 or 3100 BC

Kāśkṛtsana 51/7/28th Kali/2 or 3100 BC

Śākaṭāyana 51/7/28th Kali/100 or 3000 BC

Āśvalāyana 51/7/28th Kali/100 or 3000 BC

Kātyāyana Śrautasūtrakāra 51/7/28th Kali/102 or 3000 BC

Kāśyapa 51/7/28th Kali/100 or 3000 BC

Āpiśali 51/7/28th Kali/100 or 3000 BC

Mādhyandina 51/7/28th Kali/100 or 3000 BC

Rauḍhi 51/7/28th Kali/100 or 3000 BC

Gautama 51/7/28th Kali/100 or 3000 BC

Bhāradvāja 51/7/28th Kali/100 or 3000 BC

Chākravarmaṇa 51/7/28th Kali/100 or 3000 BC

Vyāḍi 51/7/28th Kali/150 or 2950 BC

Senaka 51/7/28th Kali/150 or 2950 BC

Sphoṭāyana (Audumbarāyaṇa) 51/7/28th Kali/150 or 2950 BC

Śaunaka 51/7/28th Kali/300 or 2800 BC

Vyāḍi Saṅgrahakāra (Dākṣāyaṇa) 51/7/28th Kali/350 or 2750 BC

Kātyāyana II Vārtikakāra 51/7/28th Kali/400 or 2700 BC

Yāska 51/7/28th Kali/400 or 2700 BC

Author of Kātantra Vyākaraṇa 51/7/28th Kali/1100 or 2000 BC

Ananta Bhaṭṭa 51/7/28th Kali/1500 or 1600 BC

Ramānātha 51/7/28th Kali/1539 or 1563 BC

Ātreya 51/7/28th Kali/1687 or 1415 BC

Sāyaṇa 51/7/28th Kali/1700 or 14th Centuy BC

Rajaśri author of Dhātuvṛtti 51/7/28th Kali/1800 or 13th Century BC

Maitreya Rakṣita 51/7/28th Kali/1900 or 12th Century BC

Deva 51/7/28th Kali/1900 or 12th Century BC

Patañjali 51/7/28th Kali/1900 or 1200 BC

Kṣiraswami 51/7/28th Kali/2000 or 11th Century BC

Chandragomī 51/7/28th Kali/2100 or 1000 BC

Durga Singh 51/7/28th Kali/2400 or 700 BC

Vararuchi 51/7/28th Kali/2400 or 7th Century BC

Kalidāsa of Abhijñāna Śākuntala 51/7/28th Kali/2400 or 7th Century BC

Varāhamihira 51/7/28th Kali/2400 or 7th Century BC

Śaṅku 51/7/28th Kali/2400 or 7th Century BC

Maṇḍana Miṣra 51/7/28th Kali/2407 or 695 BC

Vāmana 51/7/28th Kali/2500 or 600 BC

Devanandī 51/7/28th Kali/2550-2600 or 500-550 BC

Harshavardhana 51/7/28th Kali/2645 or 457 BC

Bhartṛhari 51/7/28th Kali/2700 or 400 BC

Śarva Varmā 51/7/28th Kali/2700 or 4th Century BC

Amara Singh 51/7/28th Kali/3000 or 1st Century BC

Kṣapaṇaka 51/7/28th Kali/3000 or1st Century BC

Kalidāsa of Jyotirvidābharaṇa 51/7/28th Kali/2394 or 708 BC

Bhojarāja author of

Samarāṅgaṇa Sūtradhāra 51/7/28th Kali/3438-3494 or 336-392 AD

Nārāyaṇa 51/7/28th Kali/3700 or 600 AD

Udgītha 51/7/28thKali/3800 or700 AD

Śākṭāyana II 51/7/28th Kali/3900 or 800 AD

Śivaswamī 51/7/28th Kali/3900 or 800 AD

Halāyudha 51/7/28th Kali/4000 or 900 AD

Rāmānuja Swami 51/7/28th Kali/4118 or 1016 AD

Hemachandra Sūri 51/7/28th Kali/4200 or 1100 AD

Haradatta (commentator of Kāśikā) 51/7/28th Kali/4200 or 1100 AD

Devarāja Yajvā 51/7/28th Kali/4200 or 1100 AD

Uvaṭa 51/7/28th Kali/4200 or 1100 AD

Mallinātha 51/7/28th Kali/4300 or 1200 AD

Nāgeśabhaṭṭa 51/7/28th Kali/4800 or 1700 AD

The Epoch of Āryabhaṭa

51/7/28th Kali/336 or 2766 BC

Āryabhaṭa, the famous mathematician and astronomer was born in 2766 BC. In his book Āryabhaṭīyam (3.10), Āryabhaṭa clearly provides his date of birth. Accordingly,

षष्ट्यब्दानां(षष्ट) षष्टिर्यदा व्यतीतास्त्रयश्च युगपादाः ।
त्र्यधिका विंशतिरब्दास्तदेह मम जन्मनोऽतीताः ॥

ṣaṣṭyabdānāṁ(ṣaṣṭa) ṣaṣṭiryadā vyatītāstrayaścha yugapādāḥ /
trayadhikā viṁśatirabdāstadeha mama janmano'tītāḥ //

When three yugapādas (Satyayuga, Tretāyuga, Dvāparayuga) and six times of 60 Saṁvatsaras had elapsed from the beginning of the fourth yuga, i.e. Kaliyuga, then 23 years of my life had passed, i.e I was 24 years old.

It is clear from the above śloka that Āryabhaṭa was 23 years old in (60X6=) 360 Kaliyuga or 2744 BC. It implies that Āryabhaṭa was born in 337 Kali Era or 2768 BC.

Here I would like to point out one controversy. In almost all manuscripts we come across the word षट्, but Sudhākara Dwivedi altered this word षट् as षष्टि: in his edition. Due to this alteration, 60X6=360 becomes 60X60=3600. This alteration significantly demoted the date of birth of Āryabhaṭa to 3600 Kali or 497 AD as it is clear from our table. This alteration by Sudhakara Dwivedi was openly challenged by T.N. Narayana Sastry in his book 'The Age of Shankara' to show any genuine manuscript of Āryabhaṭiyam', where altered 'षष्टि:' appears.

Note: Here it may also be noted that according to Āryabhaṭa, one yugapāda is equal to 10,80,000 years. As such three yugapādas are equal to 32,40,000 years. If we go by the statement of Āryabhaṭa, he was born 6,47,640 years before the present Kaliyuga.

The Epoch of Buddha

51/7/28th Kali/1215/ Vaiśākha Purṇimā -1295/Vaiśākha Purṇimā

or 14 May 1887 BC - 24thMay 1807 BC

As per Kalhaṇa (1.172), three Turuṣka kings namely Huṣka, Juṣka and Kaniṣka ruled Kashmir from 1657 BC to 1597 BC and founded three cities named Huṣkapura, Juṣkapura and Kaniṣkapura. Juṣka also founded Jayaswāmipura. They built Maṭhas, and Chaityas. During their period, Buddhism was prevalent in Kashmir. He also informs that 150 years before the period of Turuṣka dynasty, the parinirvāṇa of Śākya Singh also took place on this part of the earth (1.172).

तदा भगवतः शाक्यसिंहस्य परनिर्वृतेः ।
अस्मिन्महीलोकधातौ सार्धं वर्षशतं ह्यगात् ।।

tadā Bhagavatā Śākyasiṁhasya parnirvṛteḥ
asminmahilokadhātau sārdham varṣaśatam hyagāt.

Accordingly, Buddha's parinirvāṇā took place in 1657+150= 1807 BC. Huṣka, Jhuṣka, and Kaniṣka came after Buddha's death. They were Buddhist kings of Turuṣka origin.

Kalhaṇa (1.173) also informs that Nāgārjuna, who was known as a Bodhisattva also lived in Kashmir at Ṣaḍarhardvana during this period.

Gotam Buddha was born on Vaiśākha Purṇimā in 1887 BC or 9th May 1887 BC (Monday) during the reign of king Kṣemajit of Magadha. This seems to be perfectly true. During 1887 BC Saptarṣis were spending 90th year in Sravaṇa Nakṣatra.

Buddha was 72 years old at the time of Ajātśatru's coronation. Ajātśatru's coronation took place in 1815 BC.

According to Saṁyutta Nikāya, Buddha was staying in Śrāvastī about three months before his death which occurred on Vaiśākha Pūrṇimā (24th May 1807 BC). During this time, there occurred a lunar eclipse followed by a solar eclipse within the same fortnight. It clearly indicates that the lunar and solar eclipses occurred at closed interval of 15 days within the three months before the death of Buddha i.e between 19th January and 19th March and they were visible in India. Surprisingly we find that in a lunar eclipse took place on 26th Jan. 1807 BC followed by a solar eclipse on 10th Feb. 1807BC in a close succession of 15 days within the three months before the death of Buddha (24th May, 1807, Thursday) which were visible in Śrāvasti and elsewhere in India.

The diagrams of eclipses procured from NASA's website are given hereunder:

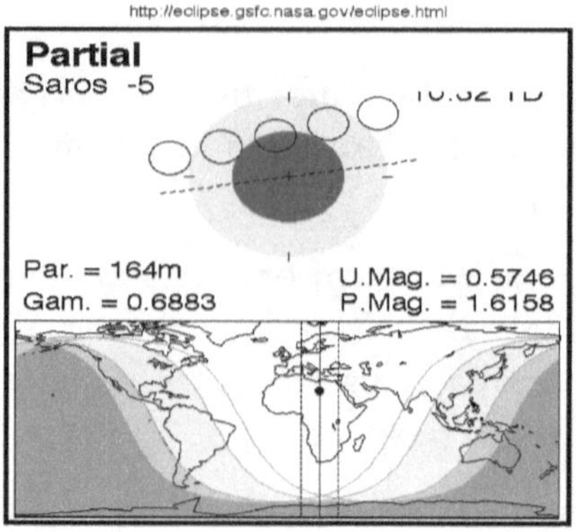

A Lunar eclipse of 26th Jan. 1807 BC

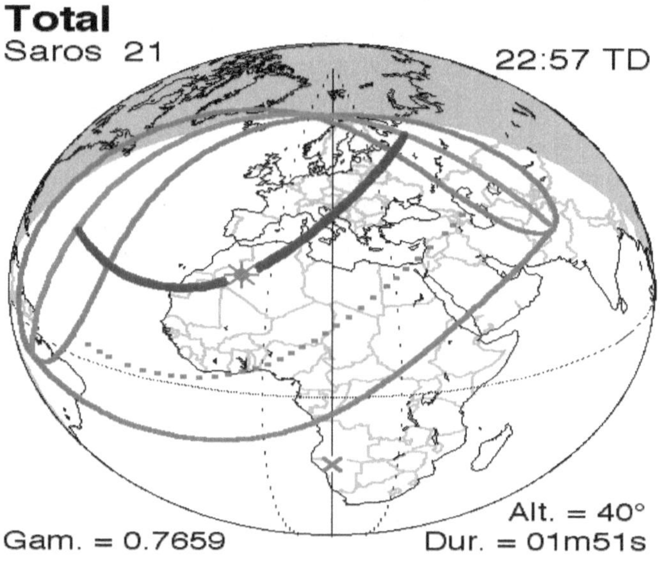

A Solar eclipse on 10th Feb. 1807 BC

Therefore, we can say with conformity that Buddha attained Mahā Parinirvāṇa in Kuśinagar 1807 BC.

The Epoch of Patañjali

51/7/28th Kali/1900 or 1200 BC

Puṣyamitra Śuṅga (1223 BC- 1163 BC) of Śuṅga dynasty of Magadha performed the Aśvamedha yajña and Patañjali says in his Mahābhāṣya, a commentary on Pāṇini's Aṣṭādhyāyī, quotes Puṣyamitra and informed that he participated in that Yajña. Thus Patañjali was contemporary to Puṣyamitra Śuṅga and he must have lived in 13th Century BC.

The Epoch of Ādi Śaṅkarāchārya

51/7/28th Kali/1933-34 to Kali/1965-66 or 1168 BC–1136 BC

The epoch of Ādi Śaṅkarāchārya serves as a pivotal reference point in Indian history. If we can ascertain the precise date of Śaṅkarāchārya, a significant portion of the riddles pertaining to the chronology of Indian history will be resolved. Despite the unambiguous records of Śaṅkara's date in Sanskrit literature, it has remained a subject of scholarly debate due to a lack of comprehensive understanding of the Indian eras. In this context, we will examine accounts from various texts that quote Śaṅkaras's date. We will exclude records of Maṭhas founded by Śaṅkara, as these records are flawed and not maintained adequately. Furthermore, every pontiff who assumed the leadership of Maṭhas has been designated as Śaṅkarāchārya. All of these Śaṅkarāchāryas dedicated their efforts to the propagation of dharma. Consequently, the diverse dates provided by historians are associated with any one of these Śaṅkarāchāryas. It is not necessary that all of these dates correspond to the initial Śaṅkarāchārya. These names can be somewhat confusing and hinder the attainment of accurate conclusions. In this context, we intend to focus on the case of the Ādi Śaṅkara.

First View

1. The most clinching evidence is provided by a book titled as *'Bāla Mayaṅkha Śekhara'* quoted by Thakur Nagina Ram Parmar in his celebrated book '*Tvārīkha-e-Kadim Āryāvartta*' published in Urdu in 1887. According to him, the above book mentions that in Tiṣya or Tikha Saṁvat 3889, when vibhava Saṁvat was in currency, Śaṅkarāchārya was born in the house

of Śivaguru in auspicious Muhurta. As already informed, Tikha Saṁvat became prevalent 1955 years before Kaliyuga. It remained in currency by the time of emperor Yudhiṣṭhira. According to our table, Tikha Saṁvat 3889 corresponds to 1934 Kali era, 2006 Yudhiṣṭhira era and 1168 BC. Our '9000 Years Calendar of Various Indian Eras' also shows that during that period Vibhava Saṁvatsara of Daivi (Northern) tradition was in currency. So according to the above evidence first Śaṅkarāchārya or Ādi Śaṅkara was born in 1168 BC.

2. The above statement is corroborated by the statement of famous Semi Puranic text '*Śiva Rahaṣya*' (Aṁśa 9. Ch. 8. Stanza 16). Accordingly, Śaṅkara was born before the end of 2nd Millenium of Kaliyuga. The Sanskrit text reads as under:

कल्यादिमे महादेवि सहस्रद्वितीयादपरम ॥
kalyādime mahādevi sahasradvitīyādaparama //

[Meaning] O Mahādevi, according to me, Śaṅkara was born prior to the 2nd Millenium of Kaliyuga.

Word-by-word meaning

कल्यादि (kalyādi) — from the beginning of Kali (Kali Yuga)

मे (me) — by me / according to me / for me (depending on context)

महादेवि (mahādevi) — O Mahādevi

सहस्रद्वितीयात् (sahasra-dvitīyāt) — from the second (2nd) millennium

अपरम् (aparam) — prior

The above date of 1168 BC corresponds to Kaliyuga year 1934 which stands prior to the end of 2nd Millenium of the Kaliyuga.

Tradition has it that Patañjali taught Gaudapada who taught Govindapada, the Guru of Śaṅkara. So, Patañjali and Śaṅkara must be separated by not more than 100 years. Patañjali's date has been arrived at 12-13th century BC. As such above date of Śivarahasya seems to be correct.

2. I may now turn to the view which is most popular among historians, that Saṅkara lived from AD 788 to AD 820. K.B. Pathak has argued for it on the basis of a manuscript of three pages which he discovered in Belgaum. Its colophon states that the giver of salvation directly incarnated himself as Śaṅkarāchārya on the earth for the destruction of evil conduct. The rise of Śaṅkara took place in the year called Vibhava in Tikha Saṁvat 3889. At the age of eight, he studied the four Vedas; at 12 he authored all Śāstras assigned to him; at 16 he composed the great commentary; at 32, the sage went away. In Kaliyuga, 3921 Tikha Saṁvat his entry into the cave took place. On the full moon day of Vaiśākha, Śaṅkara attained 'Śivahood'. The Sanskrit text goes like this:

दुष्टाचार-विनाशाय प्रादुर्भूतो महीतले ।
स एव शंकराचार्य साक्षात्कैवल्यनायकः ॥
निधिनागेभवह्न्याब्दे (3889) विभवे शंकरः ।
अष्टवर्षे चतुर्वेदी द्वादशे सर्वशास्त्रकृत् ।
षोडशे कृत्वान् भाष्यं द्वत्रिंशे मुनिरभ्यगात् ॥
कल्यब्दे चन्द्रनेत्रांक वह्न्यब्दे (3921) गुहाप्रवेशः ।
वैशाखे पूर्णिमायां तु शंकरः शिवतामियात् ॥

duṣṭāchāra-vināśāya prādurbhūto mahītale |
sa ēva śaṁkarāchārya sākṣātkaivalyanāyakaḥ ||
nidhināgebhavahnyābde (3889) vibhave śaṁkaraḥ |
aṣṭavarṣe chaturvedī dvādaśe sarvaśāstrakṛt |
ṣoḍaśe kṛtvān bhāṣyaṁ dvatriṁśe munirabhyagāt ||
kalyabde chandranetrāṁka vahnyabde (3921) guhāpraveśaḥ |
vaiśākhe pūrṇimāyāṁ tu śaṁkaraḥ śivatāmiyāt ||

[Meaning] To destroy the evil ways of conduct, He was born upon the Earth — that very Śaṅkarācārya, the direct Lord of Liberation (Kaivalya-nāyaka). In the year 3889 (in the Jovian year Vibhava), Śaṅkara was born. At the age of eight, He mastered the four Vedas; at twelve, all scriptures; at sixteen, He composed His celebrated commentaries; and at thirty-two, the sage attained His final state. In the Tiṣya (Here Kali refers to Tiṣya) year 3921, on the full moon of

Vaiśākha, Śaṅkara entered the cave (at Kedarnath) and became one with Lord Śiva."

Word-by-Word Meaning

दुष्टाचार-विनाशाय (duṣṭācāra-vināśāya) — for the destruction of evil conduct / corruption of dharma

प्रादुर्भूतः (prādurbhūtaḥ) — appeared /born

महीतले (mahītale) — upon the earth

सः एव (sa eva) — that very one / the same being

शंकराचार्यः (śaṅkarācāryaḥ) — Śaṅkarācārya

साक्षात् (sākṣāt) — directly / in person

कैवल्यनायकः (kaivalya-nāyakaḥ) — the leader or lord of liberation (mokṣa)

निधिनागेभवह्न्याब्दे (nidhi-nāge-bhava-agni-ābde) — in the year 3889, as per the chronogram (saṃvatsara) "Nidhi-Nāga-Bhava-Agni"

विभवे (vibhave) — in the year named Vibhava (a Jovian cycle year)

शंकरः (śaṅkaraḥ) — Śaṅkara (Ācārya)

अष्टवर्षे (aṣṭavarṣe) — at the age of 8

चतुर्वेदी (caturvedī) — became a knower of the four Vedas

द्वादशे (dvādaśe) — at the age of 12

सर्वशास्त्रकृत् (sarva-śāstra-kṛt) — master of all scriptures

षोडशे (ṣoḍaśe) — at the age of 16

कृत्वा (kṛtvā) — having composed

भाष्यम् (bhāṣyam) — commentaries (on the Upaniṣads, Brahmasūtras, and Gītā)

द्वात्रिंशे (dvātriṃśe) — at the age of 32

मुनिः (muniḥ) — the sage

अभ्यगात् (abhyagāt) — departed / attained (final state)

कल्यब्दे (kaly-abde) — in the Tiṣya saṁvat

चन्द्र-नेत्रांक वह्न्याब्दे (candra-netrāṅka vahny-abde) — number referring to 3921 (moon = 1, eye = 2, aṅka= 9 vagni= 3 hence reversed → for 3921)

गुहाप्रवेशः (guhā-praveśaḥ) — entry into a cave (his disappearance into Kedarnath cave)

वैशाखे (vaiśākhe) — in the month of Vaiśākha

पूर्णिमायाम् (pūrṇimāyām) — on the full-moon day

शंकरः (śaṅkaraḥ) — Śaṅkara

शिवताम् इयात् (śivatām iyāt) — attained the state of Śiva / mokṣa/ became one with Śiva

The reference to the manuscript discovered by K.B. Pathak is merely a repetition of the statement made in paragraph 1 above. This manuscript was based on the account of 'Bāla Mayaṅkha Śekhara'. However, the year 3889, as quoted by Thakur Nagina Ram Parmar, does not refer to the Kali year but rather the Tiṣya or Tikha year. In the sixth stanza, the word 'kalyabda refers to Tiṣya Saṁvatsar in Kaliyuga. Therefore, the above reference supports the notion that Śaṅkara was born after a gap of 3889 years in the Tiṣya Saṁvat, which corresponds to 1934 Kali, or 1168 BC, in the Vibhava Saṁvatsara of Jupiter, as per the Daivi or Northern tradition. It's worth noting that 788 AD also aligns with the 'Vibhava' Saṁvatsara of the Āsuri tradition. However, this interpretation does not align with other references. The aforementioned Śloka also mentions that Śaṅkara passed away after 3921 (expired) Tiṣya Saṁvat, which corresponds to 1966 Kali, or April 8th, 1136 BC, on the Vaiśākha Pūrṇimā, a Saturday. The details are as under:

30 April 1136 BC, Sunday	Chaitra Amāvasyā
2 May 1136 BC, Tuesday	Sun ingresses in Vṛṣabha
12th May 1136 BC, Tuesday	Vaiśākha S-11
16th May 1136 BC, Tuesday	Vaiśākha Pūrṇimā

30th May 1136 BC, Tuesday Vaiśākha Amāvasyā

3. Some other works may also be cited to support this view. These include Nilakaṇṭha Bhaṭṭa's 'Śaṅkara Mandāra Saurabha' and 'Śaṅkarābhyudaya'. According to these texts, when 3889 years of the Tiṣya Saṁvat had elapsed, Śaṅkara was born in the Vibhava Saṁvatsar.

नवाधिकाशीति युताष्टशक्त्या युक्ते सहस्रत्रितये (3889) व्यतीते ।
तिष्ये समानां विभवाब्दराधासिते दशम्यामुद्भूत महेशः ॥
navādhikāśīti yutāṣṭaśaktyā yukte sahasratritaye (3889) vyatīte ।
tiṣye samānāṁ vibhavābdarādhāsite daśamyāmudbhūta maheśaḥ ॥

[Meaning] After a lapse of 3889 years of the Tiṣya Saṁvat, Śaṅkara was born in the Vibhava year of Jupiter on the 10th lunation of the Śukla Pakṣa.

Similarly, Krishna Brahmananda's Śaṅkaravijaya also asserts that after 3,889 years of Tiṣya Saṁvat, Śaṅkara was born. The date was April 28th, 1168 BC. It occurred on a Sunday, the 10th and 11th Lunation of the bright half of the Vaiṣākha month. I present the original Sanskrit texts as follows:

निधिनागेभ वह्न्याब्दे (3889) विभवे शंकरोदयः ।
तिष्ये तु शालिवाहस्य सखेन्दु शत सप्तके ॥
nidhināgebha vahnyābde (3889) vibhave śaṁkarodayaḥ ।
tiṣye tu śālivāhasya sakhendu śata saptake ॥

[Meaning] After a lapse of 3889 years in the Tiṣya Saṁvat, Śaṅkara was born in Vibhava Saṁvatsar.

Here's a point to note: all the aforementioned references are quoting Tiṣya Saṁvatsara in Kaliyuga. The precision of these dates and their general agreement lend credibility to this perspective. Consequently, according to the five views mentioned above, Śaṅkara was born to Śivaguru and Mahādevī in 1168 BC during the currency of Vibhava Saṁvatsara, as per the Daivi or Northern tradition. On the other hand, Śaṅkara is believed to have passed away in 1136 BC. Notably, all these views refer to Tiṣya Saṁvat in the 'Kaliyuga,' not the Kali era. Therefore, it's crucial to distinguish between the Kali era and the Tiṣya era. Unfortunately, this confusion stems from the same obsession and preconceived notion that has led many historians and Indologists to persist in the date of 788 AD, which also coincides with Vibhava Saṁvatsara.

Second View

The second view is supported by Jain literature. According to this, Śaṅkara was born fter 2125 Jain Yudhiṣṭhira Saṁvat, which corresponds to 3294-2125=1169 BC. Śaṅkara passed away after 2157 Jain Yudhiṣṭhira Saṁvat, which is 3294-2157=1137 BC. The Yudhiṣṭhira Saṁvat of Jina Vijaya dates back to 3294 BC. Śaṅkara of Jina Vijaya was born in the Jupiter year Nandana and died in the Jupiter year Tāmrākṣa (Raktākṣa). The Jina Vijaya text mentions the death of Śaṅkara.

> ऋषिर्बाणस्तथा भूमिमर्त्याक्ष (2157) वाममेलनात् ।
> एकत्वेन लभेतांकं ताम्राक्षा तत्र वत्सरः ॥
> *ṛṣirbāṇastathā bhūmimartyākṣa (2157) vāmamelanāt ।*
> *ēkatvena labhetāṁkaṁ tāmrākṣā tatra vatsaraḥ ॥*

[Meaning] When we calculate the figures ṛṣi=7, bāṇa=5, bhūmi=1, and martyākṣi=2 in the reverse order (2157) and reckon the years in Yudhiṣṭhira Saṁvat after the Mahābhārata war, we arrive at the year Tāmrākṣa (Raktākṣa) of Jupiter as the year of Śaṅkara's death.

According to the first tradition, Śaṅkara was born in Vibhava Saṁvatsara, while the second tradition suggests Nandana Saṁvatsara. This discrepancy in Jovial years is simply a result of differing traditions. In 1168 BC, the 'Vibhava' year corresponds to the 'Daivi' tradition, while the 'Nandana' year aligns with the 'Āsuri' tradition. Consequently, both the 'Vibhava' and 'Nandana' Saṁvatsaras existed in 1168 BC, as per the 'Daivi' (North Indian) and 'Āsuri' (South Indian) traditions. Our '9000-Years' Calendar of Saptarṣi and other Indian Eras further clarifies this confusion, demonstrating that both perspectives support the same epoch.

Third View

The third perspective is presented in various Sanskrit texts written in the eulogy of Ādi Śaṅkarācharya. These texts include Śaṅkarābhyudaya, Bṛhat Śaṅkara Vijaya, Prāchina Vijaya, and Puṇya Śloka Mañjari, among others. All these works were written after Jain texts. The authors of these works adhere to the statements of Jain sources and unanimously affirm that Śaṅkara was born in the Nandana Samvatsara and passed away at the age of 32 in the Raktākṣī Samvatsara. However, they appear to be confused regarding the Tiṣya Samvat they follow, as they lack unity and make statements that align with their convenience while maintaining a central focus on the Nandana Samvatsara. For instance, I will present each of them separately. According to Prāchina Vijaya,

तिष्ये प्रयात्यनल(3)-शेवधि (9)-बाण (5)-नेत्रे (2)
अब्दे नंदने दिनमणावुदग्भाजि ॥
राधेऽसितेरुडुविनिर्गतमंगललग्नेऽस्याहूतवान् ।
शिवः शिवगुरुः स च शंकरेति ॥
tiṣye prayātyanala(3)-śevadhi (9)-bāṇa (5)-netre (2)
abde naṁdane dinamaṇāvudagbhāji ॥
rādhe'siteruḍuvinirgatamaṁgalagne'syāhūtavān ।
śivaḥ śivaguruḥ sa cha śaṁkareti ॥

Śiva, the Guru of Śiva, called Śaṅkara, was born when 2,593 years of the Tiṣya era had elapsed, with the Sun having ascended the northern horizon, during the dark half of the month under the Anuradha nakṣatra, with the stars risen, in an auspicious lagna, in the jovial year Nandana.

Prāchina Vijaya references the second Tiṣya saṁvat. Therefore, the 2593 years that have elapsed since the Tiṣya samvat equate to 3762 - 2593 = 1169 years. Consequently, the date of Śaṅkara, as per Prāchina Vijaya, can be precisely determined as 1169 (expired), or 1168 BC.

Puṇya Śloka Mañjarī mentions the emancipation period of

Śaṅkara as 2625. Śaṅkara lived for 32 years, so his birthdate, according to Puṇya Śloka Mañjarī, is 2625-32= 2593, which is almost the same as quoted by Prāchina Vijaya. This text also states that Śaṅkara's Nirvāṇa tithi is Śukla Ekādaśī (May 12, 1136 BC), while others believe it was Vaiśākha Pūrṇimā (May 16, 1136 BC). This discrepancy among scholars regarding the tithi of Śaṅkara's birth and death is the reason for the differing viewpoints expressed by different scholars. One perspective suggests that Śaṅkara was born on the 11th lunar day of the bright fortnight of Vaiśākha.

महेशांशाज्जातो मधुरमुपदिष्टाद्वयनयो महामोह।
ध्वान्तप्रशमनरविः षण्मत-गुरुः।
फले (32) स्वस्मिन् स्वायुष्यपि शरचराब्देऽपि (2625)।
च कलेः विलल्ये रक्ताषिण्यधिवृष सितैकादशी परे॥

maheśāṁśājjāto madhuramupadiṣṭādvaya-nayo mahāmoha ।
dhvāntapraśamanaraviḥ ṣaṇmata-guruḥ ।
phale (32) svasmin svāyuṣyapi śaracharābde·pi (2625) ।
cha kaleḥ vilalye raktāṣiṇyadhivṛṣa sitaikādaśī pare ॥

[Meaning] The Maheshānśa (portion of Mahesh/Śiva) was born, imparting the sweet teaching (madhuram upadiṣṭa) of the advaita path (advaya-naya), causing great bewilderment (mahāmōha).

He is the Sun (raviḥ) who dispels darkness (dhvānta-prashamana), and the guru of the six systems (ṣaṇmat-guruḥ).

In the 32nd year of his age when 2625 years of Tiṣya era (3762 BC) had elapsed in Kaliyuga (kaleḥ), he merged with Brahman (ca vilallye), in the Raktāṣiṇi jovial year, during the 11th tithi of śukla pakṣa"

The above date corresponds to May 1136 BC.

Bṛhat Śaṅkara Vijaya of Chitsukhāchārya states that Śaṅkara was born in the 31st year when 26 centuries of the Yudhiṣṭhira era had elapsed. It was the Jupiter year Nandana, the month of Vaiśākha (Chaitra), the 5th lunar day of the bright fortnight and a Sunday. The Lagna (ascendant) was Karka and nakṣatra was Punarvasu. This corresponds to 31st March 1168 BC, Sunday. Hereunder I give the horoscope for 31st March 1168 BC. prepared with the help of Astrodienst for the benefit of our readers.

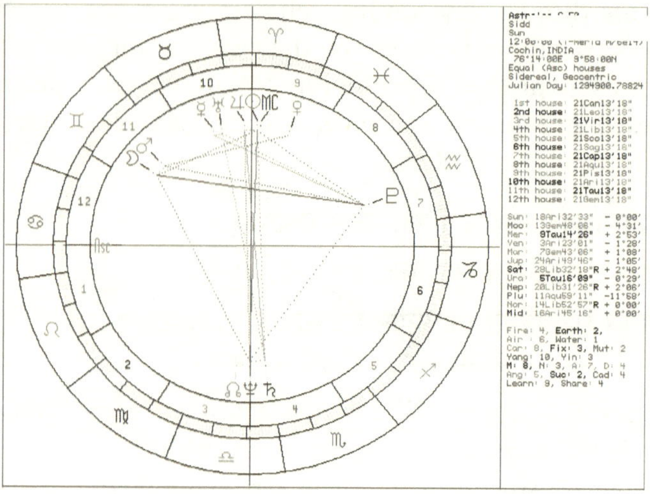

The verse of *Bṛhat Śaṅkara Vijaya* reads like this:

ततः सा दशमे मासे संपूर्ण शुभलक्षणे।
षड्विंशे शतके श्रीमद् युधिष्ठिरशकस्य वै॥
एकत्रिंशेऽथ वर्षे तु हायने नंदने शुभे।
मेषराशौ गते सूर्येवैशाखे (चैत्रे) मासि शोभने॥
शुक्लपक्षे च पंचम्यां तिथ्यां भास्करवासरे।
पुनर्वसु गते चन्द्रे लग्ने कर्कटावह्ये॥

tataḥ sā daśame māse saṁpūrṇa śubhalakṣaṇe ।
ṣaḍviṁśe śatake śrīmad yudhiṣṭhiraśakasya vai ॥
ēkatriṁśe'tha varṣe tu hāyane naṁdane śubhe ।
meṣarāśau gate sūryevaiśākhe (chaitre) māsi śobhane ॥
śuklapakṣe cha paṁchamyāṁ tithyāṁ bhāskaravāsare ।
punarvasu gate chandre lagne karkaṭāvahye ॥

[Meaning] Śaṅkara was born in the tenth month, when all auspicious marks (sampūrṇa śubhalakṣaṇe) were present. In the 26th century of the glorious Yudhiṣṭhira era (ṣaḍ-viṃśe śatake śrīmad Yudhiṣṭhira-śakasya). In the 31st year (ekatrimśe 'tha varṣe), during the auspicious period of Nandana (hāyane Nandane śubhe), when the Sun was in the sign of Aries (Meṣa-rāśau gate sūrya), in the month of Vaiśākha (or Caitra) (Vaiśākhe/Caitre māsi), on the fifth day of the bright half (śukla-pakṣe pañcamyām tithyāṁ), on Sunday (bhāskara-vāsare), and when the Moon was in Punarvasu nakṣatra, in the Karkaṭa lagna (lagne Karkaṭā-vahye).

Calculations for both the dates are as under:

25th Feb. 1168 BC	Phālguna Amāvasyā, Monday
31st March 1168 BC	Chaitra S-5, Sunday
1st April 1168 BC	Chaitra S-10, Monday
11th March 1168 BC	Chaitra Pūrṇimā, Monday
25th April 1168 BC	Chaitra Amāvasyā, Wednesday

First and foremost, let me express my skepticism about the authenticity of the provided śloka due to several metrical and astronomical errors. The śloka states that the sun was in the Meṣa rāśī and the month was Vaiśākha. However, this contradicts the fact that when the sun is in the Meṣa Saṅkrānti between two Amāvasyās, the month is known as Chaitra. Conversely, the Vaiśākha month occurs when the sun is in the Vṛṣabha rāśī. Therefore, the first technical correction required is to replace Vaiśākha with Chaitra.

Despite this correction, it appears that the writer of this śloka in the Bṛhat Śaṅkara Vijaya also quotes the second Tiṣya saṁvat 3762 BC as the first Jain Yudhiṣṭhira Śaka. To determine the exact date of Śaṅkara, we can calculate it as 3762--2600=1162 BC. This calculation is quite close to 1168 BC.

The Epoch of Kumaril Bhaṭṭa

51/7/28th Kali/1886 or 1216 BC

According to Jina Vijaya, Jina Mahāvira, Kumārila Bhaṭṭa

and Śaṅkarāchārya were contemporaries. Referring to the birth of Kumārila Bhaṭṭa, Jina Vijaya says:

ऋषिर्वारस्तथा पूर्णमर्त्याक्षौ (2077) वाममेलनात् ।
एकीकृत्य लभेतांक क्रोधी स्यात्तत्र वत्सरः ।।
भट्टाचार्यकुमारस्य कर्मकाण्डवादिनः ।
ज्ञेयः प्रादुर्भवस्तस्मिन् वर्षे यौधिष्ठिरे शके ।।
ṛṣirvārastathā pūrṇamartyākṣau (2077) vāmamelanāt ।
ēkīkṛtya labhetāṁka krodhī syāttatra vatsaraḥ ।।
bhaṭṭāchāryakumārasya karmakāṇḍavādinaḥ ।
jñeyaḥ prādurbhavastasmin varṣe yaudhiṣṭhire śake ।।

[Meaning] We obtain the Jupiter year Krodhi if we calculate the figure ṛṣi= 7, vāra=7, pūrṇa=0, and martyākṣa=2 in reverse order, which is 2077 of the Yudhiṣṭhira Saṁvat (3294 BC). Kumarila Bhaṭṭa, born in 2077 Jain Yudhiṣṭhira Saṁvat (expired) or 1216 BC).

He was older than Śaṅkara by 48 years, as mentioned by Chitsukhāchārya in his Bṛhat Śaṅkara Vijaya. Consequently, Śaṅkara was born in 1168 BC. Therefore, the exact date of Kumarila Bhaṭṭa aligns with that of Śaṅkara.

According to Jina Vijaya, two years after the death of Mahāvira, Kumārila was expelled from the terrace onto street in 2109 Yudhiṣṭhira Saṁvat or (3294-2109=1185 BC expired) in 1184 BC, Dhātā Saṁvatsara.

नन्दाः पूर्ण भूश्च नेत्रे मनुज्ञानां च वामतः ।
मेलने वत्सरो धाता युधिष्ठिरशकस्य वै ।
भट्टाचार्यकुमारस्य कर्मकाण्डवादिनः ।
जातः पराभवः तस्मिन् विज्ञेयो वत्सरे शुभे ॥
nandāḥ pūrṇa bhūścha netre manujñānāṁ cha vāmataḥ ।
melane vatsaro dhātā yudhiṣṭhiraśakasya vai ।
bhaṭṭāchāryakumārasya karmakāṇḍavādinaḥ ।
jātaḥ parābhavaḥ tasmin vijñeyo vatsare śubhe ॥

[Meaning] If we calculate nanda= 9, purṇa=0, bhūmi=1 and netra= 2 in reverse order, we obtain the year 2109 of Yudhiṣṭhira Saṁvat. It was during this Saṁvat that the Jupiter year Dhātā was in currency when Kumārila

Bhaṭṭa, a scholar of Karmakanda, met his defeat.

It is said that Kumārila Bhaṭṭa survived the fall and lost an eye.

Kumārila Bhaṭṭa was born in 2077 Jain Yudhiṣṭhira Saṁvat (expired), which is equivalent to 1216 BC. He studied under Jina (Mahāvīra) and two years later, after Jina's passing, he was expelled from the Jain Sampradāya in 2109 Jain Yudhiṣṭhira Saṁvat (expired), or 1184 BC.

The Epoch of Mahavira Jain

51/7/28th Kali/1843-1915 or 1258 BC- 1186 BC

According Jina Vijaya, Kumārila Bhaṭṭa studied under Jina (Mahāvīra) and two years later, after Jina's passing (2107), he was expelled from the Jain Sampradāya in 2109 Jain Yudhiṣṭhira Saṁvat (expired), or 1184 BC.

Jina Mahāvīra died in 2107 Jain Yudhiṣṭhira Saṁvat (expired), i.e. 1186 BC. He is said to have lived for 72 years. So, his date of birth should be 2035 Jain Yudhiṣṭhira Saṁvat (expired) or 1258 BC. Thus, we have evidence that Jina Mahāvira, Kumārila Bhaṭṭa and Ādi Śaṅkarāchārya were contemporaries. According to the Jina Vijaya, Ādi Śaṅkara had a chance to meet Kumārila Bhaṭṭa at the age of 16 in 1153 BC.

पश्चात् पंचदशे वर्षे शंकरस्य गते सति ।
भट्टाचार्यस्य कुमारस्य दर्शनं कृतवान् शिवः ॥
paśchāt paṁchadaśe varṣe śaṁkarasya gate sati |
bhaṭṭāchāryasya kumārasya darśanaṁ kṛtavān śivaḥ ||

[Meaning] When Śaṅkara attained the age of 15 years, he met Kumar Bhaṭṭāchārya.

Note: The epoch of Mahāvīra Nirvāṇa can be employed to construct the chronology of Gardabhilla and his successors.

The Epoch of Śudraka

According to Śri Yallārya, Śudraka Saṁvat was founded in Kali Saṁvat 2345, i.e. 3101-2345= 756 BC.

The śloka is quoted in the Vedavāṇī (Vikramī Saṁvat 2038: 18), as under:

बाणाब्धि गुणदस्रत्रोनाः (2345) शूद्रकाब्दाः कलेर्गताः। यल्लाचार्य

bāṇābdhi guṇadasratronāḥ śūdrakābdāḥ kalergatāḥ /

Yallāchārya

[Meaning] When 2345 years of Kali passed away, Śudraka Saṁvat was founded

The same fact is narrated in the Skanda Purāṇa (Vedavāṇī: 18). Therefore, until the Saptarṣi year 3290, King Śudraka ruled. The relevant verse is as follows:

त्रिषु वर्ष सहस्रेषु (3000) कलेर्यातेषु पार्थिवः।

त्रिशतेषु (300) दश न्यूनेषु (-10) अस्यां भुवि भविष्यति शूद्रको नाम वीराणाम्।

triṣu varṣa sahasreṣu kaleryāteṣu pārthivaḥ.
triśateṣu daśa nyūneṣuasyāṁbhūvi bhaviṣyati śudrako nāma vīrāṇām

[Meaning] Until the 3290th year of the Saptarṣi Saṁvat, the valiant Śudraka will reign supreme on this earth.

Here, the word "kali" is used to refer to Patna Saptarṣi Saṁvat, the first cycle of which began in 6776 BC. Since the year 3290 is the 3290th Saptarṣi, it belongs to the second cycle of the Saptarṣi, which commenced in 4076 BC. Therefore, by subtracting 3290 from 4076 BC, we obtain 786 BC. Analyzing both references, it becomes evident that Śudraka ruled for 30 years, from 786 BC to 756 BC.

The Epoch of Vikramaditya I of Ujjain

51/7/28th Kali/2385-2445or 717–657 BC

Vikram era 717-716 BC was started by Vikramāditya 1 was in the 470 years of the death of Mahavira Jain in 1186 BC.

Jain Paṭṭāvalis narrate that King Gardabhilla ascended to the throne of Ujjain in Mahavira-Nirvāṇa Saṁvat 453 (732 BC) and ruled for a period of 13 years. Early Jain scholars have preserved an intriguing historical account titled 'Kālakācārya-Kathānaka' within their works. This narrative provides a detailed background of the rise of Vikramāditya in the years 717-716 BC. In Jain tradition, there were three Kālakācāryas. Kālakācārya I lived during Mahavira-Nirvāṇa Saṁvat 376 (809 BC) and authored commentaries on 'Nigoḍas'. Kālakācārya II flourished during the reign of King Gardabhilla (732 BC), while Kālakācārya III lived around Mahavira Nirvāṇa Saṁvat 993 (192 BC). Notably, the renowned 'Kālakācārya-Kathānaka' is the authentic account of Kālakācārya II.

King Vairisingh of Dhārā (modern Dhar in Madhya Pradesh) had a son named Kālaka and a daughter named Sarasvati, both of whom embraced Jainism at a young age. They traveled to Ujjain, the primary center of Jainism in Madhya Pradesh. King Gardabhilla, the ruler of Ujjain at that time, was captivated by Sarasvati's beauty and forcibly took her to his palace. Despite Kālaka's numerous efforts and pleas to the king to release his sister with honor, his pleas were unsuccessful. Enraged and frustrated, Kālaka resolved to avenge this humiliation. He embarked on a journey westward, crossed the Sindhu River, and reached the region that is now modern-day Afghanistan. There, he encountered numerous Śaka kṣatraps who were subordinate to the Śāhānuśāhī kings. Through persuasion, Kālaka successfully convinced 95 or 96 Śaka kṣatraps to relocate to India and establish their own independent kingdoms, rather than continuing to serve as subordinates.

These Śaka kṣatraps arrived in Ujjain accompanied by Kālaka and vanquished King Gardabhilla, capturing him. Kālaka thus avenged his humiliation and liberated his sister Sarasvati. The Śaka kṣatraps proclaimed themselves the rulers of Ujjain in Mahavira-Nirvāṇa Saṁvat 466 (719 BC) and reigned for four years until Vikramāditya, the Great, launched an attack on the Śakas and expelled them..

King Vikramaditya, who reigned over Ujjain, lived in the 7th century BC and was contemporaneous with scholars like Varāhamihira. Jain pattāvalis, such as the Kharatara-gaccha and Tapa-gaccha, state that Vikramaditya received Jainism dikṣā from the scholar Suddhasena Divākara in the 470th year of Mahānirvāṇa of Mahavira. As previously mentioned, the Nirvāṇa of Mahavira Jain occurred in 1186 BC. Therefore, Vikramaditya was initiated into Jainism in 1186-470= 717-716 BC. Upon his initiation and subsequent conquest of the Śakas, Vikramaditya commenced his Vikrama era in 717 BC. Vikramāditya ruled for 60 years, implying that his reign spanned from 717 BC to 657 BC. Following Vikramāditya, his four successors ruled for a period of 75 years and 5 months. Consequently, the Vikramāditya dynasty ruled for 135 years and 5 months.

The chronology of King Vikramāditya and his four successors is provided in the Gurvāvali of Vṛddhagaccha.

> सुन्नमुनिवेयजुत्त ४७० जिनकल विक्कमो वरिस-सत्थि ६० ॥ धम्मैछ्छो छलिस ४० गैल पनविस २५ नहदे अत्थ ८॥ इक्किम्मि ३वससये गयमि पनतिसवछ्छरसदिये १३५ विक्कम-कलौ सग नवछ्छरो पुन वि सम्जो

> *Sunnamuniveyajutta 470 Jinakala Vikkamo varisa-satthi 60. Dhammaichcho chalisa 40 Gaila panavisa 25 Nahade attha 8. Ikkammi 3vasasaye gayami panatisavachcharasadiye 135 Vikkama-kalau saga navachcharo puna vi samjao.*

Accordingly, Vikrama, after defeating 96 Śaka Kṣatrapas in the 470th year of Mahāvira Nirvāṇa kāla (1186-470=) 717-716 BC, received initiation into Jainism. Gardabhilla, the first ruler, was killed by the 96 Śaka Kṣatrapas, accompanied by Kālkāchārya. Vikramāditya then defeated them in 717-716 BC and began his reign. The Gurvāvali states that Vikramāditya ruled for 60 years, from 717 BC to 657 BC. He was succeeded by Dharmaichhu, who ruled for 40 years, from 657 BC to 617 BC. Gaila Panvisa ruled for 25 years, from 617 BC to 592 BC. Nahade ruled for 8 years, from 592 BC to 584 BC. Ikkami ruled for 3 years, from 584 BC to 581 BC.

After 135 years and 5 months, the Śaka Kśatraps regrouped and launched another invasion of Ujjain, successfully re-occupying the city in 583 BC. It is highly likely that the Śaka Mahākśatrapa Caṣṭana was crowned the king of Ujjain during this period. In 583 BC, he established the Śaka era, which was known as 'Śaka-nṛpa-kāla', 'Śaka-nṛpa-rājyābhiśeka-saṁvatsara', and so on. Consequently, we can construct a chronology of the rulers of Ujjain that spans from the Kārtikādi Vikrama era (717 BC) to the Śaka era (583 BC).

Sr. No.	Name of the King	Mahavir Nirvāṇa Saṁvat (1186 BC) 1187BC (Expired)	Date of Coronation in the Christian Era
1	Gardabhilla (13 years)	453-466	734-721 BC
2	96 Śaka Kśatrapas invited by Kālaka (4 years)	466-470	721-717 BC
3	Vikramāditya 1 (60 years) founded Kārtikādi Vikrama era (717 BC) after defeating Śaka kṣatrapas and having taken initiation into Jainism	470-530	717-657 BC
4	Dharmaichhu (40 years)	530-570	657-617 BC
5	Gaila Panvisa (25 years)	570-595	617-592 BC
6	Nahide (8 years)	595-603	592-586 BC
7	Ikrami (3 years)	603-606	586-582 BC
8	Śaka king Caṣṭana established his rule and founded his Śaka era (583 BC)	607	583 BC

We can gather some evidence of this fact from Jain works such as Tiloyapannati by Yativṛṣabha, Harivaṁśa by Jinasena, Dhavala by Āchārya Vīrasena, Trilokasāra by Nemichandra, Mahaviracaritam by Nemichandra, and Vichāraśreṇ I by

Merutuṅga. These texts reveal that Mahāvīra attained Nirvāṇa 605 years and 5 months before the commencement of the Śaka era (583 BC) and 470 years before the beginning of the Kārttikādi Vikrama era (717 BC).

Some scholars attempt to determine the date of Mahavir's Nirvāṇa by adding 470 years to the 57 BC era established by Vikramaditya II of Ujjain. However, it's important to note that Jain texts refer to the Vikramaditya of Ujjain who embraced Jainism, not the one who did not. Therefore, it's inaccurate to calculate Mahāvīra's Nirvāṇa by adding 470 years to the era of Vikramaditya II.

Note: The era of Kārtikādi Vikrama (717 BC) was mentioned in the inscriptions of various dynasties, including the Maukharis, Aulikaras, Pratāhāras, Paramāras, Chaulukyas, Chalukyas, Chāhamānas, Gāhadwālas, and Chandrātreyas (Chandellas).

The Epoch of Varāhamihira I and other Nava Ratnas of Vikramāditya I

51/7/28th Kali/2400 or 7th Century BC

Vikramādtya I of Ujjain, in fact, patronized nine scholars known as Nava ratnas during his time. Internal evidence from Varāhamihra and Kalhaṇa's Rājataraṅginī suggests that Varāhamihira lived in 655 BC. The Bṛhat Saṁhitā (13.3) and 'Rājatariṅginī' (1.56) provide further information, stating that Yudhiṣṭhira ruled the country when the Saptarṣis were positioned in the Maghā Nakṣatra. The verse reads as follows:

आसन् मघासु मुनयः शासति पृथिवीं युधिष्ठिरे नृपतौ ।
षड्द्विक्पंचद्वियुतः शककालः तस्य राज्ञश्च ॥
āsan maghāsu munayaḥ śāsati pṛthivīṁ yudhiṣṭhire nṛpatau /
ṣaḍdvikpaṁchadviyutaḥ śakakālaḥ tasya rājñaścha //

When King Yudhiṣṭhira ruled the earth, the Great Bear, Munis, was in the Maghā constellation. Now, by the time of Varāhamihira, 2526 years had elapsed since the beginning of the Yudhiṣṭhira Śaka (in 3173 BC).

The verse cited above indicates that Varāhamihira lived during the period during 3173- 2526 = 647 BC.

In his renowned Karaṇa text, named named Pañchasidhāntika, Varāhamihira mentions that he has adopted the Śaka year 427 as the starting point for some of his calculations. Here it may be informed that Varāhamihira always used Kashmiri Saptarṣi Saṁvat in the name of Śaka year. This Śaka referenced by Varāhamihira is also the Kashmiri Saptarṣi Saṁvat, the third cycle of which commenced in 1076 BC. Therefore, the mention of Śaka 427 signifies the year 1076 BC. So, here the mention of Śaka 427 means 1076B C-427=649 BC. which again proves the presence of Varāhamihira in 649 BC.

Now, let me present another piece of evidence that is frequently cited to support his date of death. According to the statement of Āmarāja, the commentator of Brahmagupta, Varāhamihira passed away in the Śākā (Saptarṣi Saṁvat) year 509. Here's the relevant excerpt:

नवाधिकपंचशतसंख्यशाके वराहमिहिराचार्यो दिवंगतः ॥
navādhikapaṁchaśatasaṁkhyaśāke
varāhamihirāchāryo divaṁgataḥ ॥

Here again, the word Śākā is quoted, which is evidently the Saptarṣi Śaka, not the commonly known Śaka Saṁvat. Therefore, as per Āmarāja, Varāhamihira passed away in 1076 BC - 509 BC = 567 BC. This entire sequence of events strongly suggests that Varāhamihira must have lived for a span of over 80 years.

Interestingly, at another place, the same Varāhamihira mentions the points in the ecliptic where the winter and summer solstices occurred during the time of Parāśara Tantra (24th century BC) and Vedāṅga Jyotiṣa (24th century BC) and his own time. By analyzing the details provided by Varāhamihira, we can precisely determine the number of degrees (ayanāṁśa) by which the solstices in the ecliptic have shifted. To calculate the exact duration of the interval between Varāhamihira's time and Vedāṅga Jyotiṣa, we divide the difference in the precession of equinoxes (ayanāṁśa) by 72. Similarly, we can determine the exact number of years between Varāhamihira's time (as mentioned in Bṛhatsaṁhitā, 3.1-2) and the modern epoch. Varāhamihira states,

Note: Interestingly, Varāhamihira quotes Vedāṅga Jyotiṣa's statement while highlighting the time difference between them. Varāhamihira states,

आश्लेषार्द्धाद् दक्षिणमुत्तरमयनं रवेर्धनिष्ठाद्यम्।
नूनं कदाचिदासीद्येनोक्तं पूर्वशास्त्रेषु ॥ बृहत्संहिता, 3.1
āśleṣārddhād dakṣiṇamuttaramayanaṁ raverdhaniṣṭhādyam;
nūnaṁ kadāchidāsīdyenoktaṁ pūrvaśāstreṣu.

Bṛhatsaṁhitā, 3.1

The Sun's southern course began at one time from the latter half of Āśleṣā and the northern from the beginning of Dhaniṣṭhā. This must indeed have been the case, as it is so recorded in previous Śāstras (like the Vedāṅga Jyotiṣa).

साम्प्रतमयनं सवितुः कर्कटाद्यं मृगादितश्चान्यत्।
उक्ताभावो विकृतिः प्रत्यक्षपरीक्षणैर्व्यक्तिः ॥ बृहत्संहिता, *3.2*

sāmpratamayanaṁ savituḥ karkaṭādyaṁ mṛgāditaśchānyat;
uktābhāvo vikṛtiḥ pratyakṣaparīkṣaṇairvyaktiḥ.

*Bṛhatsaṁhitā,*3.1

At present, the one course of the Sun commences from the beginning of Karkaṭa (Cancer), and the other from the beginning of Mṛgaśirā. The change (vikṛti) from that earlier condition has become evident through direct observation and examination.

So at the time of Varāhamihira, the Sun had receded its southward course from the mid-point of Āśleṣā (113^0) of the previous Śāstras (Vedāṅga Jyotiṣa) to the beginning of Karka/ Cancer (90^0). This makes an interval of 113-90= 23^0 between the time of Vedāṅga Jyotiṣa and Varāhamihira which is equal to 23 x 72=1656 years. It shows that Vedāṅga Jyotiṣa was written 1656 years before the period of Varāhamihira.

Similarly, at the time of Varāhamihira, the Sun had receded its northward course from the beginning of Dhaniṣṭhā ($293^{0'}$) of the previous Śāśtras (Vedāṅga Jyotiṣa), to the beginning of Makara (270^0). This makes an interval of 293^0-270^0= 23 ^{0} between the time of Vedāṅga Jyotiṣa and Varāhamihira which is equal to 23 x 72=1656 years. It also confirms that previous Śāśtras (Vedāṅga Jyotiṣa) were written 1656 years before the period of Varāhamihira. Mṛgaśirā (53.20^0)

Now the epoch of Varāhamihira can also be worked out on a similar pattern. Today the Sun had receded its northward course from the beginning of Makara (277^0), of Varāhamihira's period, to Mula nakṣatra (240^0). This makes an interval of 277^0-240^0= 37^0 between the time of Varāhamihira and the modern epoch which is equal to 37x72=2664 years. It also confirms that Varāhamihira lived 2664 years ago or 2664-2025=639 BC

Similarly, today the sun has receded its southward course from the beginning of Karka / Cancer (90^0) of Varāhamihira's period to the Mṛgaśirā constellation (53^0). This makes an interval of 90-53=37^0 between the time of Varāhamihira and the modern epoch which is equal to 37 x 72=2664 years. It shows that Varāhamihira lived 2664 years ago or 2664-2025=639 BC.

This makes it clear that Vedāṅga Jyotiṣa was written around 639+1656=2298 BC.

We find one more śloka in Pañchasiddhāntikā (3.21) which reads as under:

अश्लेषार्धाद् आसीद्यदा निवृत्तिः किलोष्णकिरणस्य ।
युक्तमयनं तदासीद् साम्प्रतमयनं पुनर्वसुतः ॥

Aśleṣārdhād āsīd yadā nivṛttiḥ kiloṣṇakiraṇasya,
yuktamayanam tadāsīd sāmpratamayanam punarvasutaḥ.

When the Sun's (hot rays') southern turning point (nivṛtti) occurred from the middle of the constellation Āśleṣā (113^{0}), that was considered the true solstitial point (ayana). Now, however, this solstitial point lies at Punarvasu (90^{0}).

It is noteworthy that the commencement of the Karka sign is 90^{0}, which corresponds to the end of Punarvasu. Therefore, in this context, Varahamihira refers to the Punarvasu, the end of the Punarvasu.

Epoch of Bāṇabhaṭṭa

5th Century BC

The second chapter, titled "Rājadarśana," of Harshacharita narrates recounts Bāṇabhaṭṭa's encounter with King Śri Harsha. Bāṇabhaṭṭa informs us that he was personally invited by Krishna, the brother of King Śri Harsha (Mahārājādhirāja-Śri-Harasya bhrātrā Kṛṣṇaṇāmnā—). He embarked on a journey across the Gaṅgā River and arrived at the headquarters of the royal army, known as Upamaṇipura.

अन्यस्मिन् दिने स्कन्धावारम् उपमणिपुरम् अन्वजिरवति कृतसन्निवेशम् समाससाद

anyasmin dine skandhāvāram upamaṇipuram anvajiravati kṛtasannivesam samāsasāda.

[Meaning] On another day, he reached the military camp (skandhāvāra) at Upamaṇipura, which had been established near the river Ajiravatī."

Thus, it seems that the renowned Sanskrit poet Bāṇabhaṭṭa served as the court poet of Śri Harsha (457 BC). Bāṇabhaṭṭa references several literary works from different eras, including the Bṛhatkathā of Guṇāḍhya (4-5th Century BC), the Gāthāsaptaśatī of Hāla Śātavāhana (527-502 BC), the Vāsavadattā of Subandhu, the Setubandha of Pravarasena, the Harichandra, Bhāsa, and Kālidāsa. These references further solidify the fact that Subandhu, Kalidasa, and others mentioned by Bāṇabhaṭṭa were indeed flourishing around or before the 7th century BC.

Considering the previous discussion, it can be safely concluded that renowned scholars like Varāhamihira and Kalidasa were patronized by the first Vikramaditya of Ujjain (717 BC) rather than the second Vikramāditya of Ujjain (57 BC).

Varāhamihira used Saptarṣi Saṁvat as Śaka Saṁvat in his treatises

It's worth mentioning that Varāhamīhira and his commentator Bhaṭṭotpala employed Saptarṣi Saṁvat cycles in their works. I can provide a few examples here. Bhaṭṭotpala concludes his commentary on Varāhamihira's Bṛhajjātaka by stating that he completed his work in Śaka 888 (expired) on Chaitra Śukla Pañchami, which fell on a Thursday.:

चैत्रमासस्य पञ्चम्याम् सितायाम् गुरुवासरे ।
वस्वष्टाष्टमिते शाके कृतेयम् विवृतिर् मया ॥
chaitramāsasya pañchamyām sitāyām guruvāsare,
vasvaṣṭāṣṭamite śāke kṛtteyam vivṛtir mayā.

Here, Bhaṭtotpala has referred to the third cycle of the Saptarṣi saṁvat, which began in 1076 BCE, as the Śaka saṁvat. Consequently, he wrote this commentary in 888 Śaka. Therefore, this date is 888 years after the Saptarṣi (Śaka) saṁvat 1076 BCE, which means it is 188 BCE. This epoch falls on March 4, 188 BCE, a Thursday, which corresponds to Chaitra śukla pañchamī. Several other scholars have proposed different Śaka eras, such as 78 AD, but if we consider those Śaka eras, we do not find any alignment between the Vedic month, tithi, and weekday mentioned in the statement.

In Bṛhatsaṁhitā (8.20-21), while presenting a formula to determine the saṁvatsara of the 60-year yuga cycle of Jupiter, as per the daivī tradition, Varāhamihira mentions the 2nd cycle of Saptarṣi saṁvat, starting from the year 3776 BC, as the central point of his formula.

गतानि वर्षाणि शकेन्द्रकालाद्धतानि रुद्रैर्गुणयेच्चतुर्भिः ।(44)

नवाष्टपंचाष्ट (8589) युतानि कृत्वा विभाजयेच्छून्यशरागरामैः (3750)।।
लब्धेन युक्तं शकभूपकालं संशोध्य षष्ट्या (60) विषयैर्विभज्य।
युगानि नारायणपूर्वकाणि लब्धानि शेषाः क्रमशः समाः स्युः।।
gatāni varṣāṇi śakendrakālāddhatāni
rudrairguṇayeccaturbhiḥ,
navāṣṭapaṃcāṣṭa yutāni kṛtvā
vibhājayecchūnyaśarāgarāmaiḥ.
labdhena yuktaṃ śakabhūpakālaṃ saṃśodhya ṣaṣṭyā
viṣayairvibhajya,
yugāni nārāyaṇapūrvakāṇi labdhāni śeṣāḥ kramaśaḥ samāḥ
syuḥ.

[Meaning] To determine the number of years since the second cycle of Saptarṣi Saṁvat (3776 BCE), multiply the relevant (śaka) saptarṣi saṁvat by 44. Add 8589 to the product and divide the result by 3750. Add the concerned śaka (saptarṣi saṁvat) to the quotient obtained. Finally, divide the result by 60; the remainder represents the number of years of the Bṛhaspati (Jupiter) yuga cycle of 60 years that have passed, with the next one being the current year. If we further divide the remainder by 5, the quotient signifies the saṁvatsara of the 12-year yuga cycles governed by Nārāyaṇa (Viṣṇu).

The above can be illustrated as under:

Suppose we want to determine the current saṁvatsara of the 12-year yuga and the 60-year yuga cycles of 2024 AD. To do this, we need to find the corresponding year of Saptarṣi saṁvat to it, considering the second cycle of Saptarṣi saṁvat that began from 3776 BC. This corresponds to the year 5801. Now, we multiply 5801 by 44 to get the product, which is 255,244. Next, we add 8589 to the product to obtain the final result, which is 263,833. Finally, we divide this result by 3750 to get the answer.

263,833/3750= 70.35.
The quotient is 70. Add this quotient to 5801.
5801+70= 5871
Divide the result by 60.

5871/60

The quotient is 19, and the remainder is 51.

51 denotes the elapsed 51st year of the Bṛhaspati yuga cycle of 60 years of Daivī Tradition. As such, the 52nd year of the daivī cycle would represent the 2024 AD, and that is called 'Kālayukta'.

If we further divide the remainder '51' by 5, we get quotient 10 and remainder 1. This means 10 months of the 12-year yuga cycle have passed, and the 11th year (Āśvina) is in currency.

The name of Jupiter's 60-year yuga cycle saṁvatsaras has already been described. Here are the names of saṁvatsaras of the 12-year yuga cycle ruled by Nārāyaṇa, etc.

1. Viṣṇu, 2. Bṛhaspati, 3. Indra, 4. Agni, 5. Tvaṣṭā,

6. Ahirbudhnya, 7. Pitṛ, 8. Viśvedevāḥ, 9. Soma,

10. Indrāgni, 11. Aśvinī, 12. Bhga

The Epoch of Āryabhaṭa II

Pañchasiddhāntika mentions the name of Āryabhaṭa II and his work was compiled in Śaka 421 which corresponds to 1076 BC-421= 655 BC.

The Epoch of Chandragupta of Ujjain (Disciple of Bhadrabāhu)

51/7/28th Kali/2070 or 1032 BC

According to Pariśiṣṭaparva of Jain author Hemachandra (5th century AD), Chandragupta ascended the throne in Ujjain during the Mahavira-Nirvāṇa era 155, i.e. 1187-155= 1032 BC.

एवं च श्रीमहावीरमुक्तेर्वर्षशते गते ।
पंचपंचाशदधीके चन्द्रगुप्तोभवन्नृपः ॥
evaṁ ca Śri-Mahavira-mukter-varṣa-śate gate
Pañca-pañcāśadadhike Chandragupto'bhavannṛpaḥ

Apart from Hemachandra's work, other Sanskrit works like

Bṛhatkathākoṣa by Hariṣeṇa, Bhadrabāhu Charitam by Ratnanandi, and Kannada works like Munivaṁābhyudaya by Chidānandakavi, Rājāvalikathe by Devachandra (1838 AD) also mention that Chandragupta, the king of Ujjain, became a disciple of Bhadrabāhu. Additionally, Chandragiri, a cave associated with Bhadrabāhu, and a few inscriptions found at Śravaṇabelgola in Karnāṭaka, provide evidence of Bhadrabāhu's visit to Śravaṇabelgola along with his disciple Chandragupta. Here's a brief summary of Bhadrabāhu's life:

Bhadrabāhu, the son of the Brāhmaṇa Somaśarma, who served in the court of King Padmaratha in Devakotta city, North Bengal, encountered the fourth Śrutakevalin, Govardhana, while playing with his friends. Govardhana later became Bhadrabāhu's teacher and initiated him into Jainism, making him the fifth Śrutakevalin. During his travels, Bhadrabāhu visited Ujjain, where he initiated King Chandragupta, the ruler of Ujjain, into Jainism.

One day, Chandragupta sought Bhadrabāhu's interpretation of his dreams from the previous night. While explaining them, Bhadrabāhu predicted a twelve-year famine in the kingdom. Consequently, he advised his followers to leave Ujjain and head south. King Chandragupta entrusted the kingdom to his son Siṁhasena and followed his guru.

Bhadrabāhu and Chandragupta then visited Śravaṇabelgola and stayed at Chikka betta or Chandragiri, where Bhadrabāhu succumbed to a tiger attack. Chandragupta continued his stay at Chandragiri, worshipping God and passing away through the rite of Sallekhana.

Sometime after Chandragupta's death, his grandson, Bhāskara, the son of Siṁhasena, arrived at Śravaṇabelgola. He constructed Jain temples and a city near Chandragiri, which was named Belgola.

It is evident from the ancient Jain tradition that Chandragupta or Chandragupti was the king of Ujjain, not Pātaliputra. He was the father of Siṁhasena and the grandfather of Bhāskara, while Chandragupta Maurya was the father of

Hyderabad) which reads as under

मानवगोत्राणां हारीतिपुत्राणां .... स्वामी महासेनपादानुध्यातृणां चालुक्यानाम् .... निजभुजनिशितनिसिंत्रश्धारावनतप्रतीपनृपचयशिखरो श्रीविष्णुवर्धनमहाराजस्य प्रियपौत्रः श्रीविष्णुवर्धनमहाराज ... राजमहेन्द्रवरे स्थितो ..... कल्यादब्दगणेऽष्ट (8) नेत्र (2) रस (6) दो (2) स्संख्ये गते वत्सरे प्राप्तेऽथ प्रभवे तपस्यपि (फाल्गुन) सिते पक्षे द्वितीयायाम् गुरौ वारे च ... लिक्षुपरिन्ध्रनाम चेरयुरीग्रामके ....

mānavagotrāṇāṁ hārītiputrāṇāṁ .... svāmī mahāsenapādānudhyātṛṇāṁ chālukyānām .... nijabhujaniśitanisiṁtraśdhārāvanatapratīpanṛpachayaśikhar o śrīviṣṇuvardhanamahārājasya priyapautraḥ śrīviṣṇuvardhanamahārāja ... rājamahendravare sthito ..... kalyādabdagaṇe·ṣṭa (8) netra (2) rasa (6) do (2) ssaṁkhye gate vatsare prāpte·tha prabhave tapasyapi (phālguna) site pakṣe dvitīyāyām gurau vāre cha ... likṣuparindhranāma cherayurīgrāmake ....

"The Chālukyas, belonging to the Mānava gotra and descended from Haritiputra, devoted to the feet of Lord Mahāsena (Kārttikeya)...

[The king described as] the peak among the assemblage of kings, before whom the edges of hostile kings' diadems bow down, cut by the sharp edge of his own arm's valorous sword —

Śrī Viṣṇuvardhana Mahārāja's beloved grandson, the illustrious Śrī Viṣṇuvardhana Mahārāja...residing in Rājamaheṃdravara (modern Rajahmundry).

When the year counted as Kalyāba era year 2628 had elapsed, in the Prabhava samvatsara (Jovian cycle year), during the bright fortnight of Phālguna month, on the second tithi (lunar day), on Thursday, at the village named Cērāyurī (or Cerayūrī) near Likṣuparindra ... [the grant or deed is being issued]."

The date mentioned is Kaliyuga 2628 (474 BC), which includes a date Phālguna S-2, Guruvāra, and Prabhava Saṁvatsara. According to our '9000 Years Calendar', the 474

BC corresponds to Prabhava Saṁvatsara of the Āsuri tradition, which falls on February 11th, 474 BC. In his 20th regnal year (173 BC), the Ganga king Durvinīta wrote a commentary on the 15th Sarga (canto) of Kirātārjunīyam. Therefore, Bhāravi must have lived in the 5th century BC.

Epoch of Daṇḍī

51/7/28th Kali/2700 or 4th Century BC

The Sanskrit poet Danḍī recounts an intriguing tale in his work 'Avantisundarikathā' about his great-grandfather's friendship with Bhāravi. This friendship led to an introduction by Bhāravi to King Vishnuvardhana, suggesting that Daṇḍī's literary prowess flourished during the 4th century BC.

Brahmagupta

51/7/28th Kali/3000 or 1st Century BC

Brahmagupta, the renowned astronomer, authored the celebrated astronomical treatise, 'Brahma Sphuṭasiddhānta'. According to his account, he composed the Brahma Sphuṭasiddhānta during the Śaka Nṛpa Kāla 550 era, which corresponds to 33 BC when he was 30 years old. Consequently, Brahmagupta's life can be dated to 63 BC.

श्रीचापवंशतिलके श्रीव्याघ्रमुखे नृपे शकनृपाणाम्
पंचाशतसंयुक्तैर्वर्षशतै पंचभिरतीतैः ।
ब्राह्मस्फुटसिद्धान्तः सज्जनगणितज्ञगोलवित्प्रित्यै
त्रिंशत्वर्षेणकृतोजिष्णु-सुत ब्रह्मगुप्तेन ॥

śrīchāpavaṁśatilake śrīvyāghramukhe nṛpe śakanṛpāṇām
paṁchāśatasaṁyuktairvarṣaśatai paṁchabhiratītaiḥ /
brāhmasphuṭasiddhāntaḥ sajjanagaṇitajñagolavitprityai
triṁśatvarṣeṇakṛtojiṣṇu-suta brahmaguptena //

"When the illustrious king Vyāghramukha, ornament of the noble Cāpa (Chāpa) dynasty, was reigning, and five centuries and fifty years (550 years) of the Śaka kings had passed, this treatise, the Brahmasphuṭasiddhānta, was composed by Brahmagupta, son of Jishnu, for the joy of the good and for those skilled in mathematics and astronomy."

In the above verse, Brahmagupta clearly refers to the Śaka Nṛpakāla era 550 (33 BC) by stating 'Śaka-nṛpāṇām'. Brahmagupta also wrote 'Khanḍakhādyaka' in the 37th year from the date of 'Brāhma Sphutasiddhānta' (33 BC) i.e. (4 AD). We can thus fix the epoch of Brahmagupta around 1st century BC.

Lallāchārya

51/7/28th Kali/3200 or 1st Century AD

Lallāchārya was, the son of Trivikrama Bhaṭṭa and the grandson of Sāmba. was the author of 'Śiśyadhīvṛddhidatantra'. He clearly refers to the end of Śaka era 'Śakakśitīśābda', in Kaliyuga 3179 elapsed (78 AD).

नन्दाद्रिचन्द्रानल (3179)संयुतो भवेत् ।
शकक्षितीशाब्दगणोगतः कालेः ॥
दिवाकरघ्नो गतमास-संयुतः ।
खवह्निनिघ्नस्थिभिः समन्वितः ॥

nandādrichandrānala (3179)saṁyuto bhavet /
śakakṣitīśābdagaṇogataḥ kāleḥ //
divākaraghno gatamāsa-saṁyutaḥ /
khavahninighnasthibhiḥ samanvitaḥ //

In view of the above reference, Lalla's date can be fixed in the 1st century AD. Here it may also be pointed out that Bhaskaracharya (452AD–532 AD) wrote a commentary on his work.

Udyotana Sūri

51/7/28th Kali/3300 or 2nd Century AD

The Jain scholar Udyotana Sūri authored his work 'Kuvalayamālā' on astrology in Śaka 700 (117 AD) during the reign of the Pratīhāra king Vatsarāja (109-138 AD).

Jinasena

51/7/28th Kali/3224 or 122 AD

Jinasena, a renowned Jain scholar, lived during the 2nd century AD. Lokasena's praśasti in the Uttarapurāṇa mentions that Jinasena, the guru of Guṇabhadra, was a contemporary of the Rāṣṭrakūṭa king Amoghavarṣa. In the concluding praśasti of the 'Harivaṁśa', a Jain Purāṇa, Jinasena provides the date of completion in the Śaka year 705, which corresponds to 122 AD.

शाकेष्वब्दशतेषु सप्तसु दिशं पंचोत्तरेषूत्तराम्।
पातीन्द्रायुधनाम्नि कृष्णनृपजे श्रीवल्लभे दक्षिणाम्॥

śākeṣvabdaśateṣu saptasu diśaṁ paṁchottareṣūttarām /
pātīndrāyudhanāmni kṛṣṇanṛpaje śrīvallabhe dakṣiṇām //

"In the Śaka era, after seven centuries and five years had passed (i.e., in Śaka 705 = 122 CE), at the southern place named Śrīvallabha, (the event occurred) during the reign of Pātīndra Āyudha, the illustrious son of King Kṛṣṇa."

Vateśvara

51/7/28th Kali/3321 or 219 AD

Vateśvara, the author of 'Vateśvara Siddhānta', was born in 'Śakendra-kāla' in 802 AD, which corresponds to 219 AD. He was the son of Mahādatta Bhaṭṭa, a native of Ānandapura in Punjab. At the age of 24, he wrote 'Vateśvara Siddhānta' in 243 AD. Additionally, he wrote 'Karaṇasāra' in Śaka 821 (238 AD).

Guṇabhadra & Lokasena

51/7/28th Kali/3300 or 200AD

Guṇabhadra, the author of the Uttarapurāṇa, was the disciple of Lokasena. In Śaka-nṛpa-kālābhyantara 820 (237 AD), Lokasena wrote a 'praśasti' at the end of the Uttarapurāṇa, which indicates that Guṇabhadra and Lokasena were present in 200 AD.

Bhaṭṭotpala

51/7/28th Kali/3407 or 305AD

Bhaṭṭotpala wrote commentaries on the works of Varāhamihira and Brahmagupta. He wrote a commentary named 'Chintāmaṇi' on Varāhamihira's Bṛhat Saṁhitā. In the commentary named 'Vivṛti' on Varāhamihira's Brihajjātaka,

Bhaṭṭotpala stated that he completed the commentary on Chaitra Śukla pañcamī, Thursday of Śaka 888.

> चैत्रमासस्य पञ्चम्याम् सितायाम् गुरुवासरे
> वस्वष्टाष्टमिते शाके कृतेयं विवृतिर्मया।
> *chaitramāsasya pañcamyām sitāyām guruvāsare*
> *Vasvaṣṭāṣṭamite Śāke kṛteyam Vivṛtir-mayā.*

"In the Śaka year 888, on the fifth day of the bright fortnight of the month of Caitra, on a Thursday, this exposition (vivṛti) was composed by me."

Here, the term Śāke refers to Saptarṣi Saṁvat 1076 BC (third cycle of Kashmir Saptarṣi Saṁvat). As such his time period works out to be 1076-888=188 BC. So, Chaitra Śukla Pañcamī, Thursday of Saptarṣi 888 (188 BC) corresponds to 7th March 188 B.C.

The Epoch of Hariswami & Skandaswami

51/7/28th Kali/3065 or 36 BC

Vikramaditya II, the custodian of knowledge, bestowed patronage upon scholars and scientists. A striking example of this is mentioned by Hariswami, a disciple of Skandaswami, in his commentary on the Kāṇva Śatapatha Brāhmaṇa. Hariswami recounts that King Vikramaditya of Ujjain honored him by presenting him with a golden chair in his court and appointing him as a minister responsible for spiritual activities and charitable endeavors when 3740 years of Kali had elapsed. This remarkable event is quoted below:

> श्रीमतोऽवन्तिनाथस्य विक्रमार्कस्य भूपतेः।
> धर्माध्यक्षो हरिस्वामी व्याख्यातवान् शातपथीं श्रुतीम्॥
> भूभर्त्राविक्रमार्केणक्लृप्ता कनकवेदिकाम्।
> दानाध्यक्षाः यः कृतवान् श्रुत्यर्थविवृत्तिं हरिः।
> यदादीनां कलेर्जग्मुः सप्त त्रिंशत् शतानि (3700) वै।
> चत्वारिंशत् (40) समाश्चान्याः तदा भाष्यमिदं कृतम्॥
> *śrīmato'vantināthasya vikramārkasya bhūpateḥ* ।

dharmādhyakṣo harisvāmī vyākhyātavān śātapathīṁ śrutīm ||
bhūbhartrāvikramārkeṇaklṛptā kanakavedikām |
dānādhyakṣāḥ yaḥ kṛtavān śrutyarthavivṛttiṁ hariḥ |
yadādīnāṁ kalerjagmuḥ sapta triṁśat śatāni (3700) vai |
chatvāriṁśat (40) samāśchānyāḥ tadā bhāṣyamidaṁ kṛtam ||

"During the reign of the illustrious King Vikramārka (Vikramāditya), Harisvāmi, who held the office of Dharmādhyakṣa (chief of religious affairs), wrote a commentary on the Śatapatha Brāhmaṇa (a Vedic scripture). A golden platform was constructed by King Vikramārka himself, and the officer in charge of charitable donations (Dānādhyakṣa), named Hari, composed a commentary clarifying the meaning of that sacred text. This commentary was written when 3,740 years of Kali had passed. Here Kali means Saptarṣi Samvat 3776."

Therefore, as per the citation, the renowned Vedic scholars Hariswami and Skandswami lived 3776-3740= 36 B.C. They were contemporaries of the illustrious Śakārī Vikramaditya II of Ujjain.

The Epoch of Kalidasa of Jyotirvidābharaṇa

51/7/28th Kali/3068 or 33 BC

Several scholars believe that the Vikramāditya II of Malavā also patronized nine 'gems' or Navaratnas. These Navaratnas are described by Kalidasa, the author of the work titled 'Jyotirvidābharaṇa,' which was written in the 3068 Kali year, which corresponds to 33 BC. Regarding his own time-period, Kalidasa mentions as follows:

वर्षे सिन्धुदर्शनांबर गुणैः (3068) याते कलौ सम्मिते ।
मासे माधव संज्ञिते च विहितो ग्रंथ क्रियोपक्रमः ॥

varṣe sindhudarśanāṁbara guṇaiḥ (3068) yāte kalau sammite |
māse mādhava saṁjñite cha vihito graṁtha kriyopakramaḥ ||

That is, this work was composed by me in Vaiśākha month when 3068 years of Kaliyuga.

Consequently, the author of Jyotirvidābharaṇa, Kālidāsa, composed his work during the period of 3101-3068, which corresponds to 33 BC. It is indisputable that Kālidāsa was a contemporary of Vikramāditya II, who emerged victorious against the Śaka ruler of Rukma country. As recorded in Kālidāsa's Jyotirvidābharaṇa (22.14), Vikramāditya II's conquests encompassed Draviḍa, Lāṭa, Vaṅga, Gauda, Gurjara, Dhārā, and Kāmboja.

Furthermore, he successfully defeated other Śaka rulers and initiated the Śaka Saṁvat (Jyotirvidābharaṇa, 22.13). In this context, Kālidāsa referred to Vikramāditya II as Vikramārka. Additionally, he mentions that Śaṅku, Suvāk, Vararuchi, Maṇi, Aṅgudatta, Viṣṇu, Trilochana, Hari, Ghaṭakharpara, Amarsingh, and other renowned poets were honored as members of Virkama's council.

शङ्कुः सुवाग्वररुचिर्मणिरङ्गुदत्तो जिष्णुस्त्रिलोचनहरो घटखर्पराख्यः।
अन्येऽपि सन्ति कवयोऽमरसिंहपूर्वा यस्यैव विक्रमनृपस्य सभासदोऽमी।। 22.8
śaṅkuḥ suvāg-vara-rucir maṇir aṅgu-datto
jiṣṇus trilocana-haro ghaṭa-kharparākhyaḥ |
anye'pi santi kavayo'mara-siṃha-pūrvā
yasyaiva vikrama-nṛpasya sabhāsado'mī || *22.8* ||

In addition to the above-mentioned poets, he counts the names of astronomers such as Satyāchārya, Varāhamihira (different from the famous one), Śrutasena (Jain Śvetāmbara astronomer), Bādarāyaṇa, Maṇittha, Kumārasingha and he himself to have graced the court of King Vikram.

सत्यो वराहमिहिरः श्रुतसेननामा श्रीबादरायणमणित्थकुमारसिंहाः।
श्री विक्रमार्कनृपसंसदि सन्ति चैते श्रीकालतन्त्रकवयस्त्वपरे मदाद्याः।। 22.9
satyo varāha-mihiraḥ śrutasena-nāmā
śrī-bādarāyaṇa-maṇittha-kumāra-siṃhāḥ |
śrī-vikramārka-nṛpa-saṃsadi santi caite
śrī-kāla-tantra-kavayas tv apare madādyāḥ || *22.9* ||

In the Jyotirvidābharaṇa (22.19), he further reiterates the

presence of renowned scholars such as Śaṅku and astronomers like Varāhamihira in the court of Vikramārka. He identifies himself as 'nṛpasakhā,' indicating that he belonged to the same age group as the king Vikramāditya.

शंक्वादिपंडितवराः कवयस्त्वनेके। ज्योतिर्विदश्च प्रभवं च वराहपूर्वा॥
श्रीविक्रमार्कनृपसंसदि मान्यबुद्धिः। तैरप्यहं नृपसखा किल कालिदासः॥ 22.19

Śaṅkvādi-panditavarāḥ kavayastvaneke
jyotirvidaśca prabhavañca Varhapūrvāḥ
Śri-Vikramārka-nṛpa-saṁsadi mānyabuddhiḥ
tairapyaham nṛpasakhā kila Kālidāsaḥ

Furthermore, in the subsequent verse (Jyotirvidābharaṇa, 22.20), he feigns to demonstrate his identity as the renowned Kalidasa, celebrated for his compositions of Meghadutam and the other three kāvyas.

Interestingly, in the verse 22.10, he quotes the names of Dhanvantari, Kṣapaṇaka, Amarsingha, Śaṅku, Vetālabhaṭṭa, Ghaṭakharpara, Kālidasa, and famous Varāhamihira and Vararuchi as Nine gems "Navaratnas" of the court of Vikram king. The verse goes like this:

धन्वन्तरि क्षपणक अमरसिंह शंकु जेतालभट्ट घटखर्पर कालिदासः।
ख्यातो वराहमिहिरो नृपतेः सभायां रत्नानि वै वररुचिर्नव विक्रमस्य॥ 22.10

dhanvantari kṣapaṇaka amarasiṁha śaṁku jetālabhaṭṭa ghaṭakharpara kālidāsaḥ I
khyāto varāhamihiro nṛpateḥ sabhāyāṁ ratnāni vai vararuchirnava vikramasya II

In the preceding verse, two notable points emerge. The author referred to as Kalidasa, known for his compositions such as Meghaduta, as a Navaratna, is different from present author Kalidasa. Notably, the style and standard of verses of this Kalidas diverge from those of Kalidasa of Meghadutam. Additionally, the author refers to Varahamihira as "famous Varahamihira," indicating that the Varahamihira included in the Navaratnas differed from the Varahamihira mentioned in verse 22.19. Furthermore, while verse 22.8 quotes Vararuchi as a poet, Vararuchi among Nine Gems was primarily recognized as a grammarian.

The analysis presented demonstrates that the names Kalidasa, Vararuchi, and the renowned Varamihitra are distinct from the same names used in the court of King Vikram II. This analysis also reveals the existence of two Kalidasas, Vararuchis and Varahamihiras. Notably, the Kalidasa of Meghadutam, the famous Varahamihira, and the grammarian Vararuchi were not among the nine gems of King Vikram II. Instead, they belonged to King Vikramadiya I, who flourished in the city of Ujjain in the Mālava region around 717-657 BC. Conversely, King Vikramāditya II ruled over Ujjain or Avanti in Malwa during the period of 82-19 BC. Notably, both Vikramādityas successfully fought against the Śakas. King Vikramāditya I also ascended to the position of sovereign ruler of Mālava Gaṇa by defeating 96 Śaka Kṣatrapas.

The Epoch of Śri Harshavardhan of Puṣpabhuti Dynasty

51/7/28th Kali/2645 or 457 BC

Indian history has two kings named Harsha. First one is Śri Harsha of Puṣpabhūti dynasty, who was also known as Harshavardhana. According to Harshacharita of Bāṇabhaṭṭa, Puspabhūti is the originator of Pushpabhuti dynasty of North India. According to Alberuni, Śri Harsha founded an era in 457 BCE. Three grants of Śri Harsha are dated in Saṁvat 22 (435 BC), 23 (434 BC) and 25 (432 BC). Alberuni, who came to India around 1017-1031 AD, states that the Śri Harsha era was founded 400 years before the Vikrama era (57 BC):

'The Hindus believe regarding Śri Harsha....... His era is used in Mathura and the country of Kanauj. Between Śri Harsha and Vikramāditya there is an interval of 400 years, as I have been told by some of the inhabitants of that region. However, in the Kashmirian calendar, I have read that Śri Harsha was 664 years later than Vikramāditya. In the face of this discrepancy, I am in perfect uncertainty, which to the present moment has not yet been cleared up by any trustworthy information.'

'Now, the year 400 of Yazdajird, which we have chosen as a gauge (1031 AD), corresponds to the following years of the Indian eras:

1. To the year 1488 of the era of Śri Harsha (1488-1031=457 BC)

2. To the year 1088 of the era of Vikramāditya (1031-1088=57 BC)

It is evident from Alberuni's account that the Śri Harsha era commenced in 457 BC. He also calculated that the year 1031 AD corresponds to the year 1488 in Śri Harsha era. He simply stated that according to some Kashmirian sources, one Śri Harsha was ruling 664 years after Vikramāditya. Therefore, Alberuni expressed his inability to explain why the people of Mathura and Kanauj believed the existence of the rule of Śri Harsha in 457 BC whereas some Kashmirian sources tell us that Śri Harsha ruled 664 years after Vikramāditya i.e. 606. In fact, Alberuni failed to recognize the second Harsha of 606 AD of Kashmirian source.

Indian tradition doesn't mention any era of 606 AD started by Śri Harsha who ruled 664 years after Vikramāditya, but Western historians concocted the myth that Śri Harsha was supposed to have started an era from about 606 AD. Thus, they clubbed Śri Harshavardhan son of Prabhakaravardhan (457 BC) and Śri Harsha son of Rasal (606 AD) into one person and omitted the name of Śri Harshavardhan or Harsha Vikramaditya from Indian history and created a non-existent era of 606 AD.

The rulers of Puṣpabhūti dynasty flourished in the 6th and 5th centuries BC and Śri Harsha was the most illustrious king of this dynasty. Probably, Puṣpabhūti was the progenitor of this dynasty as mentioned in the Harshacharita of Bāṇabhaṭṭa. According to the genealogy given in the grants of Śri Harsha, Naravardhana was the earliest known king of the Puṣpabhūti dynasty who was succeeded by his son Rājyavardhana I and subsequently by his grandson Ādityavardhana. Prabhākaravardhana, the son of Ādityavardhana had two sons, Rājyavardhana II & Śri Harsha and one daughter, Rājyaśri.

The chronology of the Puāpabhūti dynasty may be detailed as under:

1. Naravardhana	580-550 BC
2. Rājyavardhana I	550-520 BC
3. Ādityavardhana	520-500 BC
4. Prabhākaravardhana	500-465 BC

Prabhakaravardhana was the first sovereign king of the Puspabhuti dynasty as he was referred to as 'Maharajadhiraja' in the inscriptions. He defeated the Hunas, the kings of Sindh, Gandhara, Gurjara, Lāṭa and Mālava as mentioned in Harshacharita. His capital was Sthāṇiśvara or Thanesar located in Kurukshetra district of Haryana. It seems that the Puspabhutis had family relations with the Mālava Guptas.

Mahāsena-Guptadevi, the mother of Prabhākaravardhana, was the daughter of Mālava Gupta king Mahāsenagupta (Mahāsenaguptadevyāmutpannaḥ). Later, Mahāsenagupta also sent his sons Kumāragupta and Mādhavagupta to live as companions to the Puṣpabhūti princes. Historians wrongly called the Mālava Guptas as the Later Guptas; in reality, their period was prior to the rise of the Imperial Guptas. Therefore, the Mālava Guptas must be referred to as the Early Guptas. The Aphsad inscription of the Mālava Gupta king Ādityasena, the son of Mādhavagupta is dated in Śri Harsha era 66 (391 BC).

5. Rājyavardhana II	465-458 BC
6. Śri Harsha or Harshavardhana	457-420 BC

The Epoch of Śri Harsha (Siharsha) son of Rasal

51/7/28th Kali/3708 or 606 AD

The Chinese pilgrim Hiuen Tsang visited India between 629 AD and 645 AD, whereas Śri Harsha ruled in the 5th century BC, more than 1000 years before him. Thus, Hiuen Tsang cannot be a contemporary of Śri Harshavarshana (457 BC). Western historians and their followers completely distorted the historical account given by Hiuen Tsang, because they believed that Śri Harsha flourished in the 7th century AD. Hiuen Tsang must have visited the court of King Siharasa, i.e Śri Harsha (606 AD), the son of Rasal mentioned in the Chacha Nāmā and the same king Siharasa (Śri Harsha) was mentioned in some Kashmirian sources who ruled 664 years after Vikramāditya (57 BC). In this context, we shall have a relook in the statement of Alberuni who came to India around 1017 to 1031 AD. He states:

> 'The Hindus believe regarding Śri Harsha....... His era is used in Mathura and the country of Kanauj. Between Śri Harsha and Vikramāditya there is an interval of 400 years, as I have been told bysome of the inhabitants of that region. However, in the Kashmirian calendar, I have read that Śri Harsha was 664 years later than Vikramāditya. In the face of this discrepancy, I am in perfect uncertainty, which to the present moment has not yet been cleared up by any trustworthy information.'

Alberuni simply quotes some Kashmirian sources, according to which one Śri Harsha ruled 664 years after Vikramāditya (57 BC). Alberuni was not able to understand the differing statements of the people of Mathura and Kanauj and Kashmirian sources. Kashmirian sources are not against the knowledge of people of Kannauj, rather they make it clear that a king Śri Harsha flourished 664 years after Vikramāditya (57 BC). Here it is pertinent to point out that Kashmirian sources never say that Śri Harsh known to them ever started an era 606 AD as it is speculated by some confused historians. On the other hand, Kannauj and Mathura sources informed Alberuni of Śri Harsha who started an era 400 years before Vikramāditya (57 BC). So Alberuni's statement informs us about the existence of two Śri Harshas who lived in different time spans like 457 BC and 606 AD. But confused historians clubbed both Śri Harshas into one who flourished in 606 AD and made a mess of the whole history demoting the facts by 1000 years.

According to the Chacha-Nāmā (Shyam Manohar, 1 977:38-39) Rai Harachandra, the son of Jathal, was ruling at Kanauj during the time of Muhammad bin Kasim (695-715 AD). Kasim sent his emissary to Kanauj and coerced Harachandra to acknowledge his suzerainty and embrace Islam. But Harachandra replied, 'This country (of Kanauj) for about one thousand and six hundred years has been under our rule. During our sovereignty, no enemy has ever dared to encroach on our boundary. Now go back to your master and tell him that we are ready for war.' The generals of Kasim urged him to declare war but Kasim died before any such war could take place. According to the Chacha-Nāmā, Kasim killed the Hindu-king Dāhir and annexed Sindh and Multan. He sent the daughters of King Dāhir as presents to the Khalifa. The daughters of King Dāhir tricked the Khalifa into believing that Kasim had already violated them. The furious Khalifa ordered Kasim to be stitched in ox hides which resulted in his death.

The Chacha-Nāmā clearly tells us that it was King Harachandra who was ruling at Kanauj around 715 AD and not Yaśovarman. Therefore, the Jain sources must have used Vikrama era of epoch 717 BC and not of 57 BC. Thus, Yaśovarman also flourished in the 1st century AD and cannot be a contemporary of Mohammad bin Kasim. King Harachandra was a contemporary of Kasim in the 8th century. Chacha-Nāmā also tells us that a king named Siharasa, the son of Rasal, was ruling in Kanauj in the 7th century during the reign of Chandra, the king of Sind. The Rai dynasty was supplanted by a Brāhmaṇa minister Chacha in Sind. Chandra, the brother of Chacha, succeeded him. King Dāhir was the son of the Brahmaṇa king Chacha.

17. Rulers of Hastinapur/Indraprastha/Delhi

Pāṇḍava Dynasty

51/7/28th Dvāpara/863963–28th Kali /1734
or 3137 BC–1368 BC

Yudhiṣṭhira

51/7/28th Dvāpara/863963/Mārgaśīrṣa Pūrṇimā 28th Kali 1/
Śrāvaṇa S-9
or
18 April, 3136 BC–8 August, 3101 BC

Yudhiṣṭhira regained his kingdom on December 20, 3137 BC, a Saturday on the Pūrṇimā. He ruled the earth from Indraprastha and established it as the capital of the Pāṇḍava dynasty after the victory in the Mahābhārata war. Here are some notable events that occurred during his reign:

Aśvamedha Yajña: On Chaitra Pūrṇimā, or 18 April, 3136 BC, Monday, an Aśvamedha Yajña was performed by Yudhiṣṭhira. This fact is confirmed by the following references.

चैत्र्यां हि पौर्णमास्यां च तव दीक्षा भविष्यति।
संभाराः संभ्रियन्तां ते यज्ञार्थं पुरुषर्षभ॥ महा. 14.71.4
chaitrayāṁ hi paurṇamāsyāṁ cha tava dīkṣā bhaviṣyati /
saṁbhārāḥ saṁbhriyantāṁ te yajñārthaṁ puruṣarṣabha //
Mahā. 14.71.4

Vyāsa informs Yudhiṣṭhira, "On the full moon day of Chaitra, you will be consecrated. Please ensure that all the necessary items for the Yajña are prepared, O most esteemed among men."

आगच्छेथा महाराज परां चैत्रीमुपस्थिताम्।
तदाश्वमेधो भविता धर्मराजस्य धीमतः॥। महा. 14.75.25
āgachchhethā mahārāja parāṁ chaitrīmupasthitām /
tadāśvamedho bhavitā dharmarājasya dhīmataḥ //
Mahā. 14.75.25

Arjuna, having defeated Vajradatta in the Aśvamedha yajna, invites him to attend the full moon day of the upcoming Chaitra month. At that time, the wise Dharmarāja will perform the Aśvamedha Yajña.

Retiring of Dhritrastra, Gandhari and Kunti to forest: On Kārtika Pūrṇīmā, or 10th October 3136 BC., Monday Dhṛtarāṣṭra along with Gāndhārī and Kuntī retired to the forest.

गान्धारी सहितो धीमानभिनन्द्य यथाविधि ।
कार्त्तिक्यां कारयित्वेष्टिं ब्राह्मणैर्वेदपारगैः ॥
अग्निहोत्रं पुरस्कृत्य वल्कलाजिनसंवृतः ।
वधूपरिवृतो राजा निर्ययौ भवनात्ततः ॥ महा. 15.21.2; 3

gāndhārī sahito dhīmānabhinandya yathāvidhi |
kārttikyāṁ kārayitveṣṭiṁ brāhmaṇairvedapāragaiḥ ||
agnihotraṁ puraskṛtya valkalājinasaṁvṛtaḥ |
vadhūparivṛto rājā niryayau bhavanāttataḥ ||

Mahā. 15.21.2; 3

The wise king Dhṛtarāṣṭra, accompanied by Gāndhārī, cordially invited the Pāṇḍvas and expressed his congratulations. Subsequently, he completed a small yajña on the full Moon Day of Kārtika, guided by Brahmins who were well-versed in scriptures, adhering strictly to the prescribed rules. The king also participated in the customary Agnihotra ceremony and, adorned in cloth made of bark and wool, departed the palace in the company of his queen.

Here's a chronological list of other rulers of the Pāṇḍava dynasty who ruled Hastinapur after King Yudhiṣṭhira. Yudhiṣṭhira abdicated on the 7th of Śrāvaṇa, in the year 3101 BC, which corresponds to August 8th, 3101 BC, a Wednesday. Subsequently, Prikshita was crowned the king of the Kuru Dynasty.

Parikshita

51/7/28th Kali/1/60
(8 August, 3101 BC – 18 August 3041 BC)

Parikshita, the son of Abhimanyu, who met his end in the Kurukshetra battle, was born in the same year. At the age of 36, he ascended to the throne as the emperor, following Yudhiṣṭhira's abdication. This year is considered the beginning of Kali Yuga. Parikshita diligently continued the consolidation of the empire initiated by his father. During his reign, the compilation and edition of sacred scriptures by the esteemed school of sages of Vedavyasa flourished. Sage Śuka, the son of Vedavyāsa, played a pivotal role in narrating the Bhāgavata Purāṇa, meticulously incorporating the figurative story of Astronomical Krishna. In the nineteenth year of his reign, King Parikshita engaged in a battle and successfully annexed Kashmir to his empire. He bestowed the title of king upon his second son, Harnadeva, at the time of his passing. Consequently, the Pandava dynasty was established in Kashmir in the year 3041 BC. Parikshita ruled for nearly six decades, with Hastinapur serving as his capital. Tragically, his reign came to an end due to a snakebite.

Janamejaya

51/7/28thKali/60–145

(18thAugust, 3041 BC–25 Dec. 2957 BC)

Janamejaya, the son of Parikshita, ruled the earth for 84 years, 7 months, and 23 days from Hastinapur. After the demise of King Parikshita, his son Janamejaya ascended to the throne and became the emperor.

King Janamejaya, whose father had perished from a snakebite, performed the Sarpa Yajna to eliminate as many snakes as possible.

In 3013 BC, after the 89th year of Jayābhyudaya Yudhiṣṭhira Śaka, commonly known as Kali, King Janamejaya bestowed two gift deeds upon the temples of Rama and Seeta, situated on the banks of the river Tungabhadra, and the temple of Kedarnath nestled in the northern Himalayas. These gift deeds, inscribed on copper plates, hold the distinction of being the oldest known inscriptions that employ the Jayābhyudaya Yudhiṣṭhira Śaka, also known as Kali 1 or 3101 BC.

Both the inscriptions written in Sanskrit on copper plates are about the gift of land bestowed upon Emperor Janamejaya during the 28th year of his reign on the New Moon Day of the Pausha month, which falls on December 26, 3013 BC (Julian calendar). This event occurred during the pūrṇimānta months, known as Plavanga Samvatsara. Here are the calculations:

26th Dec. 3013 BC,	Pauṣa Amāvasyā (Pūrṇimānta)
10th Jan. 3013 BC	Pauṣa Pūrṇimā
13th Jan. 3013 BC	The sun ingressed into Makara sign
24th Jan. 3013 BC	Māgha Amāvasyā

The gifts were crafted at two distinct locations: one in Kiṣkindhā and another in Kedārnāth. Remarkably, the year of Kali and other specific details of the day were precisely identical in both the inscriptions. While one of the inscriptions has been discovered by the Archaeological Department, the other was unearthed by a devoted follower of Kedārnāth who diligently recorded the contents of the copper plate preserved in Kedārnāth to this day (over 5000 years old). The whole record of grant given in Kedārnāth is given hereunder with Roman transliteration and English Translation.

"स्वस्तिश्री विजयाभ्युदययुधिष्ठिर शके प्लवंगाख्ये एकोननवतितमवत्सरे सहसिमासि अमावास्यायां सोमवासरे श्रीमन्महाराजाधिराजपरमेश्वर वैयाघ्रपद-गोत्रज श्रीजनमेजयभूपो इंद्रप्रस्थनगरीसिंहासनस्थः सकलवर्णाश्रमधर्मप्रतिपालको उत्तरहिमालये श्रीकेदारक्षेत्रं तत्रत्यमुनय उषामठस्य श्रीगोस्वामिआनंदलिंगजंगमाय श्रीमच्छिश्यनज्ञान लिङ्गजङ्गमद्वाराराधितश्रीकेदारनाथस्य पूजार्थं दत्तवंतः चतुस्सीमा परिमितिक्रमः। पूर्वभागे दक्षिणवाहिनी मंदाकिनी । पश्चिमदक्षिणभागे क्षीरगंगा उत्तरपश्चिमे मधुगंगा, पूर्वोत्तरभागे स्वर्गद्वारनदी, दक्षिणे सरस्वतीमंदाकिन्योः संगमः, एतन्मध्ये श्रीकेदारक्षेत्रं भवच्छिश्यपरंपरया चंद्रार्कपर्यंत निधिनिक्षेप।

svasti-śrī vijayābhyudaya-yudhiṣṭhira-śake plavaṅgākhye ekonanavatitama-vatsare sahasi-māsi amāvāsyāyāṃ soma-vāsare śrīman-mahārājādhirāja-parameśvara vaiyāghra-pada-gotraja śrī-janamejaya-bhūpo indraprastha-nagarī-siṃhāsana-sthaḥ sakala-varṇāśrama-dharma-pratipālako uttara-himālaye śrī-kedāra-

kṣetraṃ tatratya-munayuṣā-maṭhasya śrī-gosvāmī-ānanda-liṅga-jaṅgamāya śrīmac-chishya-najñāna-liṅga-jaṅgama-dvārārādhita-śrī-kedāra-nāthasya pūjārthaṃ dattavantaḥ catuḥ-sīmā parimiti-kramaḥ — pūrva-bhāge dakṣiṇa-vāhinī mandākinī, paścima-dakṣiṇa-bhāge kṣīra-gaṅgā, uttara-paścime madhu-gaṅgā, pūrva-uttara-bhāge svarga-dvāra-nadī, dakṣiṇe sarasvatī-mandākinyoḥ saṅgamaḥ, etan-madhye śrī-kedāra-kṣetraṃ bhava-chishya-paramparayā candrārka-paryanta nidhinikṣepa.

"Auspicious prosperity!

In the Vijayābhyudaya Yudhishṭhira Era, in the year named Plavaṅga, being the eighty-ninth year, in the month of Sahasa, on the new moon day, a Monday —

The illustrious Great King of Kings, Supreme Lord, of the Vaiyāghrapada lineage, King Janamejaya, seated on his throne in the city of Indraprastha, protector of the duties of all classes and stages of life (varṇāśrama-dharma), has made a donation (land grant) in the northern Himalaya region, at the sacred field of Śrī Kedāra (Kedārakṣetra).

The gift is made to Śrī Gosvāmī Ānanda-liṅga Jaṅgama, of the Uṣā Monastery, and to his disciple Śrī Jñāna-liṅga Jaṅgama, for the purpose of worship (pūjārtha) of Śrī Kedāranātha, the Lord who is devoutly worshipped by them.

The boundaries (catuḥ-sīmā parimitikramaḥ) of the donated land are as follows:

On the east, the south-flowing Mandākinī River,

On the south-west, the Kṣīra-gaṅgā (Milky Ganga),

On the north-west, the Madhu-gaṅgā,

On the north-east, the Svargadvāra River (the River of Heaven ' s Gate), and on the south, the confluence (saṅgama) of the Sarasvatī and Mandākinī rivers.

Within these boundaries lies the Śrī Kedāra sacred region, which, along with its deposits, waters, and treasures, is to remain in the possession of the monks and their line of disciples, enduring for as long as the sun and moon endure."

The decree of the king, Śri Janamejaya of the Śri Kuru Vaṁśa, to the Kedarnath temple, as written in the letter, is briefly as follows:

In the 89th year of Jayābhyudaya Yudhiṣṭhira Śaka (3101 BC), during the auspicious Jovial month of Plavaṅga, In the Pauṣa Month, on the Amāvasyā Day (New Moon Day), on a Monday, (26th Dec. 3013 BC) Śri Janamejaya, ruler of the earth (king), born in the Gotra of Vaiagrani Vayaghra, enthroned in the city of Indraprastha, the protector of all Varṇas and Āśramas (classes and stages), made a gift to Śri Goswami Anandalinga Jaṅgma Swami of Usha Math located in the Kedar region of North Himalaya through his disciple Śri Jñāna Liṅga Jaṅgama for the worship of Kedārnath surrounded by four rivers: Mandākini flowing to the east, Kṣirganga flowing to the southwest, Svargadvāra flowing to the northwest, and the confluence of Saraswati and Mandākini flowing to the south. The Kedāra region is situated in the middle of these rivers.

The whole record of grant gifted in Kiṣkindhā is given hereunder with original Sanskrit, Roman transliteration and English translation.

" श्रीकुरुवंशावतंस श्रीजनमेजयभूपालानां दानशासनपत्रं ।

śrī-kuru-vaṃśā-vataṃsa śrī-janamejaya-bhūpālānāṃ dāna-śāsana-patram.

॥ पांतु वो जलदश्यामाः शार्ङ्गज्याघातकर्कशाः ।

त्रैलोक्यमंडपस्तम्भाश्चत्वारो हरिबाहवः ॥

pāntu vo jalada-śyāmāḥ śārṅga-jyā-ghāta-karkaśāḥ |

trailokya-maṇḍapa-stambhāś catvāro hari-bāhavaḥ ||

"स्वस्तिश्री जयाभ्युदये युधिष्टिर शके प्लवांख्ये (ख्य) एकोननवती (८९) वत्सरे सहस्यमासि अमावास्यायां सोमवासरे

svasti-śrī jayābhyudaye yudhiṣṭhira-śake plavākhye ekona-

navati (89) vatsare sahasya-māsi amāvāsyāyāṃ soma-vāsare

श्रीमन्महाराजाधिराजपरमेश्वरो वैयग्रणी वैयाघ्र (?) पाद गोत्रजः श्रीजनमेजयभूपः किष्किंधानगर्यां सिंहासनस्थः

śrīman-mahārājādhirāja-parameśvaro vaiyagraṇī vaiyāghrapāda-gotrajaḥ śrī-janamejaya-bhūpaḥ kiṣkindhā-nagaryāṃ siṃhāsana-sthaḥ

सकलवर्णाश्रमधर्मप्रतिपालकः पश्चिमदेशस्थ सीतापुरवृकोदरक्षेत्रे तत्रव्य मुनिवृंदमठस्य

sakala-varṇāśrama-dharma-pratipālakaḥ paścima-deśa-stha-sītāpura-vṛkodara-kṣetre tatravya muni-vṛnda-maṭhasya

गरुडवाहनतीश्रीमच्छिप्यकै कयनाधैरराधितसीतारामस्यपूजार्थं कृतभूदानशासनम्

garuḍa-vāhana-tīrtha-śrīmac-chipyakai-kayanā-dhair ārādhita-sītā-rāmasya pūjārthaṃ kṛta-bhū-dāna-śāsanam

अस्मत्प्रपितामहयुधिष्ठिराधिष्ठितमुनिवृंद- क्षेत्रस्य चतुःसीमापरिमितिक्रमः -

asmat-prapitāmaha-yudhiṣṭhira-ādhiṣṭhita-muni-vṛnda-kṣetrasya catuḥ-sīmā-parimitikramaḥ —

"पूर्वभागे ....उत्तरवाहिन्यास्तुंगभद्रयाः पश्चिमे दक्षिणभागे अगस्त्याश्रमसंगमादुत्तरे । पश्चिमे पाषाणनद्याः पूर्वे । उतरभागे भिन्ननद्या दक्षिणे।

pūrva-bhāge ... uttara-vāhinyāstuṅga-bhadrāyāḥ, paścime dakṣiṇa-bhāge agastya-āśrama-saṅgamād uttare; paścime pāṣāṇa-nadyāḥ pūrve; uttara-bhāge bhinna-nadyā dakṣiṇe.

ये (ए)तन्मध्यस्थितमुनिवृंदक्षेत्रं भवच्छिष्यपरंपराचंद्रार्कपर्यंतं निधिनिक्षेपजल पाषाणाच्छिण्या (?) गामिसिद्धसाध्यतेजः स्वाम्यसहितं स्वबुध्या ऽनुकूल्येनाऽस्मता पित्रृणां विष्णुलोकप्राप्त्यर्थं

ye tan-madhya-sthita-muni-vṛnda-kṣetraṃ bhava-chishya-paramparā-candrārka-paryantaṃ nidhinikṣepa-jala-pāṣāṇa-cchinnya gāmi-siddha-sādhya-tejaḥ-svāmyasahitaṃ sva-budhyā'nukūlyenā'smatā pitṛṇāṃ viṣṇu-loka-prāpty-arthaṃ

हरिहरसन्निधावुपरागसमये सहिरण्येन तुङ्गभद्राजलधारापूर्वकं क्षेत्रं यतिहस्ते दत्तो (तवान्, अ)स्म्यहं ।

hari-hara-sannidhau uparāga-samaye sa-hiraṇyena tuṅga-bhadrā-jala-dhārā-pūrvakaṃ kṣetraṃ yati-haste datto'smyahaṃ.

एतद्धर्मसाधनस्य साक्षिणः ॥

etat-dharma-sādhanasya sākṣiṇaḥ.

॥ आदित्यचंद्रावनिलोऽनलश्च द्यौर्भूमिरापोहृदयं यमश्च ।
अहश्च रात्रिश्च उभे च संध्ये धर्मश्च जानाति नरस्य वृत्तं ॥ २

āditya-candrāvanilo'nalaś ca dyaur bhūmir āpo hṛdayaṃ ya maś ca /
ahaś ca rātriś ca ubhe ca saṃd hye dharmaś ca jānāti narasya vṛttam //

दानपालनयोर्मध्ये दानाच्छ्रेयोऽनुपालनं ।
दानात्स्वर्गमवाप्नोति पालनाद् द्विगुणं फलं ॥ ३
dāna-pālanayor madhye dānāc chreyo'nupālanam /
dānāt svargam avāpnoti pālanād dviguṇaṃ phalam // 3 //

स्वदत्ताद्विगुणं पुण्यं परदत्तानुपालने ।
परदत्तापहारेण स्वदतं निष्फलं भवेत् ॥ ४

svadattād dviguṇaṃ puṇyaṃ paradattānupālane /
paradattāpahāreṇa svadattaṃ niṣphalaṃ bhavet // 4 //

मद्दत्ता पुत्रिका ज्ञेया पितृदत्ता सहोदरी ।
अन्यदत्ता तु जननी दत्तभूमिं परित्यजेत् ॥ ५

maddattā putrikā jñeyā pitṛdattā sahodarī /
anyadattā tu jananī dattabhūmiṃ parityajet // 5 //

अन्यैस्तु छर्दितं छद्वे श्वभिश्च छर्दितं न तु ।
ततः कष्टो ततो नीचः स्वयं दत्तापहारकः ॥ ६

anyais tu charditaṃ chadve śvabhiś ca charditaṃ na tu /
tataḥ kaṣṭo tato nīcaḥ svayaṃ dattāpahārakaḥ // 6 //

स्वदत्तां परदत्तां वा ब्रह्मवृत्तिं हरेत यः ।
षष्टिर्वर्षसहस्राणि विष्ठायां जायते कृमिः ॥ ७

svadattāṃ paradattāṃ vā brahmavṛttiṃ haret yaḥ /
ṣaṣṭir varṣa-sahasrāṇi viṣṭhāyāṃ jāyate kṛmiḥ // 7 //

This inscription records a royal land grant (दानशासनपत्रम्) issued by King Janamejaya of the Kuru dynasty (श्रीकुरुवंशावतंस).

"May you be protected by the four arms of Lord Hari — dark as rainclouds, strong as the thunder of His bow, the very pillars supporting the three worlds.

Auspicious prosperity! In the Jayābhyudaya Yudhishṭhira

Era, in the year named *Plava*, being the eighty-ninth year, in the month of *Sahasya* (likely *Phālguna*), on the new-moon day, which fell on a Monday...

The illustrious *Mahārājādhirāja Parameśvara* (Great King of Kings, Supreme Lord), Janamejaya—descendant of the Viyāghrapāda lineage, and lord of the Kuru dynasty—being seated upon his throne in the city of *Kiṣkindhā*...

Protector of the sacred duties (*dharma*) of all social orders and stages of life (*varṇāśrama*), residing in the western province, at Sītāpura in the holy field of Vṛkodara (Bhīma), within which lies the monastery of the assembly of sages (*muni-vṛnda-maṭha*).

For the worship of Śrī Sītā-Rāma, who is devoutly served by the revered Chipyakai and Kayanā ascetics at the sacred *Garuḍavāhana Tīrtha*, this land-donation charter (*bhū-dāna-śāsana*) was made.

The boundaries of the *Muni-vṛnda field*—once established by my great-grandfather, King Yudhishṭhira—are as follows:

On the east—(bounded by) the northern-flowing river Tuṅgabhadrā;
on the south—by the confluence near Sage Agastya's hermitage;
on the west—by the Pāṣāṇa river;
and on the north—by the Bhinnā river.

This central area of the Muni-vṛnda field, along with all its deposits, waters, stones, treasures, fixed and moving properties, rights, and spiritual merits — is hereby granted to you and your line of disciples, enduring as long as the sun and moon, for the purpose of securing the attainment of Viṣṇu's world for my ancestors.

In the presence of Lord Hari and Hara (Viṣṇu and Śiva), during the time of a lunar eclipse, this land—together with gold, and sanctified by the waters of the Tuṅgabhadrā river—has been given by me into the hands of the ascetics (yatis).

Let all beings be witnesses to this act of righteousness.

The Sun, Moon, Wind, Fire, Heaven, Earth, Waters, Mind, Yama, Day, Night, both Twilights, and Dharma — all know the deeds of man. (2)

Between giving and preserving a gift, preservation is superior. From giving one attains heaven, from preservation, double merit. (3)

He who guards another's gift earns twice the merit; he who steals another's gift nullifies his own donation. (4)

Land given by me is like my daughter; land given by my father is like my sister; land given by another should be left untouched. (5)

Even food vomited by others may be eaten in dire need,
but not that which has been vomited by dogs;
worse than both, and most degraded of all,
is the man who seizes back land that he himself has given away. (6)

Whoever seizes land given to Brahmins—whether his own or another's—will be reborn as a worm in excrement for 60,000 years. (7)

The decree of the king, Śri Janamejaya of the Śri Kuru Vaṁsa, to the temple of Rāma and Sītā was found on the bank of the river Tuṅgabhadra, is briefly as follows:

In the 89th expired year of Jayabhyudaya Yudhiṣṭhira Śaka (3101 BC), during the Jovial month of Plavanga, In the Pauṣa Month, on the Amāvasyā Day (New Moon Day), on a Monday (26th Dec. 3013 BC), Śri Janamejaya, ruler of the earth (king), born in the Gotra of Vaiagrani Vayāghra, who also represents the imperial throne of Kishkindhā (Hampi), the protector of all Varṇas and Āśramas (classes and stages), in the western city of Sitāpura, in the Vrikodara Kṣetra, for the worship of Sita Rama who are worshipped by the honoured disciple

> Kaikaya of Garuḍavāhana Tīrtha and others of the maṭha of the group of munis, I give in the hands of the Yati, along the Gold besprinkled by waters of Tuṅgabhadrā river, the decree of the donation of land, of the area to the east of the Tuṅgbhadrā river, in the presence of Hari Hara (Viṣṇu and Siva) in the time of uparaga (eclipse), for the attainment of Moksha by my forefathers, in the order of the four boundaries of the Muni Vrinda Kṣetra, established by my great grandfather Yudhiṣṭhira.

Here, the inscription chronicles the antiquary's history. It's evident that both gifts were presented by Janamejaya during the 89th year of Jayabhydaya Yudhiṣṭhira Śaka. Let's clarify that Jayābhydaya Yudhiṣṭhira Śaka commenced in 3101 BC when Yudhiṣṭhira relinquished his throne to Parikshita. During that era, the Plavaṅga year was in vogue. Therefore, it was 3013 BC. The day fell on a Monday and was the New Moon Day of the Pauṣa Month. Consequently, it translates to December 26, 3013 BC, which marked the 28th year of Janamejaya's reign. He ascended to the throne on August 18, 3041 BC (Julian), or July 24, 3041 (Gregorian). The king is depicted seated on both the imperial throne of Indraprastha and Kiṣkindhā, which underscores Janamejaya's rule over the entire Bharat, spanning from north to south. Indraprastha represented the northern region, while Kiṣkindhā (Hampi of Vijayanagar) symbolized the southern region.

In the land gifted to Kiṣkindhā, it is evident that the king is presenting a piece of land established in the name of his great grandfather Yudhiṣṭhira during the solar eclipse as a token of reverence for his ancestors. It is customary to make offerings and gifts during the solar eclipse to honor one's forefathers.

During the reign of King Janamejaya, the sage Vaiśampāyana, belonging to the Vedavyāsa school, narrated the Mahābhārata. This was the second narration under the name Bharat and covered events up to the time of King Janmejaya. The dates are given according to the Gregorian calendar.

2957 BC Dec. 25 (Julian) or 2957 BC Dec.1 (Gregorian)– 2875 BC March 1: Ashvamedha ruled the earth from Indraprastha. He was the last ruler of Hastinapur, who used to take tributes from the rulers of various countries. Afterwards, the rulers were confined to Bharat, and the Pāṇḍava empire came to an end.

2875 BC March 1 –2786 BC Dec. 24: Dvitīya Rāma ruled Bharat from Indraprastha.

2786 BC Dec. 24 –2704 BC Dec. 28: Chhatramal ruled Bharat from Indraprastha. During Chhatramal's reign, Indraprastha city was ravaged by floods of the Ganges, and the capital was shifted to Kaushambi Puri.

2704 BC Dec. 28 –2629 BC Sept. 10: Chitraratha ruled Bharat from Indraprastha. He started expanding his empire outside Bharat. He invaded many states and annexed them to Indraprastha.

2629 BC Sept. 10 –2553 BC Oct. 17: Duṣṭa Śailya ruled Indraprastha.

2553 BC Oct. 17–2475 BC Feb. 24: Ugrasen started ruling Indraprastha.

2475 BC Feb. 24 – 2396 BC July 3: Śūrasena became the ruler of Indraprastha.

2396 BC July 3 – 2327 BC Jan. 29: Bhuvanpati took over the reins of Indraprastha from Śūrasena.

2327 BC Jan. 29 – 2261 BC March 25: Ranjit became the 12th ruler.

2261 BC March 25 – 2196 BC Aug. 21: Ṛkṣaka ruled Indraprastha.

2196 BC Aug. 21 – 2134 BC July 28: Sukhdev ruled Indraprastha.

2134 BC July 28 – 2082 Sept. 26: Narhari Dev ruled during this period.

2082 Sept. 26 – 2039 BC Oct. 24: Suchiratha ruled.

2039 BC Oct. 24 - 1980 BC Dec. 16: Śūrasena II ruled Indraprastha.

1980 BC Dec. 16 - 1925 BC April 6: Parvatasen ruled during this period.

1925 BC April 6 - 1872 BC May 27: Medhāvī took over the reins of Indraprastha.

1872 BC May 27 -1821 BC Sept. 6: Sonachīr became the 20th ruler of Indraprastha.

1821 BC Sept. 6 - 1773 BC Nov. 16: Bhim Dev ruled Indraprastha.

1773 BC Nov. 16 - 1727 BC Nov. 23: Narihari Dev was 21st ruler.

1727 BC Nov. 23 - 1683 BC March 16: Pūrṇamal was 22nd ruler.

1683 BC March 16 - 1638 BC May 8: Karadavī was the 23rd ruler.

1638 BC May 8 -1587 BC May 31: Alamika ruled as 24th ruler.

1587 BC May 31 - 1548 BC Aug. 31: Udayapal was the 25th ruler.

1548 BC Aug. 31 - 1507 BC Oct. 5: Duvanmal ruled as 26th ruler.

1507 BC Oct. 5 - 1475 BC Oct. 5: Damāt ruled for 32 years as 28th ruler.

1475 BC Oct. 5 - 1417 BC April 27: Bhimpal ruled for 58 years 5 months and 8 days as 29th ruler.

1417 BC April 27 - 1368 BC May 6: Kṣemaka ruled for 48 years 11 months and 21 days as the 30th ruler of Indraprastha. He was the last ruler of Pāṇḍava dynasty. Kṣemaka was killed by his Prime Minister named Viśrvā. After killing Kṣemaka, Viśravā declared him the ruler of Indraprastha. Thus came the end of Pāṇḍava dynasty and beginning of Viśravā dynasty in

Indraprastha.

Rule of Viśravā Dynasty

51/7/28th Kali/1734-2235 or 1368 BC- 867 BC

1368 BC May 6 -1351 BC Jan. 8: Viśravā ruled Indraprastha for 17 years 3 months and 29 days as the first ruler of Viśravā dynasty.

1351 BC Jan. 8 - 1308 BC April 17: Purseni ruled for 42 years 8 months and 21 days.

1308 BC April 17 - 1255 BC June 10: Veersenī ruled for 52 years 10 months and 7 days.

1255 BC June 10 - 1207 BC Sept. 17: Anangśāyī ruled for 47 years 8 months and 23 days.

1207 BC Sept. 17 - 1171 BC Nov. 30: Harijita ruled for 35 years 9 months and 17 days.

1171 BC Nov. 30 - 1127 BC Sept. 7: Paramseni ruled for 44 years 2 months and 23 days.

1127 BC Sept. 7 - 1097 BC June 16: Sukhpātāla ruled for 30 years 2 months and 21 days.

1097 BC June 16 - 1054 BC Aug. 23: Kadruta ruled for 42 years 9 months and 24 days.

1054 BC Aug. 23 - 1022 BC June 9: Sajja ruled for 32 years 2 months and 14 days.

1022 BC June 9 -995 BC Feb. 21: Amarchood ruled for 27 years 3 months and 16 days.

995 BC Feb. 21 - 972 BC Feb. 25: Amīpāl ruled for 22 years 11 months and 25 days.

972 BC Feb. 25 - 946 BC Sept. 13: Daśaratha ruled for 25 years 4 months and 12 days.

946 BC Sept. 13 - 915 BC Jan. 2: Veersāl ruled for 31 years 8 months and 11 days.

915 BC Jan. 2 - 867 BC Dec. 19: Veersāl Sen ruled for 47 years and 14 days. He was killed by his Prime Minister Veermahā Gotam of Magadha who annexed Indraprastha to Magadha on 19 Dec. 867 BC. This was the end of Viśravā dynasty and beginning of Gotam dynasty in Indraprastha.

Rule of Gotam Dynasty

51/7/28th Kali/2235-2691 or 867 BC - 411BC

The rulers of Gotam dynasty ruled Indraprastha from 19th Dec. 867 BC to 13 April 411 BC led by Veermahā who started ruling from Indraprastha from 19th Dec. 867 BC. Hereunder we give the list of various rulers of Gotama dynasty who ruled Indraprastha.

Sr. No.	Name of the King	Rule ends		
1	Raja Veermaha	832 BC	Feb.	11
2	Ajitsingh	804 BC	June	22
3	Sarvadatta	776 BC	March	12
4	Bhuwanpati	760 BC	Nov.	2
5	Veersen	739 BC	Aug.	20
6	Mahipal	698 BC	Dec.	13
7	Shatrushaal	672 BC	Aug.	10
8	Sanghraj	655 BC	May	31
9	Tejpal	626 BC	June	21
10	Manikchand	588 BC	Oct.	31
11	Kamseni	546 BC	May	21
12	Shatrumardan	537 BC	June	8
13	Jeevanlok	508 BC	Aug.	22
14	Harirao	481 BC	Sept.	23
15	Veersen II	446 BC	July	3
16	Adityaketu	411 BC	April	13

Rule of Mayur Dynasty

51/7/28th Kali/2691-3066 or 411 BC - 36 BC

Adityaketu, the last ruler of Indraprastha, was killed by the Dhandhara, the ruler of Prayaga. Indraprastha was annexed to Prayaga. Dhandara came from Mayur dynasty. This was the end of Gotama dynasty and beginning of Mayur dynasty. Dhandara started ruling Indraprastha from Prayaga from 13th April 411 BC.

Hereunder we give the list of various rulers of Mayur dynasty who ruled Indraprastha along with the date of the end of their rules.

Sr. No.	Name of the King	Rule ends		
1	Raja Dhandhar	368 BC	Aug.	20
2	Maharshi	327 BC	May	22
3	Sanrachhi	276 BC	July	3
4	Mahayudha	246 BC	March	26
5	Durnath	217 BC	Oct.	1
6	Jeevanraj	172 BC	July	27
7	Rudrasen	125 B.C	Feb.	27
8	Aarilak	72 BC	April	19
9	Rajpal	36 BC	April	19

Mahanpal

51/7/28th Kali/3066-3080 or 36 BC-22 BC

Rajpal, the last ruler of Mayur dynasty, was killed by his Samant Mahanpal. Thus came the end of Mayur dynasty. Mahanpal ruled Indraprastha for 14 years, i.e. till 19th April, 22 BC.

Vikramāditya of Ujjain

51/7/28th Kali/3080-3121 or 22 BC-19AD

Mahanpal was invaded by Vikramāditya of Ujjain (called Avantika) and was killed on 19 April, 22 BC. Vikramāditya of Ujjain annexed Prayaga and Indraprastha to Ujjain. Vikramāditya came from Panwar Dynasty. He ruled Indraprastha from 19th April, 22 BC to 19th April 19 AD till his death.

Yogi Dynasty of Pattan

51/7/28th Kali/3121-3493or 19 AD-391 AD

The Vikramaditya of Ujjain was later killed by Samudrapal Yogi who was the commander of Śālivāhan of Pattan, present-day Pratisthan of Maharashtra. Śālivāhan handed over the reins of Indraprastha to Samudrapal Yogi on 19 April, 19AD. This was the beginning of the rule of Yogi dynasty in Indraprastha. Śālivāhan of Pattan founded the Śaka era 78 AD

Hereunder we furnish the list of various rulers of Yogi dynasty who ruled Indraprastha along with the date of the end of their rules.

Sr. No.	Name of the King	Rule ends		
1	Samudrapal	73 AD	July	9
2	Chandrapal	109AD	Dec.	13
3	Sahaypal	121AD	April	24
4	Devpal	148AD	June	21
5	Narsighpal	166AD	July	11
6	Sampal	193 AD	Aug.	28
7	Raghupal	215AD	Dec.	23
8	Govindpal	243AD	Feb.	09
9	Amratpal	279 AD	Dec.	22
10	Balipal	292AD	June	8
11	Mahipal	306AD	Feb.	12

12	Haripal	320 AD	Oct.	16
13	Seespal	332 AD	August	29
14	Madanpal	350 AD	July	18
15	Karmpal	366 AD	Sept.	20
16	Vikrampal	391 AD	Sept.	2

Bohra Dynasty of Punjab

51/7/28th Kali/3493-3674 or 391 AD-572 AD

The last king of Yogi Dynasty Raja Vikrampal attacked Malukhchand Bohra of Punjab but was killed by Malukhchand Bohra in the war. He took over the rein of Indraprastha on 16th July 391 AD. His 10 generations ruled Indraprastha for 191 years, 1 month and 16 days. This list of rulers along with the date of the end of their rules is furnished as follows:

Sr. No.	Name of the King	Rule ends		
1	Malukhchand	445 AD	April	29
2	Vikramchand	457 AD	Dec.	11
3	Manakchand	467 AD	Dec.	16
4	Ramchand	471 AD	Nov.	24
5	Harichand	486 AD	Sept.	17
6	Kalyanchand	497 AD	Feb.	21
7	Bhimchand	513 AD	April	30
8	Lovchand	539 AD	Aug.	21
9	Govindchand, Govind Chand had no issue. So after his death, his wife became the ruler of Indraprasth	571 AD	April	12

10	Rani Padmavati	572 AD	April	12

Vairāgi Dynasty

51/7/28th Kali/3674-3724 or 572 AD-622AD

Govind Chand and Padmavati were issueless. So her advisors appointed Hariprem Vairagi for the throne on 12 April, 572 AD and the rule of Vairagi dynasty commenced in Indraprastha. The list of rulers of his generation with the dates of end of their rules is given hereunder:

Sr. No.	Name of the King	Rule ends		
1	Hariprem	579 AD	Sept.	28
2	Govindprem	599 AD	Dec.	6
3	Gopalprem	615 AD	Aug.	3
4	Mahabahu	622 AD	May	2

Adhisena Dynasty of Bengal

51/7/28th Kali/3724-3870 or 622 AD-768 AD

Mahabahu, the last ruler of Vairagi dynasty took Saṁnyāsa. Hearing the news of his Saṁnyāsa, Adhisena of Bengal attacked Indraprastha and annexed it to Bengal on 2 May, 622 AD. Thus the Adhisena dynasty started ruling Indraprastha. The list of rulers of Sena dynasty who ruled Indraprastha is furnished below.

Sr. No.	Name of the King	Rule ends		
1	Raja Adhisena	640 AD	Oct.	23
2	Vilavalsena	653 AD	Feb.	25
3	Keshavsena	668 AD	Oct.	7

4	Madhavsena	681 AD	Feb.	9
5	Mayursena	704 AD	Feb.	5
6	Bhimsena	707 AD	Dec.	14
7	Kalyansena	711 AD	Oct.	23
8	Harisena	718 AD	July	14
9	Kshemsena	730 AD	Aug.	8
10	Narayansena	739 AD	July	23
11	Lakshmisena	741 AD	Oct.	22
12	Damodarsena	768 AD	Aug.	22

Singh Dynasty

51/7/28th Kali/3870-3978 or 768 AD-876 AD

Damodarsena, the last ruler of Sena dynasty, mistreated his Commander Deep Singh who with the help of his army revolted and killed Damodarsen and took over the command of Indraprastha in his hands on 22 August 768 AD. This is how the rule of Singh dynasty commenced in Indraprastha. 6 generations of Deep Singh ruled Indraprastha for 107 years, 6 months and 22 days as follows:

Sr. No.	Name of the King	Rule ends		
1	Deepsingh	785 AD	Oct.	18
2	Rajsingh	800 AD	March	18
3	Ransingh	809 AD	Nov.	29
4	Narsingh	854 AD	Dec.	14
5	Harisingh	868 AD	March	14
6	Jeevansingh	876 AD	March	15

Tomar Dynasty

51/7/28th Kali/3978-4294 or 876 AD-1192AD

Anangapal Tomar, known as Anangpal I, the ruler of Patliputra who belonged to the line of Ksemaka the last ruler of Pandav Dynasty, took over the reins of Delhi again on March 15, 876 AD. Thus, Delhi came to the hands of its original ruler after a long span of 2127 years. Anangpal I did a lot of development work in Delhi. The list of Tomar dynasty rulers is furnished below:

Sr. No.	Name of the King	Rule ends		
1	Anangpal I	894AD	March	15
2	Vasudev	913AD	May	3
3	Prithivi Pal	932AD	Nov.	22
4	Jaideva	953 AD	July	20
5	Hirpal	967AD	Nov.	29
6	Udiraj	994AD	July	10
7	Vijaypal	1015AD	Sept.	23
8	Anangpal II	1038AD	Jan.	8
9	Rikspal	1059AD	July	13
10	Gopal	1077AD	Oct.	28
11	Sallaksana Pal	1103AD	Sept.	7
12	Jaipal	1120 AD	Jan.	10
13	Kanvar Pal	1149 AD	Oct.	28
14	Mahipal	1175AD	Jan.	20
15	Anandapal or Anangapal III	1178 AD	Nov.	23

Prithviraj Chauhan

51/7/28th Kali/4280-4294 or 1178 AD-1192 AD

Anandpal, the last Tomar ruler of Indraprastha (Delhi), had no son. His daughter, married to Someshwar Chauhan, the king of Ajmer, bore Prithviraj Chauhan. Consequently, Anandpal was Prithviraj's maternal grandfather. Prithviraj was born in 1165 and displayed exceptional intelligence and a remarkable aptitude for military training. Notably, he possessed the unique skill of hitting a target solely based on its sound. In 1178 AD, after hearing about his courage and bravery, Anandpal declared Prithviraj his heir to the throne of Delhi. Tragically, Prithviraj ascended to the throne of Ajmer at the tender age of thirteen in 1178, following his father's death in battle. He even managed to kill a lion single-handedly without any weapon, solidifying his reputation as a formidable warrior king.

When he ascended to the throne of Delhi, he constructed Qila Rai Pithora here. His entire life was a continuous chain of bravery, courage, chivalrous deeds, and glorious exploits. At the tender age of thirteen, he vanquished the formidable Bhīmadeva, the ruler of Gujarat.

His love story with his enemy, Jaichanda's daughter, Samyukta is very famous. He rode off with her on the day of her 'Swayaṁvara'.

Prithviraj Chauhan, the valiant Rajput king, expanded his empire. However, his triumphs were short-lived. In 1191, Mahmud Ghori, the formidable invader, launched a devastating attack on India. The first battle of Tarain proved decisive, resulting in Mahmud Ghori's defeat.

Despite his victory, Prithviraj was asked to pursue the retreating army. However, he refused, adhering to the strict principles of fair warfare. This act of honor angered Mahmud Ghori, who vowed revenge. The second battle of Tarain ensued, and Prithviraj Chauhan was once again defeated and captured.

Mahmud Ghori's cruelty knew no bounds. He subjected Prithviraj to unimaginable torture, burning his eyes with red-hot irons and blinding him. Yet, Prithviraj's spirit remained unbroken. With the unwavering support of his court poet and friend, Chand Bardai, he devised a daring plan to avenge his capture.

During an archery competition organized by Mahmud Ghori, Prithviraj showcased his exceptional skills. His remarkable ability to hit the target solely based on the sound it produced caught Mahmud Ghori's attention. As Mahmud Ghori praised Prithviraj, he sensed the king's presence and lunged at him. In a swift and decisive move, Prithviraj struck Mahmud Ghori with his sword, ending the invader's reign of terror.

To escape the wrath of his enemies, Prithviraj's friend Chand Bardai intervened and stabbed Mahmud Ghori to death. Thus, Prithviraj Chauhan emerged victorious, preserving his legacy as a symbol of courage and honor in Indian history.

Chand Bardai compiled the story of the life of Prithviraj Chauhan in his epic poem 'Prithviraj Rāso'. Prithviraj Chauhan died in 1192, with his death a period of bravery, courage, patriotism, and principles came to an end. In the 2nd battle of Tarin, last Śālivāhana king Gaṅgā Singh and last king of the Parihar or Pratihar dynasty, Mahipati, were also killed.

The victorious Muslim army marched to Benaras, looting and plundering the town and villages on the way. It destroyed more than 1,000 temples and raised mosques on their foundations. Thus, Ghori got success through perfidy and gave way to Islamic invaders to capture some states in India. Thus came to an end the rule of three Agni Vaṁśa Kṣatriyas, namely Parmars, Pratiharas, Chauhanas, along with Śālivāhanas in India. Had Prthviraj Chauhan killed Muḥammad Ghori in the first battle of Tarain, Muslim rule would not have started in Bharat.

18. Rulers of Magadha

51/7/28th Dvāpara/863812-28th Kali/3180

or

3920 BC-78AD

The rule of Magadha was established by Upāvasu, the brother of Āyu, the ruler of ancient Prayāga (modern Allahabad). Girivraj, also called Rajgriha, was their capital. Jahan was the most famous king in the dynasty of Upāvasu. The river Gangā was named Jāhnavī after his name. The famous Ṛṣis Jamadgni and Viśvāmitra belonged to this dynasty. The great grammarian Kātyāyana and surgeon-physician Suśruta had the honour of belonging to this dynasty. Suśruta is the father of surgery and the first discoverer of the method of manufacturing Caustic soda, also known as Sodium hydroxide and Potash, which are claimed by European scientists as their discovery. This dynasty contributed significantly to the field of science, grammar, military science, and spirituality. Purāṇas close the lineage of this dynasty in the name of Sindhu and make no mention as to how this dynasty came to an end. But when we delve deep into world history, we come across the fact that the rulers of this dynasty migrated to the part of Earth presently known as Greece. In fact, they named this land Greece after the name of 'Griha' of 'Rajagṛha', which was their capital in India. They also founded a historical region in Greece and named it after Magadha as Makedonia or Macedonia. According to Herodotus, the history of Macedonia began with the Makednoi group of people who were none other than Kṣatriyas from Magadha. This fact can be verified from E. Pockoke's book 'India in Greece' published by the author of the present lines as 'Indian Origin of Greece and Ancient World'. Thus, on the migration of the Upāvasu dynasty from Magadha to Macedonia in Greece, Sudhanvā, son of the Kuru king of Hastinapur, took over the command of Magadha in 4000 BC. He was followed by Suhotra (3920 B.C.), Chyavana (3827 BC), Kriti (3789 BC), Pratipa (3752 BC). Pratipa was dethroned by Brihadrath in 3710 BC, and Brihadrath's dynasty started ruling Magadha. In his dynasty, he was followed by Kusagra (3638 BC), Rishabh (3568 BC), Satyahit (3498 BC), Punya (3438 BC), Satyadhriti (3397 BC), Sudhanva II (3357 BC), Sarva (3319 BC), Sambhav (3278 BC), and Jarasandh (3236 BC). Jarāsandh happened to be the most famous ruler. He used to rule the entire region from the Bay of Bengal to Arabia. He was acclaimed one of the most powerful sovereigns of his times. He used to be at loggerheads with Śri Krishna, who killed his son-in-law, named Kansh, the tyrant ruler of Mathura. Śri Krishna had him killed by Bhimsen, the second son of Pāṇḍu, prior to the Mahābhārata war around 3170 B.C., reducing the powerful kingdom of Magadha to a penury state. His son, Sahadeva, was made to ascend the throne of Magadha in 3180 BC. As history goes, Sahadeva participated in the war of Mahābhārata as an associate of Duryodhana and was killed. On his death, his son, Marjari (Somadhi), was crowned as the king of Magadha. Purāṇas provide us with the information of various dynasties that ruled over Magadha after the Mahābhārata war. According to the Purāṇas, the following dynasties ruled the Magadha empire.

Brihadratha Dynasty's continuation after Mahābhārata war

51/7/28thDvāpara/863965-28th Kali/963
or
3137 BC-2139 BC

3137 BC-3081 BC: Though Brihadratha dynasty started in 3710 BC as mentioned above. Here we shall deal with its continuation after Mahābhārata war. Sahadeva son of Jarāsandha participated in the war of Mahābhārata as an associate of Duryodhana and was killed. On his death his son Marjari (Somadhi) was crowned as the king of Magadha.

3081 BC-3017 BC: Srutvat or Srutśravā ruled over Magadha.

3017 BC-2981 BC: Apratipa or Ayutyu ruled over Magadha.

2981 BC- 2941 BC: Nirāmitra ruled over Magadha.

2941 BC-2883 BC: Sukrita or Sukṣatra ruled over Magadha.

2883 BC- 2860 BC: Brihatkarm a ruled Magadha.

2860 BC- 2810 BC: Senajit ruled Magadha.

2810 BC- 2770 BC: Śrutañjaya ruled Magadha.

2770 BC-2735 BC: Mahābalaruled Magadha.

2735BC-2677 BC: Mahābala's son Śuchi ruled Magadha.

2677 BC-2649 BC: Anuvrata ruled Magadha.

2649BC-2585 BC: Dharmanetra/Dharma/or Dharmasutra) ruled Magadha.

2585 BC-2550 BC: Nirvritti or Shama ruled Magadha.

2550 BC-2492 BC: Susharma ruled Magadha.

2492 BC-2452 BC: Dhridhsena or Dyumsena ruled Magadha.

2452 BC-2396 BC: Sumati or Mahanetra ruled Magadha.

2396 BC- 2363 BC: Subala or Suchala ruled Magadha.

2363 BC- 2341 BC: Sunetra or Sunitha ruled Magadha.

2341 BC- 2301BC: Satyajit ruled Magadha.

2301 BC- 2218 BC: Vishvajit ruled Magadha.

2218BC- 2139BC: Ripunjaya ruled Magadha. Ripunjaya was killed in 2139 B.C treacherously by his minister Munika and with him, the Brihadratha dynasty came to an end.

Pradyot Dynasty

51/7/28th Kali/963-1101 or 2139 BC-2001 BC

2139 BC- 2116BC: After the demise of Ripunjaya, his minister Munika married his son Pradyota to the sole surviving daughter of the late king Ripunjaya and crowned him as the ruler of Magadha. This union marked the commencement of the Pradyota dynasty in Magadha. Pradyota successfully subjugated the Vitihotras of Avanti and conquered all the neighboring states of Magadha. However, the Puraṇas state that he deviated from the Rājadharma prescribed in the Śāstras and faced opposition from the populace. During his dynasty, five kings ruled Magadha for a total of 138 years. They are as under:

2116BC- 2092BC: Pālak or Balak ruled Magadha.

2092 BC- 2042BC: Vishkhayupruled Magadha.

2042BC-2021BC: Janak ruled Magadha.

2021 BC- 2001BC: Janak Nandivardhan ruled Magadha.

Śiśunāga Dynasty

51/7/28th Kali/1101-1464 or 2001 BC-1638BC

2001BC-1961BC: After the demise of Nandivardhan, the last king of the Pradyota dynasty, Magadha fell under the conquest of Śiśunāga, the ruler of Kashi (modern-day Banaras or Varanasi). Śiśunāga bestowed the throne of Kashi upon one of his sons and personally governed from Girivraj, the capital of Magadha. This dynasty ruled for a remarkable 360 years, with 10 kings at the helm.

1961BC-1925BC: Kākvarmā ruled Magadha.

1925BC-1899BC: Kṣemadharma ruled Magadha.

1899 BC-1859BC: Kṣemajit ruled Magadha.

1859 BC-1815BC: Kṣemajit's son Bimbisar ruled Magadha.

1815BC-1791BC: Bimbisar, a prominent ruler of the Sisunag dynasty, was succeeded by his son, Ajatsatru. Ajatsatru, a nobleman from Vaishali, sought to gain the republic's friendship by marrying into the royal family. However, his ambitions led him to usurp the throne and imprison his father, Bimbisar. Tragically, Ajatsatru had his father starved to death in prison. In a fit of rage, he also attacked and destroyed Vaishali.

However, Ajatsatru's life took a turning point when he was influenced by the teachings of Buddha. He abandoned his tyrannical ways and shifted his focus towards better administration and the expansion of his empire through peaceful means.

1791 BC-1756BC: Darbhak ruled Magadha.

1756BC–1726BC: Udayan ruled Magadha. Here it may be noted that king Udayan founded the city of Kusumpur which later came to be known as Patliputra (modern Patna).

1726BC–1684BC: Nandivardhan ruled Magadha.

1684BC–1638BC: Mahānandi ruled Magadha.

Nanda Dynasty

51/7/28th Kali/1464–1564 or 1638 BC–1538BC

The Śiśunāga dynasty came to an end in 1638 BC with the rise of the Nanda dynasty. Mahapadma, also known as Nanda, was the son of Mahanandin, born to a woman who was not a kṣatriya but was married to Mahanandin. He adopted the surname Nanda and declared himself the emperor of Magadha in 1638 BC. Various Puranic traditions based on the Saptarishi Saṁvat corroborate this historical event. We present here the relevant instances we have found.

According to the Kaliyuga Rājavṛttānta (Bhāga 3, Chapt. 3), Nanda's rule began 1500 Saptarṣī years after Parikṣita. This means that 1500 years later, after 15 Nakṣatras had progressed in retrograde order.

महापद्माभिषेकात्तु यावज्जन्म परीक्षितः ।
एवमेव सहस्रं तु ज्ञेयं पंचशतोत्तरम् ॥
mahāpadmābhiṣekāttu yāvajjanma parīkṣitaḥ /
ēvameva sahasraṁ tu jñeyaṁ paṁchaśatottaram //

Parikṣita was born in 3137 BC in Maghā, according to the Maghā chronology. If we subtract the Maghā period from the Maghā chronology in reverse order, we get Śravaṇa 39, which corresponds to 1638 BC according to our 9000 Years' calendar. This confirms that the Nanda rule began in 1638 BC.

However, according to other Puranic traditions, there is a discrepancy of 1015 Saptarishi years between Parikṣita's birth and Nanda's coronation.

यावत् परीक्षितो जन्म यावन्नन्दाभिषेचनम् ।
एतत् वर्षसहस्रं तु ज्ञेयं पंचदशोत्तरम् ॥

yāvat parīkṣito janma yāvannandābhiṣechanam |
etat varṣasahasraṁ tu jñeyaṁ paṁchadaśottaram ||

[Meaning] That is between the birth of Parikshita and coronation of Nanda, there is a difference of 1015 Saptarishi years."

The Bhāgavat Purāṇa (Skand. 12, Ch. 2.5.26) also has similar view as:

आरभ्य भवतो जन्म यावत् नन्दाभिषेचनम् ।
एतद्वर्ष सहस्त्रं तु शतं पंचदशोत्तम ॥
ārabhya bhavato janma yāvat nandābhiṣechanam |
etadvarṣa sahasraṁ tu śataṁ paṁchadaśottama ||

[Meaning] From the time of your birth up to the coronation of King Nanda, there elapsed **one thousand one hundred and fifteen years** (a thousand plus a hundred and fifteen)."

The Kashmiri school's interpretation of the Puranic reading suggests that Parikṣita was born in 3137 BC. By that time, the Saptarṣī Saṁvat had elapsed, with 639 years having passed since Maghā 39 (the 6th Nakṣatra from Rohiṇi in the normal order). The readings indicate that the difference between Parikṣita's birth and Nanda's coronation was 1015 Saptarṣī years. This means that after 1015 years of the Saptarṣī Saṁvat 639, Nanda ascended to the throne. This period would be 639 (the Saptarṣī year of Parikṣita's birth) plus 1015 (the difference in years) equals 1654 (which corresponds to the 16th Nakṣatra if counted from Maghā in the normal order). This date aligns with Pūrva-bhādrapada 54 or 1623 BC, which also corresponds to Śravaṇa 54, the 10th Nakṣatra in retrograde motion (2700-1654=1046) if counted from Rohiṇī. Therefore, the exact date of Nanda's coronation is ± 19 years. Our proposed date is 1638 or Purvabhādrapada 39, which is 15 years away from the Saptarṣī date mentioned in the Purāṇa.

According to Skanda Purāṇa (Maheśvara Khaṇḍa, 1, 40 251), Nanda rule will take place in 3310 years, which will be eliminated by Chāṇakya. The verse goes like this

ततः त्रिषु सहस्रेषु (3000) दशाधिक (10) शतत्रये (300) ।
भविष्यं नन्दराज्यम् चाणक्यो यान् हनिष्यति ॥
tataḥ triṣu sahasreṣu (3000) daśādhika (10) śatatraye (300) ।
bhaviṣyaṁ nandarājyam chāṇakyo yān haniṣyati ॥

[Meaning] Then, after **three thousand and three hundred and ten years**, there will arise the **kingdom of the Nandas**, whom **Chāṇakya (Kauṭilya)** will bring to destruction."

This calculation is based on the Revati-centric Patna School of the Saptarṣī Saṁvat. If we subtract 2700 from 3310, we obtain 610. This number corresponds to the 6th asterism in retrograde motion. According to the Patna school, the 6th asterism in retrograde motion starting from Revati is Śravaṇa. Therefore, Śravaṇa 10, which corresponds to 1667 BC, is the 6th asterism in retrograde motion. However, there is a discrepancy of 19 years in this calculation.

According to the Kaliyuga Rājavṛttānta of the Bhaviṣya Purāṇa (Bhāga 3, Chapt. 3), during the reign of Nanda, the Saptarṣīs were residing in the Śravaṇa Nakṣatra (the 15th Nakṣatra from Maghā, calculated in reverse order, of course).

सप्तर्षयो मघायुक्ताः काले यौधिष्ठिरे शतम् ।
श्रवणे ते भविष्यन्ति काले नन्दस्य भूपतेः ॥
saptarṣayo maghāyuktāḥ kāle yaudhiṣṭhire śatam ।
śravaṇe te bhaviṣyanti kāle nandasya bhūpateḥ ॥

[Meaning] These Saptarṣī-s were associated with the asterism Maghā for a duration of 100 years during the reign of Yudhiṣṭhira. Subsequently, at the beginning of King Nanda's (Mahāpadma) reign, they will be connected with the Śravana Nakṣatra.

According to the timeline I've fixed, the Nanda rule began in 1638 BC when the Saptarṣīs were in the Śravaṇa 39. This reference also corroborates the timeline we've established.

Vāyu and Matsya Purāṇas also have similar view as:

महापद्माभिषेकात्तु जन्म यावत् परीक्षितः ।

एकं वर्षसहस्रं तु ज्ञेयं पंचशतोत्तरम् ॥
mahāpadmābhiṣekāttu janma yāvat parīkṣitaḥ ।
ekaṁ varṣasahasraṁ tu jñeyaṁ paṁchaśatottaram ॥

[Meaning] From the coronation of **Mahāpadma (Nanda)** up to the **birth of King Parīkṣit**, there elapsed **one thousand and five hundred years** (a thousand plus five hundred).

The above cited references also prove the date line of Nanda rule fixed by us.

1638BC- 1538BC: Mahāpadma, along with his eight sons—Panduka, Pandugati, Bhutapala, Rashtrapala, Govishanaka, Dashasiddhaka, Kaivarta, and Sumalya—were collectively known as the Nava Nandas. They ruled Magadha for a remarkable 100 years. Among them, Nanda stood out as the most powerful and formidable king of India during that era. He was renowned as Dhanānanda, a name that aptly reflected his immense wealth. To safeguard his vast fortune, he made a daring decision—he safe-deposited it in the bed of the river Ganges.

Maurya Dynasty

51/7/28th Kali/1564-1880 or 1538 BC-1222BC

Mahāpadma Nanda was a corrupt and oppressive ruler. People used to hate him. Chāṇakya overthrew him with the help of Chandragupta Maurya and placed him on the throne of Magadha.

Chandragupta Maurya

51/7/28thKali/1564-1598 or (1538BC- 1504BC)

Chandragupta was also a son of Mahapadma Nanda by another wife named Mura whom he had banished. Since Chandragupta was the son of Murā, he was known as Chandragupta Maurya. He owed his sovereignty to a great scholar of that period called Chāṇkya alias Kauṭilya (original name Viṣṇu Gupta), the famous author of the Arthaśāstra, an excellent treatise on statecraft, economic policy and military strategy. Chāṇkya not only enthroned Chandragupta Maurya by routing out the nine Nandas but also trained him in the necessary arts and sciences. Chandragupta ruled the Magadha empire for 34 years i.e. from 1538BC to 1504BC.

1504BC– 1476BC: Bindusar's son of Chandragupta Maurya ruled Magadha for 28 years.

Aśoka

51/7/28th Kali/1626-1662 or 1476 BC to 1440BC

Aśoka, the great ruled Magadha for 36 years. Here it may be pointed out that Mauryan Aśoka did not embrace Buddhism. He fought the Kaliṅga war in which 100,000 people were killed and 150,000 were taken as prisoners. Moved by this massacre, Aśoka Vardhan decided to follow the path of peace and winning others over to his side by dharma and not by wars.

According to the Rājtaraṅgiṇī of Kalhaṇa (written in 748 AD), there was also a king named Aśoka who belonged to the Godhara dynasty in Kashmir. He was known as Dharmāśoka and was crowned in 1734 BC. It was this Kashmir Aśoka who embraced Buddhism and dedicated himself to spreading it. Later, in 1657 BC, Kanishka of the Turuṣka dynasty also supported Buddhism. Consequently, due to a mistaken identity between the Aśoka of the Godhara dynasty in Kashmir and the Maurya Aśoka, it was erroneously assumed that the Maurya Aśoka had become a Buddhist. Let us consider the Rock edict XIII of Aśoka Vardhan of the Maurya Dynasty for further clarification. I present here the precise translation of Rock edict XIII.

1. By his majesty Priyadarśī, when consecrated 8 years, the inhabitants of Kaliṅga were conquered.
2. 150,000 people were made prisoners from there, nearly 100,000 were killed there, nearly as many died.
3. After that, now the inhabitants of Kaliṅga have been taken, there is an ardent entry into practice of dharma, there is the love of dharma, there is instruction in

dharma for his Majesty.

4. But his Majesty has remorse for his conquest of the inhabitants of Kaliṅga.

5. For conquering the unconquered, when slaughter takes place there, and death and imprisonment of people, then it is thought of as extremely painful and thought of as serious by his Majesty.

6. But this is thought of as more serious than that by his Majesty.

7. Whatever scholars of Vedic dharma live there, or scholars of Buddhism or other sects, or householders who are well disposed, of whom there is obedience to authority, obedience to parents, obedience to elders, proper behaviour to friends, acquaintances, companions, relatives, servants, dasyusand firm devotion, of them there is injury there or death or separation from dear ones.

8. Those well-disposed ones, whose affection is undiminished, when their friends, acquaintances, companions, and relatives come to disaster there, then it is an injury for them indeed.

9. And that is a bad fortune for all men, and it is thought of as serious by His Majesty.

10. But that country doesn't exist where these scholars of Vedic dharma and Buddhism, do not exist, except among the Yavanas, and there is nowhere in any country where there is not a faith of men in one sect or another.

11. Therefore, however many people then, when the inhabitants of Kaliṅga were taken, were killed and died and were imprisoned, one-hundredth part, one-thousandth part of that is today thought of as serious by His Majesty.

12. Should anyone injure (him), what can be forgiven is indeed thought fit to be forgiven by His Majesty.

13. And the forest dwellers in His Majesty's territory, even on them he has compassion and wins them over.

14. And remorse is said to them by His Majesty to be the cause, in order that they may repent and may not kill.

15. For his Majesty wishes for all creatures' freedom from injury, self-restraint, impartiality and gentleness.

16. But this is thought to be the best victory by His Majesty, namely the victory of dharma.

17. But this has been obtained by His Majesty here and at all the boundaries, up to 600 yojanas, where the Yavan king Amtiyoka is beyond that Amtiyoka four kings, Tulmaya, Amtikoni, Maka and Alikiya Sudra, constantly, the Cholas and Pāṇḍyas as far as Tambapanni (Tāmraparṇī).

18. In the same way here in the territory of the king, among the Yavanas, and Kambojas, Nibhakas and Nabhapantis, the Bhojas and Pitinikas, the Āndhras and Pulindas, everywhere they conform to His Majesty's instruction in dharma.

19. Even where His Majesty's messengers do not go, they too having heard of His Majesty's practice of morality (and) order (and) instruction in morality, conform to morality and will conform to it.

20. But victory obtained by such dharma is a victory everywhere, moreover, a victory everywhere has a taste of joy.

21. I feel happy over the victory of dharma.

22. But even the victory of dharma (moral and ethical values) is indeed small.

23. His Majesty thinks that only that which concerns the next world is fruitful. (Here edict talks about the transmigration of souls or punarjanma which is not accepted in Buddhism. It stresses upon the performance of moral and good deeds which could help one's

elevation in one's future birth).

24. For this purpose, this script on dharma has been written, in order that my sons and grandsons should not think that another new victory is to be won. Let them approve of mildness and light punishment in the event of their own victory. Let them think that alone is a victory which is obtained by dharma.

25. That concerns this world and next world.

26. And let enjoy dharma.

27. For that concerns this world and the next world. (According to the Vedic philosophy, nothing accompanies human being in their next life except dharma good deeds and moral and ethical values enjoyed by him).

The following information can be deduced from this edict.

a) From the edict, it is crystal clear that after the Kaliṅga war Aśoka abjures war and started the following dharma and propagated the rule of dharma. According to him, inculcation of dharma is essential not only for this life but for life after death. Vedic philosophy lays stress on dharma and accordingly, dharma accompanies human being to their next life and everything else is left here. From this, it is crystal clear that after Kaliṅga war Aśoka did not embrace Buddhism, rather he propagated dharma.

b) From edict, is is also clear that Aśoka sent messengers ro propagate dharma. They were never charged with the propagation of Buddhism. Had it been a truth, Greece would have been a Buddhist country. We have no evidence from the Greek side which indicates that any Buddhist missionary had arrived in Greece in 250 BC. Propagation of dharma and propagation of Buddhism are two different things. I think scholars are confusing here. According to the Pāli text Mahavañśo (7.1-8) messengers for the propagation of Buddhism were sent by Moggaliputta.

c) Similarly, the edict informs that scholars of Vedic dharma and Buddhism are available in all places except Yavana countries. Here it may be pointed out that Mahābhārata and Manusmṛti speak of Yavanas together with Kambojas as the degraded Kṣatriyas or Mlecchhas devoid of Vedic dharma (morality or ethical code). Mahāvañśa (II, 149, 4-6) states that in Yavanas and Kambojas, there were only two classes, Aryas (following Vedic dharma) and Dasyus (atheists).

As per the descriptions in the epic Mahābhārata, Yavana or Yona refers here to a community under western countries along with Sindhu (Sindhu kingdom stretched along the river Indus in modern Pakistan), Madra (Sialkot region of Punjab province of Pakistan), Kekaya (Northwestern Punjab between Gandhar and river Beas in Pakistan), Gāndhāra and Kamboja (the degraded Kṣatriyas living in the countries of Tajikistan, Uzbekistan, Kyrgyzstan). Yavanas were described to be beyond Gandhara. There was another country mentioned in the epic as Parama Yona, in the far west of Yavana. This could be the Ionia of Greece, somehow related to Indian Ionians or Yavanas. The name Yavana could be the Sanskritized form of the name Ionia. So Yavanas mentioned in Rock edict XIII are not Greeks as conceived by many historians. Yavanas are northwestern countries around Gāndhāra and beyond Gāndhāra. According to the Bhaviṣya Purāṇa, the part to the west of Indus which was inhabited and resorted to by all Indians who disregarded Vedic culture and left the parent fold was known as Mlecchhasthan.

सिन्धुस्थानमिति ज्ञेयं राष्ट्रमार्यस्य चोत्तमम्।
म्लेच्छस्थानं परं सिन्धोः कृतं तेन महात्मना॥ भविष्यपुराण, 3.3.2-20&21
sindhusthānamiti jñeyaṁ rāṣṭramāryasya chottamam /
mlechchhasthānaṁ paraṁ sindhoṁḥ kṛtaṁ tena mahātmanā // Bhaviṣyapurāṇa, 3.3.2-20&21

According to the Viṣṇu Purāṇa (4.3.47-48), various Mleccha communities distinguished themselves from one another through distinct physical characteristics. For instance, the Yavans were known for their shaven heads, the Śakas had partially shaven heads, the Pardas wore long hair, and the Pahlavas were characterized by their beards.

यवनान् मुंडितशिरसोऽर्धमुंडान् शकान् ।
प्रलंबकेशान् पारदान् पहलवान् श्मश्रूधरान् । ।
yavanān mumḍitaśiraso'rdhamumḍān śakān /
pralambakeśān pāradān pahalavān śmaśrūdharān / /

As such, the five Yavan kings mentioned in the Rock Edict are not the Greek kings of the 3rd century B.C., as identified by many historians and Indologists. They must have been rulers of territories located somewhere in modern-day Pakistan, Afghanistan, Tajikistan, Uzbekistan, and Kyrgyzstan. Since Yavanas belong to the caste of outcast Kṣatriyas, their mention is not found in the Purāṇas.

Moreover, since Samudragupta of the Imperial Guptas was known as Aśokāditya, Indologists and historians mistakenly attributed his inscriptions to Maurya Aśoka to align their fanciful theories with the historical record.

1439 BC–1431 BC: According to Viṣṇu Purāṇa, Aśoka was followed by Supārśva or Suyaśa. He ruled Maghadha for 8 years.

1431BC–1423 BC: According to the Viṣṇu Purāṇa, Daśaratha, also known as Bandhupālita, followed Suyaśa and ruled Magadha for eight years. In contrast, the Matsya Purāṇa narrates that he succeeded the Mauryan empire after his uncle Kuṇāla became blind, rendering him incapable of ruling. Daśaratha was only around twenty years old when he ascended to the throne with the assistance of his ministers. The Purāṇas state that he reigned for eight years. Daśaratha also made a significant gesture by dedicating three caves in the Nagārjunī Hills to the Ajivikas. Three inscriptions, ordered by Devānāmpiya Daśaratha, confirm that these caves were dedicated immediately upon his succession.

1423BC–1353BC: According to Vāyu and the Brahmāṇḍa Purāṇa Indrapālita followed Daśaratha and ruled Magadha for 70 years.

1353BC–1345BC: Harshavardhana ruled Magadha for 8 years.

1345BC–1321BC: to Vāyu Purāṇa, Samprati ruled Magadha. He ruled almost the entire present-day Indian subcontinent.

The Jain text, Pariśiṣṭaparvan, mentions that King Samprati ruled from both Pataliputra and Ujjain. However, unfortunately, we lack any inscriptions or other evidence to support these accounts. He reigned for a period of 9 years. Samprati was influenced by the teachings of a Jain monk named Suhastin. Additionally, he dispatched Jain scholars abroad to disseminate Jain teachings.

Emperor Samprati, often overlooked in history, is revered as the "Jain Aśoka" for his unwavering patronage and tireless efforts to spread Jainism across eastern India. Jain historians hold Samprati in even higher esteem, considering him more powerful and renowned than Aśoka himself.

The Samprati Vihāra, named after the emperor, stood in Vadamānu, nestled in the Krishna Valley. Under the influence of Suhastin, a disciple of the esteemed Acharya Sthulibhadra, the leading saint of the Jain community during the Mahagiri period, Samprati underwent a profound spiritual awakening and was once again drawn back to Jainism, the ancestral religion of the Mauryas.

Driven by his unwavering devotion to Jainism, Samprati embarked on a remarkable journey to spread the faith through every possible means. He dedicated himself tirelessly to upholding the teachings of the scriptures, working relentlessly to ensure the success of his mission.

One of Samprati's most remarkable feats was his daily ritual of rinsing his mouth in the morning. This act was not merely a personal hygiene practice, but a symbolic gesture of his reverence for the new temples that were being constructed. He would eagerly await the news of each new temple's completion, and upon hearing it, he would rush to perform the Anjankala ceremony, declaring them fit for worship.

Samprati's dedication extended beyond mere temple construction. He also made it his mission to repair and renovate existing temples, ensuring that they were in a state of pristine condition. He installed magnificent gold, stone, silver, brass, and a blend of fine metals murtis, holy statues, within these temples, and performed the Anjankala ceremony to consecrate them.

It is said that Samprati's remarkable efforts resulted in the construction of thousands of Jain temples across India, many of which continue to stand as vibrant centers of worship to this day. Among these temples are the renowned Jain temples at Viramgam and Palitana in Gujarat, Agar Malwa in Ujjain, and numerous others scattered throughout his empire.

In just three and a half years, Samprati's remarkable achievements were nothing short of astounding. He constructed an incredible one hundred and twenty-five thousand new temples, repaired thirty-six thousand existing ones, consecrated twelve and a half million murtis, and prepared ninety-five thousand metal murtis. His dedication extended even to non-Aryan territories, where he founded Jain monasteries, demonstrating his inclusive and compassionate spirit.

The legacy of Emperor Samprati continues to inspire generations, and his contributions to the spread of Jainism remain unparalleled. Many ancient Jain temples and monuments of unknown origin bear his name, a testament to his enduring impact on the religious landscape of India. Notably, all the Jain monuments in Rajasthan and Gujarat, attributed to unknown builders, are also believed to be the result of Samprati's visionary efforts.

According to Jain tradition, King Samprati had no children. He considered it the consequence of earlier Karma and observed the religious customs more scrupulously.

1321BC- 1312BC: According to Viṣṇu Purāṇa, Sangat followed Samprati and ruled Magadha for 9 years.

1312BC-1299BC: According to Vāyu Purāṇa Sangat was succeeded by Śāliśuka, who according to the Yuga Purāṇa was a cruel, wicked and unrighteous ruler. He ruled for 13 years.

1299BC- 1292BC: According to Vāyu Purāṇa, Deva Varman /Deva Sharma/ Soma Sharma ruled Magadha for 7 years.

1292BC-1284BC: According to the Vāyu Purāṇa, Śatadhanvanfollowed Devasharma and ruled Magadha for 8 years.

1284BC-1223BC: According to all Purāṇas, Brihadratha, the last ruler of the Mauryan dynasty, met his demise at the hands of his Senapati, Puṣyamitra Śuṅga. Brihadratha ascended to the throne after succeeding Śatadhanvan and ruled for a period of 61 years. However, the Mauryan territories, which had flourished under the great Emperor Aśoka, had significantly diminished during Brihadratha's reign.

During his reign, northwestern India, encompassing parts of modern-day Afghanistan and Pakistan, faced invasions from the Yavanas and Śakas. These invaders established their rule in the Kabul Valley and parts of Punjab in present-day Pakistan. The Yuga Purāṇa section of the Gargī Saṁhitā specifically mentions that the Yavana army, led by King Dhamamita, launched an invasion of the Mauryan territories during Brihadratha's reign. Tragically, Brihadratha was killed in 1223 BC by his commander-in-chief, the Brahmin general Puṣyamitra Śuṅga. Following Brihadratha's demise, Puṣyamitra seized power and established the Śuṅga dynasty.

Bāṇabhaṭṭa's Harśacharita provides a different account of Puṣyamitra's actions. He claims that Puṣyamitra, while parading the entire Mauryan army before Brihadratha, feigned a display of the army's strength to impress his master. However, Puṣyamitra ultimately crushed Brihadratha, believing that the emperor was too weak to fulfill his promise of repelling the Yavanas.

Śuṅga Dynasty

51/7/28th Kali/1879-2179 or 1223 BC - 923BC

1223BC-1163BC: Puṣyamitra Śuṅga, the founder of Śuṅga dynasty, ruled Magadha.

1163BC-1113BC: Puṣyamitra's son was Agnimitra. He reigned for 50 years from 1163BC to 1113BC.

1113BC-1077BC: Vasujyeṣṭha ruled Magadha

1077BC-1060BC: Vasumitra ruled Magadha

1060BC-1030BC: Bhadrak ruled Magadha

1030BC-997BC: Pulindak ruled Magadha

997BC-994BC: Ghoṣa ruled Magadha

994BC-965BC: Vajramitra ruled Magadha

965BC-933BC: Bhāgavatruled Magadha

933 BC-923BC: Devabhuti ruled Magadha. Devabhuti addicted to the life of pleasure, entrusted the kingdom to his minister Vasudev. Devabhuti was so blinded in the pleasure that he seduced Vasudev's beautiful daughter and killed her husband. On hearing this, Vasudev sent a Viṣakanyā and had him killed.

Kaṇva Dynasty

51/7/28th Kali/2179-2264 or 923 BC-838 BC

923BC-884 BC: Vasudeva took over the reins of Magadha and become the founder of the Kaṇva dynasty, being descendant of Kaṇvāyana Brāhmaṇa family. This dynasty lasted for 45 years and four kings ruled Magadha during this period.

884BC-860BC: Bhūmi Mitra ruled Magadha.

860BC-848BC: Narayan ruled Magadha.

848BC-838BC: Suśarmā was the last king of Kaṇva dynasty. He was killed by his general and minister Śrimukh, an Andhra Brāhmaṇa, who ascended the throne of Magadha in 1247BC.

This was the end of Kaṇva dynasty and beginning of Āndhra Sātavāhan.

Andhra Sātvāhana Dynasty

51/7/28thKali/2264-2765or 838BC-327BC

According to '*Kali Yuga Rāja Vṛttānta*' (15th verse), 'By the time of the beginning of the rule of the Andhras, the Saptarishis will be in the 24th star.

चतुर्विंशेऽथ नक्षत्रे भविष्यन्ति शतं समाः ।
आन्ध्रराज्यारम्भकालादारम्यैते सुरर्षयः ॥
chaturviṁśe'tha nakṣatre bhaviṣyanti śataṁ samāḥ ।
āndhrarājyārambhakālādāramyaite surarṣayaḥ ॥

[Meaning] From the commencement of the Andhra Dynasty (at Magadha) the Saptarṣīs will be found in conjuction with with (Chitrā) the 24th constellation (when calculated in retrograde order from and inclusive of Māgha).

This counting begins from Maghā Nakṣatra. Counting backward from Maghā, we discover that Chitrā is the 24th star. The aforementioned statement indicates that during the reign of the Andhras, the Saptarishis were positioned in Chitrā Nakṣatra. Our table reveals that the Saptarishis entered Chitrā Nakṣatra in 877 BC. Therefore, the date of the commencement of the Āndhra dynasty, as calculated by our methods, is accurate. During 838 BC, the Saptarishis were in Chitrā 40.

This statement is found in all the Purāṇas, and there's nothing in this verse that can be attributed to any conjectures or inferences. The 16th verse of the '*Kali Yuga Rāja Vṛttānta*' further supports our claim, stating, "Those who know (authoritative elders) say that the interval between Nanda's coronation and the beginning of the Āndhra empire is 800 years or 8 constellations.".

आन्ध्रराज्योपक्रमात्तु यावन्नन्दाभिषेचनम् ।
अन्तर तच्छतान्यष्टौ प्रमाणज्ञै समा स्मृता ॥
āndhrarājyopakramāttu yāvannandābhiṣechanam ।

antara tachchhatānyaṣṭau pramāṇajñai samā smṛtā II

[Meaning] According to competent authorities (Pramāṇajñas), the duration between Mahapadma Nanda's coronation and the beginning of the Andhra Dynasty is precisely 800 years.

Nanda ascended the throne of Magadha in 1638 BC when Saptarṣis was in Śravaṇa 40. Chitra Nakṣatra is 8th Nakṣatra away from Śravaṇa. As such Āndhra dynasty commences in 1638-800=838BC, which is Chitra 40. If you take the difference between Śravaṇa 40 (1638 BC) and Chitra 40 (838 BC), it is exactly (1638-838 = 800 years).

The Vāyu Purāṇa explicitly states that the Saptarṣīs were in the Maghā constellation for a century during the reign of King Parīkṣita, approximately between 3176 and 3076 BC. They will once again be in the 24th Nakṣatra from Maghā (specifically, the Chitrā Nakṣatra) by the time the Āndhra (Śātavāhana) dynasty begins around 838 BC.

सप्तर्षियो मघायुक्ताः काले परिक्षिते शतम् ।
आन्ध्रांशे स चतुर्विंशे भविष्यन्ति मते मम ॥
saptarṣiyo maghāyuktāḥ kāle parikṣite śatam I
āndhrāṁśe sa chatuviṁśe bhaviṣyanti mate mama II

[Meaning The **Saptarṣis**, when positioned with the **Maghā constellation**, will remain so for **one century during the time of King Parīkṣit**.
In my opinion, they will again occupy the the **twenty-fourth Nakṣatra during the Andhra (Sātavāhana) era**.

The Vāyu Purāṇa also supports the beginning of the Andhra dynasty's rule in the 9th century BC.

838BC–814BC: Simukh or Śrimuka Sātakarṇī founded the Āndhra Sātavāhana dynasty after killing the Suśarmā, the last king of Kaṇva dynasty in 838BC he ruled for 23 years. One inscription at Naneghat mentions the king Simuka Śātavāhana. Most probably, the inscriptions found in the cave of Naneghat belong to the reign of the Śātavāhana king Śri Śātakarṇi and the Nāgānikā mentioned in the inscriptions was his mother.

814BC–796BC: Śri Krishna Sātakarṇi or Kanha the younger brother of Śrimukh Sātakarṇī ruled next for 18 years and he extended the kingdom up to Nāsik, near the source of Godavari in western Ghats. An inscription at the Nāsik cave refers to the name of the king Kānha.

796BC–786BC: Śri Malla Sātakarṇi was the next powerful emperor who extended the empire up to South India including Mahārāṣṭra, Mālvā and the Deccan. One of his artisans was responsible for the construction of one of the gateways at Sāñchī. He ruled for 10 years.

786 BC–768BC: Pūrnotsaṅga ruled for 18 years.

768BC–712BC: Sātakarṇī II ruled for 56 years.

712BC–694BC: Skandhastambhi ruled for 18 years

694BC–676BC: Lambodara ruled for 18 years.

676BC–664BC: Āpīlaka ruled for 12 years.

One coin found in the village Bālpur in Raipur District, Chattisgarh mentions the name of the king Āpīlaka.

664BC–646BC: Meghasvāti ruled for 18 years.

646BC–628BC: Svātiruled for 18 years.

628BC–621BC: Skandasvāti ruled for 7 years.

621BC–610BC: Mṛgendra Sātakarṇi ruled for 11 years.

610BC–602BC: Kuntala Sātakarṇi ruled for 8 years.

The name of the 13th king Kuntala Sātakarṇi was referred to in Vātsyāyana's Kāmasūtrā and Rājaśekhara's Kāvyamīmāṁsā.

602BC–590BC: Saumya Sātakarṇi ruled for 12 years.

590BC–589BC: Sāta Śātakarṇi ruled for 1 year.

589BC–565BC: Pulumavi I ruled for 24 years.

565BC–527BC: Megha Śātakarṇi ruled for 38 years.

527BC- 502BC: Ariṣṭ Sātakarṇi ruled for 25 years.

Ariṣṭ Sātakarṇī and Hāla Śātakarṇi were contemporaries of

the Śaka king Rudradāman (531 BC-493 BC)

502BC–497BC: After Ariṣṭ Sātakarṇī, Hāla ruled for only five years. He was a patron of Prakṛta languages and literature. He composed the renowned 'Sapta Śataka' and 'Gāthā Saptasati'. This compilation also includes the works of women writers such as Anulabda, Anulakṣamī, and Revā. One of Hāla's ministers, Guṇāḍhya, wrote the famous 'Bṛhat Kathā' in Prākṛta. These stories gained immense popularity and were later translated into Sanskrit. They also served as the basis for the stories in 'Kathā Sarit Sāgara' and other works. During his reign, a Prākṛta grammar titled 'Kātantra Vyākaraṇa' was written. Hāla's name is mentioned in various literary works, including Līlāvatī, Abhidhāna Cintāmaṇī, Deśināmamālā, and others. After Hāla and before Gautamīputra Sātakarṇī, the western Kṣatrapās occupied parts of Mahārāṣṭra and Malwa. Bhumaka and Nahapana ruled these regions.

497BC–492BC: Mandalakaor Puttalaka ruled for 5 years.

492BC–480BC: Purindrasena ruled for 12 years.

480BC–479: Sundara Sātakarṇī ruled for one year.

479BC–467: Śivasvāti ruled for 12 years

467BC–446BC: Gautamīputra Sātakarṇī ruled for 21 years. He was the most important rulers of this dynasty. He dislodged the Kṣatrapas and eliminated them. His other victories over Śakas, Yavanas and Pahalvas are described in the inscription at Nasik.

446BC–418BC: Vasisthiputra ruled for 28 years.

418BC–411BC: Śivaśri Sātakarṇī ruled for 7 years.

411BC–404BC: Śivaskanda Sātakarṇī ruled for 7 years.

404BC–359BC: Śri Yajña Sātakarṇī ruled for 25 years. He was a powerful ruler. He ruled the Deccan for a long time. Later several kings who served Sātvahanas became independent due to not having central control. For example, Scythians, Parthians and Kuṣāṇas ruled over different parts of Bharatvarṣa.

359BC–347BC: Vijaya Sātakarṇi ruled for 12 years.

347BC–344BC: Chandra Śri Sātakarṇialso known as Chandramas Śātakarṇi. He ruled for three years and left behind his son Pulumavi III, a minor.

344BC–337BC: Pulumavi III was minor. The Gupta family of Prayaga was in the service of Sātavāhana rulers. That is why they are called 'Āndhrabhṛtyas'. Śri Gupta became the caretaker of the minor son of Chandra Śri Sātakarṇi after his death. He placed Pulumavi III on the throne and ruled on his behalf as a regent for 7 years.

337 BC-327 BC: Śri Gupta's son Ghaṭotkacha followed him. He served Magadha as a regent for another 10 years till 327 BC.

Imperial Gupta Dynasty

51/7/28th Kali/2765–3020 or 327BC–82BC

327 BC– 322BC: In 327 BC, Ghaṭotkacha, the regent of Magadh rulers, was succeeded by his son Chandragupta I. However, Chandragupta's ambitions led him to assassinate Pulomavi III and seize power for himself, becoming the founder of the Gupta Empire. While Śri Gupta is often referred to as the founder of the Gupta dynasty and the first ruler of the Gupta Empire as a regent of the Sātavāhana rulers, Chandragupta I's actions were driven by a desire to strengthen his power and establish his sovereignty. To achieve this, he married Kumar Devi, the princess of the Licchavi dynasty of Nepal. This strategic alliance further solidified Chandragupta's position and contributed to the expansion of the Gupta Empire. The Allahabad Pillar inscription of Samudragupta further corroborates this fact, describing Chandragupta as the Licchavi-dauhitra (the grandson of the Licchavis from his mother's side).

Chandragupta I ruled Magadha for 7 years. This era is known after his name as the Gupta era. For his prowess and valour, he was known as 'Vijayāditya'. Since the Gupta dynasty was established by the subordinates of Andhra Sātavāhanas, the dynasty was also known as Andhra Bhṛtya dynasty.

Samudra Gupta
(Sandrocottus of Greek History)

51/7/28th Kali/2782–2833 or 322 BC to 269BC

Samudra Gupta, the son of Chandra Gupta I from Kumāra Devī, ruled the Magadha empire for an impressive 51 years, from 322 B.C. to 269 B.C. He was revered as the supreme emperor of great India and affectionately known as 'Aśokāditya.' A formidable and ambitious monarch, Samudragupta set out on a mission to expand his empire.

Samudragupta was a remarkable ruler, possessing exceptional capacity and a diverse range of talents. He was a skilled warrior, a gifted poet, and a talented musician. Under his leadership, he conquered vast territories, extending his empire from Oxus to Ceylon. During his three-year southern campaign, Samudragupta and his formidable army marched an astonishing 3000 miles, battling through challenging terrain against formidable adversaries without a single defeat.

Harisena, a renowned poet in the court of Samudragupta, penned an account of his remarkable accomplishments. To proclaim the vastness of his dominion, Samudragupta graced the occasion with grandeur by performing the Aśvamedha Yajña. He also bestowed upon esteemed Vedic scholars an abundance of gold coins and medals, a testament to his appreciation for their knowledge. The inscription etched on the stone pillar at Allahabad, erroneously attributed to Aśoka of the Mauryas by Indologists, serves as a testament to Aśokāditya Samudragupta's achievements. Regarded as the most significant historical document of the classical Gupta era, it stands as a remarkable piece of literature written in exquisite Sanskrit, employing the refined Gupta script (a later iteration of Brahmi). Harishena, the poet and minister, played a pivotal role in crafting this panegyric, which offers a comprehensive praising of Samudragupta and chronicles his political and military triumphs, including his expeditions to the southern regions.

This inscription provides a unique glimpse into the Gupta empire and its neighboring territories, serving as a valuable source of information about the geopolitical landscape of that era. Below is the translation of the inscription.

Allahabad stone pillar inscription of Samudragupta.

(Verse 3) Whose mind is surcharged with happiness in consequence of his association with the wise, who is thus accustomed to retain the truth and purpose of (any) science . . . . . . fixed . . . . . . upraised . . . . . . who, removing impediments to the grace of good poetry through the very injunction (ājñā) of (poetic) excellence (guṇa) clustered together (guṇta) by the experts, enjoys, in the literate world, in an attractive fashion, sovereignty, in consequence of fame for copious lucid poetry.

(Verse 4) (Exclaiming) "Come, oh worthy (one)", and embracing (him) with hair standing on end and indicating (his) feeling, (his) father, perceiving (him) with the eye, overcome with affection, (and) laden with tears (of joy), (but) discerning the true state (of things) said to him "so protect (thou) the whole earth", while he was being looked up with sad faces by others of equal birth, (but) while the courtiers were breathing cheerfully.

(Verse 5) Beholding whose many super-human actions, some felt the thrill of marvel and burst into horripilation, some relishing with feeling . . . . . ., some afflicted with his prowess sought (whose) protection after performing obeisance. . . . . .

(Verse 6) (Whose enemies), whose offence was always

great, being conquered by his arm in battles . . . . . . day by day . . . . . . pride . . . . . . (develop) repentance with their minds filled with delight and expanding with much and evident pleasure and affection.

(Verse 7) By whom, with the impetuosity of the prowess of (his) arm, which grew to overflowing, having singly and in a moment uprooted Achyutaand Nāgasena and [Gaṇapati] come together in a battle (against him) thereafter, causing, indeed, the scion of the Kota family to be captured by (his) forces, (while) amusing himself at (the city) named Pushpa, while the sun. . . . . . the banks . . . . . .

(Verse 8) (Being) the enclosing structure of Dharma (Sacred Law), (his) multifarious sprouting fame is as bright as the rays of the moon; (his) erudition pierces down to Truth . . . . . . quiescence . . . . . ., the course of (his) wise utterances is worthy of study; (his) again is poetry which outdistances the greatness of the genius of (other) poets. What excellence is there which does not belong to him? So has he alone become a fit subject of contemplation with the learned?

(**Verse 9**) Fame, ever ascending higher and higher masses, and travelling by many paths, (namely) by liberality, prowess of arm, sobriety and utterance of scriptural texts, purifies the three worlds, like the white water of the (holy river) Gaṅgā, dashing forth rapidly when liberated from the confinement in the inner hollow of the matted hair of Paśupati, (which rises up in ever higher and higher masses and flows through many paths).

(Lines 17-18) Of him (who) was skilful in engaging in hundreds of battles of various kinds, whose only ally was valour (prākrama) through the might of his own arm, and who (has thus) the epithet prākrama, whose body was most charming, being covered over with the plenteous beauty of the marks of hundreds of promiscuous scars, caused by battle-axes, arrows, spikes (śaṅku), spears (śakti), barbed darts (prāsa), swords, iron clubs (tomara), javelins (bhindipāla), barbed arrows (narācha), span-long arrows (vaitastika) and many other weapons.

(**Verses 19-20**) Whose magnanimity blended with valour

was caused by (his) first capturing, and thereafter showing the favour of releasing, all the kings of Dakshiṇāpatha such as Mahēndra of Kōsala Vyāghrarāja of Mahākāntāra, Maṇṭarāja of Kurāḷa, Mahēndragiri of Pishṭapura, Svāmidatta of Kōṭṭūra, Damana of Ēraṇḍapalla, Vishṇugōpa of Kāñchī, Nīlarāja of Avamukta, Hastivarman of Vēṅgī, Ugrasēna of Pālakka, Kubēra of Dēvarāshṭra, and Dhanañjaya of Kusthalapura.

(**Verse 21**) (Who) is great through the extraordinary valour, namely, the forcible extermination of many kings of Āryāvarta such as Rudradēva, Matila, Nāgadatta, Chandravarman, Gaṇapatināga, Nāgasēna, Āchyuta-Nandin and Balavarman; who has made all the kings of the forest regions to become his servants.

(**Verse 22**) (Whose) formidable rule was propitiated with the payment of all tributes, execution of orders and visits (to his court) for obeisance by such frontier rulers as those of Samataṭa Ḍavāka, Kāmarūpa, Nēpāla, and Kartṛipura, and, by the Mālavas, Ārjunāyanas, Yaudhēyas, Mādrakas, Ābhīras, Prārjunas, Sanakānīkas, Kākas, Kharaparikas and other (tribes).

(**Verse 23**) (Whose) fame has tired itself with a journey over the whole world caused by the restoration of many fallen kingdoms and overthrown royal families.

A Samudragupta coin featuring the Garud banner.

(**Verse24**) The unimpeded flow (prasara) of the prowess of (whose) arm (was arrested) by an earth embankment (dharaṇi-bandha) put up by means of service through such measures as self-surrender, offering (their own) daughters in marriage and a request for the administration of their own districts and provinces through the Garuḍa badge, by the Dēvaputra-Shāhi-Shāhānushāhi and the Śaka lords and by (rulers) occupying all Island countries, such as Siṁhala and others.

(**Verses 25-26**) He was without an antagonist on earth; he, by the overflowing of the multitude of (his) many good qualities adorned by hundreds of good actions, has wiped off the fame of other kings with the soles of (his) feet; (he is) Purusha (Supreme Being), being the cause of the prosperity of the good and the destruction of the bad (he is) incomprehensible; (he is) one whose tender heart can be captured only by devotion and humility; (he is) possessed of compassion; (he is) the giver of many hundred-thousands of cows; (his) mind has received ceremonial initiation for the uplift of the miserable, the poor, the forlorn and the suffering; (he is) resplendent and embodied kindness to mankind; (he is) equal to (the gods) Kubēra, Varuṇa, Indra and Yama; (his) Āyukta officers are always engaged upon restoring wealth (titles, territories, etc.) to the many kings conquered by the might of his arms.

(**Verses 27-28**) (He) has put to shame Bṛihaspati by (his) sharp and polished intellect, as also Tumburu, Nārada and others by the graces of his musical performances; (his) title of 'King of Poets' has been established through (his) many compositions in poetry which were a means of subsistence to the learnedpeople; (his) many wonderful and noble deeds are fit to be praised for a very long time; (he is) a human being, only as far as he performs the rites and conventions of the world, (otherwise he is) God whose residence is (this) world.

A Samudragupta coin depicting his parents who are mentioned in the inscriptions

(**Verses 28-30**) This lofty column, (is) the raised arm of the earth, proclaiming as it was, that the fame having pervaded the entire surface of the world with (its) rise caused by the conquest of the whole earth, has acquired an easy and graceful movement in that it has repaired from here (i.e. from this world) to the abode of (Indra) the lord of the gods (the fame) of that prosperous Samudragupta the Mahārājādhirāja, son of the prosperous Chandragupta (I), the Mahārājādhirāja, born of the Mahādevī Kumāradevī, (and) daughter's son of the Lichchhavi, son's son of the prosperous Ghaṭōtkacha, the Mahārājā and the son of the son's son of the prosperous Gupta, the Mahārājā.

(**Verses 31-32**) And may this poetic composition (kāvya) of Harishēṇa, the servant of the very same venerable Bhaṭṭāraka, whose mind has been enlightened through the favour of dwelling near (him), who is the Sāndhivigrahika, Kumārāmātya (and) Mahādaṇḍanāyka, (and who is) a native of Khādyaṭapāka, and son of the Mahādaṇḍanāyaka Dhruvabhūti, lead to the welfare and happiness of all beings!

(**Lines33**) and (it) was executed by the Mahādaṇḍanāyaka Tilabhaṭṭaka who meditates on the feet of the Paramabhaṭṭaraka.

From the above-cited inscription, it is clear that (I) Samudra Gupta was a valiant king who subdued 13 kings of the south namely,

1. Achyuta Nagsena
2. Mahendra of Kosala
3. Vyāghra Rāja of Mahākāntāra
4. Mantra Rāja of Kurālā (Kerala)
5. Mahendra Giri of Piṣṭapura
6. Svāmidatta of Kottūra (Kottara)
7. Damana of Erandpalla
8. Vishnugopa of Kanchi

9. Nilarāja of Avamukta

10. Hastivaran of Vengi

11. Ugrasena of Pālakka

12. Kubera of Devarāṣṭra

13. Dhanañjaya of Kusthalapura and all the other kings of the southern region.

(II) He also conquered 9 kings of Āryāvarta such as Rudradēva, Matila, Nāgadatta, Chandravarman (Xandrammes of Greek accounts), Gaṇapati Nāga, Nāgasena, Āchyuta-Nandin and Balavarman.

(III) He also conquered all the chiefs of the wild forest regions and made them his servants. (IV) In addition, he also conquered the rulers of the frontier kingdoms and republics and married their daughters. The above eulogy demonstrates Samudra Gupta's relationship with various indigenous powers who settled in the Western parts of India from the frontiers of Persia, such as the Śaka, the Tuṣāras, the Yavanas of Abisāra and Urṣa, etc. These people were degraded as Mlecchas because they abandoned Vedic Dharma, but not the Greeks, as modern historians believe, the Marundas, who began to enter the country from the northwestern parts of India, crossing the Indus River, almost from the kingdoms of Samtasta, Kasa, and Kāvaka, as well as other border countries in the East, including those of Malava and Khandesh. Even the Sakas of Sakastan, the Yavanas of modern Afghanistan, and the Devaputras submitted to him.

Greek Accounts

Megasthenes, a Greek ambassador sent by Seleucus Nicator in 302 BC, was stationed in Palimbothra, the capital city of the Indian kingdom, where he and the Greeks referred to the king as "Sandrocottus." Megasthenes's stay in India is uncertain, but he documented his experiences in an account titled "Indica." Unfortunately, the original manuscript has been lost, and no copies are available. However, during its time of existence, many other Greek writers referenced passages from "Indica" in their own works. Dr. Schwanbeck meticulously collected these quotations in the nineteenth century, and they are now available in English (J.M. McCrindle: Ancient India as Described by Megasthenes and Arrian). During the nineteenth century, when European Indologists were attempting to date Indian history (after arbitrarily rejecting the Purāṇas), the Megasthenes account proved invaluable to their research.

Megasthenes

Sir William Jones, according to Indian accounts, was skeptical about the antiquity of the Mahābhārata War due to his Christian faith, which held that Creation occurred at 9:00 AM on October 23, 4004 BC. In an attempt to find evidence, he sought out Greek and Roman accounts. These accounts provided some insights into India during the time of the Macedonian king Alexander. They mentioned the names of three successive Indian kings: Xandrammes, Sandrocottus, and Sandrocyptus. Xandrammes (Chandravarman), a ruler from the northern region, was assassinated by Sandrocottus, whose son was Sandrocyptus (Chandra Gupta II).

William Jones, as mentioned at the outset of this work, under the influence of Max Müller, significantly reduced the Indian chronology to align it with the Greek and Biblical chronologies. This resulted in a misinterpretation of the Greek synchronism between Sandrocottus and Chandragupta of the Maurya Dynasty, instead of the Samudragupta of the Gupta Dynasty.

Later scholars confirmed the identity of Sandrocottus with

Chandragupta Maurya and continued their research. James Princep, an employee of the East India Company, deciphered the Brahmi script and read the inscriptions of Piyadassana. Turnour, another employee of the Company in Ceylon, discovered in the Ceylonese chronicles that Piyadassana was a surname of Aśoka, the grandson of Chandragupta Maurya. The inscription bearing Aśoka's name was not found until Turnour's discovery. In 1838, Princep identified five names of Yona kings in Asoka's inscriptions and matched them with the five Greek kings near Greece from the third century BC who were contemporaries of Aśoka.

Alexander The Great

In the Greek accounts, Sandrocottus of Palimbothra is described as a contemporary of Alexander the Great, who invaded India between 327 BC and 323 BC. This information determines the approximate date of Chandragupta Maurya. Princep's research suggests that Asoka, the grandson of Chandragupta Maurya, lived in the 3rd century BC. Both these dates were adjusted based on the reign periods of the three successive Magadha kings: Chandragupta, Bindusara, and Aśoka, as mentioned in the Purāṇas. Consequently, the date 320 BC was fixed as the coronation date of Chandragupta Maurya. This date serves as a foundation, and from then on, it has been used as a reference point to construct the timeline of Indian history.

Max Müller, in 1859 AD, finally identified Sandrocottus with Chandragupta Maurya and declared 320 BC as the date of Chandragupta Maurya's coronation, marking the beginning of Indian history. However, M. Troyer disagreed with this conclusion and mentioned it in the introduction to his translation of Rājataraṅginī by Kalhaṇa (748 AD). Troyer even expressed his views to Professor Max Müller in a letter, but he never received a response.

Historian V.A. Smith, building upon the chronological identity established by his predecessors in this historical hierarchy, employed numismatics and epigraphy to calculate the precise dates of the various dynasties that ruled over Magadha after and before the Mauryas. However, he was unable to overcome his compulsion to deviate from the Purāṇas in the enumeration of kings and their dynasties. Nevertheless, he reduced their reign periods. The cumulative reduction achieved by these British scholars, from Jones to Smith, amounts to 1300 years, as per some Indian chronologists.

On the other hand, a keen study of Megasthenes' Indica tells us that Chandra Gupta Maurya never met Megasthenes.

1. Megasthenes has nowhere mentioned the word Maurya.
2. He makes absolutely no mention of a person called either Chaṇakya or Kauṭilya.
3. Indian historians have recorded two Chandra Gupta, one of the Maurya dynasty and another of the Gupta dynasty. Both of them had a grandson called Aśoka. While the Mauryan Chandragupta's son was called Bimbisara (sometimes Bindusara), the Gupta Chandragupta had a son called Samudragupta. Interestingly Megasthenes has written that Sandracottus had a son called Samdrocyptus. Sandrocottus is phonetically nearer to Samudra Gupta and Samdrocyptus to Chandra Gupta and not Chandra Gupta and Bindusara as allegedly taken.

4. Megasthenese himself says 137 generations of kings have come and gone between Krishna and Sandrakuttos, whereas the Purāṇas account for only 83 generations only between Jarasandha's son (Krishna's contemporary) to the Nandas of the Magadha kingdom. If we pull on this chain upto Gupta Dynasty the list of kings come close to 137. As such, Megasthenese's statement itself proves that Sandrocottus of Greek account was corresponding to the Samudra Gupta of Gupta period instead of Chandra Gupta of Maurya period.

5. According to the Greek accounts, Xandrammes was deposed by Sandrocottus and Sandrocyptus was the son of Sandrocottus. In the case of Chandragupta Maurya, he had opposed Dhanananda of the Nanda dynasty and the name of his son was Bindusara. Both these names, Dhanananda and Bindusara, have no phonetic similarity with the names Xandrammes and Sandrocyptus of the Greek accounts, whereas from Allahabad pillar inscription attributed to Eulogy of Samudra Gupta we are informed that Northern king Chandravarman was deposed by Samudra Gupta. Chandravarman had some phonetic similarity with Xandrammes of Greek account. Similarly, Chandra Gupta II, son of Samudra Gupta has phonetic similarity with the Sandrocyptus of Greek account.

Allahabad Iron Pillar

Aśoka's empire was bigger than that of Chandragupta Maurya and he had sent missionaries to the so-called Yavana countries. But both of them are not mentioned. Colebrook has pointed out that the Greek writers did not say anything about the Buddhist Bhikkus though that was the flourishing religion of that time with the royal patronage of Aśoka of Kashmir. That is why Greek accounts are silent on Buddhism. This fact surprised historians like Roychaudhari.

The empire of Chandragupta Maurya, also known as the Magadha Empire, had a long history even during its time. In Indian literature, this powerful empire is extensively described by this name, but it is notably absent in the Greek accounts. It is perplexing why Megasthenese chose to use the word "Prassi" (synonymous to Sanskrit Prāchī) instead of the more commonly used "Magadha," which lacks a direct equivalent or counterpart in Indian historical records..

To determine whether Pataliputra served as the capital of the Mauryas, the Purāṇas are the sole source of information. The Purāṇas provide details about the eight dynasties that ruled Magadha after the Mahabharata War, from 3067 BC onwards. These dynasties are listed and Girivraja is mentioned as their capital. However, the name Pataliputra is not even mentioned anywhere in the Purāṇas.

Chandra Gupta of the Gupta dynasty conquered Pataliputra in 323 BC and established it as his capital. Megasthenese, who visited Pataliputra during the Gupta period, refers to Polibothra. Therefore, the association between Palibothra and Pataliputra holds true for Samudra Gupta of the Gupta period, not for Chandra Gupta of the Maurya period.

Western scholars and their followers in India have consistently demanded concrete evidence for the ancient Indian chronology, yet they have been unable to provide any such evidence for the foundation of their beliefs.

Samudragupta Coin

All the evidence presented so far is speculative. There's no numismatic or inscriptional proof to support the date. The same was the case during V.A. Smith's time. He had written, "Regrettably, no monuments have been discovered that can be definitively linked to the period of Chandragupta Maurya, and the archaeologist lacks any tangible evidence provided by excavations."

269 BC–233BC: Chandragupta II, the son of Samudra Gupta and Datta Devi, ruled Magadha for an impressive 36 years. He earned the title of 'Vikramāditya' and made significant military strides. His most notable achievement was his conquest of the Arabian Sea through Malva and Gujarat, followed by the subjugation of the Saurashtra peninsula, also known as Kathiawar. This region had been ruled by the Śakas known as Satraps for over a century. Additionally, Chandragupta II defeated the Bahlika nation in battle. The elegant and poetic description of the celebrated iron pillar of Mehrauli in Delhi, now known as the Qutub Minar, vividly captures his victories.

Iron Pillar of Mehrauli, Delhi

This iron pillar, a marvel of the forger's art during the early Gupta period, stands as a testament to the ingenuity of its creators. Its base is a foot and a half thick, while its height is twenty-three feet. Estimated to weigh over six tons, it is forged from a single piece of pure rustless iron. Remarkably, more than two thousand years of exposure to various weather conditions have not caused any deterioration in the metal. Despite advancements in modern technology, it remains an impossible feat to replicate the 99.95% purity of iron achieved during that era.

233 BC– 191 BC: Kumar Gupta I, son of Chandra Gupta II by his queen Dhruva Devi ruled Magadha Empire for 42 years.

The Mandasor inscription of Bandhuvarman, engraved during the reign of the Gupta king Kumāragupta I (*Kumāragupte prithivām praśāsati*) goes like this.

मलवाणाम् गण-स्थित्या याते शत-चतुष्ट्ये ॥
त्रि-नवत्यधिकेऽब्दानाम् ऋतौ सेव्य-घन-स्वने ॥
सहस्य-मास शुक्लस्य प्रशस्तेऽह्नि त्रयोदशे
Malavāṇām gaṇa-sthityā yāte śata-catuṣṭaye.
tri-navatyadhike'bdānām ṛtau sevya-ghana-svane.
Sahasya-māsa śuklasya praśaste'hni trayodaśe.

[Meaning] When, according to the reckoning of the Malava era, four centuries and ninety-three years had passed, in the season resounding with clouds worthy of worship (the monsoon), on the auspicious thirteenth day of the bright fortnight (śukla-pakṣa) of the month of Sahasya (Pauṣa).

It is dated to the year 493 of the Mālava-gaṇa era or Kārtikādi Vikrama era, which corresponds to 717-493=224 BC. The 13th tithi of the bright fortnight of Sahasya (Pauṣa) month falls on November 21st, 224 BC.

He also performed the Aśvamedha Yajña, a grand sacrifice to assert his supreme sovereignty and to successfully drive out the Hunas who were invading through the Northwestern passes.

191 BC–166BC: Skanda Gupta, the son of Kumar Gupta 1 and his senior queen Ananta Devi, ascended to the throne in 191 BC. During his reign, the Hunas wreaked havoc and destruction across western India. Skanda Gupta dedicated his life to a successful war against them, establishing peace in the country. The people celebrated his conquests through songs and ballads during that era. According to Kaliyuga Rāja Vṛttānta, Skandagupta ruled for 25 years. Renowned for his valor and prowess, he was celebrated as 'Vijayāditya'. The Gupta dynasty, founded by the subordinates of the Andhra Sātavāhanas, was also known as the Andhra Bhṛtya dynasty. Although Gupta dynasty practically ceased to exist upon his passing, it endured for two to three generations.

According to the Jūnāgarh inscription of Skandagupta, the embankment of the Sudarśana lake in Saurāṣṭra collapsed due to relentless rains during the Gupta Saṁvat 136 (327-136=191 BC). During the reign of the Western Śaka Kṣatrapa Rudradāman I in Śaka 72 (583-72=511 BC), extensive repairs were undertaken to restore the lake. Skandagupta's Governor in Saurāṣṭra, Chakrapālita, the son of Parṇadatta, took on the task of repairing Sudarśana lake and completed it by Gupta Saṁvat 137 (327-137=190 BC). During the period from 166 BC to 126 BC, Skanda Gupta, who lacked a son of his own, adopted Narasiṁha Gupta Bālāditya, the son of his half-brother Purugupta or Sthiragupta Prakāśāditya and Chandradevi. According to Kaliyuga Rāja Vṛttānta (Kota, 1957: p.226-228), Sthiragupta (Purugupta) and Narasiṁha Gupta ruled for a combined period of 40 years from 166 BCE to 126 BC.

ततो नृसिंहगुप्तश्च बालादित्य इति श्रुतः ।
पुत्रः प्रकाशादित्यस्य स्थिगुप्तस्य भूपतेः ॥
नियुक्तः स्वपितृव्येन स्कन्धगुप्तेन जीवता ।
पित्रैव साकं भविता चत्वरिंशत समाः नृपः ॥
tato nṛsiṁhaguptaścha bālāditya iti śrutaḥ I
putraḥ prakāśādityasya sthiguptasya bhūpateḥ II
niyuktaḥ svapitṛvyena skandhaguptena jīvatā I
pitraiva sākaṁ bhavitā chatvariṁśata samāḥ nṛpaḥ II

[Meaning] Then came Nṛsiṃhagupta, also known as Bālāditya, the son of Prakāśāditya, son of Sthigupta, the noble king. He was appointed to rule by his paternal uncle, Skandagupta, while the latter was still alive. Together with his father, he will reign as king for forty years.

126 BC–82 BC: Kumar Gupta II was the last Gupta emperor. He assumed the title of Kumārāditya. Kumāragupta II, the son of Narasiṁha Gupta and Mittradevi, ruled for 44 years from 126 BC to 82 BC. He had a tough time resisting the Huṇas who utterly destroyed the Gupta empire by 82 BC. According to Kaliyuga Rāja Vṛttānta, when the Saptarṣī-s reached Punarvasu Nakṣatra (in its second revolution after the Mahābhārata War), the Empire of the great Gupta Kings began to decline.

यदा पुनर्वसु यास्यन्त्येते सप्तर्षयः पुनः ।
तदा श्रीगुप्तवंश्यानां राष्ट्रं दैन्यं गमिष्यति ॥

yadā punarvasu yāsyantyete saptarṣayaḥ punaḥ I
tadā śrīguptavaṁśyānāṁ rāṣṭraṁ dainyaṁ gamiṣyati II

[Meaning] When these Seven Sages (Saptarṣis) once again move into the Punarvasu constellation, then the kingdom of the illustrious Gupta dynasty shall fall into misery and decline.

After Mahabharata War, Saptarṣīs came in conjunction with Punarvasu Nakṣatra (in retrograde order) in 2876 BC. Second time they came in conjunction with Punarvasu stars in 176 BC and remain there till 76 BC.

During the rule of Kumar Gupta II (126 BC-82 BC) Saptarṣīs lived in Punarvasu Nakṣatra from 51-95 years.

The Gupta period stands as the greatest unifying era in Indian history, during which the enlightened Gupta kings brought northern India and a significant portion of the Deccan under their suzerainty. This period of their rule, spanning 250 years, is celebrated as the golden age of Bharat. The exceptionally intelligent and capable kings of the Imperial Gupta dynasty generously patronized scholars, scientists, and various intellectual and artistic endeavors. Notably, they played a pivotal role in language reform, elevating Sanskrit to the status of an official language.

Panwar or Parmar Dynasty

51/7/28th Kali/3020–4294 or 82 BC–78AD

After the fall of Gupta dynasty, the Panwar or Parmar Dynasty came into prominence from 82 BC led by famous Vikramaditya. He belongs to one of the Agnivaṁśa Kṣatriyas. Agnivaṁśa Kṣatriyas were those Brāhmaṇas who were dedicated to their profession and were performing routine Yajñas. But who were forced to leave their original profession of Brāhmaṇa and took arms to protect the country from invaders when Kṣatriyas became weak. The three other Agnivaṁśa Kṣatriyas are Śuklas or Chalukyas, Pariharas or Pratiharas and Chahamanas/Chauhanas or Tomaras.

Vikramaditya II

51/7/28th Kali/3020–3121 or 82 BC–19 AD

Vikramaditya, the son of Gandharvasena, the seventh king of Ujjain from the Panwar dynasty, was born in 102 BC. Gandharvasena, after rigorous penance and prayer to Lord Śiva, was blessed with a son. From the age of five for a period of twelve years, Vikramāditya was educated in a hermitage, where he acquired spiritual powers. At the age of twenty, in 82 BC, he was crowned the king of Ujjain. In 24 years, he subjugated several independent principalities. Magadha was already weakened, and most of the neighboring kingdoms sought Vikramaditya's help in their rivalry. Taking advantage of the situation, he established a strong hold over the entire country without resorting to major wars. However, there were savage wars fought between Vikramaditya's army and invaders from the west known as the Śakas. In these wars, King Vikramaditya emerged victorious and gained wealth from the invaders.

Vikramādtya II, the second king of the Vikramāditya dynasty, engaged in a conflict with the Śakas in the northwestern region. He successfully defeated a Śaka king of 'Romaka'. Additionally, Alberuni mentions that Vikramāditya II marched against another Śaka king and eliminated him in the region of Karur, situated between Multan and the castle of Loni.

यो रुमकेशाधिपतिं शकेश्वरम्।

जित्वा गृहितोऽज्जयिनीं महाहवे ॥

आनीय संभ्राम्य मुमोच तं त्वहो।
श्रीविक्रमार्कसमसह्यविक्रमो ॥

yo Rummakeśādhipatim śakeśvaram
jitvā gṛhito'jjayinīm mahāhave
ānīya saṁbhrāmya mumoca tam tvaho
Śri-Vikramārka-samasahyavikramaḥ

[Meaning] He who, having conquered the lord of the Romakas and the ruler of the Śakas, captured the city of Ujjayinī in a great battle; having brought (the enemy) back in humiliation, yet magnanimously released him — such was Śrī Vikramāditya, whose valor equaled the brilliance of the Sun."

Since he expelled the Sakas from the country, he gained fame as Śakārī, meaning "foe of Sakas." He consolidated his power as the emperor of the entire Indian subcontinent, extending his dominion up to Herat. In 3044 Kali or 57 BC, the king of Nepal recognized his suzerainty, leading to him becoming the unchallenged emperor of the entire Indian subcontinent. This event is recorded in the Nepali Rāja Vaṁsāvali, where it is mentioned that to commemorate the occasion, he established a new Samvat (era) in 3044 Kali or 57 BC, which is now known as the Chaitrādi Vikrama era.

The empire of Vikramāditya ultimately stretched from Indo-China in the east to the Arab world in the west. In addition to diplomacy and warfare, matrimony was also employed as a tool for both expansion and consolidation of the empire. Vikramāditya had married several princesses from prominent royal families, including a princess from China.

The city of Mecca, founded by him, became a significant center of Śiva worship and an annual carnival. The holy stone of Kaba held immense importance as the most revered Śiva linga in the entire western Asian region. Vikramāditya's influence extended across the seas, reaching Śri Laṅkā and the islands now known as Indonesia. Notably, these islands did not constitute part of his empire. Vikramāditya's reign is celebrated as the harbinger of a new era of abundance and prosperity in

India. It marked the zenith of advancements in sciences, medicine, astronomy, and other fields.

This Vikramaditya II of Ujjain was later killed by Samudrapal Yogi who was the commander of Śālivāhana of Pattan in present-day Pratisthan of Maharashtra. Śālivāhana handed over the rule of Indraprastha which was under Vikramāditya to Samudrapal Yogi and took himself the control of Ujjain.

Śaka Dynasty

51/7/28th Kali/3121–3181or 19AD–1192 AD

Thus came an end to Parmar dynasty and Śaka started ruling Ujjain. Having heard the news of the death of Vikramāditya, Śakas, Tartaras, Chinese, Balhikas, Kamrupas, Romakas and Khurasanas again became active and started invading and plundering India. Śakāri king decided to teach them a lesson like that of Vikramāditya and conquered all the foreigners, drove all of them back to their country. He recovered the plundered booty and established a rule of peace and prosperity for his countrymen.

According to Skanda Purāṇa (Maheśvara Khaṇḍa, 1, 40.254), the name Śaka will be associated with the alleviation of poverty in the Saptarṣī year 1100. The verse goes like this:

तत शतसहस्रेषु शतेनाप्यधिकेषु च ।
शको नाम भविष्यश्चासौऽतिदारिद्यहारकः ।।
tata śatasahasreṣu śatenāpyadhikeṣu cha ।
śako nāma bhaviṣyaśchāsau'tidāridryahārakaḥ ।।

[Meaning] Then, when one hundred and thousand and one hundred (1100) years have passed, there shall arise a ruler named Śaka, who will be a remover of great poverty and distress.

The above calculation is according to third cycle of Saptarṣi Saṁvat according to the Kahsmir school which started in 1076 BC. If we deduct 1100 from 1076 BC, we get 1076 BC-1100= 24 AD.

The above statement refers to Śaka named king who established Śaka era 78 AD after eliminating the rule of Śakas from India.

Śaka Era

(Śaka Nṛpa Kālātīta)

51/7/28thKali/3180 or 78 AD

To commemorate his triumph, Śālivāhana established a Vijayastambha in Paithan/Pattan (Pratiṣṭhāna) and inaugurated a new era known as Śaka Saṁvat in 78 AD. He ruled over a vast territory spanning from the Himalayas to Cape Comorin and conducted Aśvamedha Yāga to solidify his authority.

Vijaya Stambha of Paithan

The great emperor Śaka established the boundaries between Āryāvartta and Mleccha desha, with the river Sindhu serving as the dividing line. The land to the east of the river was known as Sindhu-sthan, while the land to the west was called Mleccha-sthan. Later, Sindhusthan evolved into Hindusthan when the river was referred to as Sindu in Hindu literature. Śaka not only demarcated the border of Mlecchasthan but also made arrangements to prevent the Mlecchas from crossing the river Sindhu. He ruled for an impressive 60 years until 79 AD. In his lineage, there were ten rulers, with Bhoja being the last one. The first nine rulers ruled from 79 AD to 637 AD, and they were known for their weakness. Their names are as follows:

Shalihotra, Shalivardhan, Suhotra, Havirhotra, Indrapal, Malaya-van, Shambhudatta, Bhauma-raj, Vatsaraj

After the decline of the Śaka dynasty, the influence of the dynasty waned significantly. Most kingdoms declared their independence, while others accepted nominal suzerainty from the king of Magadha. There were also invasions from the west by Mleccha rulers. Despite these challenges, the last ruler, Bhojraj, emerged as a formidable and powerful king. He unified the entire country under his rule and conquered northwestern provinces such as Gandhar, Kashmir, Ariya (whose capital was Herat), and imposed taxes on the defeated Śaka rulers. Bhoja ruled from 637 AD to 693 AD. Following Bhoja's reign, there were ten rulers who ruled from 693 AD to 1192 AD. Their names are as follows: Shambhudatta, Bindupal, Rajpal, Mahinara, Somavarma, Kamavarma, Bhumipal, Anangpal, Kalpa Singh, and Ganga Singh.

Last King Ganga Singh of the Śaka dynasty and Mahipati, the last king of the Parihar/Pratihar dynasty, fought as allies of Prithviraj Chauhan against Mohammad Ghori and his ally Jayachandra of the Chalukya dynasty in the 2nd Battle of Tarain in 1192 AD. Tragically, they were all killed in battle. Jayachandra, too, committed suicide for trusting the Muslims. Following their deaths, the kingdoms of the Śaka dynasty, along with those of the Parihar and Chalukya dynasties in northwestern India, fell under Muslim rule.

19. Rulers of Kashmir

51/7/28th Dvāpara/863652–28th Kali/1734

or

3450 BC–1535 AD

The chronology of the rulers of Kashmir is derived from the "Rājataraṅgiṇī," written by Kalhaṇa. He cited several earlier works that chronicled the history of Kashmir. Notable among these sources are the writings of Suvrata, Kṣemendra's "Nṛpāvali," and eleven other works by earlier scholars that recorded the names of kings. Additionally, he references the "Nīlamat Purāṇa" (Rāj. 11-14).

According to Kalhaṇa (1.44), the history of 52 Kashmiri kings, up to Gonand II—who was a contemporary of the Kauravas and Pāṇḍavas—remains undocumented.

तत्र कोरवकौन्तेय समकालभवात् कलौ।
आ गोनन्दात् स्मरन्ति स्म न द्वापंचाशतं नृपान्।। 1.44
tatra koravakaunteya samakālabhavāt kalau /
ā gonandāt smaranti sma na dvāpaṁchāśataṁ nṛpān // 1.44

[Meaning] In that country, fifty-two rulers, up to the time of Gonanda II, who lived during the Kaliyuga alongside the Kurus and the sons of Kunti (the Pāṇḍavas), have not been recorded.

The absence of their historical records is attributed to the shortcomings of those fifty-two kings. As a result of their failings, there was no scholar of creative talent born in Kashmir during that time who could have chronicled their glory.

तस्मिन्काले ध्रुवं तेषां कुकृत्यैः काश्यपीभुजाम्।
कर्तारः कीर्तिकायस्य नाभुवन्कविवेधसः।।
tasminkāle dhruvaṁ teṣāṁ kukṛtyaiḥ kāśyapībhujām /
kartāraḥ kīrtikāyasya nābhuvankavivedhasaḥ //

[Meaning] In that age, assuredly because of the failings

of the descendants of Kāśyapa (the kings of that lineage), there shall no longer born scholar who could have chronicled their glory.

These 52 kings, beginning with Gonand II (3137-3082), ruled for a total of 1,266 years (Rāj. 1.54). According to Kalhaṇa, the history of the rulers of Kashmir dates back 4,403 years, calculated as 3137 + 1266 (653 years of the Tiṣya saṁvat).

However, we are given to understand that around 3,500 years before Christ, the last king of Ayodhyā, Agnivarṇa, began living a life of luxury, neglecting his responsibilities to the people. His brother advised him to change his ways, as per the ideals established by their ancestors, to uphold the glory of the Sūryavaṁśa dynasty. Unfortunately, Agnivarṇa ignored this counsel. Frustrated by his brother's indifference, Agnigarbha left Ayodhyā. He traveled through Rajasthan and Kangra, eventually reaching the Punjab region, which is now known as Kathua in Jammu and Kashmir. There, he took control of some areas and began ruling. His son, Babu Rao, later conquered the entire region along the Tawi River, thereby expanding their territory.

The history of the 52 kings, starting with Gonand II (3137-3082), accounts for a total of 1,266 years of rule (Rāj. 1.54).

वर्षाणां द्वादशशती षष्टिः षड्भिश्च संयुता ।
भूभुजां कालसंख्यायां तद्द्वापंचाशतो मता । ।

varṣāṇāṁ dvādaśaśatī ṣaṣṭiḥ ṣaḍbhiścha saṁyutā /
bhūbhujāṁ kālasaṁkhyāyāṁ taddvāpaṁchāśato matā / /

Thus as such, as per information of Kalhaṇa, the lineage of Kashmir's rulers stretches back 4,403 years, derived from the sum of 3137 and 1266 (or Tiṣya Saṁvat 653, that commences from 5056 BC).

It is noted that around 3,500 years before Christ, Agnivarṇa, the last king of Ayodhyā, led a life of luxury, neglecting his duties towards his people. His brother urged him to reconsider his ways in alignment with the values established by their ancestors to maintain the honor of the Sūryavaṁśa dynasty.

Regrettably, Agnivarṇa dismissed this advice. In frustration over his brother's apathy, Agnigarbha departed from Ayodhyā. He journeyed through Rajasthan and Kangra, ultimately arriving in the Punjab region, which is now known as Kathua in Jammu and Kashmir. There, he seized control of certain territories and began his reign. His son, Babu Rao, later expanded their dominion by conquering the entire region along the Tawi River. The available record of rulers of the Īkṣvāku dynasty shows that they ruled for 368 years (from 3450-3082).

Īkṣvāku Dynasty

3450 BC- 3082 BC

1. 3450 BC-3407 BC: Lakho, the grandson of Agnigarbha and son of Babu Rao captured the whole North-western region and started ruling from Kashmir instead of Kathua in 3450 BC.

2. 3407 BC-3364 BC: Lakho was succeeded by Khiyat.

3. 3364 BC- 3312 BC: Arjuna ruled Kashmir

4. 3312 BC-3254 BC: Arjuna had two sons, viz. Bahulochana and Jammulochan. Bahulochan is credited with having built the Bahu fort, but he died issueless. So, Jamulochan succeeded him to the throne of Kashmir. He is credited with having built Jammu city after his name. He had two sons Dharmakarṇa and Dayākarṇa. He divided his vast empire spanning over Iran and Iraq into two parts: Jammu and Kashmir. He handed over the reins of Jammu to Dharmakarṇa and Kashmir to Dayākarṇa.

4. 3254 BC-3228 BC: Dayākarṇa made Babilla or Babylon (built on the Euphrates River in Iraq) his capital and ruled Kashmir.

5. 3228 BC-3188 BC: Gonanda I, the son of Dayākarṇa, succeeded his father and ruled for 40 years. He expanded his empire by annexing most of the Turkish regions. At the time, the regions of Yarkand, now a county and historical town in the Xinjiang Uyghur Autonomous Region of China, and Khiva, known as Khorasan and currently located in the Xorazm region of Uzbekistan, were already part of his domain. Gonanda I was

a powerful king who lived during the time of Śri Kṛṣṇa (3225 BC - 3101 BC) and was a friend of Jarasandha, an enemy of Śri Kṛṣṇa.

Jarāsandha invited him to assist in an invasion of Mathura, the capital of Kansa (Rāj. 1.59). With a large army, they besieged the city and camped on the banks of the Yamuna, causing great fear among their opponents. At one point, Kansa's army was defeated in battle, but Balarama managed to regain control during the chaos and launched a vigorous counterattack on the allied forces. For a long time, the outcome of the battle remained uncertain until Gonanda I, wounded, ultimately fell dead on the battlefield. In the end, the army of Śri Kṛṣṇa emerged victorious (Rāj. 1.63).

6. 3188 BC-3138 BC: After Gonanda I, Damodara I ruled (Rāj. 1.64). Damodara, deeply affected by his father's death, learned that the Gandhar king had invited the Vṛṣṇis to the Svayaṁvara of his daughter (Rāj. 1.66). In response, he invaded the Vṛṣṇis but was ultimately killed by Śri Kṛṣṇa in the ensuing battle on the banks of the river Sindhu. At the time of Damodara's death, his wife, Queen Yashovati, was pregnant. Therefore, Śri Kṛṣṇa appointed her to ascend the throne of Kashmir (Rāj. 1.70).

7. 3137 BC: Yaśovatī ruled for six months.

8. 3136 BC-3082 BC: When Yashovati delivered the child, he was called Gonanda II after the name of his grandfather. Then, the 12-day-old child named Gonanda II was installed as king. After one year of his coronation (3136 BC), the Mahābhārata war was fought (3137 BC). This shows that Gonanda II was coronated in 3137 BC. According to Kalhaṇa (Rāj. 1.51) Mahābhārata war was fought when 653 years of Kashmir Saptarṣi Saṁvat (3776 BC) passed, i.e. 3776-653=3123 BC. So, there is a difference of 14 years between the widely accepted date of war and Kalahaṇa's date of war. The *Rājataraṅgiṇī* (1.82) says that Kauravas and Pāṇḍvas did not see his support for the war as he was an infant. However, King Parikṣita (3101 BC-3041 BC) of Hastinapur killed him in a battle

and annexed Kashmir to the Hastinapur Empire. Thus, the rule of Pāṇḍva dynasty was installed there. It marked the end of the rule of Sūryavaṁśa and the commencement of the rule of Chandravaṁśa in Kashmir.

After Gonand II, the thirty-five kings of the Paṇḍava dynasty ruled. Their records were unavailable by the time of Kalhaṇa, as per his statement (Rāj. 1.83). However, Mulla Ahmed's 'History of Kashmir,' written in Persian, provides the names of these lost kings. Mulla Ahmad hailed from the village of Pindori, and his book is said to be a translation of an ancient work called the Ratnakar Purana, which detailed the accounts of 47 kings of Kashmir not included in Kalhaṇa's Rajatarangini.

During the reign of Badshah Zain-ul-Abidin (1422-1474), a search was initiated to locate old Puranas and Taranginis to produce an updated version of Kashmir's history in Persian, again by Mulla Ahmad, who was the court poet of Zain-ul-Abidin. They discovered references to about 15 different Rājataraṅgiṇīs, but only four could be located: Kalhaṇa, Kṣemendra, Wachhulakar, and Padmamihar. Although Kṣemendra's Rājataraṅgṇī was found to be significantly unreliable, a translation of Rājataraṅgiṇī was prepared using the other texts.

A few years later, some birch bark leaves of an ancient Rājataraṅgṇī written by Pandit Ratnakar, known as Ratnakar Purana, were discovered by a scholar named Praja Pandit. From those leaves, accounts of 47 'lost' kings of Kashmir were made available and included in Mulla Ahmad's History of Kashmir. Unfortunately, Ratnakar Purana was later lost again and now exists only in Mulla Ahmad's translation.

It is said that Moulvi Ghulam Hasan Shah (1832-1898) managed to obtain a copy of Mulla Ahmad's translation from a Kashmiri immigrant in Rawalpindi named Mulah Mahmud. Hasan Shah later incorporated this work into his three-volume 'Tarikh-i-Hasan.' However, he eventually lost Mulla Ahmad's History of Kashmir under peculiar circumstances: while traveling by boat, the vessel capsized. Hasan Shah was saved, but Mulla Ahmad's book was lost forever.

In 1902, the Kashmir Durbar sought to acquire a copy of Mulla Ahmad's work, but by then, Mulah Mahmud had passed away, and his family had relocated to Kabul at the invitation of Amir Abdul Rahman Khan, the Emir of Afghanistan from 1880 to 1901. As a result, the only record of the 'lost' kings of Kashmir is derived from Hasan Shah, who is a seventh-generation descendant of one Koul.

In the history of Kashmir written by Western authors in English, the first mention of Hasan Shah comes from Walter Rooper Lawrence, who served as the land settlement officer in Kashmir from 1889 to 1895. Lawrence was taught the Kashmiri language by Hasan Shah and acknowledged, 'What else I learned (in the Kashmiri language) I owe to Pir Hasan Sah, a learned Kashmiri, whose work has entirely been among the villagers.'

When Lawrence became the Private Secretary to the Viceroy of India, he invited Hasan to meet the Viceroy. Unfortunately, by the time the invitation was extended, Hasan had passed away a few days earlier.

This account is based on a brief biography of Hasan Shah written by Pandit Anand Koul for the Journal and Proceedings of the Asiatic Society of Bengal in 1913. Anand Koul also provided an account of eight 'lost' kings based on Hasan Shah's writings. A few years earlier, in 1910, for the same journal, Pandit Anand Koul authored a lengthy article titled 'History of Kashmir,' also based on Hasan's writings, which presented the accounts of 47 kings. This account of missing kings is linked to the Pandavas.

We have tried to fill up the chronological gaps of the above rulers with the help of Hasan Shah's writings based on Mulla Ahmed's history of Kashmir. They ruled from 3082 BC to 1958 BC for 1124 years. Their Chronology is given as under:

Pāṇḍava Dynasty

3082 BC-2077 BC

1. 3082 BC-3041 BC: King Parikṣita of Hastinapur ruled Kashmir for 4 years. He crowned his first son Janmejaya as king of Hastinapur and his second son Haraṇadeva as the king of Kashmir.

2. 3041 BC- 3036 BC: Haraṇadeva was the grandson of Arjuna.

03. 3036 BC - 3016 BC: Rāmdeva succeeded Haraṇadeva. He was famous for tax reforms. He reduced tax from 16% to 10%. He married the daughter of Shiva Rai, ruler of Gandhara.

04. 3016 BC- 3007 BC: Vyasadeva married Kalabhawani daughter of King Jaswant of Marwar.

05. 3007 BC- 2981 BC: Droṇadeva ruled. His wife Margidevi built the temple of Margeshvara at village Kuther.

06. 2981 BC- 2927 BC: Singhdeva ruled. Village Simhpur was founded by him

07. 2927 BC- 2914 BC: Gopaldeva was brother-in-law of Vijayananda, the chief of Kashgar. Chief of Khuttan won the war from Chief of Kashgar

08. 2914 BC- 2889 BC: Vajayananda was younger brother of Gopaldeva. Won back Kashgar. Defeated Khuttan. He built the temple of Vijayeshvara at Bijbihara.

09. 2889 BC- 2845 BC: Sukhdeva was son of Gopaldeva. He lost territories in Punjab to king of Delhi, Chitrath. Also, lost Turkistan. He was murdered while hunting in mountains of Amarnath by drawing in Liddar river by Rama Nanda, son of Vijayananda.

10. 2845 BC- 2788 BC: Rāmānand ruled. He subjugated ruler of Jammu.

11. 2788 BC - 2723 BC: Sandhiman was son of Rama Nanda. He founded the city at a place which is now the bed of Wular Lake, known as Sandimatnagar (still known as Salabatnagar). He built the temple of Zeshteshvara. Invaded territories as far a Kanauj. Married Partidevi, the daughter of king of Kandhara. She died at Attock, on way to Kashmir when her boat capsized.

12. 2723 BC- 2668 BC: Marhan Deva & Kamandeva were sons of Sandhiman. In their hostility, the country got divided into two. South-Eastern went to Marhandeva and North Eastern to Kamandeva.

Karmandeva founded the village named Marhama. Kamandeva (unjust king) made Sandimatnagar his capital. A comet appeared that year. In the same year, the rains were heavy. Also, a huge snake appeared at Chakdar which died but its carcass stayed for a year. Based on the divisions made by two kings Kashmir is still divided as Maraj and Manraj.

13. 2668 BC- 2616 BC: Chandradeva was son of Marhandeva. He killed Kamandeva. He was a debauch king, he had 360 wives, one for each lunar day.

14. 2616 BC- 2588 BC: Ānanda Deva was brother of Chandardeva. He was a cruel king.

15. 2588 BC- 2581 BC: Drupada Deva was son of Ananda. He was a kind king. He built the temple of Jwalamukhi at the village Shar.He was killed by his brother Harnamdeva with an arrow to the eye.

16. 2581 BC- 2542 BC: Harnam Deva built vineyards and distillers. He was an unjust king who was almost defeated by his commander-in-chief named Durga. Durga almost defeated Harnamdeva but people backed Harnamdeva and helped defeat Durga. Repentant Harnamdeva remitted two years' revenue. Later Durga's son named Rangu killed Harnamdeva while he was on a hunting expedition.

17. 2542 BC- 2514 BC: Sulakshan Deva was son of Harnamdeva. He was pleasure loving king worked only on Saturdays.

18. 2514 BC- 2497 BC: Senaditya was a foolish king who paid ten million dinars for a celestial virgin. He was killed in bed by his brother Mangaladitya.

19. 2497 BC- 2458 BC: Mangladitya was a bad ruler. In his time a mist appeared, the inhalation of which caused many deaths.

20. 2458 BC- 2392 BC: Kṣemendra Datta son of Mangaladitya. He was killed by minister Druna for outraging the modesty of his wife.

21. 2392 BC- 2330 BC: Bhimasen son of Kṣemendra. He was an unjust king. He built the temple of Koteshvara on Jhelum bank and founded the village of Simpur.

22. 2330 BC- 2284 BC: Indrasen was son of Bhimsena. He was unjust king.

23. 2284 BC- 2238 BC: Sundersen was son of Indrasena. Sandimatnagar drowned due to earthquake as prophesied by Nanda Gupta. Only a potter survived and took refuge at Kralasangar hillock. The earthquake also created Khadanyar hillock at Baramulla. He reigned for 41 years. This is the end of Pāṇḍava dynasty.

24. 2238 BC- 2232 BC: Galgendra founded a city in Maraj, named Naunagar which had 13,0000 houses and brought a stream to this city from the river Rambiara. His reign lasted 45 years.

25. 2232 BC- 2189 BC: Baldeva was son of Galgendra. He founded the village Balapur Suparsuman. Bhigham, the king of Ujain or modern Delhi sent a force to invade Kashmir but was defeated by Baladeva. Himal of the folklore Himal-Nagrai was the daughter of Baladeva. His reign lasted 43 years.

26. 2189 BC- 2168 BC: Nalsen was son of Baladeva. He was very cruel. Nalsen in Kashmiri still means a very cruel person. He died with family in a fire after a reign of 25 years.

27. 2168 BC- 2132 BC: Gokarana was a noble from Jammu Rajas elected king. He made the temple of Sharkadevi at the foot of Pradyumna-pitha (Hari Parbat) built by him. Villgae Brand (Bren in Phak) given as grant for maintenance of this temple. He reigned for 36 years.

28. 2132 BC- 2121 BC: Prahlada was the son of Gokarna. He built the temple of Priteshvara on Shirakut hip in Khuihama formerly called Bu Sangri and now Baba Shukruddin hill. Became a Saṁnyāsī ayer coming in touch with a saint named

Druna. Gave the kingdom to his minister Bambru. He reigned for 11 years.

29. 2121 BC- 2113 BC: Bambru fell in love with maternal cousin's wife named Lolare. He would song out 'Lo.Lo.Lo'. From them it is assumed comes the folklore of Bambur ti Lolare. He ruled for 8 years.

30. 2113 BC- 2077 BC: Pratapsheel was the descendent of Galgendra. He founded the city at the foot of the hill in Vular called Pratapa-Nagar. He built the temple of Pratabeshvara at Bhawan. He ran off with a woman to never return. His reign lasted 36 years.

31. 2077 BC- 2076 BC: Sangram Chandra was son of Pratāpaśīla. He founded a village named Sangrampura in Pattan. His reign lasted 1 year and 4 months.

32. 2076 BC- 2045 BC: Brother of Pratāpaśīla. Built the city Larik-nagar (Lar) at the foot of the Vatargang hill. The city was said to be so dense you could walk the roofs from east to west. Larkul stream was dug on his order in village Lar. His reign lasted 31 years.

33. 2045 BC- 2000 BC: Viram Chand son of Larik Chandra. His reign lasted 45 years.

34. 2000 BC- 1983 BC: Babighan was the son of Biram Chandra. Actual ruler his wife Chakra Rani. His reign lasted 17 years

35. 1983 BC- 1958 BC: Bhagvanta's reign lasted for 14 years. He was son of Biram Chandra and Chakra Rāni.

Here it may be noted that followed by 35 unrecorded rulers Kalhaṇa gives the names of rulers starting from the Parmar dynasty to the Turuṣka dynasty but fails to point out their years of rules or any dateline. As such their tentative dateline has been fixed by the present author based upon various other sources.

Parmar Dynasty

1958 BC-1596 BC

36. 1958 BC- 1938 BC: Lava ruled (1.84). He founded the city named Lalau in Lolab valley [which contained 84 lakh houses according to Kalhana (1.84) but 80 thousand according to Ratnakar.

37. 1938 BC- 1931 BC: Kush ruled (1.88). He was the son of Lava. He granted the village of Karuhara (Kolar) to Brahmins.

38. 1931 BC- 1901 BC: Khagendra ruled (1.89). He founded Khagi and Khonamusha (now called Kakapur and Khunmuh)

39. 1901 BC- 1878 BC: Surendra ruled Kashmir. He founded in the neighbourhood of the Darad country a town called Soraka, and built the vihāra called Narendrabhavana (1.93). With him, his dynasty came to an end as he had no son and the king Godhara of the Godhara dynasty became the new ruler of Kashmir.

Godhara Dynasty

1878 BC- 1657 BC

40. 1878 BC- 1841 BC: Godhara. He went to heaven after bestowing on Brahmaṇas the Agrahāra of Godharā-Hastiśālā.

41. 1841 BC- 1806 BC: Suvarṇa. He used to gift gold to needy persons and made a canal called Suvarṇamaṇi.

42. 1806 BC- 1774 BC: Janaka was Suvarṇa's son. He established the Vihāra and Agrahāra of Jālora.

43. 1774 BC- 1734 BC: Śachinara was Janaka's son. He founded the Agrahāras of Śamāṅgāsā Śanāra. He died without male issue.

44. 1734 BC-1710 BC: Aśoka or Dharma Aśoka was the son of Śachinara's grand uncle and great-grandson of Śakuni. He covered Śuṣkaletra and Vitastātrā with numerous Stupas. He built the city of Srinagar, with ninety-six lakhs of houses, resplendent with wealth. He was a poet. In his days, the mlechchhas (foreigners) overran the country, and he took Saṁnyāsa. Kalhaṇa (747-748 AD) also states that this king had adopted the doctrine of Jina, constructed stupas and Śiva temples, and appeased Bhuteśa (Śiva) to obtain his son Jalauka.

Despite the discrepancies, multiple scholars identify Kalhaṇa's Aśoka with the Mauryan emperor Aśoka (1476-1440 BC), who adopted Buddhism. Although "Jina" is a term generally associated with Jainism, some ancient sources use it to refer to the Buddha.

45. 1710 BC-1682 BC: Jalauka son of Aśoka became king. (1.108) He was a staunch Śaivite, who constructed several Śiva temples. He freed the country from the Mlechchhas. He created conditions like the Yudhiṣṭhira did.

46. 1682 BC-1657 BC: Damodar II was a devout Śaivite. He built a new city called Damodarasauda, and a dam called Guddasetu. He descended from Aśoka's race or belonged to some other family.

Turuṣka Dynasty

1657 BC- 1582 BC

47. 1657 BC–1597 BC: Kalhaṇa (1.172) states that three Turuṣka kings namely Huṣka, Juṣka and Kaniṣka ruled Kashmir and founded three cities named Huṣkapura, Juṣkapura and Kaniṣkapura. Juṣka also founded Jayaswāmipura. They built Maṭhas, and Chaityas. During their period, Buddhism was prevalent in Kaśmir. He also informs that 150 years before the period of Turuṣka dynasty, the parinirvāṇa of Śākya Singh also took place. on this part of the earth (1.172).

तदा भगवतः शाक्यसिंहस्य परनिर्वृतेः ।

अस्मिन्महीलोकधातौ सार्धं वर्षशतं ह्यगात् ।।

tadā Bhagavatā Śākyasiṁhasya parnirvṛteḥ

asminmahilokadhātau sārdham varṣaśatam hyagāt.

Accordingly, Buddha's parinirvāṇā took place in 1657+150= 1807 BC. Huṣka, Jhuṣka, and Kaniṣka came after Buddha's death. They were Buddhist kings of Turuṣka origin.

Kalhaṇa (1.173) also informs that Nāgārjuna, who was known as a Bodhisattva also lived in Kashmir at Ṣaḍarhardvana during this period.

48. 1597 BC–1582 BC: Abhimanyu was a Śaivite ruler during whose reign Buddhism also flourished. Under his instructions, Chandrāchārya and others revived the study of Mahābhāṣya and wrote his Vyākaraṇa called Chāndra Vyākaraṇa. This proves the Mahābhāṣya was written before the 16th century BC. Because of the rising Buddhist influence, people stopped following the Śaivite Nāga rites prescribed in the holy text 'Nīlamat Purāṇa'. This angered the Nāgas, who heavily persecuted the Buddhists. To avoid this disorder, the king retired. A Brahmin named Chandradeva restored Śaivite rites by worshipping Śiva.

From the Gonandiya dynasty onward Kalhaṇa provides the years of their rules, based upon which their dateline is fixed as under:

Gonandiya Dynasty

1582 BC–579 BC

49. 1582 BC-1492 BC: Gonanda III ruled till 1492 BC. Kalhaṇa (1.53) informs that Gonanda III lived 2330 years before his times. This fixes the dateline of Kalhaṇa as 747-748 AD.

प्रायस्तृतीयगोनन्दादारभ्य शरदां तदा।
द्वे सहस्रे गते त्रिंशदधिकं च शतत्रयम्।
prāyastritīya-Gonandādārabhya śaradām tadā.
dve sahasre gatetriñśadadhikam cha śatatrayam.

Gonanda III restored the Nāga rites. He ruled for 35 years. (1.191)

1546 BC- 1492 BC: Vibhiṣaṇa I, son of Gonanda III ruled for 53 and half years. (1.192)

1492 BC-1457 BC: Indrajit ruled for 35 years. (1.193)

1457 BC- 1426 BC: Rāvaṇa son of Indrajit ruled for 30 and half years (1.193). A Śivaliṅga attributed to Rāvaṇa could still be seen at the time of Kalhaṇa.

1426 BC- 1390 BC: Vibhiṣaṇa II son of Rāvaṇa rule for 35 and half years (1.196).

1390 BC- 1350 BC: Kinnara or Nara son of Vibhiṣaṇa II. His

queen eloped with a Buddhist monk, so he destroyed the Buddhist monasteries and gave their land to the Vedic priests. He tried to abduct a Nāga woman, who was the wife of a Vedic priest. Because of this, the Nāga chief burnt down the king's city, and the king died in the fire. He ruled for 39 years and 9 months. (1.273)

1350 BC-1290 BC: Siddha was the son of Nara. He was saved from Nāga's fury because he was away from the capital at the time when city was burnt down. He was a religious king and followed a near-ascetic lifestyle. He ruled earth for 60 years. (1.282)

1290 BC- 1259 BC: Utpalākṣa was the son of Siddha. He ruled for 30 and half years. (1.286)

1259 BC-1222 BC: Hiraṇyākṣa was the son of Utpalākṣa. He ruled for 37 years and 7 months. (1.287)

1222 BC- 1162 BC: Hiraṇyakula was a son of Hiraṇyākṣa. He ruled for 60 years. (1.288)

1162 BC-1102 BC: Vasukula was the son of Hiraṇyakula. He also ruled for 60 years. During his reign, the Mlechchhas (possibly Śakas and Huṇas) overran Kashmir.

1102 BC-1032 BC: Mihirakula was the son of Vasukula (1.289). Stein and other historians identify this Mihirkula with Huna Mihircule also known as Mihiragula, but they are confused. According to Kalhaṇa (747 AD), Mihirakula was a cruel ruler who ordered killings of a large number of people, including children, women and elders. He invaded the Siṅhala Kingdom, and replaced their king with a cruel man. As he passed through Chola, Karnataka and other kingdoms on his way back to Kashmir, the rulers of these kingdoms fled their capitals and returned only after he had gone away. On his return to Kashmir, he ordered killings of 100 elephants, who had been startled by the cries of a fallen elephant. Once, Mihirakula dreamt that a particular stone could be moved only by a chaste woman. He put this to test. The women who were unable to move the stone were killed, along with their husbands, sons and brothers. He was supported by some immoral Brahmins who received grants from him. He goes down most cruel ruler in the history of Kashmir who killed three crore persons. In his old age, the king committed self-immolation after the rule of 70 years. (1.309).

1032 BC-969 BC: Baka was the son of Mihirkula. But he was a virtuous king, he was seduced and killed by a woman named Bhaṭṭā, along with several of his sons and grandsons. He ruled for 63 years and 13 days. (1.330)

969 BC-939 BC: Kṣitinanda, the only surviving son of the king became the ruler. He ruled for 30 years. (1.336)

939 BC-887 BC: Kṣitinanda was followed by his son Vasunanda. Vasunandana was a poet and author of Samara Śāstra. He ruled for 52 years and two months. (1.337)

887 BC-827 BC: Nara II was the son of Vasunanda. He ruled for 60 years. (1.338)

827 BC-767 BC: Akṣa was the son of Nara II. He also ruled for sixty years. He founded the village of Akṣavāla.

767 BC-707 BC: Gopāditya ruled. He took care of all Varṇas and Āśramas without any discrimination. People started thinking that the Satyayuga had come. He established Agrahāras bearing the names of Khola, Khāgika Hāḍigrāma and Skandapura. He ruled for 60 years and 6 days. He founded several temples and Agraharas. He was also a poet. He was the son of Akṣa. He gave lands to Brahmins. He expelled several irreligious Brahmins who used to eat garlic (non-Sattvic diet); in their place, he brought others from foreign countries.

707 BC-649 BC: Gokarna was the son of Gopāditya. He ruled for fifty-eight years less thirty days. (1.346)

649 BC-613 BC: Khiṅkhila or Narendraditya I was the son of Gokarṇa. He ruled for 36 years and 100 days. (1.349)

613 BC-579 BC: His son Yudhistira I ruled. He was called Andha Yudhistira by the people, because of his small eyes. In fact, he was not blind. In the later years of his reign, he started

patronizing unwise persons, and the wise courtiers deserted him. He was deposed by rebellious ministers and granted asylum by a neighbouring king. His rule is counted for 34 years. According to Kalhaṇa (Rāj. 1.48), Gonanda II (3137BC-3082 BC) and his successors till Yudhiṣṭhira I (613 BC - 579 BC) ruled Kashmir for 2268 years in the Kaliyuga.

अष्टषष्ट्यधिकामब्दशतद्वाविंशतिं नृपाः ।
अपीपलंस्ते कश्मीरान्गोनन्दाद्याः कलौ युगे ।।
aṣṭaṣaṣṭyadhikāmabdaśatadvāviṁśatiṁ nṛpāḥ ।
apīpalaṁste kaśmīrāngonandādyāḥ kalau yuge ।।

Here Gonanda means Gonanda II whose rule started in the year of war, i.e. 3137 BC, and ended in 3082. Further in Śloka 49, Kalhaṇa himself admits that this calculation is thought to be wrong by those who consider that Bhārat war occurred at the end of Dvāpara yuga.

भारतं द्वापरान्तेभूद्वार्तयेति विमोहिताः ।
केचिदेतां मृषा तेषां कालसंख्यां प्रचक्रिरे ।।
bhāratam dvāparāntebhūdvārtayeti vimohitāḥ ।
kechidetāṁ mṛṣā teṣāṁ kālasaṁkhyāṁ prachakrire ।।

Kalhaṇa has rightly quoted the above view, when we take 3137 BC as the year of war, Gonanada II and his successors till Yudhiṣṭhira I ruled for 2568 years and not 2268 years. There is apparently a difference of 300 years.

Dynasty of Pratāpāditya

579 BC-479 BC

579 BC-547 BC: Pratapaditya ruled for 32 years (2.9). This king Pratapaditya is mentioned in the Rājataraṅgiṇī as a relative of Vikramāditya (2.5). He was brought to the Kashmir throne by his ministers from a distant land (Ujjain). Kalhaṇa (747-48 AD) clarifies that the Vikramāditya related to Pratapaditya was not the Śakārī Vikramāditya II (2.6). According to Kalhaṇa (2.7), from that period onward, the region suffered from internal conflicts and was at times subject to Harṣa Vikramāditya of Pushpabhūti dynasty (457BC) and other (Śaka) kings.

Kalhaṇa, here, refers to the rule of western kṣatrapas who united under Śaka Mahākṣatrapa Chaṣṭana (583 BC-531 BC). After the reign of the dynast of Vikramāditya I of the Kārtikādi Vikram era, the rule of Śaka Nṛpa Kāla (583 BC) was initiated by Chaṣṭana. It is likely that Chaṣṭana may have adopted the title of Vikramāditya. This is why Kalhaṇa (2.6) points out that people often confuse this Vikramāditya with Śakāri Vikramāditya.

शकारिर्विक्रमादित्य इति स भ्रममाश्रितैः ।
अन्यैरत्रान्यथालेखि विसंवादकदर्थितम् ।।
śakārirvikramāditya iti sa bhramamāśritaiḥ ।
anyairatrānyathālekhi visaṁvādakadarthitam ।।

[Meaning] Some individuals, under the mistaken belief that this figure referred to as Vikramāditya was the adversary of the Śakas (known as Śakāri), have erroneously documented conflicting accounts that are now regarded as insignificant.

He further clarifies (in section 2.7) that after this ruler, the land was governed by Harṣa Vikramāditya (457 BC) and other rulers (Śakas).

इदं स्वभेदविधुरं हर्षादीनां धराभुजाम् ।
कंचित्कालमभूद्भोज्यं ततः प्रभृति मंडलम् ।।
idaṁ svabhedavidhuraṁ harṣādīnāṁ dharābhujām ।
kaṁchitkālamabhūdbhojyaṁ tataḥ prabhṛti maṁḍalam ।।

We know that Chaṣṭana and his followers ruled this land till 246 BC.

Thus, we may unhesitatingly say that this Pratāpādity was the relative of Chaṣṭana.

547 BC-515 BC: Jalaukas son of Pratāpāditya also ruled for 32 years. (2.10)

515 BC-479 BC: Tuñjīna I the son of Jalaukas ruled. He shared the administration with his queen Vākpuṣṭā. The couple sheltered their citizens in the royal palace during a severe famine resulting from heavy frost. After his death, the queen committed sati (died at the funeral pyre of her husband). The

couple died childless. They ruled for 36 years. (3.56)

Vijaya Dynasty

479 BC-387 BC

479 BC- 471 BC: Vijaya became ruler. He was not from the Pratāpāditya dynasty. He ruled for 8 years (2.62).

471 BC-434 BC: Jayendra, son of Vijaya was coronated after his death. His long arms reached to his knees. His flatterers instigated him against his minister Sandhimati, a saint minister. The minister was persecuted and ultimately imprisoned because of rumours that he would succeed the king. Sandhimati remained in prison for 10 years. In his old age, the childless king ordered the killing of Sandhimati to prevent any chance of him becoming a king. He died after hearing about the false news of Sandhimati's death after a rule of 37 years. (2.81)

434 BC-419 BC: Sandhimati ruled. Sandhimati was selected by the citizens as the new ruler. He ascended the throne reluctantly, at the request of his guru. He was a devout Śaivite, and his reign was marked by peace. He filled his court with riṣis (sages), and spent his time in forest retreats. Therefore, his ministers replaced him with Meghavāhana from Gāndhār. He ruled for 15 years.

Ikşvāku Dynasty

419 BC-200 AD

419 BC-385 BC: Meghavāhana was the son of Andha Yudhisthira's great-grandson, who had been granted asylum by Gopāditya, the king of Gandhara. Meghavāhana had been selected as the husband of a Vaiṣṇavite princess at a Svayaṁvara in another kingdom. The ministers of Kashmir brought him to Kashmir after Sandhimati proved to be an unwilling king. Meghavāhana banned animal slaughter and compensated those who earned their living through hunting. He patronized Vedic priests and set up a monastery. His queens built Buddhist viharas and monasteries. He subdued kings in regions as far as the Siṁhala Kingdom, forcing them to abandon animal

slaughter. He ruled for 34 years. (3.96)

385 BC-355 BC: Pravarasena or Sreșțhasena or Tuñjīna II was the son of Meghvahana. He ruled for 30 years. (3.101)

355 BC-327 BC: Hiraṇya the son of Sreșțhsena became ruler. He died issueless. He ruled for 30 years. (3.124) He was the elder brother of Toramāṇa, who along with his wife and son were in exile. Kalhaṇa (3.125) mentions that Hirañya lived during the period of Vikramāditya, i.e. Chandragupta I of the Gupta Dynasty (327BC-320 BC) whose other name was also called Harṣa.

तत्रानेहस्युज्जयिन्यां श्रीमान्हर्षापराभिधः ।
एकच्छत्रश्चक्रवर्ती विक्रमादित्य इत्यभूत् ।।
tatrānehasyujjayinyāṁ śrīmānharṣāparābhidhaḥ /
ēkachchhatraśchakravartī vikramāditya ityabhūt / /

[Meaning] At that period there lived at Ujjayinī as the sole sovereign of the world the glorious Vikramāditya who [also] bore the second name of Harṣa.

Here the mention of Vikramāditya with another name Harṣa points out to the Chandragupta 1 of Gupta Vaṁśa (327BC-322 BC).

This is the period of the Gupta dynasty in Ujjain. Gupta era was also started by Chandragupta (327BC-322BC) of the Gupta dynasty. In 322 BC Samudragupta became ruler whose regnal year is mentioned by Kalhaṇa as 322 BC.

लौकिकेऽब्दे चतुर्विंशे शककालस्य साम्प्रतम् ।
सप्तत्यभ्यधिकं यातं सहस्रं परिवत्सराः ॥
laukike'bde chaturviṁśe śakakālasya sāmpratam /
saptatyabhyadhikaṁ yātaṁ sahasraṁ parivatsarāḥ //

At present in the 24th Laukika Era, 1070 years of Śaka kāla (regnal year) of Samudragupta (322 BC) have elapsed.

327 BC-321 BC: When Kashmir king Hiranya died issue less, his ministers informed the news to Harśa Vikramaditya of Ujjain who destroyed Śakas. This Vikramaditya was

Chandragupta 1 of the Gupta dynasty. He also ousted Śakas from Saurāṣṭra and another place. Mātṛgupta was also patronized by Chandragupta I of Gupta dynasty. Kalhaṇa Pandit describes in detail in his Rājataraṅgiṇī how Chandragupta 1 (of Gupta dynasty called Vikramāditya by Kalhaṇa) chose Mātṛgupta, a learned poet and administrator to install him as the king of Kashmir (3.129). This Mātṛgupta ruled Kashmir for 5 years less three months and one day (3.264). Hearing the demise of Vikramāditya he retired to Varanasi and became a yati. According to Raghunatha Singh, Hindi Translator of Rājatariṅgiṇī, a Phd. Thesis submitted to BHU, Varanasi, published from Hindi Pracharaka Sansthan Varanasi (p. 498) emperor Samudragupta (322-269 BC) mentions Mātṛgupta.

> मातृगुप्तो जयति यः कविराजो न केवलम्।
> कश्मीरराजोऽप्यभवत् सरस्वती प्रसादतः ।।
> *mātṛgupto jayati yaḥ kavirājo na kevalam |*
> *kaśmīrarājo'pyabhavat sarasvatī prasādataḥ ||*
>
> [Meaning] Glory to Mātṛgupta, who was not only a poet-laureate, but, by the grace of Goddess Sarasvatī, also became the king of Kashmir."

The above mention also proves that Mātṛgupta was contemporary of Samudragupta.

321 BC-260 BC: Pravarasena II (Toramana's son) ascended the throne of Kashmir. He was very much impressed by Mātṛgupta and used to send the whole revenue to Mātṛgupta at Varanasi. He wanted to kill Chandragupta 1 of Gupta dynasty called Vikramāditya of Ujjain by Kalhana for installing Mātṛgupta as the king of Kashmir, when he was on the way to fight the war with Vikramāditya, he heard the news of his demise. He was known as the most courageous king next to Vikramāditya and Śudraka. He ruled for 60 years (3.364)

260 BC-221 BC: Yudhiṣṭhira II son of Pravarsena became ruler. He ruled for 39 years (3.379).

221 BC-208 BC: Lahkhaṇa or Narendrāditya son of Yudhiṣṭhira II became ruler. He ruled for 13 years (3.385).

208 BC-122 AD: Tuñjina or Raṇāditya, the brother of Narendrāditya ascended on the throne after his death. He was a poet. He ruled the earth for 300 years (3.470). One person's rule for 300 years is not possible. Keeping in view of the Saptarṣi eras mention the year 300 has been modified to 86 so that it may coincide with the Saptarṣi era.

122 AD-164 AD: Vikramāditya in the family of Rāṇāditya ruled for 42 years (3.475).

164 AD-200 AD: Bālāditya, the younger brother of Vikramāditya. He subdued several enemies. An astrologer prophesized that his son-in-law would succeed him as the king. To avoid this outcome, the king married his daughter Anaṅgalekha to Durlabhavardhana, a handsome but non-royal man from Aśvaghama Kāyastha caste. Bālāditya ruled for 37 years less four months.

Karkota Dynasty

200 AD-454 AD

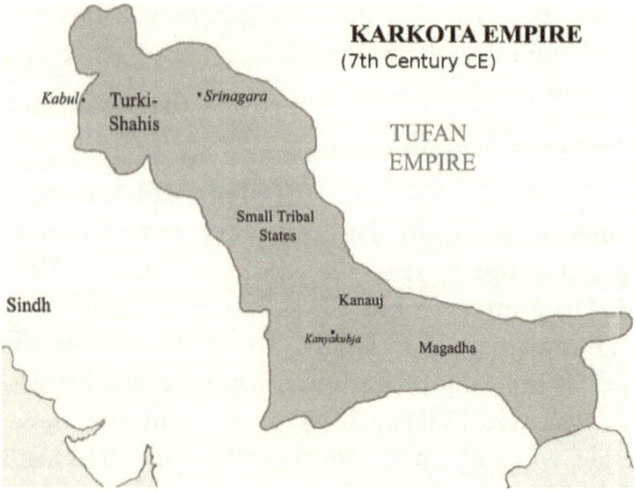

200 AD-236AD: Durlabha Vardhana (Son-in-law of Bālāditya). Born to Nāga Karkoṭa (a deity), Durlabhavardhana was Bālāditya's officer in charge of fodder. Bālāditya married his daughter Anaṅgalekhā to him. As the royal son-in-law, he

became known as a just and wise man and was given the title "Prajñāditya" by the king. His wife Anaṅgalekha became involved in an extra-marital affair with the minister Kharga. Despite catching them sleeping together, Durlabhavardhana forgave Kharga and won over his loyalty. After Bālāditya's death, Kharga crowned him the new king. Durlabhvardhan ruled for 36 years (4.6)

236 AD-286 AD: Durlabhaka or Pratāpāditya II son of Durlabhavardhana and Anaṅgalekhā. He was adopted as a son by his maternal grandfather and assumed the title Pratāpāditya after the title of the grandfather's dynasty. He ruled for 50 years (4.44).

286 AD-295 AD: Chandrāpīḍa or Varṇāditya son of Durlabhaka. He ruled for 8 years and 8 months (4.118)

295 AD- 299 AD: Tārāpīḍa or Udayāditya was the younger brother of Chandrāpīḍa. Chandrāpīḍa and Tārāpīḍa are the characters of Kādambarī of Bāṇabhaṭṭta. It appears that Bāṇabhaṭṭta (3rd century AD) was a contemporary to Tārāpīḍa. He ruled for 4 years less days (4.123).

299 AD- 336 AD: Lalitāditya or Mukatāpīḍa (Poet) was the younger brother of Chandrāpīḍa and Tārāpīḍa. This Lalitāditya built the famous Martaṇḍa (Sun) temple in Kashmir. Kalhaṇa states that Lalitāditya Muktāpḍa invaded the tribes of the north and after defeating the Kambojas, he immediately faced the Tuṣāras. The Tuṣāras did not give a fight, but fled to the mountain ranges leaving their horses on the battlefield. Then Lalitāditiya met the Bhauṭṭas in Baltistan in western Tibet, north of Kashmir, then the Dardas in Karakoram/Himalaya, the Vālukāmbudhi and then he encounters Strīrājya (Amazons), the Uttarakurus and the Pragjyotiṣa respectively (4.165-175). The illustrious poet Bhavabhūti belonged to his period. He ruled for 36 years, seven months and 11 days. (4.366)

336 AD- 337 AD: Kuvalayāpīḍa son of Lalitāditya from Kamaladevī ascended the throne. His short reign was marked by a succession struggle with his half brother Vajrāditya II. He abdicated the throne in one year and half a month (4.392) and

became a hermit to seek peace.

337 AD-344 AD: Vajrāditya or Bappiyaka or Lalitāditya the son of Lalitādity from Chakramardikā became king. He was a cruel and immoral person, who introduced the evil habits of Mlecchas to Kashmir. He ruled for 7 years (4.398).

344 AD-348 AD: Prithivyāpīḍa son of Vajraditya and Mañjarikā became the ruler. He ruled for 4 years and one month (4.399). He was deposed by his half-brother Saṅgrāmapīḍa.

348 AD: Sangramapīḍa I son of Vajraditya and Mammā. He deposed his half-brother to become the king but died after a week (4.400).

348 AD-351 AD: Jajja ruled.

351 AD-382 AD: Jayāpīḍa (Pandit and poet) was the youngest son of Vajrāditya. He erected a monument at Prayāga, which existed at Kalhaṇa's time. His wife Kalyāṇadevī was the daughter of Jayanta, the king of Pundravardhana in the Gauda region. Jayāpīḍa subdued five kings of Gauda and made them vassals of his father-in-law. On his way back to Kashmir, he also defeated the king of Kānyakubja. While Jayāpīḍa was in Gauda, his brother-in-law Jajja usurped the throne in Kashmir. After three years of ruling Kashmir, Jajja was killed by Śrideva, a supporter of Jayapīḍa. Jayāpīḍa became the king once again and patronized scholars. He waged wars against Bhīmasena, king of the Eastern region and Aramuḍi of Nepal. In both instances, he was first imprisoned by the enemy kings but managed to escape and defeat the enemy. During the last years of his reign, he imposed excessive taxes on the advice of Kāyasthas and treated his subjects cruelly. He died because of a curse by a Brahmin. He revived the study of Mahābhāṣya which was interrupted and he learnt grammar from a grammarian called Kṣīra. He ruled for 31 years (4.657).

382 AD-394 AD: Lalitapīḍa son of Jayāpīḍa born from the queen Durgā. He devoted his time to sensual pleasures and neglected royal duties. He ruled for 12 years (4.673).

394 AD-401 AD: Saṅgrāmapīḍa II or Pṛthivyāpīḍa son of Jayāpiḍa born from queen Kalyāṇadevī assumed the power. He ruled for 7 years (4.675)

401 AD- 412 AD: Chippṭa-Jayāpīḍa also called Bṛhaspati, the child son of Lalitāpīḍa and his mother Jayādevī, a concubine of Lalitāpīḍa became started ruling. The actual power was in hands of Jayādevī's brothers Padma, Utpalaka, Kalyāṇa, Mamma and Dharma. He was killed after a rule of 12 years (4.687).

412 AD-449 AD: Ajitāpīḍa son of Lalitāpiḍa and Jayādevi, was made king by his maternal uncle Utpalaka. He was dethroned by Utpalaka's rival Mamma and the latter's son Yaśovarman.

449 AD- 452 AD: Yaśovarman and Mamma made Anaṅgpīḍa son of Saṁrāmpīḍa II, king. Kalhaṇa (4.703) mentions that Ajitapīda, the king of the Karkoṭ dynasty and Anaṅgapīḍa both reigned from the Laukika year 89 (412AD) to 26 (452 AD). This is the first reference of the Saptarṣi saṁvat by Kalhaṇa. From 412 AD onwards, Kalhaṇa has given the exact datelines, based upon Kashmiri Saptarṣi Saṁvat.

एकोननवते वर्षे स्वस्रीये शान्तिमागते।
निर्विघ्नभोगास्तेभूवन्षड्विंशाब्दात्ययावधि।।
ekonanavate varṣe svasrīye śāntimāgate /
nirvighnabhogāstebhūvanṣaḍviṁśābdātyayāvadhi / /

[Meaning] From the Laukika year eighty-nine (A.D. 412)) when their nephew died, in the year twenty-six (A.D. 452), they ruled unrestrained

452 AD- 454 AD: Utpalapīḍa son of Ajitāpīḍa was made king by Sukhavarman, the son of Utpala. He was deposed by the minister Śūra in the laukika year 31.

Utpala Dynasty

454 AD-538 AD

454 AD- 482 AD: Avantivarma son of Sukhavarman was made king in the year 31 (454 A.D.) by the minister Śura

(5.716). Established the city of Avantipura. In his court flourished many poets like Anandavardhana of Dhvanyāloka, Ratanakara etc. He died in the Laukika era 59 (482 AD). [5.126]

482AD-500AD: Śaṅkaravarma ruled. He was contemporary to Lalya Sahi, Brahmin king of the Yavanas in Uttara Jyotisha, Divya Kataka and Siṅhapura, now part of Afghanistan. He died in Laukika era 77 (500 AD) when hit by an arrow. (5.220-222)

500 AD- 503 AD: Gopālavarman son of Śaṅkaravarman ruled under the guardianship of his mother Sugandha, two years after his rule he was Murdered.

503 AD: Saṅkaṭa, the minor brother of Gopālavarman was picked up for the coronation under the guardianship of his mother Sugandhā. But he died 10 days after ascending the throne.

503 AD-505 AD: Sugandhā herself assumed royal power after the death of all male heirs. But deposed by Tantrin soldiers, who had earlier served as the royal bodyguards. She waged a war against the Tantrins with the help of their rivals (known as Ekāṅgas), but was defeated and killed. She could rule for 2 years (5.249).

505 AD- 520 AD: Partha son of Nirjitavarman was placed on the throne by the Tantrins. He was a then 10-year old. Nirjitavarman acted his guardian. In the month of Pauṣain the Laukika year 97 (520 AD), Pārtha was overthrown (5.287) by his father with the support of Tantrins and became the king.

520 AD-522 AD: Nirjitavarman, the half-brother of Avantivarman started ruling, but died in the month of Māgha in the Laukika year 98 (5.288), i.e. 521 AD after having placed his child son Chakravarman in the throne.

522 AD-532 AD: Chakravarman, started ruling for some time under the guardianship of his mother Bappaṭadevī and then for 10 years under the that of his grandmother, Kṣillikā. He was wicked and unpopular king, Tantrins overtrew Chakravarman in Laukika year 9, i.e. 532 AD (5.292).

532 AD- 533 AD: Tantrins made Sūravarman I, the son of

Nirjitavarman from Mṛgāvalī, king. But he was also deposed by Tantrin foot soldiers when a year had passed. They made Pārtha once more king.

533 AD-534 AD: Pārtha ruled for one year.

534 AD: In the month of Āṣāḍha of the Laukika year 11, i.e. 534, Chakravarman purchased rulership from Tāntrins. But for want of money, he could not pay to the Tantrins, he fled in fear in the month of Pauṣa of the same year. He stopped in Maḍvarājya. There Śaṅkarvarvardhana aspired to the throne. He sent his younger brother Śaṁbhuvardhana to negotiate with the Tantrin foot soldiers.

534 AD-535 AD: Śaṁbhuvardhana deceived his elder brother, he himself bribed Tantrins and got himself installed king.

535 AD-536 AD: Chakravarman with the help of Dāmaras defeated Śaṁbhuvardhana and Tantrins and became king for the third time. He was characterless and so was killed by Dāmaras on the 8th day of the bright half of Jyeṣṭha in the Laukika 13, i.e. 536AD.

536 AD-538 AD: Unmattavanti the son of Partha was raised as the king by Śarvaṭ and other ministers. He died in the month of Āṣāḍha of the Laukika year fifteen, i.e. 538 AD.

538 AD-538 AD: Unmattavanti the son of Partha was raised as the king by Śarvaṭ and other ministers. He died in the month of Āṣāḍha of the Laukika year fifteen, i.e. 538 AD. Thus came an end to the Utpala dynasty.

Gupta Brahmin Kings Dynasty

538 AD-602 AD

538 AD-547AD: Yaśaskara elected by a council of Brahmins. He was famous for his good governance. He was successful in restoring the law and order established by the former kings (Raj. 6.6). He ensured safety and security for all. There was no fear of robbery and there was no need to lock the shops in the night. Villagers were absorbed in farming and the Brahmaṇas

never had to carry arms (Raj. 6.9). Ignorant Gurus did not perform tāntrika yāgas like Matsyāpūpa Yāga [in which fish and cake offerings were made], and did not by texts of their composition revise traditional doctrines (6.11). No housewives were henceforth consecrated to be a Guru in Tāntrika rituals to criticize their husbands' conduct. According to Kalhaṇa (6.114), he died on the 3rd tithi of the dark fortnight of Bhādrapada month in the 24th Laukika year (547AD).

547AD: Varnata (1 month)

547AD-548AD: Sangramadeva (5 months). He was murdered by the divira (clerk or writer) Parvagupta, who had become a regent minister.

548AD-549AD: Kalhaṇa (6.129; 6.148) informs that Parvagupta ascended the throne on the 10thtithi of the dark fortnight of Phālguna month in the 24th year of the Laukika era (547 AD) and died on the 13th tithi of the dark fortnight of Āṣāḍha month in the 26th year of the Laukika era (549 AD). He was a strong but unpopular ruler.

549AD-557 AD: Kṣemagupta son of Parvagupta became ruler. He married Didda, daughter of King Siṅharāja, a member of the Lohara dynasty) (6.176). Didda overpowered the king and she and/or her relatives ran the administration (6.177). He died on the ninth tithi of the bright half of Pauṣa, in the Laukika era 34 (557 AD).

557AD-571 AD: Abhimanyugupta. Abhimanyu was a minor, ruled by mother Didda, wife of Kṣemagupta. Didda was a contemporary of Bhima Sahi of Kabul, a descendant of Lalya Sahi. Didda was the grand-daughter of Bhima Sahi (Daughter's daughter). Didda was a corrupt lady. She had illicit relationships with her ministers (6.188). Abhimanyu died on the 3rd tithi of the bright half of Kārttika in the Laukika year 48 (571 AD)

571 AD- 572 AD: Nandigupta (second son of Didda) assumed the throne. She employed witchcraft agninst her little grandson. On the twelfth day of the bright half of Mārgaśīrṣa in the Laukika era forty-nine (A.D. 572), he died.

572 AD- 574 AD: According to Kalhaṇa (6.311-312), Tribhuvanagupta (3rd grandson of Didda) became king on the 12th tithi of the bright fortnight of Mārgaśirṣa month in the 49th year of the Laukika era (572 AD) and died on the 5th tithi of the bright fortnight of Mārgaśirṣa month in the 51st year of the Laukika era, (574 AD) on account of the same practice of witchcraft against him.

574 AD-579 AD: Bhimagupta (4th grandson of Didda). All sons were minors. So, ruled by mother Didda. At last Bhimgupta was killed by her subjecting to various tortures and usurped power herself in Laukika era 56, i.e. 579 AD (6.332).

579 AD-602 AD: Diddā, herself reigned. Diddā was the daughter of Simharaja of Lohar and wife of Kṣemagupta. This Lohar family belongs to the Andhra Satavahana dynasty. This Simharaja, the father of Diddā, is the son-in-law of Bhima Sahi of Kabul, who belonged to the Tomara Dynasty, one of the four Agni Vaṁśi. According to (6.332 & 6.365), Diddā ascended the throne in the 56th year of the Laukika era, i.e. 579AD, and died on the 8thtithi of the bright fortnight of Bhādrapada month in the 79th year of the Laukika era i.e. 602 (6.365). Diddā had already raised the son of her brother Udayarāja, called Saṅgrāmrāja to the rank of Yuvarāja (6.355).

Lohar Dynasty

602 AD-700AD

602 AD- 627 AD: Sangramaraja became king after the death of Diddā. It was the third change of dynasty through marriage in the history of Kashmir (6.366). He was the contemporary of Trilochanapāla of Kabul.

627 AD: According to Kalhaṇa (7.127), Saṅgrāmarāja died on the first day of Āṣāḍha in the Laukika era four (627 AD), and his son Harīrāja ascended on the throne. He ruled for 22 days only and died on the eighth day of the bright half of Āṣāḍha (7.131). It was a rumour that the licentious queen mother, Śrilekhā, herself used witchcraft against her son, who was dissatisfied with her conduct. It is said that while the king's

mother, Śrilekhā, who wished the throne for herself, was coming after taking a bath [where] the arrangements or the installation had been made, the assembled Ekāṅgas and the [king's] milk-brother, Sāgara, made her another child-son Ananta king (7.134-135).

627 AD-662 AD: Anantadeva ruled. He took out many foreign expeditions. He defeated the king Sāla of Champā and placed a new ruler on the throne. But Kalaśa was very disrespectful to his father, so his prime minister Haladhara made the king again resume royal powers (7.234-243). Kṣemendra writes in the colophon to the 'Samayamātrikā' that he completed that work during the reign of Ananta in the 25th year of the Laukika era (648 AD). Anantdeva left Śrinagar and shifted to Vijayakṣetra in the month of Jyeṣṭha of the laukika year 55 (678 A.D.) and Kalaśa occupied the rulership of Śrinagar.

It appears that Hiuen Tsiang (cir. A.D. 631-635) visited Kashmir during the reign of Anantadeva. Hiuen Tsiang found all adjacent territories on the west and south, down to the plains, subject to the sway of the king of Kashmir. He thus distinctly records that Taksaśilā east of the Indus, Uraśā or Hazāra, Siṅhapurā or the Salt Range, with the smaller hill-states of Rājapurī and Parṇotsa, had no independent rulers, but mere tributary to Kashmir.

662 AD-688 AD: Kalaśa or Ranaditya (Pandit and Poet) ruled Kashmir. On the sixth day of the bright half of Kārttika in the Laukika era thirty-nine, i.e. 662 (7.233) the Anantadeva had his son Kalaśa crowned. He rebelled against his parents, leading to the suicide of his father Ananta on the full moon day of the month Kārtika in the laukika era of 57, i.e. 680 A.D. (7.452), followed by sati-suicide by his mother. His son Harsha revolted against him (7.627) and was imprisoned on the 6th day of the bright half of Pauṣa in the laukika year 64, i.e. 687 A.D. Kalaśa died on the sixth day of the bright half of Mārgaśīrṣa in the laukika year 65, i.e. 688 A.D.

688 AD: Utkarśa was coronated (few days only). He was the

second son of Kalasha. His half-brother Vijaymalla rebelled against him and got Harsha released from prison. Utkarsha was imprisoned and committed suicide.

688 AD-700 AD: Harsha ruled. In his early years, he was a sagacious king and a patron of art and literature. The later years of his reign were marked by unsuccessful military campaigns, resulting in excessive taxation and plundering of temples. Revolts by his generals Uchchala and Sussala (of the Lohara family) ended his reign. His son Bhoja was killed, and Harsha himself was killed by Uchchala's men while hiding in a village. Kalhaṇa (7.171) says that Harshadeva died on the 5th tithi of the bright fortnight of Bhādrapada month in the 77th year of the Laukika era i.e. 700 AD.

Second Lohar Dynasty

700 AD-748 AD

700 AD-710AD: After Harsha's death Uchchla usurped power. He ruled for 10 years. But his own ministers Raḍḍa and others hatched a conspiracy against him and murdered him by cutting him into pieces on the sixth day of the bright half of Pauṣa in the laukika year 87, i.e. 710 AD.

710 AD: Saṅkarāja or Raḍḍa usurped the throne. He claimed himself the descendent of Yaśaskara's family, but he could reign for one night and one prahar [watch] of the day (8.356) and was defeated and killed along with other conspirators by Gargachandra.

710 AD- 711AD: Uchchala's infant son Salhaṇa was consecrated as king by Gargachandra and Gargachandra started ruling as a shadow king. But Sussal the younger brother of Salhaṇa captured Salhaṇa. Having reigned for four months less three days, Salhaṇa fell into captivity on the 3rd day of the bright half of Vaiśākha in the laukika era 88, i.e.711 AD (8.480).

711 AD- 719 AD: Sussala occupied the throne. He won several territories and made Gargachandra his minister. Lastly, Gragchandra was imprisoned and executed in the month of Bhādrapada of the laukika era of 94, i.e. 717 A.D. (Rāj. 8.617).

In the laukika era 96, i.e. 719 A.D. Dāmaras revoled (8.661-671) and Sussala was defeated. His own soldiers also revolted and the king had to leave his palace in Śrinagar on 6th day of the dark half of Mārgaśīrṣa in the year 96, 719 A.D. and retired in Lohara (8.819).

719AD-720 AD: Bhikṣāchara gained power. Real power was in the hands of Bimba, who was prime minister while Bhikṣāchara enjoyed the mere title of king. There arose dissensions among the Bhikṣāchāra's supporters Pṛthvīhara and Mallakoṣṭha. He also sent Bimba with an army against Lohara by the route of Rājapurī to attack Sussala, but they were defeated. Sussala restored his power.

720 AD -727 AD: Sussala returned to Śrinagar after an absence of 6 months and 12 days on the 3rd day of the bright half of Jyeṣṭha in the year 97, i.e. 720 AD. (8.954). He made Yaśorāja governor, but he defected. The enemies burnt a house and the fire spread in the whole of Śrinagar, this disappointed Sussala who desired an early death. Sussala crowned his son Jaisingh but was imprisoned. Utpala, Praśastarāja, and Vyāghra murdered Sussal on the new moon day of Phālguna in the laukika year three (727 A.D.).

727 AD - 748 AD: Jaisingh, son of Sussala occupied the throne. Utpala, the murderer of the father of Jaisingh was caught and killed. During the reign of Jayasingh, Kalhaṇa wrote the historic treatise Rājatariṅgiṇī, the history of Kashmir. He mentions (Rāj. 8.3404) that twenty-two years had the king passed before he obtained the throne, and for the same [number of years] he has been on the throne in the [present] year twenty-five (A.D. 748).

लौकिकेऽब्दे चतुर्विंशे शककालस्य साम्प्रतम्।
सप्तत्यभ्यधिकं यातं सहस्रं परिवत्सराः ॥
laukike'bde chaturviṁśe śakakālasya sāmpratam I
saptatyabhyadhikaṁ yātaṁ sahasraṁ parivatsarāḥ II

At present in the 24th Laukika Era, 1070 years of Gupta Śaka Saṁvat (322 BC) have elapsed.

747-748 AD is the epoch of Kalhaṇa. He also sums up the

list of Kashmir kings till his period.

748 AD- 800 AD: Rajadeva

800 AD- 860 AD: Sangramdeva

860 AD- 920 AD: Ramdeva

920 AD-980AD: Lakṣmandeva

980 AD- 1060 AD: Singhdeva

1060 AD- 1120 AD: Suhadeva

1120 AD-1175 AD: Śāraṅgadeva moves to Deccan

1175AD-1212AD: Singhana II

1223AD-1257 AD: Sangramdeva

1257 AD-1276 AD: Lakṣmaṇadeva

1276AD-1295 AD: Singhdeva

1295 AD-1320 AD: Suhadeva

1320 AD- 1323 AD: During the reign of Suhadeva, a Tatar chief Dulucha (Zulju) invaded Kashmir and ravaged it. King Suhadeva fled the country and his general Ramchandra occupied the throne. In the confusion Rinchan, a Tibetan Buddhist refugee in Kashmir, established himself as the ruler after Zulju, the Ladhaki prince organized an internal rising and seized the throne. He married Kota Rani, the daughter of Ramchandra. The Hindu religious leaders of the time refused to admit him into their fold. Rinchan embraced Islam and took a Muslim name called Sultan Sadruddin. He was attacked by rebels and was badly wounded and died in 1323 AD.

1323 AD-1339 AD: Just before his death Sultan Sadruddin (Rinchan) summoned his trusted minister, Shah Mir, and entrusted his son, Hyder, and wife, Kotarani, to his care. He had a son, Haidar by his queen named Kota Rani. After the death of Rinchan, who was assassinated, Kotarani married Udayanadeva, the brother of Suhadeva.

The last Hindu ruler of Kashmir was Udyanadeva. It was his chief Queen named Kota Rani, who practically governed the state. She was a very brave, shrewd and an able ruler. Though she tried her best to save her kingdom, odds were too heavy for her. The Kashmir Valley was again invaded by a Mongol-Turk invader named Achalla, and Udayanadeva fled to Tibet. But the Queen defeated (killed) Achalla and drove away all the foreign troops.

Finally, in this age of chaos, Shah Mir organized an uprising against Queen Kota Rani and defeated her at Jayapur (modern Sumbal). The defeat upset her and seeing the indifference of the Hindu grandees and the general public, she stabbed herself to death, because Shah Mir wanted to marry her. Her death in 1339 paved the way for the establishment of Shah Mir dynasty rule in Kashmir.

Shah Mir Dynasty

51/7/28th Kali/4441–4637or1339 AD–1535AD

1339 AD- 1342 AD: Shah Mir worked to establish Islam in Kashmir and was aided by his descendant rulers, specially Sikandar Butshikan. He reigned for three years and five months. He was the ruler of Kashmir and the founder of the Shah Mir dynasty. He was followed by his two sons who became kings in succession.

1342 AD- 1344 AD: Shah Mirwas succeeded by Jamshed

1344 AD- 1355 AD: Alau-ud-Din

1355 AD–1373 AD: Shahab-ud-Din

1373 AD–1389 AD: Qutub-ud-Din

1389 AD–1413 AD: Sikandar ruled. He imposed taxes on non-Muslims, forced conversions to Islam, and earned the title Butşikan for destroying idols.

1413 AD–1420AD: Alishah

1420AD–1470 AD: Zain-ul-Abdin ruled. He invited artists and craftsmen from Central Asia and Persia to train local artists in Kashmir. Under his rule, the arts of wood carving, papier-mâché, shawl and carpet weaving prospered. For a brief period in the 1470s, states of Jammu, Poonch and Rajauri which paid tributes to Kashmir revolted against the Sultan Hajji Khan. However, they were subjugated by his son Hasan Khan who took over as ruler in 1472 AD.

1470 AD– 1472 AD: Haidershah

1472 AD–1484 AD: Hassan Khan

1484 AD– 1486 AD: Mohammadshah

1486 AD–1495 AD: Fatehshah

1495 AD–1496 AD: Mohammadshah

1496 AD–1497 AD: Fatehshah

1497 AD–1509 AD: Mohammadshah

1509 AD–1529 AD: Ibrahimshah s/oMohammadshah

1529 AD– 1530 AD: Nazukshah s/o Fatehshah (one year)

1530 AD– 1535 AD:Mohammad Shah

20. Rulers of Nepal

Gopala Dynasty

51/7/28th Dvāpara/862,943-28th Dvāpara/863,291
or 4159 BC-3709 BC

Nepal Rājavanśāvali is the main source of Nepal rulers. Nepal Rājavanśavali records the list of rulers from 4159 BC. Accordingly, the first dynasty to rule Nepal was Gopala dynasty. The names of kings along with the years of their coronation is given below:

Name of the King	Year of the coronation
1. Bhukta Mangat Gupta	4159 BC
2. Jaya Gupta	4071 BC
3. Parama Gupta	3999 BC
4. Harsha Gupta	3919 BC
5. Bhima Gupta	3826 BC
6. Mani Gupta	3788 BC
7. Vishnu Gupta	3751 BC
8. Yaksha Gupta	3709 BC

Yaksha Gupta died childless. So, Vara Singh, the first king of Ahir dynasty was brought from India. He was coronated in 3637 BC. Some prominent names of Ahir dynasty kings are as follows:

Ahir Dynasty

51/7/28th Dvāpara/863,465-28th Dvāpara /863,765
or
3637 BC-3437 BC

Name of the King	Year of the coronation
9. Vara Singh	3637 BC
10. Yamat Singh	3557 BC
11. Bhuvana Singh	3437 BC

Kirat Dynasty

51/7/28th Dvāpara/863,765-28th Kali/782
or
3437 BC-2320 BC

After Bhuvana Singh, Nepal was conquered by Yalambara who established the Kirata dynasty in 3437 BC. He made Gokarna as his capital. Kirat dynasty ruled for 1118 years, i.e. till 2319 BC. The names of the first seven kings of Kirat dynasty are as follows:

Name of the King	Year of the coronation
12. Yalambara	3437 BC
13. Pavi	3392 BC
14. Skandara	3352 BC
15. Valamba	3317 BC
16. Hriti	3275 BC
17. Humati	3219 BC
18. Jitedasti	3151 BC

Humati abdicated in 3151 in favour of Jitedasti and accompanied Pāṇḍavas to the forest for 12 years during the period of exile. Jitedasti fought on the side of Pāṇḍavas and was killed during Mahabharata war in Kurukshetra in Dec. 3139 BC. After the death of Jitedasti, his son Gali was crowned as the king of Nepal. The rest of the kings of Nepal and their coronation years are given hereunder.

Name of the King	Year of the coronation
19. Gali	3138 BC
20. Pushak	3101 BC
21. Suyama	3064 BC
22. Parva	3027 BC
23. Thunka	2990 BC
24. Svananda	2953 BC
25. Stunco	2915 BC
26. Gidhri (Gighri)	2882 BC
27. Nane	2844 BC
28. Luk	2809 BC

29.	Thor	2769 BC
30.	Thoko	2734 BC
31.	Varma	2690 BC
32.	Guja	2653 BC
33.	Pushka (Pushkara)	2616 BC
34.	Kesu	2579 BC
35.	Snusa	2542 BC
36.	Sammu	2505 BC
37.	Gunana	2468 BC
38.	Kimbu	2431 BC
39.	Patunka	2394 BC

During the reign of king Patunka, Nepal was attacked by Somavanshi Rajputs. The king withdrew to Shankmula Tirtha and built a new fort there.

40.	Gasti	2357 BC

Invasions of Somavanshi Rajputs also continued during the reign of Gasti. King Gasti also built a new fort at Bhutochha near Godavari, close to Lalita Pattana. In the year 2320 BC he lost his kingdom to the Somavanshi dynasty.

Somavanshi dynasty ruled Nepal for 607 years, i.e. till 1713 BC. Names of some prominent kings of Somavanshi dynasty are quoted hereunder.

Somavaṁśī Dynasty

51/7/28th Kali/783–1389or 2320 BC–1713 BC

	Name of the King	Year of the coronation
41.	Nimisha	2320 BC
42.	Manaksha	2211 BC
43.	Kaka Varman	2026 BC
44.	Pashupreksha Deva	1868 BC

King Pashupreksha Deva restored Pashupati's temple brought over by people from India in Kali 1234 or 1868 BC. He inspired people from India to migrate in Nepal and helped them settle over there.

45. Bhaskar Varman 1713 BC

King Bhaskar Varman conquered the whole of India, enlarged Devapattan, caused the rules for the worship of Pashupati to be engraved on a copper plate which he deposited in the Charumati Vihar. Being childless, he adopted a prince from the Suryavanshi dynasty, Bhumivarman who was crowned king in Kali 1389 or 1713 BC.

Sūryavañśī Dynasty

51/7/28th Kali/1389-3002or 1713 BC-100BC

Name of the King	Year of the coronation
46. Bhumi Varman	1713 BC
47. Chandra Varman	1645 BC
48. Jaya Varman	1584 BC
49. Varsha Varman	1502 BC
50. Sarva Varman	1441 BC
51. Prithivi Varman	1368 BC
52. Jyestha Varman	1287 BC
53. Hari Varman	1212 BC
54. Kuber Varman	1136 BC
55. Siddhi Varman	1048 BC
56. Haridatta Varman	987 BC
57. Vasudatta Varman	906 BC
58. Pati Varman	843 BC
59. Sivavriddhi Varman	790 BC
60. Vasanta Varman	736 BC
61. Siva Varman	675BC
62. Rudra Varman	613 BC
63. Vrisha Deva Varman	547 BC

Vrisha Deva (991 BC-930 BC) built viharas and erected images of Lokeshwar and other Buddha divinities. Actually, image erection and image worship were started first by Buddhists in India followed by Jains. Later people believing in Paurāṇic faith also adopted it and started making images of divinities and worshipping them.

64. Sankara Deva 486 BC

Sankara Deva was the son of Vrisha Deva. He named his son Sankara Deva after Ādi Śaṅkrāchārya. Sankara deva erected Trident at Pashupati.

Name of the King	Year of the coronation
65. Dharma Deva	461 BC
66. Māna Deva	437 BC
67. Mahi Deva	417 BC
68. Vasanta Deva	397 BC
69. Udaya Deva Varman	382 BC
70. Māna Deva Varman	377 BC
71. Guṇakāma Deva Varman	347 BC
72. Śiva Deva Varman	338 BC

Śiva Deva Varma's inscription records Śri Harsha Saṁvat 119 which shows that Śiva Deva Varma ascended the throne in 457-119= 338 BC. This also shows that Śri Harsha Saṁvat (457 BC) was in vogue in Nepal.

73. Narendra Deva Varman	277 BC
74. Bhimdeva Varman	234 BC
75. Viṣṇudeva Varman	198 BC
76. Viśvadeva Varman	151 BC

He had no son and gave his daughter to Aṁśu Varman of Thakuri dynasty.

First Thakuri Dynasty

51/7/28th Kali/3002-3880or100BC-682 AD

The names of kings of Thakur dynasty that were available to the author of Nepal Rāja-vaṁśāvalī are given hereunder:

Name of the King	Year of the coronation
77. Aṁśu Varman	100 BC

Vikramaditya of Ujjain visited Nepal in 57 BC and the king of Nepal came under his suzerainty. Vikramaditya celebrated this occasion by founding the Vikram era in 57 BC.

78. Kritvarman	51 BC
79. Bhimārjuna	9 BC

80.	Nanda Deva	30AD
81.	Viradeva	79 AD
82.	Chandraketu Deva	144 AD
83.	Narendra Deva	192AD
84.	Varadeva	249 AD
85.	Naramudi	295 AD
86.	Sankara Deva	335AD
87.	Vardhamāna Deva	381 AD
88.	Balideva	420 AD
89.	Jayadeva	463 AD
90.	Balārjuna Deva	519 AD

Some Śaṅkrāchārya (not to be confused with Ādi Śaṅkarācharya) and Avalokiteśvara visited Nepal in 520 AD or Kali Saṁvat 3623.

91.	Vikrama Deva	559 AD
92.	Guṇakāma Deva	597 AD
93.	Bhoja Deva	626 AD
94.	Lakshmikāma Deva	660 AD
95.	Jayakāma Deva	682 AD

Second Thakuri Dynasty of Aṁśuvarman

51/7/28th Kali/3852-3989or702AD-887 AD

Name of the King	Year of the coronation
96. Vāmadeva	702 AD
97. Harsha Deva	735 AD
98. Sadāśivadeva	750 AD

He built Kirtipura on a hill south-west of Kāṭhamanḍu and golden roof of Pashupati's temple in Kali 3851 or 750 AD. He introduced coins of copper alloyed with iron, marked with a figure of a lion.

99.	Mānaveva	760 AD
100.	Narsinghdeva	782 AD
101.	Nanad Deva	803 AD
102.	Rudra Deva	822 AD

Rudra Deva became a Buddhist monk.

103.	Mitra Deva	843 AD
104.	Arideva	865 AD

A son was born to him. He made him engaged in wrestling, so he was given a title 'Malla' i.e. a wrestler.

105.	Abhaya Malla	870 AD
106.	Jayadeva Malla	879 AD

Jayadeva Malla with the help of Sakhwal established the Nepal Saṁvat beginning 879 AD. He ruled over Kāntipurā and Lalitpaṭṭaṇa.

107.	Ananda Malla	887 AD

Ananda Mall was the younger brother of Jayadeva Malla. He founded Bhaktapura or Bhātagām and seven other towns, Venipura, Pānāti, Nala, Dhomakhel, Khadpu or Shadpu, Chankat and Sanga. He used to reside in Bhātagām. During the reign of these two brothers, Nānyadeva came from the south and founded the Karnataka Dynasty.

Karnataka Dynasty

51/7/28thKali/3990-4424or888AD-1322AD

Name of the King	Year of the coronation
108. Nānyadeva	888 AD

Nānyadeva conquered the whole country on Śrāvaṇa Sudi 7 of Nepal Samvat 9, i.e. 888 AD. and expelled the Malla brothers of Tirhut. He ruled at Bhātagām for 50 years.

109. Gangādeva	938 AD
110. Narasingh Deva	978 AD

In his reign, on Phalgun Sudi 6 of Nepal Samvat, 111 or 989 AD, king Malla Deva and Kātyamalla of lalitapaṭṭaṇa founded Chāpagām or Champāpuri.

111. Śaktideva	1017 AD
112. Ramsingh Deva	1056 AD
113. Harideva	1114 AD

Harideva transferred his capital to Kathmandu. The

army of Pattan (Lalitapattana) rose in rebellion and drove Harideva to Thambal. It is said that a Magār (low caste servant) was dismissed from king Harideva's service. On being furious at this act, king Mukundasena invaded Harideva and defeated him. His soldiers destroyed the sacred images and took Bhairava from the temple of Matoyendravadha away to Pālpa. Mukundasena's whole army died of cholera, he alone escaped in the guise of an ascetic and died in Devighāṭ. It was considered that this all happened due to the anger of Pashupati.

As Nepal had been completely devastated, an interregnum of 7 or 8 years followed. 22 Thakuris of Navakoti came back to occupy the country. In the reign of Śaṅkardeva (1018 AD - 1130 AD), a widow Brāhmṇi 'Kaphi' in Ganda, who lived in a village of Jhal in Nepal, caused a Manuscript titled 'Prajñā Parmitā' to be written with golden letters in Nepali Saṁvat 245, i.e 1124 AD.

In Lalitapattana, every ward had its own king and in Kantipura, 12 kings ruled at once. Bhātagām was too held by Thakuri king. The Thakuris ruled the country for 200 years, i.e. till 1322 AD. They built many Buddha temples and Viharas. In 1322 AD king Harisingh Deva of the solar dynasty was driven away by Muslims from Ayodhya. He established himself in Simrongarh in Terai. His guardian deity Tulja Bhawani commanded him in a dream to capture Nepal, so he invaded Nepal and founded 10th Sūryavaṁśī Dynasty of Bhātagām in 1322 AD.

Sūryavaṁśī Dynasty of Bhātagām

51/7/28th Kali/4424-4512or1322 AD-1410 AD

Name of the King	Year of the coronation
120. Harisigh Deva	1322 AD

Harisingh Deva conquered the valley in Śaka (Śālivāhana) Saṁvat 1245 or Nepal Samvat 444 (i.e. 1322 AD).

121. Matisingh Deva	1347 AD
122. Śaktisingh Deva	1362 AD

Śaktisingh Deva received a letter from the emperor of China with a seal bearing the name Śaktisingh Rama in Chinese year 535, he abdicated the throne.

123. Śyāmasingh Deva 1395

In his reign, a devastating earthquake occurred on Bhādrapada Sudi 12 of Nepal Saṁvat 528, i.e. 1406 AD. His daughter married a descendant from Mallas who ruled Tirhut before Nānyadeva. He had no son, so after his death in 1410 AD, Nepal came under the rule of Mallas.

The Third Thakuri Dynasty

51/7/28th Kali/4512-4572 or 1410 AD-1470 AD

Name of the King	Year of the coronation
124. Jayabhadra Malla	1410 AD
125. Naga Malla	1415 AD
126. Jayajagat Malla	1418 AD
127. Nāgendra Malla	1420 AD
128. Ugra Malla	1422 AD
129. Aśoka Malla	1424 AD

He drove the 22 Thakuris from Pattana and founded near Svayanbhunadha the town of Kassipura between the rivers Mānmati, Vāgmati and Rudramati.

130. Jayastiti Malla 1427 AD

He made laws for castes and families. He built many temples. One of his inscriptions is found in Lalitapaṭṭana dated Nepal Saṁvat 547 or 1425 AD. He died on Kartika Badi 5 of Nepal Saṁvat 549 or 1427 AD

131. Yakṣa Malla 1470 AD

He built the walls of Bhātagām, where to the right of the principal gate an inscription is put which bears a date Śrāvaṇa Sudi of Nepal Saṁvat 573 or 1451 AD. He and his successor built a temple of Dattatreya in Tāchapātol of Bhātagām. He died in Nepal Saṁvat 592 or 1470 AD. He was survived by 3 sons, the eldest and youngest of whom founded two separate dynasties of Bhātagām and Kathmandu, while the second Rana Malla held the town Banepa.

Bhātagām line

51/7/28th Kali/4572–4822 or 1470 AD–1720 AD

Name of the King	Year of the coronation
132. Jayarāya Malla	1470 AD
133. Suvarṇa Malla	1485 AD
134. Prāṇa Malla	1500 AD
135. Viśva Malla	1515 AD
136. Trailokya Malla	1530 AD
137. Jagajyotir Malla or Jayajyotir Malla	1558 AD
138. Narendra Malla	1610 AD
139. Jagatprakash Malla	1661 AD

In his time Harasimha Bhāro and Vasimha Bhāro built a temple of Bhīmasena, inscribing the date Nepal Saṁvat 775, i.e. 1653 AD on a stone lion. On Mārgaśīrṣa Sudi 6 of Nepal Saṁvat 772, i.e. 1660 AD the king inscribed five Hymns in honour of Bhavani.

140. Jitamitra Malla	1681 AD
141. Bhūpatīndra Malla	1702 AD
142. Ranjit Malla	1720 AD

In his time Gorkha Rāja Nara Bhūpāla Sha invaded Nepal and with him, the dynasty rule came to an end.

Kāthmāṇḍu line

51/7/28th Kali/4822–4868 or 1720 AD–1766 AD

Name of the King	Year of the coronation

143. Ratna Malla 1470 AD

Ratna Malla was the youngest son of Yakṣa Malla (1427-1470 AD). He defeated 12 Thakuri Rājās of Kantipura in Nepal Saṁvat 611 or 1489 AD. Later, he also defeated the Thakuris of Navakot and Bhotiyas (Tibetans) with the help of Śiva, king of Palpa. During his reign Muslims first invaded Nepal. Somaśekharānanda, a southern Brāhmaṇa became High Priest of Pashupati, a temple of Tuljadevi which was dedicated in Nepal Saṁvat 621 or 1499 AD and a new copper currency with a sign of a lion was introduced.

144. Amara Malla 1517 AD

He ruled over 28 towns and villages. In his reign, a great temple on the model of that at Gaya was built at Lalitapaṭṭana.

145. Sūrya Malla 1528 AD

146. Narendra Malla 1536AD

147. Mahindra Malla 1540 AD

He received permission from the Muslim emperor of Delhi to issue silver coins. He was the friend of Trailokya Malla of Bhātgām and dedicated a temple of Tulja Devi in Kathmandu in Nepal Saṁvat 699, i.e. 1547 AD. During his period, Purandara Rajavanshi built a temple of Narayana close to the palace of Lilitapaṭṭana in Nepal Saṁvat 686, i.e.1564 AD.

148. Sadāsiva Malla 1569 AD

He was compelled by his subjects to escape to Bhātagām where he was imprisoned.

149. Sivasingh Malla 1570 AD

He was the younger brother of Sadāsiva Malla. According to an inscription, he repaired a temple of Svayambhū in Nepal Saṁvat 714, i.e. 1592 AD. His queen Ganga restored the temple of Changu Narayana in Nepal Saṁvat 705, i.e. 1583 AD. He had two sons, the elder of whom ruled over Kantipura and the younger one occupied the throne of Lalitapattana during the life-time of his father.

150. Lakshminarasingh Malla 1593 AD

During his reign, the modern temple of Gorakhnath called Kathmandu was built in Nepal Saṁvat 715, i.e.1593 AD. following which the town of Kantipura was named as Kathmandu. He has some mental problem, so he was dethroned by his son and kept in confinement for 16 years.

151. Pratap Malla 1637 AD

He was a poet. There are four inscriptions associated with his reign, the last one was prepared in Nepal Saṁvat 777, i.e. 1655 AD.

152. Mahipatīndra Malla 1660 AD

He died in Nepal Saṁvat 814, i.e.1692 AD.

153. Bhaskar Malla 1692 AD

In Nepal Saṁvat 822, i.e. 1700 AD, he died childless at the age of 22.

154. Jagajjaya Malla 1700 AD

He was a distant relative of Bhaskar Malla. He was placed on the throne by the wife of Bhaskar Malla on 1700 AD. He had five sons. He died in Nepal Samvat 852, i.e. 1730 AD.

155. Jaya Prakash 1730 AD

He was deposed by the Gorkha king Prithvi Narayana in Nepal Saṁvat 888, i.e. 1766 AD.

Lalitapaṭṭana line

51/7/28th Kali/4686–4868or1584 AD–1766 AD

Name of the King **Year of the coronation**

156. Hariharasingh 1584 AD

He was the younger son of Sivasingh of Kantipura (Kathmandu).

157. Siddhi Nrisingh 1630 AD

He became an ascetic in Nepal Saṁvat 777, i.e. 1655 AD.

158. Srinivas Malla 1655 AD

He had a war with Pratap Malla of Kathmandu in Nepal Saṁvat 778, i.e. 1656 AD. His latest inscription dates Nepal Saṁvat 821, i.e. 1699 AD.

159. Yoga Narendra Malla 1655 AD

He lost his son and became an ascetic.

160. Mahipatīndra or Mahindra Malla 1700 AD

He died in Nepal Saṁvat 842, i.e. 1720 AD.

161. Jayayoga Prakash 1720 AD

He founded an inscription dated 1723 AD.

162. V iṣṇu Malla 1729 AD

Viṣṇu Malla son of Yoganarendra Malla's fourth daughter died without issue shortly after 1737 AD.

163. Rājya Prakash 1737 AD

Third son of Jagajjaya Malla (1700 AD-1730 AD) of Kathmandu was appointed as king at the age of 7, but he was blinded by the Pradhanas and expelled from the throne.

164. Jaya Prakash 1752 AD

165. Viśvajita Malla 1754 AD

166. Dalamardana Shah 1767 AD

167. Teja Narayana Singh 1773 AD

Teja Narayana Singh was descendent of Viśvajita Malla. During his reign, the country was conquered by Gorkha king Prithvi Narayana in 1766 AD. Thus in 1766 AD Gorkha rule was established in Nepal.

21. Chālukya Rulers

The origin of the Early Chalukyas of Rājamahendravaram

The grant of Vāra Chola contains valuable information about the origin of the Chalukyas. At the outset, it gives the genealogy of Soma Vaṁśa (Lunar dynasty) from Atri Muni to Pāndavas and Arjuna to Udayana. Starting from King Udayana, total of 59 kings ruled over Ayodhyā. Vijayāditya was the 60th king of Ayodhyā. He went on to conquer 'Dakśiṇāpatha' and attacked Trilochana Pallava but unfortunately got killed in the battle. His queen, who was pregnant (ṣaṇamāsagarbhiṇī), reached an 'agrahāra' called Muḍivemu along with the family-priest and the old ministers. Viṣṇubhaṭṭa-somayājin protected her like a daughter and she gave birth to a son, Vishṇuvardhana. After coming of age, Vishṇuvardhana founded a kingdom in Dakśiṇāpatha.

Thus, Vishṇuvardhana founded the rule of Chalukya dynasty.

Two grants of the Early Chalukyas who ruled at Rājamahendravaram are available today. These grants are dated in the Kaliyuga era. One grant available at the Govt Museum of Hyderabad is unambiguously dated in Kali year 3628 elapsed (527 AD). It was issued by King Vishṇuvardhana II, the grandson of King Vishṇuvardhana I. Historians have identified this grant with Vishṇuvardhana I or Vishṇuvardhana II of the Eastern Chalukyas and assumed that the Kali year given is incorrect. However, there should be no doubt that these grants belong to the Early Chalukyas who ruled at Rājamahendravaram, much before the establishment of the Eastern Chalukya kingdom at Veṅgi. It appears that the Chalukyas were attempting to establish a kingdom in Dakśiṇāpatha from the beginning of the 6th century AD till the end of the 9th century AD.

The Early Chālukyas of Badami

51/7/28th Kali/3628–3198 or 527 AD - 97AD

Early Chalukya dynasty ruled from Vātāpi or Badami (in Bagalkot district of Karnataka) as their capital. Ptolemy (140 AD) mentions Badami as 'Badiamaioi' which indicates that Badami was in prominence during the 1st and 2nd centuries AD. Pulakeśin I, the founder of the Chalukya Empire in Vātāpi, according to the Altem or British Museum copper plates, Pulakeśin I was the grandson of Jayasiṁha and son of Raṇarāga. The Aihole inscription 13 also gives a similar lineage of the Chalukyas. Pulakeśin I ruled from Śaka 411 (489 AD) to Śaka 466 (544 AD). Chronology of early Chalukya kings is based upon 'Śaka Kālātīta Saṁvatsara' which is given below.

	Date of the coronation	
Name of the King	**Śaka era** (78 AD)	**Christian Era**
1. Jayasiṁha	358	436 AD
2. Raṇarāga	383	461 AD
3. Pulakeśin I	411	489 AD
4. Kīrtivarman I	466	544 AD
5. Mangaliśvara	489	567 AD
6. Pulakeśin II	515	593 AD

Pulakeśin II defeated Śri Harsha Śilāditya (606 AD) who was defeated by the Rāṣṭrakuṭa Dantidurga.

काण्चाश-केरल-नराधिप-चोल-पाण्ड्य श्रीहर्ष-वज्रट-विभेद-विधानदक्षम्
kāṇchāśa-kerala-narādhipa-chola-pāṇḍya śri harsha-vajraṭa-vibheda-vidhānadakśam.

7. Kokkulla Vikramāditya		
(elder son of Pulakeśin II)	531-561	609AD-639AD
8. Vijayabhaṭṭārikā		

(wife of Chandrāditya)	562-576	640 BC- 654 BC
9. Vikramāditya I (Younger son of Pulakeśin II)	577-601	655 BC-679 AD
10. Vinayāditya	602-618	680 AD -696 AD
11. Vijayāditya	619-655	697 AD-733 AD
12. Vikramāditya II	655-666	733 AD -744 AD
13. Kīrtivarman II	666-680	744 AD - 758AD

The Chinese pilgrim I-tsing travelled in India around 671-695 AD. He referred to a king named Chi-li-ki-to who ruled five hundred years before his time as having built a temple exclusively for Chinese priests.

The Early Chalukyas of Gujarat

51/7/28th Kali/3711–3870 or 610AD–769 AD

Kokkulla Vikramāditya, the elder son of Pulakeśin II, was the founder of the Gujarat branch of the early Chalukyas. He was appointed the Viceroy of Gujarat region around Śaka 532 (610 AD) by his father Pulakeśin II. He was supported by his paternal uncle Buddhavarasarāja, his father's younger brother. Many inscriptions of the early Chalukyas referred to Kalachuri-Chedi era, because Kalachuri-Chedi era was popular in this region.

The chronology of early Chalukyas of Gujaratas available in various inscriptions which is cited in a table given below:

Name of King	Śālivāhana Śaka era (78 AD)	AD
Kokkulla Vikramāditya (elder son of Pulakeśin II)	532-573	610-651
Dharāśraya Jayasiṁha	573-616	651 -694

Śryāśraya Sīlāditya	616-623	694-701
Jayāśraya Vinayāditya	623-653	701-731
Avanijanāśraya Puṇakeśirāja	653-670	731-748
Satyāśravadeva	670-691	748-769

The Eastern Chalukyas of Veṅgi

51/7/28th Kali/3716–4232 or 615 AD–1131 AD

Vishnuvardhana I (Kubja Vishnuvardhana) was the founder of the Eastern Chalukya Dynasty. He was the younger brother of early Chalukya king (Satyaśrava) Pulakeśin II (593 AD-609 AD) who established the strongest empire of the Chalukyas between the Narmadā and Kāveri rivers. Pulakeśin II extended his territory towards east from Viśākhapaṭnam to Nellore. He appointed his brother Vishnuvardhana I as Viceroy in the coastal Andhra region. In a short period, Vishnuvardhana I became independent and established his capital at Veṅgi and ruled for 18 years. Satārā grant of Vishṇuvardhana I dated in the 8th year (601 AD) of the rule of Mahārāja Pulakeśin II gives the title of 'Yuvarāja' to Vishṇuvardhana I. Hyderabad plates are dated in the 3rd year of rule of Pulakeśin II (596 AD) which was 518th year of Śaka.

Chipurupalle plates mention the lunar eclipse on the full moon day of Śrāvaṇa month in the 18th year of the rule of Vishṇuvardhana I. In 44 BC he was declared as 'Yuvarāja' We find that from 44 BC onward only three lunar eclipses occurred on full moon day of Śrāvaṇa. They are on 25 July 48 BC (penumbral), 4 July 46 BC (penumbral) and 26 July 29 BC (total). So, 18 years of the rule can take place on 26th July 29 BC. Considering 29th BC as the 18th year of the rule, the first year of rule would be 46 BC. As such Vishṇuvardhana I ruled from 46 BC to 29 BC. The chronology of all the Chalukya rulers of Veṅgi can be relocated as under:

Sr. No	Name of King	Years of rule	Period
1	Vishnuvardhana I (Brother of Satyāśraya Pulakeśin II)	18 years	615-633 AD
2	Jayasiṁha (Brother of Kubja Vishnuvardhana)	30 years	633AD-663 AD
3	Indrarāja	7 days	663 AD
4	Vishnuvardhana II (elder son of Indrarāja brother of Jayasiṁha)	9 years	663 - 672 AD
5	Maṅgi Yuvarāja (son of Vishnuvardhana II)	25 Years	672 - 697 AD
6	Jayasiṁha II (Son of Maṅgi Yuvarāja)	13 Years	697 - 710 AD
7	Kokkili (Jayasiṁha's brother, the son of his stepmother)	6 Months	710 AD
8	Vishnuvardhana III (Elder brother of Kokkili and younger Son of Indra Bhaṭṭāraka)	37 Years	710 - 747 AD
9	Vijayāditya Bhaṭṭāraka (Son of Vishnuvardhana III)	18 Years	747-765 AD
10	Vishnurāja (Vishnuvardhana IV)	36 Years	765-801 AD
11	Vijayāditya Narendra Mrigarāja	40 Years	801-841 AD
12	Kali Vishnuvardhana	1.2 year	841-842 AD
13	Guṇagāṅka Vijayāditya	44 Years	842-886 AD
14	Chalukya Bhāma I (Drohārjuna)	30 Years	886-916 AD

15	Kollabigaṅda Vijayāditya	6 Months	916 AD
16	Amma Rāja I Vishnuvardhana Sarvalokāśraya	7 Years	916-923 AD
17	Taḍapa	1 Month	923 AD
18	Vikramāditya (Son of Chalukya Bhāma I)	11 Months	924 AD
19	Yuddhamalla (Son of Taḍapa)	7 Years	924-931 AD
20	Bhāma II (Brother of Amma Rāja I)	12 Years	931-943 AD
21	Amma Rāja II Vijayāditya (Son of Bhāma II)	25 Years	943-968 AD
22	Indrarāja	7 days	968 AD
23	Dānārṇava (Son of Bhāma II & Aṅkidevi and half-brother of Amma Rāja II)	3 years	968-971 AD
24	Baḍpa and his brother Tala II	28 years	971-999 AD
25	Śaktivarman or Chalukya Candra (son of Dānārṇava)	12 years	999-1011 AD
26	Vimalāditya (Brother of Śaktivarman) Vimalāditya married Rājendra Chola's sister Kundava Mahādevi)	7 years	1011-1018 AD
27	Rājarāja I (son of Vimalāditya)	41 years	1018-1059 AD
28	Kulottuṅga Choladeva I (Son of Rājarāia I)	16 years	1059-1075 AD
29	Vāra Chola (son of Kullottuṅga Choladeva I)	33 years	1075-1108 AD

30	Vikrama Chola (Son of Kulottuṅga Choladeva I)	15 years	1108-1123 AD
31	Kulottuṅga Choladeva II (Son of Vikrama Chola)	8 years	1123-1131 AD

The Eastern Chalukya kingdom gradually became a part of the Chola kingdom during the 12th century AD and slipped into its deepest internal crisis during the reign of Dānārṇava. Jaṭā Chola Bhāma, the brother-in-law of Amma Rāja II, killed Dānārṇava. Consequently, the succession struggle between the sons of Dānārṇava and Jaṭā Chola Bhāma ensued for 27 years. Vimalāditya, the younger brother of Śaktivarman and the son of Dānārṇava, took refuge in the court of Rājarāja Chola. Rājarāja invaded Veṅgi and killed Jaṭā Chola Bhāma. Rājarāja ensured that Veṅgi was part of Chola Kingdom and appointed Śaktivarman as the King of Veṅgi under his control. He also married off his daughter Kundava Mahādevi to Vimalāditya, the younger brother of Śaktivarman.

Rājarāja also ensured that his grandson Rājarāja II, the son of Kundava Mahādevi and Vimalāditya, took over the reins of Veṅgi. Thus, the successors of the Eastern Chalukya kingdom became more Cholasthan Chalukyas and gradually, the territory of Veṅgi was absorbed by the Chola Empire. By this period, the Western Chalukyas re-established themselves in Northern Karṇātaka by overthrowing the Rāṣṭrakuṭas. They were outraged by the absorption of Veṅgi into the Chola Empire. Veṅgi became a bone of contention resulting in repeated conflicts between the Cholas and the Western Chalukyas.

Western Chalukyas of Kalyāṇī (Phase II)

51/7/28th Kali/3500-3600
or 4th century AD-5th century AD

The chronology of the Western Chalukyas of Kalyāṇī (phase II) is as follows:

Genealogy by Bilhaṇa	Genealogy given in Inscriptions	Christian Era
1. Tailapa I	Tailapa I Āhavamalla	290-320 AD

2. Satyāśraya I	Bhimarāja?	320-325 AD
3. Jayasingh	Ayyanārya?	325-330 AD
4. Āhavamalla Trailokyamalla	Vikramāditya?	330-345 AD
5. Someśvara		345-346 AD
6. Vikramāditya Tribhuvanamalla		346-405 AD
7. Bhulokamalla?	(Śaka 1047)	450-480 AD?

Western Chalukyas of Kalyāṇī (Phase III)

51/7/28th Kali/4082–4300 or (980 AD–12th century AD)

The chronology of the Western Chalukyas of Kalyāṇi Phase III is as follows:

Name of the King	**In Śālivahana Era (78AD)**	**In Christian** Era
1. Tailapa II		970-980 AD
2. Satyāśraya II		980-1000 AD
3. Vikramāditya (Son of Dāsa Varmā, the younger brother of Satyāśraya)		1000-1016 AD
4. Jagadekamalla Jayasingh (Younger brother of Vikramāditya)	938-967	1016-1045 AD
5. Āhavamalla Trailokyamalla	967-986	1045-1064 AD
6. Bhuvanaikamalla (Son of Trailokyamalla)	986-998	1060-1076 AD
7. Vikramāditya Tribhuvanamalla (Younger brother of Bhuvanaikamalla)	998-1049	1076-1127 AD

22. The Pratīhāras

51/7/28th Kali/3177-3487or 75 AD-385 AD

Epigraphic records of Pratiharas used mainly Kārtikādi Vikrama era (717 BC), Śaka Nṛpa rājyabhiṣeka era (583 BC). Sometimes, Chaitrādi Vikrama era (57 BC) is also found to be used by them. The Pratīhāras trace their origin from Lakśmaṇa who acted as the 'Pratīhāra' (Door-keeper) of his elder brother Rāma during his fight with Meghanāda. Pratīhāras are one of the four Agnivaṁśī dynasties. The Pratīhāras occupied Avanti and established their kingdom at Ujjain in the 1st century AD. The chronology of Pratīhāra rulers is as under:

1. Nāgabhaṭa I (73-93 AD)

Nāgabhaṭa I established his kingdom by defeating Valacha, the Mleccha king and became the first Pratīhāra king of Ujjain. He also conquered the invincible Gurjaras. The Rāṣṭrakūta king Dantidurga probably defeated Nāgabhaṭa I around 85-90 AD.

2. Kakkuka or Kākustha (93-103 AD)

According to the Gwalior Praśasti of Mihira-Bhoja, Kākustha or Kakkuka succeeded Nāgabhaṭa I. He was the son of the brother of Nāgabhaṭa I.

3. Devarāja or Devaśakti (103-109 AD)

Devarāja was the Kakustha's younger brother.

4. Vatsarāja (109-138 AD)

Devarāja's son Vatsarāja was the famous Pratīhāra king who forcibly wrested the empire from the Bhāṇḍi clan. Udyotana Sūri, the author of Kuvalayamālā, mentions that King Vatsarāja was ruling Avanti in Śaka 700 (117 AD). An inscription of king Vatsarāja tells us that he wasruling in Śaka 717 elapsed (134 AD) [muni-śaśi-nāga (717) saṁsthe yānti kāle śakānām]. It appears that Pratīhāra Vatsarāja ruled between 109 AD to 138 CE.

According to a Jain Purāṇa 'Harivaṁśa' written by Jinasena, Vatsarāja was ruling in Avanti, Indrāyudha in the North and

Śrivallabha in the South around Śaka 705 elapsed (122 AD). An inscription of Vatsarājais dated in Śaka 717 elapsed (134 AD).

5. Nāgabhaṭa II (138 -168 AD)

Vatsarāja's son Nāgabhaṭa II was the most successful Pratīhāra king. He defeated the Āndhra, Saindhava, Vidarbha and Kaliṅga kings. He also defeated Chakrāyudha and the king of Vaṅga. He took away the hill forts of the Ānarta, Mālava, Kirāta, Turūṣaka, Vatsa, Matsya and other kings. The Pathari pillar inscription of Rāṣṭrakūṭa Parabala mentions that Parabala's father Karkarāja fought with the king Nāgāvaloka. According to Vedveer (2015:191) Nāgabhaṭa II was probably referred to as Nāgāvaloka. The Buchkala inscription of Nāgabhaṭa II is dated in Kārtikādi Vikrama era 872 (153-154 AD). The Pratīhāras took control over Kānyakubja or Kanauj during the reign of Nāgabhaṭa II.

6. Rāmabhadra (168-172 AD)

7. Bhoja I or Mihira-Bhoja (172-232 AD)

Rāmabhadra's son Bhoja I or Mihira-Bhoja expanded the Pratīhāra kingdom from Sind in the West to Vaṅga in the East and Narmadā in the South. The earliest inscription of Bhoja I was dated in Kārtikādi Vikrama era 893 (172 AD). The Deogarh pillar inscription of Bhoja I is dated in Śaka era 784 (200 AD) and also in Kārtikādi Vikrama era 919 (200 AD). Interestingly, the Ahar inscription of the time of Bhoja I consists of 10 documents with 10 different dates. One date is given in the Kārtikādi Vikrama era and other nine dates are given in the Chaitrādi Vikrama era. The fourth document is dated in Kārtikādi Vikrama era 943 (222 AD) while the third, eighth & tenth documents are dated in Chaitrādi Vikrama era 298 (241 AD). The earliest inscription of Bhoja I's son Mahendrapāla is dated in 955 (234 AD). Thus, Bhoja I may have ruled for at least 60 years from 172 AD to 232 AD and died in 239 AD. The Ahar inscription is the earliest epigraphic evidence that the Chaitrādi Vikrama era came into use at the beginning of the 3rd century CE. Historians speculated that the nine documents of the Ahar Inscription are dated in the Śri Harsha era considering the fictitious epoch of the Śri Harsha era in 606 AD. In reality, the Śri Harsha era commenced, as discussed above, in 457 BC. It appears that Partīhāra empire started declining after Bhoja I.

8. Mahendrapāla I	232-252 AD
9. Bhoja II	252-262 AD
10. Vināyakapāla	262-272 AD
11. Mahendrapāla II	272-283 AD
12. Vijayapāla	284-319 AD
13. Rajyapāla	319-359 AD
14. Trilochanapāla	359-372 AD
15. Yaśahpāla	372 -379 AD

23. Paramāra Rulers

The Paramāras of Mālava (Phase I)

51/7/28th Kali/3312–3712 or 200AD–610AD

Paramāras also belong to Agnivaṁśī Kṣatriyas or Rajputs. They also used Kārtikādi Vikrama era in their inscriptions.

1. Upendrarāja (?)

According to the Udaypur Praśastiand the Navasāhasāṅka Charita of Padmagupta, Upendrarāja was the founder of the Paramāra kingdom of Mālavā.

2. Vairisingh I (?)

3. Siyaka I (?)

4. Vākpati I or Krishnarāja or Bopaiyyarāja (Kārtikādi Vikrama 950-975 or 229-254AD)

He was the first independent ruler of Parmāra dynasty. Dhāra city in Madhya Pradesh was the capital of Parmāra dynasty.

5. Vairisingh II or Vajrata (Kārtikādi Vikrama 975-1000 or 254-279AD)

6. Siyaka II or Śri Harshadeva (Kārtikādi Vikramaera 1000-1027 or 279-306AD)

The Udaypur Praśasti refers to Siyaka II as Śri Harshadeva who defeated Khoṭṭigadeva and annexed his kingdom. Khoṭṭigadeva mentioned in the Paramāra inscriptions was probably a Chediking.

7. Vākpati II or Muñja (Kārtikādi Vikramaera 1027-1043 or 306 -322AD)

Vākpati II was also referred to as Muñjain the Nagpur Praśasti. According to the Udaypur Praśasti, Vākpatirāja II established his authority in Karṇāṭa, Lāṭa, Kerala and Chola.

कर्णाट-लाट-केरल-चोलशिरोरत्न-रागीपादकमलः ।

karṇāṭa-lāṭa-kerala-cholaśiroratna-rāgīpādakamalaḥ ।

It seems that the Chedi king Yuvarāja challenged Vākpatirāja II whom he successfully defeated in Tripuri, the capital of Chedi kingdom.

युवराजं विजित्याजौ हत्वा तद्वाहिनीपतीन् ।
खड्गमूर्ध्वकृतं येन त्रिपूर्यां विजिगिषुणा ॥

yuvarājaṁ vijityājau hatvā tadvāhinīpatīn ।
khaḍgamūrdhvakṛtaṁ yena tripūryāṁ vijigiṣuṇā ॥

8. Sindhurāja (Kārtikādi Vikrama (1043-1057 or 322-336AD)

He was the younger brother of Vākpatirāja II. Hismajor achievement was his victory over the Hūṇas.

तस्यानुजोनिर्जितहुणराजः ।
tasyānujonirjitahuṇarājaḥ ।

Padmagupta, the author of Navasāhasāṅka Charitam was in thecourt of Sindhurāja and according to him, Sindhurāja conquered Kuntala, Vāgada, Murala, Lāṭa, Aparānta, Kosala and Hūṇas.

9. Bhojarāja (Kārtikādi Vikramaera 1057-1113 or 336-392AD)

Bhojadeva, the son of Sindhurāja, was one of the most celebrated kings of Indian history. The Kalvan grant of the time of Bhojadeva tells us that he ruled over Karṇāṭa, Lāṭa, Gurjara, Chedi and Koṅkaṇa.

कर्णाट-लाट-गुर्जर-चेद्याधिपकोंकणेशप्रभृतिरिपुवर्गनिर्धारितजनितत्रासयशो ध्वलितभुवनत्रयः ।

karṇāṭa-lāṭa-gurjara-chedyādhipakoṁkaṇeśaprabhṛtir-ipuvarganirdhāritajanitatrāsayaśo dhvalitabhuvanatrayaḥ ।

Bhojadeva issued the Betmagranton the occasion of his victory over Koṅkaṇa. According to Udaipur Praśasti, Bhojadeva subjugated the kings of Chedi, Indraratha, Karṇāṭa, Lāṭa, Gurjara and Turuṣka.

चेदीश्वरेन्द्ररथ.......कर्णाटलाटपतिगुर्जरात्तुरुष्कान् ।

chedīśvarendraratha...karṇāṭalāṭapatigurjarātturuṣkān ।

Kalhaṇa (487 AD: 1.170), mentions that Huṣka, Juṣka and Kaniṣka were born in the dynasty of Turuṣka.

ते तुरुष्कान्वयोद्भूताः ।
te turuṣkānvayodbhūtāḥ ।

Thus, the Turuṣkas existed since ancient times in what is today modern North-western Pakistan. Turuṣkas were not Arabs as some historians speculate. The Udaipur Praśasti also tells us that Bhojadeva ruled from Kailāśa in the North to Malayagiri in the South and from the Western ghats to the Eastern Ghats.

आकैलाशान्मलयगिरितोऽस्तोदयाद्रिद्वयादाभुक्तपृथिवीं पृथु ।

His kingdom was protectedby Kedāranātha in the North, Rāmeśvaram in the South, Somanātha in theWest and Śuṇḍīra-Kālānala-Rudra in the East.

केदाररामेश्वरसोमनाथशुण्डीरकालानलरुदसत्कैःसुराश्रयैर्व्याप्य च यः समन्ताद्यथार्थसंज्ञं जगतिं चकार ।

kedārarāmeśvarasomanāthaśuṇḍīrakālānalarudasatkaiḥsurāśr ayairvyāpya cha yaḥ samantādyathārthasaṁjñaṁ jagatiṁ chakāra ।

According to the Pattana Manuscript Catalogue, Bhojadeva subjugated the kings of Draviḍa, Lāṭa, Vaṅga, Gauḍa, Gurjara, Kīra and Kāmboja and also terrorised the kings of Chola, Āndhra, Karṇāṭa, Gurjara, Chedi and Kānyakubja.

It is evident from the Paramāra inscriptions that Bhojadeva ruled over the whole of North India and Karṇāṭaka in South India. Bhojadeva's inscriptions are dated in Kārtikādi Vikramaera from 1067 (346AD) to 1103 (382AD). The Rājamṛgāṅkakaraṇa mentions that Bhoja was ruling in Śaka 964 (381 AD). Bhoja was still on the throne when the 'Cintāmaṇi-Sāraṇika' was composed by his court-poet Daśabalain Śaka 977 (394 AD). According to Merutuṅga and Bhojaprabandha of Ballaladeva, Bhoja ruled for fifty-five years, seven months and three days. Therefore, the time of Bhojadeva can be fixed around 336-392AD. Thus, in the 4th century AD, the Paramāra dynasty established a powerful empire in North India and in Karnataka & Bengal as well. Bhoja was the most illustrious king of the Paramāras and he may well have been the most successful king of India after Samudragupta and Chandragupta II. The Vadanagar Praśasti of Kumārapāla refers to Bhoja as 'Mālava Chakravartin'. Bhoja was a learned king and a great Sanskrit poet who wrote the 'Saraswatīkaṇṭhābharaṇa' on poetics, the 'Samarāṅgaṇa-sūtradhāra' on architecture and the 'Rājamārtaṇḍa' on Yogaśāstra etc. He authored a Karaṇa treatise 'Rājamṛgāṅka' in Kārtikādi Vikrama era 1100 (379AD). He was a great patron of learning and according to the Patna inscription, Bhaskaracharya's great grandfather Bhāskarabhaṭṭa received the title of Vidyāpati from him. He rebuilt the city of Dhārā and also constructed a Sanskrit Mahāvidyālaya (college) in Dhārā, now occupied by a mosque.

10. Jayasingh (Kārtikādi Vikrama era1113-1118 or 392-397AD)

11. Udayāditya (Kārtikādi Vikrama era1118-1151 or 397-430AD)

It is recorded in the Udaipur Praśasti that Bhojadeva's successor Udayāditya killed the ruler of Dāhala deśa or Chedi kingdom.

दाहलाधीशसंहारवज्रदण्ड इवापरः ।
dāhalādhīśasaṁhāravajradaṇḍa ivāparaḥ /

According to the Udaipur Praśasti, the Dhārā kingdom was filled with dense darkness after thedeath of Bhojadeva. Emboldened by his death, the Chedi king invaded Dhārā and various other enemy kings also tried to regain their lost territories until Udayāditya, the bandhu or a relative of Bhojadeva (asmentioned in the Nagpur Museum stone inscription of Naravarman), killed the Chedi king and re-established the authority of the Paramāras.

12. Naravarman (Kārtikādi Vikramaera 1143-1190 or430-

469AD)

13. Yaśovarman (Kārtikādi Vikramaera 1190-1214 or 469-493AD)

14. Jayavarman I or Ajayavarman (Kārtikādi Vikrama era 1214-1255 or 493-534AD)

15. Vindhyavarman (Kārtikādi Vikrama era 1255-1262 or 534-541AD)

16. Subhaṭavarman (Kārtikādi Vikramaera 1262-1266 or 541-545 AD)

17. Arjunavarman (Kārtikādi Vikramaera 1266-1274 or 545-553AD)

18. Devapāla (son of Hariśchandra) (Kārtikādi Vikramaera 1274-1290 or 553-569AD)

19. Jaitugideva (Elder Son of Devapāla) (Kārtikādi Vikramaera 290-1312 or 569-590AD)

20. Jayasingh? (Kārtikādi Vikramaera 1312-1314 or 590-592AD)

21. Jayavarman II (Younger son of Devapāla) (Kārtikādi Vikrama era 1314-1331 or 592-610 AD)

The above-mentioned complete genealogy of the Paramāra dynasty is available in the Mandhata grant of Jayavarman II dated in Vikrama 1 era 1331 (610 AD). The Parmāras lost their power in 610 AD.

The Later Paramāras of Mālava (Phase II)

51/7/28th Kali/4158or 1056 AD

Parmāra dynasty was again revived by later Paramāra descendant king Udayāditya II, known as 'Aribalamathana', destroyer of the power of enemies, the son of Gāndala or Gondala or Gondila and (the grandson of Sāravira?), went to Mālava and recovered Madhyadeśa which had been formerly governed by his ancestors and usurped by enemy kings. It is evident that king Udayāditya II re-established the Paramāra kingdom in 1056AD. Interestingly, an inscription of the Later Paramāras found at Sagarin Madhya Pradesh is dated in Chaitrādi Vikrama era 1116 (1058AD), Śālivāhana Śaka era 981 (1058 AD) and Kaliyuga era 4160 (1058 AD) which informs us that Udayāditya II re-established the Paramāra kingdom after 446 years, i.e. in 610+446= 1056 AD.

गतपदवेदशताधिकचत्वारिंषत्गतेय सैरज्ञ 446 पूर्वनृपगत संह्यतकनप्रभृति...
gatapadavedaśatādhikachatvāriṁṣatgateya sairajña 446 pūrvanṛpagata saṁhyatakanaprabhṛti...

Being unaware of the real facts, historians could not understand the reference to 446 years in the inscription of Udayāditya II. H. T. Prinsep thought it was a new era established by Udayāditya II with the epoch around 618 AD. Some historians ridiculously added 446 years to 1116 years to establish the rule of Udayāditya II around 1506 AD which is nothing but a sheer absurdity. The chronology of later Parmāras of Mālava may be constructed as under:

1. Gondala or Gandala (?)

Gondala had a son named as Udayāditya II. He was the uncle of Bhojadeva II. Bhojadeva II was very talented. He was enthroned after the death of Gondala.

1. Bhojarāja II (1025-1050 AD)

The Dongargaon stone inscriptionof the time of Jagaddeva dated in Śālivāhana Śaka 1034 (1112 AD) tells us that Bhojadeva II of the Paramāra dynasty became the king who was like Rāma.

तद्वंशे .....बभूव भोजदेवाख्यो राजा रामसमोगुणैः ।
tadvaṁśe .....babhūva bhojadevākhyo rājā rāmasamoguṇaiḥ /

After him, the Mālava kingdom was subjugated by three enemies.

Alberuni mentions Bhoja, the ruling king of Dhārā when he visited India during 1017-1030 AD. It was Bhojadeva II who was ruling in Dhārā around 1025 AD and therefore, the Bhoja referred to by Alberuni was Bhojadeva II and not the great

Mālava king Bhojadeva I who flourished in the 4th entury AD.

3. Udayāditya II (Śālivāhana Śaka981-1120 or1058-1098 AD)

Udayāditya II was the cousin of Bhojadeva II. According to Inscription found at Kolanupaka, Gondala was the father of Udayāditya II and the uncle (tasya pitṛvyaḥ) of Bhojadeva II.

4. Jagaddeva (Śālivāhana Śaka 1026-1051 or 1104-1129 AD)

Udayāditya II had many sons. Though Jagaddeva had the opportunity to become the king after the death of his father, here linquished his claim in favour of his elder brother Yogarāja and became a close associate of the Kuntala king i.e. the Kalyāṇ I Chalukya king Tribhuvanamalla.

दिवं प्रयाते पितरि श्रियं परिवित्तिभयं त्यक्त्वा योगराज्याय न्यवेदयत्।
divaṁ prayāte pitari śriyaṁ parivittibhayaṁ tyaktvā yogarājyāya nyavedayat I

The earliest inscription of Jagaddeva is dated in the year 29 of the Chalukya Vikrama era (1104 AD) and the Kamagiri inscription of Jagaddeva is dated in Śālivāhana 1051 (1129 AD). Historians wrongly identified the elder brother of Jagaddeva to be Naravarman and Lakśmadeva. In fact, Lakśmadeva and Naravarman were the sons of Udayāditya I whereas Jagaddeva was the son of Udayāditya II.

Three inscriptions found at Kolanupaka, Bhuvanagiri, Nalgonda District in Telangana, which tell us that Jagaddeva, the son of Udayāditya II and the grandson of Gondala, was ruling as the feudatory of the Kalyāṇi Chalukya king Tribhuvanamalla around 1104 AD (the 29th year of Chalukya Vikrama era).

24. Rāṣṭrakūṭa Rulers

The Rāṣṭrakūṭas were the descendants of Raṣṭrikas or Raṭhikas as mentioned in the edicts of Aśoka. According to a Tamil chronicle namely 'Koṅgu-deśa-rājakkal', seven Raṭṭa kings ruled over the Koṅgu region (the modern districts of Salem, Dharmapuri and Coimbatore in Tamilnadu). Koṅgani Varmande throned the last Raṭṭa (Rāṣṭrakūṭa) king Śri Vikrama Deva Chakravarty and established the Gaṅga Kingdom in Koṅgudeśa in Śaka 111. It shows that Rāṣṭrakūṭas were present in before 472 BC. The Uṅgikavāṭikā grant of Abhimanyu is the earliest available copper plate inscription of early Rāṣṭrakūṭa as. Mānāṅka was the founder of the early Rāṣṭrakūṭa dynasty of Mānapura (later Mānyakheṭa or Malkhed).

The genealogy of the Malkhed Rāṣṭrakūṭas is as under:

Mānāṅka	250 BC
Devarāja	230 BC
Vibhurāja and Bhaviāya	215 BC
Abhimanyu	200 BC

The Nagardhan plates of Swamirāja and the Tiwarkheda plates of Nannarāja (Epigraphica Indica, 11, pp. 276-281) indicate that the Rāṣṭrakūṭas also ruled over Achalpur, the region of Vidarbha around Śaka 553.

शककालसंवत्सरशतेषु (100) पंचसु (5) त्रयःपंचाशद्वर्षाधिकेषु (53) अष्टमासेभ्यः अतीतेषु.......
śakakālasaṁvatsaraśateṣu (100) paṁchasu (5) trayaḥpaṁchāśadvarṣādhikeṣu (53) aṣṭamāsebhyaḥ atīteṣu.......

Rāṣṭrakūṭas used Śaka Nṛpa kāla Saṁvat. As such this period corresponds to 30 BC. The Rāṣṭrakūṭas might have shifted their base to Vidarbha following the establishment of the Chalukya kingdom in Northern Karṇātaka.

The chronology of the Achalapura branch of the early

Rāṣṭrakūṭas is as under:

Name of Ruler	Śaka Saṁvat	Christain era
Durgarāja	500-515	83-68 BC
Govindarāja	515-530	68-53 BC
Swamikarāja	530-550	53-33 BC
Swamirāja	550-573	33-10 BC
Nannarāja	573-615	10BC-32 AD
Nandarāja Yuddhāsura	615-632	32 - 49 AD

The Main Branch of Early Rāṣṭrakūṭas

Govindarāja was the earliest king of this branch and was succeeded by his son, Karkarāja. Indrarāja was the son of Karkarāja. Indrarāja defeated the Western Chalukya king and married his daughter. Dantidurga, the Son of Indrarāja, was the first founder of Rāṣṭrakūṭa Empire. He built the Daśāvatāra temple at hiscapital Elīpura (Ellora). He defeated the Chalukya king Vallabha i.e. Kārtivarman II, the kings of Kāñchi (Pallava), Kerala, Chola, Pāṇḍya, Śri Harsha (Śālivāhana), Vajraṭa and Karṇāṭaka between Śaka 671-675 (88-92 AD) (Indian Antiquary, XI, pp. 109-115).

कांचीशकेरलनराधिपचोलपांड्यश्रीहर्षवज्रटविभेदविधानदक्षं कर्णाटकं....
kāṁchīśakeralanarādhipacholapāṁḍyaśrīharṣavajraṭavi bhedavidhānadakṣaṁ karṇāṭakaṁ....

He defeated the kings of the Gurjara dynasty in Ujjain and made them his 'Pratīhāra' or door-keepers. He also extended his empire up to the Konkan region.

The chronology of the Early Rāṣṭrakūṭa Dynasty

The chronology of Early Rāṣṭrakūṭ as reconstructed by Vedveer (2015:55) based on the inscriptions dated in Śaka coronation era (583 BC) is as follows.

	Śaka era (583 BC)	AD

Govindarāja	600-620	16-37 AD
Karkarāja	620-640	37-56 AD
Indrarāja	640-661	57-77 AD
Dantidurga (also known as Sāhasatuṅga, Khaḍgāvaloka)	662-676	78-93 AD
Krishnarāja (also known as Akālavarṣa, Shubhattuṅga)	677-692	94-109 AD
Govindarāja II (also known as Prabhātavarāa)	692-706	109-123AD
Dhruvarāja (also known as Dhārāvarṣa, Nirupama)	706-724	123 -140AD
Govindarāja III (also known as Prabhātavarā, Jagattuṅga)	724-740	140-157AD
Amoghavarāa I	740-796	157-213AD
Akālavarṣa Krishnaraja II	797-832	213-249AD

The Later Rāṣṭrakūṭas

The Rāṣṭrakūṭas were conquered by the early Chalukya Jayasiṁha I in 225-200 BC to establish the Chalukya kingdom.

योराष्ट्रकुटकुलमिन्द्र इति प्रसिद्धम् ।
कृष्णाह्वयस्य सुतमष्टशतेभसैन्यम् ॥
निर्जित्य दग्धनृपपंचशतो बभार ।
भूयश्चालुक्यकुलवल्लभराजलक्ष्मीम् ॥ The Miraj plates

yorāṣṭrakuṭakulamindra iti prasiddham I
kṛṣṇāhvayasya sutamaṣṭaśatebhasainyam II
nirjitya dagdhanṛpapaṁchaśato babhāra I
bhūyaśchālukyakulavallabharājalakṣamīm II

However, Rāṣṭrakūṭa- Yādava king Vīranārāyaṇa regained and re-established the Rāṣṭrakūṭa Empire in the 6th century AD which was lost to the Chalukyas.

Some later inscriptions of the Rāṣṭrakūṭas claim that the Rāṣṭrakūṭas were the Yādavas and the descendants of Yadu. It seems that the Vīranārāyaṇa re-established the rule of the

Rāṣṭrakūṭas again. The Tadakal (Gulbarga) inscription of Amoghavarṣa, the earliest inscription of the later Rāṣṭrakūṭas to mention Vīranārāyaṇa, is dated in Śālivāhana 651 (729 AD). This inscription starts with the invocation नमस्तुंग चिरश्चुम्बी which is commonly found in Yādava inscriptions. The rise of the Kalyāṇi Chalukyas in the 10th century AD ended the rule of the later Rāṣṭrakūṭas.

The inscriptions of the later Rāṣṭrakūṭas and the Gujarat branch of the Rāṣṭrakūṭas use Śālivāhana era. Their chronology is listed here.

The chronology of the later Rāṣṭrakūṭas

	Sālivāhana era (78 CE)	AD
Amoghavarṣa II	650-675	728-753 AD
Akālavarṣa III (Krishna III)	675-695	753-773 AD
Dhruva II Dhārāvarṣa Dhruvadeva	695-714	773-792 AD
Govinda IV Prabhātavarṣa Govindarāja	714-740	792-818 AD
Amoghavarṣa III	741-799	819-877 AD
Krishna IV - Akālavarṣa Kannaradeva	800-835	878-913 AD
Nityavarṣa	836-849	914-927 AD
Suvarṇavarṣa	850-856	928-934 AD
Amoghavarṣa IV	856-860	934-938 AD
Krishna V-Akālavarṣa V	861-889	939-967 AD
Koṭṭiga	889-893	967-971 AD
Karka	893-894	971-972 AD

25. The Gaṅga Rulers

The Gaṅgas of Talakad (Tālavanapura)

The Gaṅga was one of the oldest dynasties of South India. Early Gaṅgas started ruling over the Koṅgu region of Tamilnadu (the modern districts of Salem, Dharmapuri and Coimbatore) Anantapur and Kolār districts. They gradually established the empire of the Gaṅgas in Gaṅgavādi i.e. Bangalore, Tumkur and Mysore districts. The elephant was the emblem of Gaṅga dynasty. The majority of Early Gaṅga inscriptions were found in this region. Greek accounts of the 3rd century BC mention the region of Gaṅgadhikara as Gaṅgaridae which was ruled over by the king of Presii. Pliny also refers to the rulers of Gaṅgadhikara as Gaṅgaridae Kalingae, thereby reinforcing the evidence that the Eastern Gaṅga dynasty of Kaliṅga was ruling prior to the 3rd century BC.

According to later Gaṅga inscriptions, Hariśchandra had a son named Bharata. Vijayamahādevi, the wife of Bharata, took a bath in the Gaṅga River at the time of conception and the son born subsequently was named Gaṅāgādatta. The descendants of Gaṅgādatta were known as the Gaṅgas.

Koṅgani Varman was the founder of Gaṅga dynasty. Kudlapura stone inscriptiongives date as Śaka 25 elapsed, Śubhakṛt saṁvatsara, Phālguna Śuddha pañcamī, Rohiṇī nakṣatra and Śanivara (Saturday) referring to Prathama Gaṅga (First Gaṅga) Koṅgani Mādhava Varman.

शकवर्षाणां गतेषु पंचविंशति (25) नेय ।
śakavarṣāṇāṁ gateṣu paṁchaviṁśati (25) neya ।

This corresponds to 12th March, 558 BC. This day qualifies all parameters. Bārhaspatya Saṁvatsara was Śubhakṛt, Phālguna Śuddha pañcamī, Rohiṇī nakṣatra and Śanivara (Saturday).

The forefathers of Koṅgani Varman established the Gaṅga kingdom in Śaka 25 (558 BC). According to the Hebbata grant of Durvinīta, Mādhava Varmā or Madivarmā was the father of Koṅgani Varman. A Tamil Chronicle called 'Koṅgu-deśa-Rājakkal' places the reign of Koṅgani Varman in Śaka 111 (472 BC). Earlier, seven kingsof Raṭṭa lineage had ruled over the Koṅgu region. Koṅgani Varmande throned the last Raṭṭa (Rāṣṭrakūṭa) king Śri Vikrama Deva Chakravarty and established the Gaṅga Kingdom in Koṅgudeśa in Śaka 111.

The chronology of the Early Gaṅga kings

	Śaka era (583 BCE)	BC
1. Mādivarmā or Mādhava Varman	25	558 BC
2. Koṅgani Varman	111-134	472-449 BC
3. Mādhava I	135-167	448-416 BC
4. Harivarman	168-218	415-365 BC
5. Vishnugopa	219-269	364-314 BC
6. Elder son of Vishnugopa	270-280	313-304 BC
7. Mādhava II (Younger son of Vishnugopa)	280-324	304-259BC
8. Avinīta (Youngest son of Vishnugopa)	325-389	258-194 BC
9. Durvinīta	390-445	193-138 BC
10. Muṣkara	446-501	137-82 BC
11. Śripuruṣa I	501-531	82-52 BC
12. Bhāvikrama	531-600	52 BC-17AD
13. Śivamāra I, also known as Navakāma, Śrivallabha	601-648	18-65 AD
14. Śripuruṣa II	649-699	66-116 AD
15. Śivamāra II also known as Saygotta	700-719	117-136AD
16. Mārasiṁha	719-733	136-150 AD

17. Vijayāditya (Youngest Brother of Śivamāradeva)	733-739	150-156 AD
18. Rājamalla I (Satyavākya Koṅganivarman)	739-780	156-197 AD
19. Nātimārga I	780-810	197-227 AD
20. Rājamalla II (Satyavākya Koṅganivarman)	810-824	227-241 AD
21. Butuga I (Youngest Brother of Rājamalla II)	824-825	241-242 AD
22. Nītimārga II (Eragaṅgadeva) Narasiṅghadeva (Satyavākya	825-826	242-243 AD
23. Koṅganivarman(Satyavākya)	826	243 AD
24. Rājamalla III or Nītimārga III (son of Narasiṁghadeva)	826-830	243-247 AD
25. Butuga II (brother of Rājamalla III)	830-863	247-280 AD
26. Puṇuseya Gaṅga son of Butuga II (also known as Marula)	863-870	280-287 AD
27. Mārasingha-Guṭṭīya Gaṅga (Younger brother of Puṇuseya Gaṅga and son of Butuga II)	870-890	287-307 AD

Guṭṭīya Gaṅga was probably the last sovereign ruler of the Gaṅga dynasty. Gangas lost their sovereignty by the 4th century AD. All early Gaṅga inscriptions are available in the form of copper plates and dated in Śaka-kāla era (583 BC) except three grants (Kudlur, 168 Kadalur 169 & Kukkanur 170) of Mārasiṁha which are dated in Śaka-nṛpa-kālātīta era (78 AD). Most of the Gaṅga lithic inscriptions are dated in Śaka-kālātīta era (Śālivāhana Śaka 78 AD). It appears that the Gaṅgas re-emerged as feudatories of the Rāṣṭrakūṭas during 9th & 10th centuries AD with control restricted to the regions of Kuvalālapura (Kolār) and Nandagiri (Nandidoorg. The author of the Kudlurgrant claimed that he was coronated by the Rāṣṭrakūṭa king Krishnarāja. After the 10th century AD, Gaṅgas attained important positions under the Chalukyas and Hoyasalas. A community of Mysore is still known today as the Gaṅgādikār Vokkalingārs. Amazingly, the descendants of this glorious dynasty of Karṇātaka are still surviving.

The chronology of the Eastern Gaṅga rulers

Many inscriptions found in Orissa and Andhra Pradesh are datedin the Gāṅgeya era. Actually, the kings of the Eastern Gaṅga dynastyrecorded the regnal year starting from the initial year of the establishmentof their dynasty in their inscriptions, which has been named as Gāṅgeyaera by modern historians. The Eastern Gaṅgas ruled from the city of Kaliṅga. Kaliṅga deśa is well known from the Mahābhārata era.

Khāravela's Mahāmeghavāhana dynasty was reigning in Kaliāga aroundthe 13th century BC. Seventeen inscriptions of the Māṭharas of Piṣthāpura are found till date which indicate that the Māṭharas also ruled the Kaliṅga region and the Pitṛbhaktas were their contemporaries. Probably, the Māṭharas and Pitṛbhaktas ruled around the 8th and 7th centuries BC.

It appears that the eastern Gaṅgas were the successors of the Māṭharasand Pitṛbhaktas.

The chronology of the Eastern Gaṅgas

	Gāṅgeya era (657-656 BCE)	BC/AD
1. Father of Indravarman I	1-25	657-632 BC
2. Indravarman I	25-55	632-602 BC
3. Sāmantavarman I	55-70	602-587 BC
4. Hastivarman	70-85	587-572 BC
5. Indravarman II Rājasiṁha	85-120	572-537 BC
6. Indravarman III (also known as Lokārṇava)	120-148	537-509 BC
7. Indravarman IV		

(The son of Dānārṇava)	148-180	509-477 BC
8. Devendravarman I (son of Guṇārṇava)	180-200	477-457 BC
9. Anantavarman I (son of Devendravarman I)	200-220	457-437 BC
10. Nandavarman (son of Anantavarman I)	220-240	437-417 BC
11. Devendravarman II (son of Anantavarman I)	240-270	417-387 BC
12. Rājendravarman I	270-300	387-357 BC
13. Anantavarman II (son of Rājendravarman I)	300-306	357-343 BC
14. Devendravarman III (son of Rājendravarman I)	306-310	343-347 BC
15. Rājendravarman II (son of Anantavarman II)	310-342	347-315 BC
16. Satyavarman I (son of Devendravarman III)	342-357	315-300 BC
17. Anantavarman III (son of Devendravarman III)	357-365	300-292 BC
18. Bhāpendravarman	365-375	292-282 BC
19. Anantavarman IV (son of Bhāpendravarman)	375-385	282-272 BC
20. Devendravarman IV (son of Bhāpendravarman)	385-393	272-264 BC
21. Manujedravarman (son of Devendravarman IV)	393-398	264-259 BC

No epigraphs available between the year 397 to 520 (259-137 BC)

22. Anantavarman V

23. Devendravarman V (son of Anantavarman V)	520	137 BC
24. Madhukāmārṇava (son of Anantavarman V)	526-528	131-129 BC
25. Anantavarman VI	550	107 BC

Evidently, the kingdom of the eastern Gaṅgas had weakened due to the rise of the Imperial Guptas. This is the reason why no eastern Gaṅgas epigraphs are available between the year 397 to 520 (259-137 BC). They attempted to re-establish themselves along with the Kadaṁbas but the rise of the Chalukyas in the south and the rise of the Maukharis in the north finally ended the rule of the eastern Gaṅgas by 107 BC. The Imperial Guptas were ruling Kaliṅga indirectly through their feudatories and the Gupta era was introduced in Kaliṅga during the reign of Chandragupta II. Gradually, the Gupta era became popular and the Gāṅgeya era was forgotten by the 1st century BC.

26. The Pallava Rulers

The Pallavas were one of the earliest rulers of South India. The rise of Pallavas ended the rule of Ikṣavāku dynasty in the lower Andhra regions. The earliest inscriptions of the Pallavas are written in Prākrit. Thus, theearly Pallava inscriptions must be dated in the 6th century BC. Based on these inputs, the chronology of the Pallavas is deduced by Vedveer (2015) as under:

	Śaka era (583 BC)	BC/AD
1. Siṁhavarman I	83-108	500-475 BC
2. (Śiva) Skandavarman I	108-138	475-445 BC
3. Kumāravishnu (Elder son of Skandavarman I)	138-163	445-420 BC
Siṁhavarman II (Younger son of Skandavarman I who coronated		
4. Gaṅga king Aryavarman)	163-173	420-410 BC
Skandavarman II (who coronated the Gaṅga king Mādhava Siṁhavarman)	173-203	410-380 BC
5. Viravarman	203-218	380-365 BC
6. Skandavarman II	218-248	365-335 BC
7. Siṁhavarman III	248-253	335-330 BC
8. Viṣṇugopavarman (who fought against Samudragupta)	253-283	330-300 BC

The following kings were the probable descendants of Viṣṇugopavarman.

9. Siṁhavishnu I (contemporary to the Gaṅga king Avinīta)	323-358	260-225 BC
10. Siṁhavarman (Siṁhasūri translated		

'Lokavibhāga' in his 22nd year of rule)

358-403 225-180 BC

11. Siṁhavishnu II

(Bhāravi met him in Kāñchi) 403-443 180-140 BC

12. Siṁha? (who was defeated by Viṣṇukuṇḍin king)

443-488 140-95 BC

13. Nandivarman (a descendant of Siṁhavarman III and the one who coronated Gaṅga king Śivamāradeva)

703-733 120-150AD

References

1. Ali, S.M. (1966). Reprinted 1973. *Geography of Purāṇās.* People's Publishing House, New Delhi.

2. Edward C. Sachau (1910). *Alberuni's India*,2nd edition,

   Kegan Paul, Tubner and Co., London

3. Edwin Bryant (2001). *The Quest for the Origins of VedicCulture: The Indo-Aryan Migration Debate.* OxfordUniversity Press.

4. Georgina Adelaide Mueller (1902). The Life and Letters of the Right Honourable Friedrich Max Mueller, Longmans, Green, Vol.1

5. Ghasi Ram: *Maharsi Dayanda ka Jeevan Charit*

6. Jaspers, Karl (1963). *The origin and goal of history,* NewHaven and London, Yale University Press.

7. Kota Venktachalam (1956). *Indian Eras.*

8. Kota Venktachalam (1953). *Chronology of Nepal History.*

9. Kota Venktachalam(1953b). *The Plot in IndianChronology.*

10. Kota Venkatchalam (1955). The Chronology of Kashmir History Reconstructed.

11. Kota Venktachalam (1957). The *Chronology of Indian History,* Part 1 & 2.

12. Macdonell, A.A. (1900). History of Sanskrit Literature, D Appleton and Company, New York

13. Max Mueller (1859). History of Ancient Sanskrit Literature, Williams and Norgate, LondonShri Ram Sharma (Edited): Śiva Purāṇa

14. Ravi Prakash Arya (2019): 9000 Years Old Calendar of Various Indian Eras. Indian Foundation for Vedic Science, Rohtak, Haryana.

15. Ravi Prakash Arya (2019 a): 7000 Years' Calendar of Lunar

Months (7 vols), Amazon Books, USA

16. Shyam Manohar Mishra (1977). *Yaśovarman of Kanauj, A study of Political History, Social and cultural life of Northern India During the reign of Yaśovarman, Abhinav Publications, New Delhi.*
17. Skanda Purāṇa, Chaukhamba Prakashan, Sanskrit Series Office, Varanasi, 2019.
18. Vedveer Arya (2015). *The Chronology of Ancient India,* Aryabhata Publications, Hyderabad.
19. Vedavāṇī Journal, edited by Pt. Yudhiṣṭhir Mimansaka and published by Ramlal Kapoor Trust, Bahalgarh, Sonepat, Haryana
20. Williams, Monier (1879). English-Sanskrit Dictionary,
21. Williams, Monier (1879). '*Modern India and Indians,* Third Edition, Tubner and Co. London
22. William Jones (1799). *The Works of William Jones,* G.G. and J. Robinson, London
23. Winternitz, M (1927). '*A History of Indian literature',* Vol. 1', University of Calcutta.

www.ingramcontent.com/pod-product-compliance
Lightning Source LLC
Chambersburg PA
CBHW030641260626
47157CB00007B/2439
9788187710851